Litigating the Rights of the Child

Ton Liefaard · Jaap E. Doek
Editors

Litigating the Rights of the Child

The UN Convention on the Rights of the Child in Domestic and International Jurisprudence

Springer

Editors
Ton Liefaard
Department of Child Law
Leiden Law School
Leiden University
Leiden
The Netherlands

Jaap E. Doek
Faculty of Law
VU University
Amsterdam
The Netherlands

ISBN 978-94-017-7975-3 ISBN 978-94-017-9445-9 (eBook)
DOI 10.1007/978-94-017-9445-9

Springer Dordrecht Heidelberg New York London

Printed on acid-free paper

Springer is part of Springer Science+Business Media (www.springer.com)

Foreword

Relatively little has been written about children's rights litigation or the obligations of States parties under the Convention on the Rights of the Child (CRC), notwithstanding that it is a binding agreement on 194 countries around the world. In this vein, I sometimes have the impression, when speaking to governments either in Geneva or in follow-up missions abroad, that the view is that because the CRC deals with children's rights, it can be applied *à la carte* and that the proposed menu itself is no more than a '*Kid's menu*'—one offering small meals, and small rights, for the little customers and little persons.

Nevertheless, it is clear from human rights theory that the CRC belongs to the human rights family and that the principles which apply to all international human rights treaties are equally applicable to 'our' Convention. The rights enshrined in it amount to more than just an exhaustive list; they also enumerate the obligations that States parties have towards children from the moment at which they ratified the CRC, because the act of ratification expresses the commitment of states to accept these very obligations.

It is worth mentioning, then, that we are in a unique position with the CRC, which is the only convention to have achieved nearly universal ratification, given that 194 states have agreed to be bound by obligations towards all persons under 18 years of age. Moreover, this is the first time in modern history when all states are speaking the same language when dealing with children.

We should recall that Article 4 of the CRC clearly establishes the obligations incumbent on states, which are required to 'undertake all appropriate legislative, administrative, and other measures for the implementation of the rights recognized in the present Convention'. The same provision further requires that 'with regard to economic, social and cultural rights, States parties shall undertake such measures to the maximum extent of their available resources and, where needed, within the framework of international co-operation'. In addition to the obligations to ensure the full enjoyment of the rights of the child, States parties are obliged to submit regular reports on their achievements and challenges in implementing the CRC to the UN Committee on the Rights of the Child (Article 44).

The CRC is a uniquely broad instrument safeguarding children's civil, political, economic, social and cultural rights, many of which are not covered by provisions in the International Covenants or other international instruments. Some articles in the CRC mirror guarantees established for 'everyone' in other instruments, thereby underlining the fact that these rights apply equally to children. By the same token, however, there are many provisions in the Convention that provide unique rights for children.

As such, it seems important to highlight a selection of rights (and concomitant obligations on States parties) that are specific to children and which are **not** found under other treaties:

- The obligation to protect the child from all forms of discrimination or punishment on the basis of the status, activities, expressed opinions or beliefs of his or her parents, guardians or family members; the CRC also adds disability and ethnic origin as specifically prohibited grounds for discriminating against children (Article 2).
- The obligation to respect the right of the child to have his or her best interests taken as a primary consideration in all actions [Article 3(1)].
- The obligation to respect the principle of evolving capacities (Article 5).
- The obligation to ensure the maximum survival and development of the child (Article 6).
- The right of the child to know and be cared for by his or her parents (Article 7).
- The obligation to preserve the child's identity (Article 8).
- The obligation not to separate children from parents unless it is in the children's best interests; if it is deemed so, this decision is in turn subject to judicial review (Article 9).
- The obligation to give due weight to children's expressed views in all matters affecting them; children must also be given an opportunity to be heard in any judicial or administrative proceedings that affect them (Article 12).
- Obligations to support parents in their child-rearing responsibilities, including by means of providing child-care services; in addition, the child's best interests should be a basic concern for parents (Article 18).
- A special obligation to protect the rights of children deprived of family environment (Article 20), including adoption (Article 21).

It should be underlined as well that the two Optional Protocols to the CRC—on the sale of children, child prostitution and child pornography, and on the involvement of children in armed conflict—stipulate further unique rights and safeguards.

The recent entry into force of the third Optional Protocol on Individual Communications (OPIC) will add a new dimension to the reality that states have obligations towards children. As subjects of this new right, children will be in a position to complain before the UN CRC Committee in cases of non-compliance with, or violation of, their rights. This is certainly an important step towards better implementation of the CRC, but it will also pave the way for the notion of establishing domestic bodies where children may lodge complaints. OPIC therefore stands to have a direct effect on children's ability to litigate at the national level, and even possibly the international one.

Implementation of the Convention should mean that the provisions of the CRC can be directly invoked before the courts, applied by all national authorities, and done so in such a manner that the Convention prevails in the event of conflict with national legislation or practice. This was clearly pointed out by the General Comment No. 5 (2003)[1] on measures to implement the Convention, but in reality the incorporation of children's rights is often weak or incomplete, and while it is possible in theory to invoke the CRC's principles and articles before judicial or administrative authorities, in practice lawyers ignore this possibility and judges and magistrates are reluctant to justify their decisions on the basis of the provisions of the Convention.

It is important, therefore, to reiterate what the General Comment No. 5 mentions in paragraph 24 in relation to the meaning of the phrase '[to] have rights':

> For rights to have meaning, effective remedies must be available to redress violations. [...] So States need to give particular attention to ensuring that there are effective, child-sensitive procedures available to children and their representatives. These should include the provision of child-friendly information, advice, advocacy, including support for self-advocacy, and access to independent complaints procedures and to the courts with necessary legal and other assistance. Where rights are found to have been breached, there should be appropriate reparation, including compensation, and, where needed, measures to promote physical and psychological recovery, rehabilitation and reintegration, as required by article 39.

It is a notable area in which states have delayed their implementation of the CRC. This book by our colleagues, Professors Ton Liefaard and Jaap Doek, comes hence as a clear and timely reminder of these obligations, showing that while examples of good practice are to be found, there is still a very long way to go before children are fully recognised as bearers and agents of human rights.

So thanks are due to the two initiators of this work for having taken up the challenge and to all the authors for their encouraging contributions. May this book then inspire legislators, the judiciary, administrative decision-makers, lawyers and all other relevant professionals in their daily practice!

Jean Zermatten
Former Chair
UN Committee on the Rights of the Child

[1] CRC/GC/2003/5.

Acknowledgments

This book has been developed with the assistance of many. We would like to express our gratitude to everyone who has been involved in one way or the other. We are very grateful to the authors for their invaluable contributions to this book and their professional and constructive attitude towards the drafting (and redrafting) of their chapters. In addition, we would like to thank Dr. Jean Zermatten for his willingness to write the foreword of this book. Furthermore, we would like thank Mr. André Wiesner, Firebreak Studios, South Africa, for the editing of this book, and Ms. Jill Stein for her assistance in finalizing the manuscript. Finally, we thank Ms. Esther Otten, Senior Publishing Editor at Springer and Ms. Miranda Dijksman, Senior Assistant at Springer, for their support and trust in this book. We hope that it will used by many and that it will serve as a source of inspiration for academics, students and practitioners.

Leiden, July 2014

Ton Liefaard
Jaap E. Doek

Contents

Acronyms

ACERWC	African Committee of Experts on the Rights and Welfare of the Child
ACHPR	African Charter on Human and Peoples' Rights
ACHR	American Convention on Human Rights
ACRWC	African Charter on the Rights and Welfare of the Child
CEDAW	Convention on the Elimination of All Forms of Discrimination against Women
CRC	Convention on the Rights of the Child
ECHR	European Convention for the Protection of Human Rights and Fundamental Freedoms
ECtHR	European Court of Human Rights
HRC	Human Rights Committee
ICCPR	International Covenant on Civil and Political Rights
ICESCR	International Covenant on Economic, Social and Cultural Rights
INGO	International Non-Governmental Organisation
NGO	Non-Governmental Organisation
NHRI	National Human Rights Institutions
OAS	Organization of American States
OPAC	Optional Protocol on the Involvement of Children in Armed Conflict
OPIC	Optional Protocol to the Convention on the Rights of the Child on a communications procedure
OPSC	Optional Protocol on the Sale of Children, Child Prostitution and Pornography
UNCAT	Convention Against Torture and Other Cruel, Inhuman, Degrading Treatment or Punishment

About the Authors

Anant Kumar Asthana is a New Delhi based lawyer who specialises in children related laws, particularly juvenile justice. Prior to litigating in the Delhi High Court and Supreme Court of India, he practised juvenile justice law for four years before various Juvenile Justice Boards in New Delhi and as a panel lawyer for Delhi State Legal Services Authority. He has represented thousands of juveniles so far. In addition to litigation, he travels across the Country to impart technical trainings on juvenile justice, anti-trafficking and child sexual offences laws to police, judicial officers, lawyers, teachers, law students and activists associated with various civil society organisations. Since 2009, he has been serving as Convener of Delhi High Court Appointed Committee for Supervision of Observation Homes. He drafted national guidelines for training of juvenile welfare officers and also guidelines for legal aid in Juvenile Justice Boards, which were issued by the National Legal Services Authority for nation-wide application. He compiled India's first ever compendium of significant orders of Juvenile Justice Boards, which was published by HAQ: Centre for Child Rights as a book titled "Juvenile Justice: Law and Practice". He is also an active public interest lawyer. He was counsel for HAQ: Centre for Child Rights in eight writ petitions in the Supreme Court of India (known as Salil Bali Case) in which he successfully argued to defend constitutional validity of India's Juvenile Justice Act, which had come under challenge after 16 December 2012 Gang Rape incident in Delhi.

Prof. Dr. Mariëlle Bruning lectures on child law, children's rights and juvenile justice at Leiden University, Leiden Law School, where she is director of the Child Law Department. She is also director of the LL.M Programme on Child Law, a Dutch Master's programme (2012) designed to provide specialism to those working with and for children in the legal field. She regularly publishes on various topics in the area of children's rights and family and child law. Her research focuses on the legal position of the child and the triangle between rights and duties of parents, children and the state, with particular attention for child protection, youth care and welfare, children in alternative care, information sharing and privacy issues, legal aspects of child abuse and neglect and child abduction from an international perspective.

She supervises several Ph.D. students on various issues relating to child law and children's rights, including the rights of children in foster care, children in closed youth care and the rights of children in the context of international commercial surrogacy. She collaborates in projects with partners such as Defence for Children International-ECPAT in the Children's Rights House in Leiden, KidsRights and the Dutch Children's Ombudsman and acts as a consultant on various projects concerning child law and children's rights. Mariëlle Bruning is furthermore a (part-time) juvenile judge in the District Court of Amsterdam.

Meda Couzens LL.M is a Romanian lawyer currently working as a Senior Lecturer at the School of Law, University of KwaZulu-Natal, Durban, South Africa, where she teaches child rights-related subjects, Constitutional law and Human rights. She has published on a variety of child rights topics, such as child participation, child-headed households, inter-country adoptions, local authorities and children, the best interests of the child, independent human rights institutions and the rights of children, and children of incarcerated parents. Her latest international publications are 'The contribution of the South African Constitutional Court to the jurisprudential development of the best interests of the child' (forthcoming chapter in Diduck, A., Peleg, N. and Reece, H. *Law and Michael Freeman* (Brill Publishers 2014)) and 'Exploring public participation as a vehicle for child participation in governance: A view from South Africa' *International Journal of Children's Rights* 2012 (20) 4, 674. Meda publishes both in English and Romanian. She is currently reading, as an external candidate, for a Ph.D. with Leiden Law School, investigating the role of national courts in applying the UN Convention on the Rights of the Child.

Prof. Dr. Alfred de Zayas is a retired senior lawyer with the Office of the UN High Commissioner for Human Rights, where he was Chief of the Petitions Section and Secretary of the UN Human Rights Committee. Since 2012 he is UN Independent Expert for the Promotion of a Democratic and Equitable International Order, and reports annually to the Human Rights Council and UN General Assembly. He has taught as full Professor of Law and as guest lecturer inter alia at the Universities of British Columbia (Vancouver), DePaul (Chicago), Graduate Institute (Geneva), and Universidad de Alcalá de Henares (Madrid). At present he lectures at the Geneva School of Diplomacy and International Relations, where he also supervises masters and doctoral students. He has published nine books on international law and historical topics, including a *Handbook on the Case Law of the UN Human Rights Committee* (together with Judge Jakob Th. Möller), N.P. Engel, 2009. He was President of PEN International, Centre Suisse romand from 2006 to 2010 and is again its President since 2013.

Prof. Dr. Jaap E. Doek is an Emeritus Professor in Family and Juvenile Law at the VU University of Amsterdam and an extraordinary Professor in Children's Rights at the Anton de Kom University of Suriname. He is the special legal advisor of ECPAT and is a member of the board of various international NGO's, e.g. the African Child Policy Forum and Child Helpline International. He regularly serves as a consultant for UNICEF country offices. He was a member of the UN Committee on the

Rights of the Child from 1999 until 2007 and the chairperson of that committee from 2001 until 2007. He was Dean of the Law Faculty at the VU University of Amsterdam from 1988 to 1992. He has been a juvenile court judge in the District Courts of Alkmaar and The Hague (1978–1985) and a deputy justice in the Court of Appeal of Amsterdam (2005–2012). He wrote or edited books and contributed to many books. Examples of books are: *The Rights of the Child in International Law. Rights of the Child in a Nutshell and in Content: All About Children's Rights*. Bern: Stampfli Publishers 2012 (together with Nevena Vukcovic-Sahovic and Jean Zermatten); *Child Poverty: African and International Perspectives*. Antwerp/Oxford/Portland: Intersentia 2009 (together with A.K. Shiva Kumar, David Mugawe and Shimetis Tsegaye). Examples of contributions to books: 'The Child's Right to Freedom from Violence. The UN Convention on the Rights of the Child and UN CRC General Comment 13' (together with Kim Svevo), in: Jon Conte (ed.), *Child Abuse and Neglect Worldwide*. Volume 1 Understanding, Defining and Measuring Child Maltreatment, Santa Barbara, Denver, Oxford: Praeger 2014; and 'The CRC: Dynamics and Directions of Monitoring its Implementation', in: Antonella Invernizzi and Jane Williams (eds), *The Human Rights of Children from Vision to Implementation*, Farnham/Burlington: Ashgate Publishers 2011.

Prof. Bernardine Dohrn is a retired Clinical Associate Professor at the Northwestern University School of Law, and was the founding director of the Children and Family Justice Center. The Center represents young people in court, and is a national policy center for the comprehensive needs of adolescents and their families, matters associated with the administration of justice, and the preparation of professionals who advocate for children. Dohrn is an author and co-editor of three books: "Race Course: Against White Supremacy (2009); "A Century of Juvenile Justice" (2002); and "Resisting Zero Tolerance: A Handbook for Parents, Teachers and Students" (2001) and the author of 'I'll Try Anything Once: Using the Conceptual Framework of Children's Human Rights Norms in the U.S.', Univ. of Mich. Journal of Law Reform (2007); 'Something's Happening Here: Children and Human Rights Jurisprudence in Two International Courts', UNLV L. Rev. Summer 2006; and 'All Ellas: Girls Locked Up in Feminist Studies' (Summer 2004). She serves of the boards of Human Rights Watch's Children's Rights Division; the W. Haywood Burns Institute; and the Campaign for the Fair Sentencing of Youth. She teaches, writes and lectures on international human rights law, children in conflict with the law, racism and youth justice, school law, and torture. Dohrn taught at Northwestern, was visiting professor at Leiden University, Leiden Law School and at the VU University of Amsterdam in the Netherlands, and is currently a lecturer at the University of Chicago.

Mónica Feria-Tinta LL.M. (with merit) (London), Diploma of the Hague Academy of International Law (2000), is a practising international lawyer specialising in public international law. She has represented victims before the Inter-American organs of protection of human rights since 1997. Her work as legal counsel litigating cases before the Inter-American system created landmarks in international justice including, groundbreaking jurisprudence on the protection of children in times of war. She is the author of *The Landmark Rulings of the Inter-American Court of Human Rights on the Rights of the Child* (Martinus Nijhoff 2008) and lectures regularly at the Master of Advanced Studies in Children's Rights Programme of the Institut Universitaire Kurt Bösch (IUKB) and University of Fribourg, Switzerland. Feria-Tinta was awarded the Inge Genefke International Award for her work as an international lawyer in 2006 and was co-recipient of the Gruber Justice Prize 2007, for her contributions advancing the cause of justice as delivered through the legal system. She is a member of Middle Temple (Inn of Court), England.

Prof. Dr. Kamel Filali teaches at the Law School of the University of Constantine (Algeria). He teaches courses on international human rights law particularly the protection of children's rights at the international and regional level. He received a Ph.D. in international law from the University of Miami (FL, USA) and was a Director of Studies at the International Institute of Human Rights in Strasbourg (France). Dr. Filali was a Member of the UN committee on the Rights of the Child and its Vice Chair from 2007 to 2011. He is currently a member of the International Board of Trustee of the African Child Policy Forum (ACPF) and member of the African Union Commission of International Law. At the national level, he is a member of the National Consultative Commission on the promotion and protection of human rights. He also contributed as a professor to the training of Algerian juvenile judges on the meaning and the use by the judiciary of the Convention on the Rights of the Child. He supervises a number of Masters and Ph.D. students on various issues relating to human and children's rights, such as on the international and African Union system of protection of children's rights. Dr. Filali has written several articles and given numerous presentations on the CRC and its Optional Protocols. Among his recent publication are: 'Regional child rights instruments on the African continent: The African Charter on the rights and welfare of the Child', AUCIL Journal of International law, 2013, No. 1; 'Une Magna Carta en faveur des enfants' El Watan, Algeria 19 December 2013; 'SOS enfants en danger' in le Soir Algeria. 19 March 2013. Furthermore, Dr. Filali is a practicing lawyer and international human rights expert involved in pleading cases before Algerian Tribunals and Courts and providing legal consultations to individuals, private and public institutions.

Prof. Dr. Ursula Kilkelly holds a Chair in Law at the School of Law, University College Cork, Ireland where she is also Dean. She teaches children's rights, child law and juvenile justice and has published widely on the implementation of children's rights. Some of her key publications are: The Child and the ECHR (Ashgate 1999); Children's Rights in Ireland (Tottel 2008) and journal articles in *Youth Justice, the Child and Family Law Quarterly, the Human Rights Quarterly* and the *International Journal of Children's Rights*. Recent publications include commissioned research for UNICEF UK on the legal implementation of the UN Convention on the Rights of the Child (with L. Lundy et al. 2013), on child-friendly healthcare for the (Irish) Ombudsman for Children (with E. Savage 2013) and a children's rights study of European Constitutions for the Council of Europe Venice Commission (with C. O'Mahony 2014). She is currently conducting a 2 year study of children's rights advocacy, with L. Lundy in Queen's University Belfast, for the

Atlantic Philanthropies. At Cork, she directs the Child Law Clinic, which provides student-led legal research services to lawyers litigating children's issues and developed the LLM in Child and Family Law. She was appointed to the Board of Management of Ireland's Children Detention School by the Minister for Children and Youth Affairs in 2012, reappointed in 2014, and is co-founder and chairperson of the Law Centre for Children and Young People in Dublin.

Prof. Dr. Ton Liefaard holds the UNICEF Chair in Children's Rights at Leiden University, Leiden Law School. He teaches children's rights, child law and juvenile justice and has published widely on the UN Convention on the Rights of the Child and its meaning for children at the national level. Some of his key publications are: *Deprivation of Liberty of Children in Light of International Human Rights Law and Standards* (Intersentia 2008); 'Juveniles in transition from juvenile justice to adult criminal justice' (in: R. Loeber et al. (eds.). *Persisters and Desisters in Crime from Adolescence into Adulthood: Explanation, Prevention and Punishment.* Ashgate 2012); 'Child Soldiers: Towards A Rights Based Imagery' (in: C. Brants et al. (eds.). *Transitional Justice. Images and Memories.* Ashgate 2013); and 'Juveniles' Right to Counsel during Police Interrogations. An Interdisciplinary Analysis of a Youth Specific Approach, with a Particular Focus on the Netherlands', *Erasmus Law Review* 2014 (with Y. van den Brink). He supervises Ph.D. research on various children's rights issues and regularly advises governments and international organisations (UN, Council of Europe, European Union, INGO's), on issues related to children's rights, juvenile justice, child friendly justice, child protection and alternative care, and violence against children. Ton Liefaard is furthermore a deputy juvenile judge at the District Court of Amsterdam and a member of the State Commission advising the Dutch Government on changing parental relationships and the position of children.

Manuela Limbeek LL.M works as a lecturer at the Child Law Department of Leiden University. She studied law at the University of Amsterdam and finished her Master's in Private Law with a thesis focusing on the child's guardian ad litem. During her studies, she worked at the Child and Youth Law Centre in Amsterdam (Kinder—en Jongerenrechtswinkel Amsterdam), first as a volunteer and later as project manager/advisor. Also, she has worked as student–assistant of Dr. J.H. de Graaf, University of Amsterdam. After her Masters, she remained affiliated with the Centre for Children's Rights Amsterdam as a researcher. Manuela Limbeek is one of the authors of J.H. de Graaf et al. *De toepassing van het Internationaal Verdrag inzake de Rechten van het Kind in de Nederlandse rechtspraak.* Nijmegen: Ars Aequi Libri 2012.

Ivana Savić LL.M is Executive Director of the Centre for Human Rights and Development Studies (CHRDS), an organisation focused on advancing global, regional and national policies in the areas of human rights, especially of the rights of the child and youth rights, and sustainable development. Since 2009, she has been one of the Organising Partners for the United Nations Major Group for Children and Youth (MGCY) with a mandate to coordinate and facilitate young people's participation in the international sustainability negotiations, namely the UN Commission on Sustainable Development, Rio+20 and the post-2015 process, the UN High Level Political Forum on Sustainable Development and the Open Working Group for Sustainable Development Goals. Ivana Savić is also a member of the UNDP Civil Society Advisory Committee, and CIVICUS Youth Advisory Group. Additionally, she has been involved in different youth initiatives worldwide and has been internationally recognized as expert in the field of the rights of the child, youth rights, human rights and environment, sustainable development and young people's participation. Ivana Savić holds an LLM degree in the Rights of the Child and is a Doctoral candidate in the Rights of the Child at the Union University, Faculty of Law in Belgrade, Serbia. Some of Ivana Savić's key published work are: Savic. I., Loftus, S. et al. *Rio+20 Participation Guide—An introduction for children and youth.* Brussels: Rioplustwenties, 2011; Savic. I. 'Youth Participation in Environmental Activities', in: Institut international des Droits de l'Enfant, *Climate Change: Impacts on Children and on their Rights*, Sion 2012, 162–170; Savic. I., 'Best practices in youth engagement with intergovernmental organisations: a case study from the Rio+20 process', in: CIVICUS State of Civil Society Report 2014; Savic. I., 'Partnering with and catalysing young innovators', in: *The Challenges of Climate Change: Children on the front line*. UNICEF Office of Research/Innocenti (in print).

Prof. Dr. Ann Skelton is the Director for Child Law at the University of Pretoria in South Africa. She obtained her doctorate in law in 2005, which was on restorative justice and children. She continues to publish in these areas of interest—some of her recent publications are 'The South African Constitutional Court's restorative justice jurisprudence' 2013 1(1) *Restorative Justice: An International Journal* 122–145 and 'The role of the courts in ensuring the right to a basic education in a democratic South Africa: a critical evaluation of recent education case law' 2013 46(1) *De Jure* 1–23. She is an internationally recognised expert in child law, and frequently attends UN expert meetings. She supervises doctoral and masters students on a range of subjects relating to child law and human rights. She is an advocate who regularly appears in the superior courts of South Africa, including the Constitutional Court, arguing prominent children's rights matters. In 2012 she was presented with the honorary World's Children's Prize by Queen Silvia of Sweden. In 2013 she was appointed into the University of Pretoria's UNESCO Chair: Education law in Africa.

Prof. Dr. Julia Sloth-Nielsen is a senior professor at the Faculty of Law, University of the Western Cape. She also holds the Chair on Children's Rights in the Developing World at Leiden University, Leiden Law School. She teaches children's rights, child law and juvenile justice and has published widely on both the UN Convention on the Rights of the Child and the regional treaty the African Charter on the Rights and Welfare of the Child. She has worked on child law reform at national level in South Africa, Mozambique, Kenya, Botswana, South Sudan, Tanzania, Zanzibar and Namibia to name a few examples of regional work. Some of her key publications are *Children's Rights in Africa: A Legal Perspective* (Ashgate 2009), and

Trials and tribulations, tends and triumphs (with Z du Toit; Juta and Co, Cape Town). She supervises a number of Ph.D. students on various issues relating to children's rights in African context, including birth registration, kinships care, the rights of children with disabilities to early childhood education, and implementation of the rights of children with disabilities to education in Kenya and South Africa. Prof. Sloth-Nielsen was elected to the African Committee of Experts on the Rights and Welfare of the Child by the Heads of State of the African Union in January 2011 and currently serves as second vice chair. She currently enjoys a rating as an internationally recognised researcher with South Africa's National Research Foundation.

Prof. Dr. Helen Stalford is Professor of Law at the University of Liverpool and is founding director of the European Children's Rights Unit. Her work for the past 15 years or so has focused on examining the status and experiences of children under European law, and particularly under EU law. An important part of this work has been to develop mechanisms to measure the impact of European law on children's lives and she has led projects on behalf of the EU Fundamental Rights Agency, UNICEF and the Council of Europe in developing children's rights indicators. To complement this, she has worked directly with children and young people on a number of empirical projects, to explore their experiences of the law in the context of migration, family violence, education and access to justice. Key publications include the books 'A Community for Children?: Children, Citizenship and Migration in the European Union' (Ashgate 2004); and 'Children and the European Union: Rights Welfare and Accountability' (Hart 2012).

Enakshi Ganguly Thukral is a human rights activist and child rights advocate, researcher and trainer for the past three decades, working on wide-ranging socio-legal issues, such as development induced displacement, women in the unorganised sector, reproductive health, child labour, child trafficking, laws and policies governing women and children, education and violence. Since co-founding HAQ: Centre for Child Rights, in 1998, she has been working in focused manner on children's rights. She has been part of drafting committees of laws, polices and plans of the government of India, including the for the government's 5 Year Plans. She is currently the president of Society for Rural and Tribal Initiatives (SRUTI), Delhi, on the board of among others, the National Gender Centre of the Lal Bahadur Shastri Academy of Administration, Government of India; member of the Editorial Board of "Children, Youth and Environments", A Journal of Research, Policy and Applications, University of Colorado, the thematic group for the World Congress on Juvenile Justice, Geneva, 2015, Scientific Committee of the sixth IJJO International Conference, Brussels 2014. She has authored and co-authored a number of books, articles, manuals and handbooks on a wide range of issues; she has been invited as a technical expert on issues related to children, presented papers at various national and international meets, worked closely with the UN system, is connected with child rights experts around the world. She has been awarded the Ashoka Fellowship in 2002 in recognition of HAQ's work on children.

Prof. Dr. Wouter Vandenhole teaches human rights and holds the UNICEF Chair in Children's Rights—a joint venture of the University of Antwerp and UNICEF Belgium—at the Faculty of Law of the University of Antwerp (Belgium). He is the spokesperson of the Law and Development Research Group and chairs the European Research Networking Programme GLOTHRO. He has published widely on economic, social and cultural rights, children's rights, transnational human rights obligations and human rights and development. Vandenhole is a founding member of the Flemish Children's Rights Knowledge Centre and co-convener of the international interdisciplinary course on human rights for development (HR4DEV). More information on www.uantwerp.be/wouter-vandenhole.

Prof. Dr. Nevena Vučković Šahović is Professor at the Law Faculty, UNION University in Belgrade, Serbia, teaching International Public Law with International Organizations and Family Law with Rights of the Child. She is the coordinator of the Master on the Rights of the Child. Nevena Vučković Šahović is the Founder and Director of Child Rights Centre—Belgrade, which was the first and the only organization in Serbia exclusively devoted to the promotion and implementation of the Convention on the Rights of the Child. She served on the Committee on the Rights of the Child (2003–2009). She is active in many countries in Europe, Asia and the USA, regarding human rights and the rights of the child. Nevena Vučković Šahović is the author of numerous articles, books and research. Some include: *Implementation of the General Measures of the CRC and the Role of Civil Society,* (WP, UNICEF Innocenti Research centre, Florence 2010, p. 61); *Measures to Implement the Convention on the Rights of the Child and Good Governance: the case of Serbia*, (in: Ganguly Thukral, Enakshi: "Every Right for Every Child", Routledge Taylor and Francis Group, pp. 65–89, 2011); *ENOC Study Report on National Human Rights Institutions and Child/Juvenile Delinquency,* (ENOC/Council of Europe, Strasbourg, 2012, p. 61); *The Rights of the Child in International Law* (with Jaap Doek and Jean Zermatten), Bern: Stampfli Publishers, 2012.

Jane Williams MA, LL.M is an Associate Professor in the College of Law, Swansea University. She teaches public law, family law and children's rights. Relevant publications include *The United Nations Convention on the Rights of the Child in Wales* (University of Wales Press, 2013) and, with Dr. Antonella Invernizzi, *Children and Citizenship* (Sage 2008) and *The Human Rights of Children: From Visions to Implementation* (Ashgate 2011). She supervises research students on issues relating to human rights implementation, including but not limited to human rights of children and young people. With Dr. Simon Hoffman, she co-directs the Wales Observatory on Human Rights of Children and Young People, based at Swansea University. She is a member of the Wales UNCRC Monitoring Group and of the Rights of the Child UK (ROCK) coalition.

Chapter 1
Litigating the Rights of the Child: Taking Stock After 25 Years of the CRC

Ton Liefaard and Jaap E. Doek

Abstract The 1989 UN Convention on the Rights of the Child (CRC) is the guiding legal framework for the development and implementation of legislation and policies concerning the human rights of children in 194 countries. This human rights treaty has contributed to universalising children's rights globally and regionally. It has had significant impact on domestic legal systems throughout the world and on domestic legislation in particular. The CRC has also had an impact on domestic and international human rights jurisprudence, but due to the absence of global studies a clear picture of the extent and nature of this impact is lacking. This book is a first step in a process of systematically compiling and analysing international, regional and national jurisprudence concerning the rights of the child. This chapter presents the key findings and provides guidance on how to proceed from here.

1 Children's Rights in Domestic and International Case Law

The 1989 UN Convention on the Rights of the Child (CRC) is the guiding legal framework for the development and implementation of legislation and policies concerning the human rights of children in 194 countries. This human rights treaty, which celebrated its twenty-fifth anniversary on 20 November 2014, has contributed to universalising children's rights globally and regionally. It has had

T. Liefaard (✉)
Department of Child Law, Leiden Law School, Leiden University, Leiden, The Netherlands
e-mail: t.liefaard@law.leidenuniv.nl

J.E. Doek
Faculty of Law, VU University, Amsterdam, The Netherlands
e-mail: jaap@jaapedoek.nl

T. Liefaard and J.E. Doek (eds.), *Litigating the Rights of the Child*,
DOI 10.1007/978-94-017-9445-9_1

significant impact on domestic legal systems throughout the world (Arts 2010; Stalford 2012) and on domestic legislation in particular (Sloth-Nielsen 2012; Arts 2010: 22 with reference to UNICEF 2007a, b). The CRC has also had an impact on domestic and international human rights jurisprudence (for example, see Kilkelly 1999; Ruitenberg 2003; Fortin 2004; Van Bueren 2007; Feria-Tinta 2008; Sloth-Nielsen and Mezmur 2008; Nolan 2011; De Graaf et al. 2012; Sloth-Nielsen and Kruuse 2013; Sandberg 2014), but due to the absence of global studies a clear picture of the extent and nature of this impact is lacking.

Regional human rights courts, such as the European Court of Human Rights (ECtHR) and the Inter-American Court of Human Rights, increasingly refer to the CRC and related children's rights standards as the relevant legal framework in cases where the interests of children are at stake (Kilkelly 2001; Van Bueren 2007). The number of domestic court cases in which the CRC has been used as a significant and/or decisive legal framework to determine legal matters affecting children's interests seems to have increased as well (for example, see De Graaf et al. 2012). Some jurisdictions provide interesting examples of domestic courts using the international children's rights framework for the interpretation of domestic constitutional principles and/or legislation. The South African Constitutional Court, for instance, has issued several important judgments in which the international rights of the child were further explored and implemented within the domestic legal order. This 'domestication of the CRC in South African Jurisprudence' (Sloth-Nielsen and Mezmur 2008) has been instigated by the South African Constitution, which stipulates that courts must consider international law when interpreting the Bill of Rights and may consider foreign law [section 39(1)].

Nevertheless, there are also jurisdictions where courts either show reluctance to accept the CRC as the relevant human rights framework for children or do not reveal a clear child-rights-oriented approach, be it in general or in individual cases. It might happen that courts do not see the CRC as pertinent to cases involving children, or it could be that they dispute its potential supremacy over national law and jurisprudence. In this regard, what may be detrimental as well is the absence of national laws that have incorporated international children's rights instruments. Moreover, the justiciability of certain categories of children's rights may come into question.

Other relevant, but arguably more practical, factors concern awareness, knowledge and time. It seems crucial that courts and the professionals acting in and around them, such as lawyers, have sufficient knowledge of the CRC and its potential implications for, and applicability to, legal proceedings. Furthermore, courts may not recognise the self-executing force of at least- some of the CRC provisions or may not be explicit and/or consistent in this regard. In addition, their judgments may not clarify the extent to which the CRC played a role in the decision-making process and—ultimately—in the rulings. The ECtHR, for example, often refers to relevant international treaties and standards, including the CRC, without indicating to what extent it actually used them in the interpretation and application of the provisions of the European Convention on Human Rights (ECHR; see Kilkelly in Chap. 12 of this book).

2 Functions, Challenges and Limitations of the CRC in Litigation

Despite the ambiguity in courts' attitudes towards the CRC as a relevant substantive and procedural human rights framework for children, it is fair to assume that attention to the CRC framework in domestic and international jurisprudence has increased since the CRC's entry into force in 1990; indeed, a growing body of case law exists to illustrate its potential for the rights of children in domestic jurisdictions. This is true even of the United States, one of the few countries not to have ratified the CRC (see Dohrn in Chap. 5 of this book).

At the same time, the practical experience of having litigated children's rights during the first 25 years of the CRC also sheds light on the challenges and limitations of the CRC and related international and regional children's rights instruments in legal proceedings at the domestic, regional and international level. These challenges and limitations are related to a variety of factors, including the nature of the (domestic) legal order; the presence or absence of a domestic constitution in which children's rights have been embedded or on the basis of which international law is regarded as the higher law; the legal tradition (for example, civil law, common law or Islamic law); and the existence or not of strategic-litigation initiatives, including education and training of legal professionals.

This book aims to study these jurisprudential developments and provide insight into the possible functions, challenges and limitations of using the CRC in litigation. Its core objective is to examine the CRC's potential impact on domestic and international human rights jurisprudence in order to foster better understanding of how the CRC functions in domestic and international law and thereby advances implementation and enforcement of children's rights at the domestic level (see art. 4 CRC). These functions include, inter alia, the CRC as a tool for interpretation of domestic law or other human rights standards; the CRC as a 'gap-filler' closing gaps in domestic or international law; the CRC as the higher standard; the CRC as a limiting standard, for example with regard to local custom and practices or religion; and the CRC as an embodiment of principles of international customary law.

In addition, the book seeks to highlight a variety of experiences in children's rights litigation, experiences which legal professionals working in and around courts can draw on for reference purposes and inspiration, and which can be used in the training and education of professionals and students.

3 Outline of the Book

The book is divided into four parts. The first three consist of country studies divided along the lines of legal tradition. The first two parts accommodate countries with a common law system and civil law system, respectively. The third part of the book contains one study of an Islamic law system, namely Algeria (Chap. 10). The fourth consists of international and regional legal systems, including studies of the communications procedures under the International Covenant on Civil and Political Right (ICCPR), the Convention on the Elimination of All Forms of Discrimination against Women (CEDAW) and the African Charter on the Rights and Welfare of the Child (ACRWC), as well as studies of the use of the CRC and related instruments by the European Court of Human Rights (Council of Europe), the European Court of Justice (EU) and the Inter-American Court of Human Rights.

In the first part, four country studies are presented. Skelton (Chap. 2) shows that the South African constitutional democratic legal order has created a 'favourable climate for child rights litigation', and points in particular to the creativity of the South African Constitutional Court. Supported by the South African Bill of Rights, in which children's rights have been acknowledged explicitly (art. 28), the Court has paved the way for its children's rights jurisprudence, which relies significantly on the CRC and related documents, including General Comments of the Committee on the Rights of the Child and the ACRWC. Skelton also stresses the critical role that child rights litigators have played in this regard.

The study of India by Ganguly and Asthana (Chap. 3) provides another example of active children's rights litigation. The authors point to the incremental use of the CRC by litigators and courts at all levels, including the Supreme Court, High Courts and sometimes also lower Courts. They conclude that the CRC 'has contributed significantly to the growth and evolution of jurisprudence on child rights, serving in particular as a guiding force in filling gaps that existed in domestic legislation'. At the same time, they note that 'there is still tremendous scope for identifying areas in existing laws, policies and practices where the standards set by the CRC are yet to be realised and for which judicial intervention will be required'.

A third example of such litigation is found in Dohrn's thought-provoking case study of the United States (Chap. 5), the only country in this book which has not ratified the CRC. She argues that '[t]he unlikely element of success in the US campaigns challenging the juvenile death penalty and extreme sentencing of children is the express recognition, by the US Supreme Court in two germinal cases, of the standards of the Convention on the Rights of the Child (CRC), the role of international human rights law, and the practices of other nations'. Dohrn, who has been at the heart of these campaigns, explains how litigators managed to persuade the US Supreme Court, in the absence of CRC ratification, to adopt international children's rights standards as a frame of reference supporting and confirming the Court's interpretation of the US Constitution.

All three country studies show that the domestic constitutional or supreme courts, supported or even stimulated by the domestic constitutional framework, acted as significant generators for the inclusion of international law and related legal documents as well as judicial practices of other jurisdictions. In addition, the studies underscore the importance of active and/or strategic litigation, a practice that presupposes both a degree of knowledge about the potential of the CRC and related international standards as well as the skills to litigate in a strategic manner. Moreover, it should be noted that the examples of case law found in these studies of common law countries can be discussed as thoroughly as they are thanks to the existence of extensive court clarifications, a legal feature one will not always encounter in countries with a civil law tradition.

The fourth country study of this part of the book is Williams's account of England and Wales (Chap. 4). She highlights the different ways in which the CRC has found its way into domestic law in England and Wales even though it has not yet been incorporated in domestic legislation—a prerequisite, given the United Kingdom's dualistic system. To illustrate this development, Williams refers to Baroness Hale's statement: 'When two interpretations … are possible, the interpretation chosen should be that which better complies with the commitment to the welfare of children which this country has made when ratifying the UNCRC'. In another case, it was argued that '[u]nless we in this jurisdiction are to fall out of step with similar societies as they safeguard art 12 rights, we must, in the case of articulate teenagers, accept that the right to freedom of expression and participation outweighs the paternalistic judgment of welfare'. However, Williams argues that, despite the influence the CRC has had on courts' decisions, '[l]egislative incorporation is vital to deliver the necessary systemic changes', and goes on to cite Wales as an example of a novel legislative model.

The second part of this book consists of four studies of civil law countries. Limbeek and Bruning (The Netherlands, Chap. 6) and Vandenhole (Belgium, Chap. 7) present comprehensive studies of the use of the CRC in domestic jurisprudence. While these reveal an increasing use of the CRC in case law in both countries, Vandenhole finds that the denial of direct effect is a major obstacle impeding the CRC from making a substantive impact on Belgian jurisprudence; the self-executing force of CRC provisions plays a role in the Netherlands as well, and is perceived differently by the courts.

The authors of both studies nevertheless observe that courts need not depend on the issuance of direct effect (a typical feature of monistic systems such as Belgium and the Netherlands) and can use the CRC to fill gaps in domestic legislation and as a tool of interpretation when applying it in relevant matters. With regard to migration cases, for instance, in Belgium the expulsion of unaccompanied children without a concrete, sustainable solution in their country of origin has been considered a violation of the best interests of the child and articles 3 and 20 CRC. The Dutch Council of State decided in 2012 that article 3 CRC obliges administrative decision-makers to take into account the best interests of the child even when this is not in line with specific legislation.

However, neither country's jurisprudence reflects a comprehensive and unambiguous approach to the use of the CRC; moreover, Vandenhole argues that the 'full potential of the CRC and the interpretative work of the CRC Committee has not yet been fully capitalised upon by Belgian judicial bodies'. Limbeek and Bruning underline the need for specific training of law professionals in order to improve the quality of the influence of the CRC on Dutch case law.

Vandenhole also points out the tendency for courts to use 'open concepts', such as the best interests of the child principle, rather than specific rights laid down in the CRC. Couzens makes a similar observation in a study of France (Chap. 8). Her analysis of the case law of the country's two supreme courts indicates that in this jurisprudence the application of art. 3(1) CRC is dominant and has made the best-interests principle a 'direct source of legal entitlements and obligations'. Couzens notes that, despite the direct application of a general principle of the CRC, courts have not been mobilised by the CRC to deal with controversial issues in a more child-oriented manner. According to her, this may well be due to the fact that the CRC has not been used as an interpretive tool in relation to the French Constitution.

The fourth study in this part of the book concerns Serbia (Chap. 9). Vučković Šahović and Savić provide examples of promising children's rights case law in a legal system that has not yet embraced children's rights, in particular children's rights to access to justice and to effective remedies. The authors explain, in addition, that the justiciability of children's rights is virtually impossible in a system in which the rule of law is weak, corruption is high and the judiciary inefficient. Vučković Šahović and Savić outline a number of important steps that need to be taken in order to enable children's rights litigation in Serbia.

Filali addresses similar challenges in his study of Algeria (Chap. 10), the only survey of an Islamic legal system in this book. He explains that although the CRC would take precedence over Algeria's domestic law after ratification and publication, there are significant challenges to the implementation of children's rights, including the use of the CRC in litigation. Sharia law takes precedence over civil family law, and this places major legal and cultural limitations on the implementation of children's rights in Algeria. Filali underscores the need for a specific Code on Children's Rights and the presence of an engaged and dedicated judiciary. However, he also points to the need for cultural change, arguing that legislative and juridical changes will not be enough.

The final and fourth part of this book examines the role that children's rights play in the decisions and judgments of international treaty bodies such as the Human Rights Committee (HRC), the Committee for the Elimination of Discrimination against Women, and the African Committee of Experts on the Rights and the Welfare of the Child (African Committee), and regional judicial bodies, including the European Court of Human Rights, the European Court of Justice, and the Inter-American Court of Human Rights.

Zayas (Chap. 11) shows that both the HRC and CEDAW have provided significant guidance on the interpretation of provisions under the ICCPR and CEDAW with particular relevance for children. According to Zayas, this may be due to the absence (until April 2014 when the Third Optional Protocol to the CRC entered into force) of an individual complaints mechanism for children under the CRC. Zayas's analysis, however, also shows that neither the HRC nor the CEDAW Committee make any reference to the CRC and/or the general Comments of the CRC Committee in their interpretation of the child-specific provisions of the ICCPR and CEDAW. Furthermore, he emphasises that in view of the non-binding decisions of the treaty bodies, it remains important that states parties are willing to implement these decisions. National legislation may well be needed for domestic judicial authorities to incorporate these decisions into domestic case law. Zayas argues that this will be relevant as well for the Third Optional Protocol to the CRC on a Communications Procedure.

Sloth-Nielsen (Chap. 15) provides concrete examples of the early case law developments of the African Committee of Experts on the Rights and Welfare of the Child as a source of inspiration for the Committee on the Rights of the Child on how to deal with individual communications of children. She stresses the importance of awareness of the communications procedure; the need for room for grass-roots organisations and individual child complainants to be able to lodge complaints; and the need for technical and financial resources to exhaust domestic remedies and pursue a complaint at the international level. The experience under the African children's rights system provides for interesting insights, as pointed out by Sloth-Nielsen. She draws attention in particular to the need for expeditious processes; the challenges human rights treaty bodies face inasmuch as they are not full-blown courts with extensive investigating powers; and the need for a continuum between national litigation, judicial decision-making and the complaints mechanism before the African Committee.

At the European level, the ECtHR has developed a growing body of legally-binding case law that incorporates children's rights standards, notwithstanding that the European Convention of Human Rights contains only few references to children. With the focus on article 12 CRC, Kilkelly (Chap. 12*)* shows that, even though it lacks explicit clarification, the ECtHR's case law has unmistakably been informed by the principle and substance of article 12 CRC. However, she also emphasises that the ECtHR is far from having realised the potential of the CRC and should go beyond listing international standards to make explicit reference to particular CRC provisions. Kilkelly argues that there is a 'need for regional and international bodies to engage with and respond to each other's jurisprudence'. This would enable courts 'to make a further, important contribution to the wider understanding of the application of children's rights in specific contexts'.

In her chapter on the case law of the European Court of Justice (Chap. 13), Stalford explains that although the European Union has made efforts to integrate references to CRC provisions in its standard-setting activities and a mainstreaming strategy for children has become apparent, the Court of Justice 'has so far evaded any serious scrutiny when it comes to the actual implementation of children's rights measures'. According to Stalford, this is a missed opportunity, because if the court were to adopt a different approach this would provide 'an invaluable mechanism for stimulating dialogue between the Member States as to how they should apply uniform EU children's rights measures'. In addition, it would reinforce the international obligations in respect of children's rights to which all EU Member States are bound.

Finally, Feria-Tinta addresses the use of the CRC by the Inter-American Court of Human Rights in her study (Chap. 14), observing that the CRC has been a substantive tool for construing obligations for States parties under the American Convention on Human Rights. As far as the use of the CRC as a procedural tool is concerned, she concludes that it has indeed been used as an important tool to better state the law in the Americas and thereby maintain the unity of international law. In doing so, this Court has provided an interesting example for other legal systems in dealing with children's rights issues.

4 Concluding Observations

4.1 The CRC in Litigation at National Level

It may be too early to identify clear and emerging trends in the way the CRC is used in litigation at the national level. However, some developments can be noted:

- The significant impact of the CRC on explicit constitutional recognition of the rights of the child (South Africa and, to a certain degree India).
- The growing use of the CRC in countries with dualistic systems even when it has not been incorporated legislatively into their national laws (England and Wales), and its use in court decisions in countries that are not states parties to the CRC (United States). This can be seen as an indication of the truly world-wide impact the CRC could make and of its increasing recognition as the global and—arguably—universal frame of reference for children's rights.
- Growing acceptance of the self-executing nature of the articles 2, 3 and 12 of the CRC. This is important because the Committee on the Rights of the Child considers these articles (together with art. 6) as the CRC's general principles, meaning that they should be taken fully into account in the implementation of the other articles of the CRC. A significant number of the cases presented in the different studies of this book show that these articles are indeed taken into account by domestic courts in different areas of law such as family law, migration law and administrative law.
- The viewpoint, expressed by all the authors, that there is still a long way to go, particularly in countries strongly influenced by Islamic law (Algeria), to establish a practice in which the CRC is used systematically as a key tool for respecting, protecting and fulfilling the rights of the child. This seems especially true of the child's economic, social and cultural rights.

4.2 The CRC in Litigation at Regional and International Level

The chapters on the CRC's use in litigation at the regional and international level identify a number of encouraging developments, but there are notable differences among the latter. Given that regional courts have the power to issue binding decisions, they are discussed first, after which some remarks are made on the activities of human rights treaty bodies.

The Inter-American Court on Human Rights turns out to be the most progressive regional court in this survey. In using the CRC as a tool for interpreting the provisions of the American Convention on Human Rights, the Court states that both this Convention and the CRC are part of a broad international *corpus iuris* for the protection of children. This position supports the Court in establishing the content and the scope of general provisions defined in article 19 of the American Convention. The CRC forms an integral part of the Court's activities in its interpretation of the American Convention (see Chap. 14). In this regard, it is noteworthy that the Inter-American Court does not work according the margin-of-appreciation doctrine, one which is embraced by the European Court of Human Rights and which affords States parties a certain amount of discretion, subject to judicial scrutiny. The Inter-American Court, thanks to its power enshrined in article 63(1) of the American Convention, is also able to provide specific, and rather creative, remedies and compensation for violations of children's rights, including investment and trust funds for victims as well as public apologies and acknowledgements in which, for instance, public places such as streets and squares are named in honour of the affected children.

The two European Courts dealt with in Chaps. 12 and 13 show in their judgments a growing use of the CRC as a guiding legal instrument. While the ECtHR seems more advanced in this respect than the European Court of Justice (ECJ), both of these courts have also drawn considerable criticism for, among other things, the unpredictability of the recently applied and developed legal formulas (see also Nissen 2013). Other scholars have addressed the legal uncertainty in the ECtHR's application of the best-interests principle in family law cases, and judges have been called upon to clarify the relevant factors in determining the best interests and the weight to be attached to these factors (Van Bueren 2007). The ECJ has been criticised on the grounds that its case law has become so individualistic and fact-specific as to raise the accusation of arbitrariness (Nic Shuibhne 2012).

In the light of these criticisms (see also Kilkelly and Stalford in their respective contributions to this book), it can be concluded that further action is needed in order to use the CRC as an important standards-setting instrument for the interpretation of both the European Convention on Human Rights as well as EU Law. As Kilkelly states in Chap. 12, there is clearly a need for regional and international courts and treaty bodies to engage with and respond to each other's jurisprudence (for example, see Zayas's analysis of the recommendations of the HRC and CEDAW Committee, which lack explicit reference to the CRC and the work of the CRC Committee).

Finally, the experiences of the African Committee of Experts on the Rights and Welfare of the Child in dealing with individual communications provide useful lessons for the CRC Committee when it starts to handle the communications submitted under the Third Optional Protocol to the CRC. The decision-making process can be very lengthy, and it is necessary to take effective measures for producing the final decisions as soon as possible. Children would have undergone already the long process of exhausting national remedies and should not have to face another protracted wait before hearing a final decision.

5 Litigating the Rights of the Child: How to Proceed from Here?

This book is a first step in a process of systematically compiling and analysing international, regional and national jurisprudence concerning the rights of the child. States parties to the CRC play a vital role in encouraging and supporting analytical compilations of domestic court decisions on the implementation of the provisions of the CRC, compilations which can be used to assess the degree to which children can have meaningful access to justice and find adequate remedies for violations of their rights. In addition, these compilations should stimulate education and ongoing training for judges and other legal professionals (for example, lawyers) in and around courts on the use of the CRC in their work. The sources of information provided to (future) professionals should not only focus on the significance of litigation, but also connect the use of the CRC and related international, regional and domestic standards to legislative measures and effective enforcement mechanisms.

Furthermore, the regional courts discussed in this book can make significant progress by integrating the CRC in their decision-making processes and by paying greater attention to the underlying clarification. This could also contribute considerably to the inclusion of international children's rights law in domestic jurisprudence. In addition, it is recommended that human rights treaty bodies dealing with communications develop a practice of using each other's experiences and jurisprudence in order to make the communications procedure a more effective instrument for protecting children's rights. In this regard, the Committee on the Rights of the Child could play a leading role under its new mandate since the entry into force of the Third Optional Protocol to the CRC on a Communications Procedure in April 2014.

References

Arts, K. (2010). *Coming of age in a world of diversity. An assessment of the UN convention on the rights of the child.* The Hague: International Institute of Social Studies.

Van Bueren, G. (2007). *Child rights in Europe: Convergence and divergence in judicial protection.* Strasbourg: Council of Europe.

De Graaf, J. H., et. al. (2012). *De toepassing van het internationale verdrag inzake de rechten van het kind in de Nederlandse Rechtspraak.* Nijmegen: Ars Aequi Libri.

Feria-Tinta, M. (2008). *The landmark rulings of the Inter-American court of human rights on the rights of the child.* Leiden: Martinus Nijhoff Publishers.

Fortin, J. (2004). Children's rights: Are the courts now taking them more seriously? *K.C.L.J.*, *15*, 253.

Kilkelly, U. (1999). *The child and the European convention on human rights.* Aldershot: Ashgate.

Kilkelly, U. (2001). The best of both worlds for children's rights: Interpreting the European convention on human rights in the light of the UN convention on the rights of the child. *Human Rights Quarterly, 23*, 308–326.

Nolan, A. (2011). *Children's socio-economic rights, democracy and the courts*. Oxford: Hart Publishing.

Nic Shuibhne, N. (2012). (Some of) the kids are all right: Comment on McCarthy and Dereci. *Common Market Law Review, 491*, 349–379.

Nissen, E. (2013). *The rights of minor EU member state nationals wishing to enjoy family life with a non-EU parent in their country of nationality: A study in the light of the UN convention on the rights of the child*. Nijmegen: Wolf Legal Publishers.

Ruitenberg, G. C. A. M. (2003). *Het internationaal kinderrechtenverdrag in de Nederlandse rechtspraak*. Amsterdam: SWP.

Sandberg, K. (2014). The role of national courts in promoting children's rights: The case of Norway. *International Journal of Children's Rights, 1*, 1–20.

Sloth-Nielsen, J. (2012). Modern African childhood: Does law matter? In M. Freeman (Ed.), *Law and childhood studies (current legal issues volume 14)*. Oxford: Oxford University Press.

Sloth-Nielsen, J., & Kruuse, H. (2013). A maturing manifesto: The constitutionalisation of children's rights in South African jurisprudence 2007–2012. *The International Journal of Children's Rights, 4*, 646–678.

Sloth-Nielsen, J., & Mezmur, B. D. (2008). 2 + 2 = 5? Exploring the domestication of the CRC in South African jurisprudence (2002–2006). *The International Journal of Children's Rights, 16*, 1–28.

Stalford, H. (2012). *Children and the European Union: Rights, welfare and accountability*. Oxford: Hart.

UNICEF. (2007a). *Protecting the world's children: Impact of the convention on the rights of the child in diverse legal systems*. Cambridge: Cambridge University Press.

UNICEF. (2007b). *Law reform and implementation of the convention on the rights of the child*. Florence: UNICEF Innocenti Research Centre.

Chapter 2
South Africa

Ann Skelton

Abstract The Bill of Rights in the South African Constitution contains a powerful children's rights clause, the wording of which was shaped by the Convention on the Rights of the Child (CRC). Since the introduction of the Bill of Rights, the CRC has continued to wield influence through litigation. This chapter describes the favourable climate for child rights litigation provided by South Africa's constitutional democratic legal order, including progressive rules on standing, costs, and the obligation on the courts to consider international law in Bill of Rights cases and to prefer an interpretation compatible with it. The courts have embraced the CRC to the extent that a description of every case mentioning it is beyond the scope of this chapter. Cases where the CRC was clearly evoked and had an influence on the outcome of cases are discussed according to thematic groups. The courts have also used the African Charter on the Rights and Welfare of the Child, as well as UN guidelines, resolutions and general comments. The chapter concludes by observing that these sources of international law create a rich store of ideas for child rights litigators to bring before the courts, ideas to which the courts fortunately appear to be receptive.

1 Introduction to the South African Constitutional and Legal System

South Africa is a constitutional democracy. The Constitution contains a progressive Bill of Rights comprising civil, political and socioeconomic rights. These rights are justiciable—any law or conduct inconsistent with them may be declared invalid by the superior courts.

A. Skelton (✉)
Centre for Child Law, University of Pretoria, Pretoria, South Africa
e-mail: Ann.Skelton@up.ac.za

T. Liefaard and J.E. Doek (eds.), *Litigating the Rights of the Child*,
DOI 10.1007/978-94-017-9445-9_2

The legal system is a hybrid one based on British common law and Roman-Dutch civil law. African customary law is recognised, provided it accords with the Bill of Rights. Procedurally, the law takes a largely common law approach, incorporating the rule of *stare decisis*, meaning the law is developed through precedents set by case law.

2 Children's Rights in the South African Bill of Rights

South Africa's Bill of Rights has been hailed internationally as a good example of a constitution providing for protection and advancement of children's rights (Alston and Tobin 2005). A range of obligations is placed on the state for the promotion, protection and realisation of children's rights. With the exception of the right to vote or stand for public office, children are entitled to all rights contained in the Bill of Rights (Friedman et al. 2009).

In recognition of children's vulnerability, section 28 provides additional protections. These include the rights to name and nationality; to family care or parental care or appropriate alternative care when removed from the family environment; to basic nutrition, shelter, basic health care services and social services; to be protected from maltreatment, neglect, abuse or degradation; to be protected from age-inappropriate or exploitative labour; not to be detained except as a measure of last resort and then only for the shortest appropriate time, separately from adults and in conditions that take account of the child's age; to legal representation at state expense in civil proceedings if substantial injustice would otherwise result; and not to be used in armed conflict. Section 28(2) provides a further layer of protection by specifying that a child's best interests are of paramount importance in every matter concerning the child. A child is a person below the age of 18 years.

3 The Influence of International Law and Foreign Law

A major factor that influenced the constitution-drafting process was South Africa's signature in 1993, and ratification in 1995, of the CRC. This signified the country's acceptance of the international body of human rights regarding children, and provided the legal backing for the children's section in the Bill of Rights. Children's rights activists and political parties relied on the CRC as an authority in their submissions to the technical committees drafting the Bill of Rights (Skelton and Proudlock 2013). The committees in turn relied on the CRC when making choices as to how the section should be worded (Du Plessis and Corder 1994). As a result, the influence of the CRC can be seen throughout the text of section 28.

Section 39(2) of the Constitution obliges courts to consider international law when interpreting a right in the Bill of Rights. Rosa and Dutschke (2006) argue that, based on this provision, the CRC is directly applicable in any case involving an interpretation of children's rights. If the text of a right in the Constitution has its roots in an international human rights instrument, the courts should prefer 'any reasonable interpretation of legislation that is consistent with international law'.[1] As will be demonstrated in this chapter, the South African courts have frequently relied on the CRC.

South Africa is described as having a monist legal system because section 231(4) of the Constitution states that an international agreement becomes law once it is enacted by national legislation. The CRC has not directly been enacted into law, although the Preamble to the Children's Act 38 of 2010 does refer to the CRC and other instruments. At the same time, the courts are enjoined to 'consider international law'.[2] According to the international law expert John Dugard, a treaty that has been signed and ratified is binding on South Africa, regardless of whether it has been signed into law (Dugard 2005). Sloth-Nielsen and Kruuse (2013) argue that South Africa has 'crossed the line from dualism and monism' in relation to child law. Part of the evidence for this, in their view, is that the courts go further than referring to binding instruments by invoking even 'soft law' in their judgments. The courts have also frequently relied on and cited the African Charter on the Rights and Welfare of the Child (ACRWC).[3]

The Constitution provides that the court *must* consider international law, and *may* consider foreign law, when interpreting the Bill of Rights.[4] Foreign law would include examples of legislative approaches from other countries, legal research and, in particular, foreign case law.

In the field of children's rights the Constitutional Court has relied far less on foreign law than international law. There are examples, which will be considered in this chapter, where the Court has made reference to Canadian, United States and European Union case law, but it has been sparing compared to the significant attention paid to the international law. This may point to the fact that the South African Bill of Rights is unique in certain respects and has a powerful children's rights clause. Case comparisons with foreign jurisdictions are hence arguably of limited application. The Constitutional Court seems confident to build its own child rights jurisprudence, but roots it in international and regional law.

4 Children and Children's Rights Organisations as Litigators

The South African Constitution takes a broad approach to the question of who may bring cases before the courts. Section 38 of the Constitution, which applies where someone is alleging that a right in the Bill of Rights has been or may be

---

1 S 233.

2 S 39(1).

3 South Africa ratified the ACRWC in 2000.

4 S 39(1).

infringed, sets out the rules on standing. A matter may be brought by (i) persons acting in their own interest, (ii) persons acting on behalf of other persons, (iii) persons acting on behalf of a group or class of persons, (iv) persons acting in the public interest, and (v) associations acting in the interests of their members.

It is therefore evident that under South African law children can act in their own name and litigate all the way to the Constitutional Court. The case of *MEC for Education, KwaZulu-Natal v. Pillay*[5] was brought by the mother of Sunali, a teenage girl, who claimed that her daughter had been discriminated against on the grounds of culture and religion because she wore a nose stud contrary to school rules. The respondent claimed that the fact that Sunali had not given evidence nor deposed to any affidavits was fatal to the applicant's case. The Court found that this was not fatal, even though it would have liked to hear from Sunali herself. Langa CJ observed as follows[6]:

It is always desirable, and may sometimes be vital, to hear from the person whose religion or culture is at issue. That is often no less true when the belief in question is that of a child. Legal matters involving children often exclude the children and the matter is left to adults to argue and decide on their behalf.

Langa CJ also referred to Sachs J's 'postscript' to *Christian Education SA v. Minister of Education*,[7] a case about corporal punishment in schools. Noting that the Court would have liked to hear from the children, Sachs said their 'actual experiences and opinions would not necessarily have been decisive, but they would have enriched the dialogue, and the factual and experiential foundations for the balancing exercise in this difficult matter would have been more secure'. These judgments demonstrate the Constitutional Court's understanding of children's right to participate.

In the case of *Centre for Child law v. Minister of Justice and Constitutional Development and Others (NICRO as amicus curiae)*,[8] section 38 of the Bill of Rights was invoked. The Centre brought the application in its own interest, on behalf of all 16- and 17-year-old children at risk of being sentenced under the new provisions on minimum sentences, and in the public interest. In the High Court the Minister had unsuccessfully challenged the Centre's legal standing, contending that the issues were academic. In the Constitutional Court the Minister abandoned this aspect of the challenge. Cameron J approved of this, and made the following clarification:

> Although the Centre did not act on behalf of (or join) any particular child sentenced under the statute as amended, its provisions are clearly intended to have immediate effect on its promulgation. So the prospect of children being sentenced under the challenged provisions was immediate, and the issue anything but abstract or academic. The Centre's stated focus is children's rights, and in this case it has standing to protect them. It was thus

---

[5] 2008 (1) SA 474 (CC).

[6] Para. 56.

[7] 2000 (4) SA 757 (CC).

[8] 2009 (6) SA 632 (CC).

> entitled to take up the cudgels. To have required the Centre to augment its standing by waiting for a child to be sentenced under the new provisions would, in my view, have been an exercise in needless formalism.[9]

The broad approach to standing has been important in children's rights cases. By contrast, an application to the Northern Ireland Court of Appeal brought by the Commissioner for Children to develop the common law to exclude the defence of reasonable chastisement of children was rejected due to lack of standing because she could not be classed as a victim under the UK Human Rights Act (*Northern Ireland Commissioner for Children and Young Peoples' Application*).[10]

Another favourable factor is the courts' approach to costs in constitutional litigation. The rule is that where the litigation raises genuine constitutional issues, the applicants are not at risk of a costs order against them if they are unsuccessful; if successful, they are entitled to costs [*Biowatch v. Registrar Genetic Resources* (*Centre for Child Law & Others as Amici Curiae*)].[11] Thus, a broader range of public interest litigants, including children and child rights organisations, can approach the courts in order to enforce and advance the rights in the Bill of Rights.

In the early days of litigation under the Bill of Rights, several cases were brought by adults in which children's rights were invoked but were not necessarily central (Sloth-Nielsen 2002). During the second decade of litigation, children's rights organisations became more active in bringing litigation before the courts (Sloth-Nielsen and Mezmur 2008). Interventions by various *amici curiae*—friends of the court—have proved to be an effective vehicle, because in South Africa the *amicus curiae* plays a significant role and can shape the outcome of a case through written and oral submissions (Budlender 2006).

5 Cases Relying on the CRC

South African courts have embraced the CRC to such an extent that it goes beyond the scope of this chapter to discuss all of the many judgments referring to it. The chapter therefore focuses on Constitutional Court judgments, as well as those of High Courts where the reasoning was directly influenced by the CRC.

The Constitutional Court has clearly stated that section 28 of the Constitution must be seen as responding in an 'expansive' way to the international obligations as a State party to the CRC, and that the CRC has become the international standard against which to measure legislation and policies.[12] In what follows, the cases that have relied on the CRC are discussed under a number of themes. Dominant among them, and cutting across private and public law cases, is the principle of the

---

[9] Para. 18.

[10] 2009 NICA 10.

[11] 2009 (6) SA 232 (CC).

[12] *S v M* (*Centre for Child Law as Amicus Curiae*) 2008 (3) SA 232 (CC), para. 16.

best interests of the child. Other crucial subject areas are children's right to family care and alternative care, socioeconomic rights, the right to education, and children in the criminal justice system.

5.1 Best Interests

The best interests principle has been an established principle in South African law since the 1940s,[13] but its influence was previously limited to family law and care proceedings. It is clear that section 28(2), following the lead of the international instruments,[14] expands the meaning and application of section 28(2) to all aspects of the law that affect children.

The Constitutional Court has delivered several important judgments regarding the best interests of the child and what the principle means. In *Minister of Welfare and Population Development v. Fitzpatrick and Others*[15] the Court declared section 18(4)(f) of the Child Care Act[16] invalid because it prohibited the adoption of a South African child by non-citizens. The Court found the law too restrictive because it limited the best interests of the child, which would sometimes be achieved through the child's being adopted by non-South African parents. The Fitzpatrick case made it clear that section 28(2) does not only refer to the rights enumerated in section 28(1) but that section 28(2) is also a right, not merely a guiding principle.

In addition to being a self-standing right, it also strengthens other rights. Thus, the Constitutional Court has drawn the best interests of the child into cases pertaining to the right to family or parental care[17]; international child abduction[18]; child pornography[19]; the right to housing or shelter[20]; adoption of children by unmarried fathers,[21]

---

13 *Fletcher v Fletcher* 1948 (1) SA 130 (A).

14 Art. 3 of the CRC, art. 4 of the ACRWC.

15 2000 (3) SA 422 (CC).

16 Act 74 of 1983.

17 *Grootboom v Government of South Africa* 2001 (1) SA 46 (CC); *Bannantyne v Bannantyne* 2003 (2) SA 363 (CC); *Du Toit v Minister of Welfare and Population Development* (*Lesbian and Gay Equality Project as Amicus Curiae*) 2003 (2) SA 198 (CC); *C and Others v Department of Health and Social Development and Others* 2012 (2) SA 208 (CC).

18 *Sonderup v Tondelli* 2001 (1) SA 1171 (CC).

19 *De Reuck v Director of Public Prosecutions* (*Witwatersrand Local Division*) 2004 (1) SA 406 (CC).

20 Government of the Republic of South Africa v Grootboom 2001 (1) SA 46 (CC). See also Van den Burg 2012 (2) SACR 331 (CC) where the court applied best interests in a case where parents were facing forfeiture of their home to the state because they refused orders to stop operating a tavern on the premises.

21 *Fraser v Children's Court, Pretoria North* 1997 (2) SA 261 (CC).

by same-sex couples[22] and by foreign couples[23]; inheritance under customary law[24]; the right to access health care in the form of preventive anti-retroviral medicines[25]; the right to social assistance[26]; the right of children to privacy and dignity[27]; the testimony of child victims and witnesses[28]; the rights of children to be detained only as a measure of last resort[29]; and the right of children to a basic education.[30]

In the case of *AD v. DW*[31] the Court weighed up the best interests of the child against other important international law principles pertaining to inter-country adoption. In the Supreme Court of Appeal, the majority judgment had given substantial weight to the principle of subsidiarity encapsulated in article 21(2) of the CRC, which requires that sufficient efforts must be made to find a suitable family placement for a child in his or her country of origin before proceeding with inter-country adoption. This principle had not been followed in the case at hand. It is interesting that the *AD v. DW* case is one where the Court looked at foreign case law, in this instance in an attempt to better understand the concept of subsidiarity. The Court referred to the EHRR case of *Pini and others v. Romania*[32] and to a judgment of the British Columbia Supreme Court, *J (AL) v. M (SJ); ALJ v. SJM.*[33] However, little turned on the foreign law because ultimately the Court's approach was that, as important as the subsidiarity principle is, it is less important than the best interests of the child.

This decision demonstrates the power of the best interests clause in South Africa's Bill of Rights. Moreover, the Court found that the best interests of each child must be examined on an individual basis and not in the abstract. Sachs J stressed that 'child law is an area that abhors maximalist legal propositions that preclude or diminish the possibilities of looking at and evaluating the specific circumstances of each case'.[34]

---

[22] *Du Toit v Minister of Welfare and Population Development (Lesbian and Gay Equality Project as Amicus Curiae)* 2003 (2) SA 198 (CC).

[23] *AD v DW (Centre for Child Law as Amicus Curiae, Department for Social Development as Intervening Party)* 2008 (3) SA 183 (CC).

[24] *Bhe v Magistrate, Khayelitsha (Commission for Gender Equality as Amicus Curiae)* 2005 (1) SA 480 (CC).

[25] *Minister of Health v Treatment Action Campaign* 2002 (5) SA 721 (CC).

[26] *Khosa v Minister of Social Development; Mahaule v Minister of Social Development* 2004 (6) SA 505 (CC).

[27] *Johncom Media Investments Limited v M (Media Monitoring Project as Amicus Curiae)* 2009 (4) SA 7 (CC).

[28] *Director of Public Prosecutions, Transvaal v Minister of Justice* 2009 (2) SACR 130 (CC).

[29] *Centre for Child Law v Minister of Justice (NICRO as Amicus Curiae)* 2009 (6) SA 632 (CC).

[30] *Governing Body of the Juma Musjid Primary School v Essay NO (Centre for Child Law and Another as Amici Curiae)* 2011 (8) BCLR 761 (CC).

[31] Note 23 above.

[32] 2005 40 EHRR.

[33] (1994) 98 BCLR (2d) 277.

[34] Note 23 above, para. 55.

Section 28(2) has also been used to limit rights. *Sonderup v. Tondelli*[35] dealt with the rule of 'peremptory return' in the Hague Convention on the Civil Aspects of International Child Abduction, meaning that as a general rule children must be returned to their countries of origin as soon as possible so that the courts in those countries can deal with the legal disputes concerning care and contact. The rule was found by the court to satisfy the long-term best interests of all children. If a child's short-term best interests were limited by the Hague Convention, such limitation would be justifiable in terms of section 36 of the Constitution, largely because of the important purpose of the Convention to protect all children from the negative effects of their being unlawfully moved across international borders.

In *De Reuck v. Director of Public Prosecution (Witwatersrand Local Division)*[36] the Constitutional Court made it clear that the word 'paramount' in section 28(2) does not mean that children's best interests can never be limited by other rights. The High Court judgment of *De Reuck* had found that a child's best interest is the single most important factor to be considered when balancing or weighing competing rights concerning children and that all competing rights must defer to the rights of children unless unjustifiable.[37] This was overruled by the Constitutional Court. To say that section 28(2) of the Constitution 'trumps' other provisions of the Bill of Rights was 'alien to the approach adopted by this Court that constitutional rights are mutually interrelated and interdependent and form a single constitutional value system'.[38]

The Court thus found that section 28(2), like the other rights enshrined in the Bill of Rights, is subject to reasonable and justifiable limitations and that it was over-simplistic to interpret the child's best interests as a concept always overriding other competing rights. However, in the De Reuck case the Court found that while, on the face of it, the law banning child pornography limits rights to privacy and freedom of expression, this limitation is justifiable due to the importance of the purpose of protecting children's best interests.

The meaning of 'paramount importance' was expanded upon in *S v. M*.[39] A single mother of three children was facing a short term of imprisonment for fraud. She appealed, claiming that when sentencing primary caregivers the courts should take into account the effects of imprisonment on the caregivers' children. The competing rights, therefore, were, on the one hand, children's rights to parental care and consideration of best interests, and, on the other, the rights of the community to be protected from crime.

Sachs J pointed out that the very expansiveness of the paramountcy principle appears to promise everything but deliver little in particular. The best interests concept is indeterminate, resulting in various interpretations. Sachs J went on to

---

[35] 2001 (1) SA 1171 (CC).

[36] 2004 (1) SA 406 (CC).

[37] 2003 (3) SA 389 (W), para. 10.

[38] Note 19 above, para. 55.

[39] Note 12 above.

say that it is precisely the contextual nature and inherent flexibility of section 28 that constitutes the source of its strength. The determination of best interests will depend on the circumstances of each case, and this is not a weakness but a strength. A truly child-centred approach requires an in-depth consideration of the needs and rights of the particular child in his or her 'precise real-life situation'; applying a predetermined formula for the sake of certainty, irrespective of the circumstances, would in fact be contrary to the best interests of the child.

A more difficult question is establishing what Sachs J referred to as 'an operational thrust for the paramountcy principle'. *S v. M* went further than any previous judgment in explaining paramountcy, though it still defines the principle more by stating what it is not rather than what it is (Skelton 2008). It is not an 'overbearing and unrealistic trump', and it cannot be interpreted 'to mean that the direct or indirect impact of a measure or action on children must in all cases oust or override all other considerations'. Sachs J concluded that 'the fact that the best interests of the child are paramount does not mean that they are absolute'. Acknowledging these realities is important because if the best interests principle is spread 'too thin', it risks becoming devoid of meaning instead of promoting the rights of children as it was intended to do.[40]

The *S v. M* case has attracted worldwide attention (Robertson 2012), and has been followed in South African law in a range of criminal matters relating to sentencing and bail decisions (Skelton and Courtenay 2012). The Constitutional Court's analysis of best interests and paramountcy has been applied in a wide array of cases across the public law/private law spectrum. In a similar case heard in 2011, the Constitutional Court narrowed the scope of the judgment to single primary caregivers in a case where a mother still living with the children's father was facing prison. The Court nevertheless saw fit to appoint a curator *ad litem* to investigate and report on the children's circumstances.

In *Centre for Child Law v. Minister of Justice*, which will be discussed in more detail later, Cameron J made the point that the constitutional injunction that a 'child's best interests are of paramount importance in every matter concerning the child' does not entirely preclude sending child offenders to jail, though this must always be done as a measure of last resort. According to Cameron J, paramountcy means that 'the child's interests are "more important than anything else", but not that everything else is unimportant'.

5.2 Family Care, Parental Care and Appropriate Alternative Care

Many children in South Africa live in the care of extended family members rather than their biological parents, which explains the rather unusual arrangement of section 28(1)(b) placing 'family care' in front of 'parental care'. The Bill of Rights

---

40 Para. 42.

does not include a right to family life, although the courts have forged such a right using the right to dignity.[41] The people who do have a clearly expressed right to family are children, making the concept of family life in the Bill of Rights a uniquely child-centred one. Section 28(1)(b), like the best interests right, has been used frequently by the courts in cases relating to parenting and same-sex couples, to interventions by the state that separate families (for example, deportation, imprisonment and forfeiture of the family home), and to drawing the line regarding the state's obligation on socioeconomic rights.

An important case regarding separation of children from their parents rested on a lacuna in the Children's Act to do with automatic review of decisions to remove children from their parents where there are concerns that they are in need of care and protection.[42] The factual context was that children were removed from parents who were working or begging at the side of the road. The parents approached the High Court for relief, and their children were returned to them. They further challenged the law as being unconstitutional because it did not allow for automatic review of decisions by social workers or police to remove children from their parents. They based their case in part on article 9 of the CRC (and article 19(1) of the ACRWC) to ensure that a child is not separated from his or her parents unless necessary for the best interests of the child and subject to judicial review, with an opportunity to participate in the proceedings.

The Court split three ways. The majority of the Constitutional Court upheld the challenge, finding that the law was unconstitutional insofar as it failed to provide judicial review of decisions to remove. The majority judgment, penned by Yacoob J, held that while removal of children was not per se an infringement of the right to parental care, removal without the opportunity to review did amount to a rights violation.

A separate but concurring judgment, written by Skweyiya J, went further, finding that any removal of a child is, on the face of it, a rights violation but one which may be reasonable and justifiable depending on the facts; however, it could never be reasonable if it was not subject to immediate review by the courts. Skweyiya J referred to article 19(1) of the ACRWC and article 9(1) of the CRC dealing with the separation of a child from parents, and the conditions related thereto. The judge also referred to the Canadian Supreme Court case of *New Brunswick [Minister of Health and Community Services v. G(J)]*,[43] which held that parents' participation is essential in hearings to determine whether the state should take children into care. In addition, the Constitutional Court noted that although South African law allows a general right of review of any administrative action, this would be too onerous for parents and children, and review should therefore happen automatically, not only at the behest of the affected parties.

---

[41] *Ex parte Chairperson of the Constitutional Assembly: In re certification of the Constitution of the Republic of South Africa*, 1996 (4) SA 744 (CC); *Dawood v Minister of Home Affairs* 2000 (3) SA 936 (CC); *Booysen v Minister of Home Affairs* 2001 (4) SA 485 (CC).

[42] *C and Others v Department of Health and Social Development and Others* 2012 (2) SA 208 (CC).

[43] 1999 (3) SCR 46.

A minority judgment written by Jafta J gives rise to some concern with regard to international law. While recognising that the international and regional instruments are binding, the judge found that although the right of review of such decisions is clearly set out in the CRC, there is no specific right to review of removal decisions set out in section 28 of the Constitution. The minority thus found that a constitutional challenge could not be mounted on that basis.

It is submitted, however, that this is a narrow, legalistic interpretation of how the Bill of Rights' provisions should be read against international law. Children do have the right to family and parental care in the Bill of Rights. All persons have a right to just administrative action as well as the right to be heard. It is the amalgamation of these rights which indicates why the right of review must be safeguarded in law. In the minority view, the current law had sufficient safeguards to prevent wrongful removal. However, the facts of the case clearly demonstrated that, despite the legal provisions, social workers and police had violated the rights of children and parents in the manner by which they removed the children; the facts also showed that no automatic right of recourse was open to these parents and children. The apparently protective law was, in other words, ineffective.

The majority of the Court correctly saw that the right of automatic review was intrinsic to a fair process that allows children's best interests to be considered properly. The law was therefore changed to incorporate provisions requiring that the matter be brought before court on the first court day after removal and that the parent and child be notified and be present. In future this would allow parents (and children of sufficient age and maturity) an opportunity to ask the children's court to reconsider the decision to remove the child, and, where appropriate, reverse the order.

5.3 Children's Socioeconomic Rights

5.3.1 Children Living with Their Parents

One of the Constitutional Court's most famous judgments is *Government of the Republic of South Africa v. Grootboom*,[44] which concerned a group of people who challenged the government's policy on housing. They based their argument in part on the fact that some of the families had children, and that children, in terms of section 28(1)(c), have a right to shelter which, unlike the right to housing in section 26, is unqualified; this means that it does not contain terms such as 'progressive realisation' or 'within available resources'.

The Constitutional Court began its examination of the question whether children had a direct and immediately enforceable right by considering the CRC. Yacoob J, writing for a unanimous Court, found that the CRC seeks to impose obligations on States parties to ensure the proper protection of children's rights. The court found that the state delineates these obligations by ensuring that parents fulfil their

44 2001 (1) SA 46 (CC).

obligations in relation to their children. This appears to be linked to article 18 of the CRC which places the primary responsibility to care for children on their parents. The court found that the obligation to provide shelter therefore falls first to parents.

In turn, the obligations on the state in relation to children who live with their parents or families are limited to providing the legal framework to prevent abuse and neglect, and, more broadly, to providing families with access to housing and other services. The full obligation would rest on the state only where parental care was 'lacking'. The Court did in fact find that all the families had a right to housing, a right to be realised progressively when sufficient funds became available, and that the government's plan was unreasonable. However, it declined to prioritise families with children, as it was of the view that children should not be used as 'stepping stones' for the realisation of the socioeconomic rights of their parents.

The Grootboom judgment left space to explore the possibility that children's socioeconomic rights would be directly and immediately enforceable (and not subject to progressive realisation) if they were 'lacking parental care'. The *Treatment Action Campaign* (*TAC*) case[45] dealt with access to treatment to avoid mother-to-child transmission of HIV-AIDS. The Court held that the state is obliged to ensure the protection of children's section 28 rights when the implementation of the right to parental or family care is lacking—and the *TAC* case dealt with children born in public hospitals to indigent mothers.

So, whilst *Grootboom* had ruled that children living with their parents would have to look to their parents rather than the state for the fulfilment of their section 28(1)(c) rights, in the TAC case the Court found that, although these children were living with their mothers, the latter were not able to provide medical treatment to them, and that it was the state's responsibility to do so.

5.3.2 Children Not Living with Their Parents

Since the judgments of *Grootboom* and *TAC*, the Centre for Child Law brought two matters before the High Courts which developed the law in this regard. The first case[46] dealt with unaccompanied foreign children who had come to South Africa from neighbouring countries on their own. The case determined that they were without parents and were therefore immediately entitled to social services. The second dealt with children in the care system who had been placed by a Court order in a school of industries, a secure residential care centre where they were physically and psychologically neglected and abused.[47] The Court made a series of orders to ensure their safety and protection. Although the state argued that it had insufficient funds, the Court was adamant that children who are wards of the state have an enforceable right to social services.

---

[45] *Minister of Health v Treatment Action Campaign* 2002 (5) SA 703 (CC).

[46] *Centre for Child Law v. Minister of Home Affairs* 2005 (6) SA 50 (T).

[47] *Centre for Child Law v. MEC for Education, Gauteng* 2008 (1) SA 223 (T).

In both cases the Court laid emphasis on the fact that if children are not living with their parents, they have a direct and immediate claim on the state for the fulfilment of their socioeconomic rights. The CRC was specifically invoked in the case about unaccompanied foreign children, with the judge pointing out that it affords every child the right to health, social security and education.

5.3.3 Education

An important socioeconomic right for children is the right to education. Until recently, education litigation has centred mainly around governance questions regarding admissions and language policy. However, in recent years the focus of litigation has moved to direct consideration of the right to a basic education, including issues of availability and accessibility. The right to education is included in the Bill or Rights at section 29, which guarantees everyone the right to a basic education. The section does not include any internal qualifiers such as 'progressive realisation' or 'within available resources'.

In *The Governing Body of the Juma Musjid Primary School and another v. Essay NO and Others* (*Centre for Child Law and Another as Amici Curiae*),[48] the Court interpreted section 29(1)(a), as follows (at para. 37):

> It is important, for the purposes of this judgment, to understand the nature of the right to 'a basic education' under section 29(1)(a). Unlike some of the other socioeconomic rights this right is immediately realisable. There is no internal limitation requiring that the right be 'progressively realised' within 'available resources' subject to 'reasonable legislative measures'. The right to a basic education in section 29(1)(a) may be limited only in terms of a law of general application which is 'reasonable and justifiable in an open and democratic society based on human dignity, equality and freedom'.

The Court also contextualised section 29(1)(a) within the broader international and regional human rights framework. Nkabinde J referred to the CRC, the ACRWC, the Universal Declaration of Human Rights and the International Covenant on Economic, Social and Cultural Rights, as well General Comment 13 issued by the Committee on Economic, Social and Cultural Rights. She quoted articles 28 and 29 of the CRC in full in footnotes. In particular, she drew attention to the fact that article 29(1) of the CRC spells out that the right to a basic education is aimed at promoting and developing a child's personality, talents and mental and physical abilities to her or her fullest potential.

In a different case, an organisation called the Western Cape Forum for Intellectual Disability[49] challenged the constitutionality of a policy that excluded children with severe intellectual disabilities from accessing education. The High Court invoked article 23 of the CRC, pointing out the obligations it creates to provide properly for disabled children. The Court also quoted from article 13(1) of

---

[48] Note 30 above.

[49] *Western Cape Forum for Disability v Government of the Republic of South Africa* 2011 (5) SA 87 (WCC).

the ACRWC, which provides the right of mentally or physically disabled children to special protection measure that ensure their dignity and promote self-reliance and active participation. The court handed down a structured interdict requiring a plan and regular reports to ensure the required programmes would be provided.

In South Africa, work on the justiciability of children's rights to education is at a relatively early stage of development. The next few years will no doubt see cases being brought on the complex issues of quality and equality in education (Skelton 2012). The country's education system is failing to produce the required results (Spaull 2013), making this is a crucial area of work, one in which international law and foreign law are likely to be highly influential.

5.4 Children in the Criminal Justice System

5.4.1 Child Offenders

The South African Courts have paid particular attention to articles 37 and 40 of the CRC, together with the non-binding instruments relating to juvenile justice. A raft of cases has incorporated these into South African jurisprudence.[50]

In an early case of the *Constitutional Court, S v. Williams*,[51] judicial whipping of child offenders was declared unconstitutional. The Court did consider foreign case law,[52] and noted judgments from neighbouring countries.[53] It went on to remark that it was necessary to follow a purposive approach in South Africa, a country which had been 'subjected to an unprecedented wave of violence' and where the political negotiations that resulted in the Constitution demonstrated a rejection of violence.[54]

In particular, the courts have paid attention to the principle incorporated in section 28(1)(g) of the Constitution (modelled on article 37(b)) that the detention of children should be a measure of last resort and that, if they are detained, it should be for the shortest appropriate period of time.

The *Centre for Child Law v. Minister of Justice*[55] was a challenge to the constitutionality of the minimum sentences law, insofar as it applied to 16- and 17-year-olds. The Constitutional Court held that the minimum sentencing legislation should

---

[50] *S v Z en vier ander sake* 1999 (1) SACR 427 (E); *S v Kwalase* 2000 (2) SACR 135 (C); *S v Nkosi* 2002 (1) SA 494 (W); *Director of Public Prosecutions, Kwa-Zulu Natal v P* 2006 (1) SACR 243 (SCA) and *S v N* 2008 (2) SACR 135 (SCA); *S v B* 2006 (1) SACR 311 (SCA).

[51] 1995 (3) SA 632.

[52] *Tyrer v United Kingdom* (1979–1980) 2 EHRR 1; *Ireland v United Kingdom* (1979–1980) EHRR 25; *Cosans v United Kingdom* (1980) 3 EHRR 531 (particularly the dissenting judgment of Klecker J).

[53] Ex Parte Attorney-General, Namibia: In re corporal punishment by organs of state 1991 (3) SA 76 (NmSC); S v F 1989 (1) SA 460 (ZHC).

[54] *S v Williams* par 51 and 52.

[55] 2009 (6) SA 632 (CC).

not apply to children aged 16 and 17 years old. The majority of the Constitutional Court found that the minimum sentencing legislation limited the discretion of sentencing officers by directing them to hand down long sentences (including life imprisonment) as a first resort. Furthermore, the legislation discouraged the use of non-custodial options, prevented courts from individualising sentences, and was likely to cause longer prison sentences. All of these features of the law amounted to an infringement of child offenders' rights in terms of section 28(1)(g).

In addition to relying on article 37(b) on which the section is based, the Court found that the following instruments 'count in favour of the view that minimum sentences should not be applied to child offenders': the United Nations Standard Minimum Rules for the Administration of Juvenile Justice (Beijing Rules); the United Nations Rules for the Protection of Juveniles Deprived of their Liberty (JDLs); and the United Nations Guidelines for the Prevention of Juvenile Delinquency (Riyadh Guidelines). The court specifically emphasised Rule 17(1)(a) of the Beijing Rules, which in relation to sentencing provides that '[t]he reaction taken shall always be in proportion not only to the circumstances and gravity of the offence but also to the circumstances and needs of the juvenile as well as the needs of society'. The court also quoted article 40(1) of the CRC in full in a footnote.

From all of these instruments the Court distilled the following principles: proportionality; imprisonment is a measure of last resort and for the shortest period of time; children must be treated differently from adults; and the well-being of the child is the central consideration.[56] The international principles are 'amply' embodied in the Bill of Rights, which leads directly to the conclusion by the Court that the law was unconstitutional.

The Court's interpretation of the last resort principle is interesting. The judgment pointed out that the Constitution does not prohibit Parliament from dealing effectively with child offenders—the fact that detention must be used only as a last resort in itself implies that imprisonment is sometimes necessary. However, the Bill of Rights mitigates the circumstances in which such imprisonment can happen. It must be a last (not a first or intermediate) resort, and it must be for the shortest appropriate period. The Court stated:

> If there is an appropriate option other than imprisonment, the Bill of Rights requires that it be chosen. In this sense, incarceration must be the sole appropriate option. But if incarceration is unavoidable, its form and duration must also be tempered, so as to ensure detention for the shortest possible period of time.[57]

The Court referred to the US Supreme Court case of *Roper v. Simmons*[58] to support the contention that children are less culpable than adults and that they are more susceptible to outside pressures, including peer pressure, than adults. It went on to cite with approval the Canadian Supreme Court case of *R v. B (D)*[59], in which the

---

[56] Para. 61.

[57] Para. 31.

[58] *Roper, Superintendent, Potosi Correctional Centre v Simmons* 543 US 551 (2005).

[59] 2008 SCC 25.

Court allowed a challenge based on the Canadian Charter of Rights to a law sentencing young offenders to adult penalties in serious cases unless the young offender could justify why an adult sentence should not be imposed. In this case, foreign law, as well as international law, was used to good effect.

Another criminal case that relied on the CRC dealt with the requirement that children should be tried in a closed court environment.[60] The case was a murder trial where the victim was an infamous right-wing leader. One of the two charged was a 15-year-old boy. The media wanted to sit in on the trial due to enormous public interest in the matter. The general rule is that children's trials must be held in private, though the law allows applications to be made. Relying on article 40 of the CRC, the judge upheld the general principle that for the child accused the courtroom should be closed and entry be permitted only in exceptional circumstances. The Court allowed the media to watch the trial via closed-circuit television, but took care to ensure that the child's identity was protected.

5.4.2 Child Victims

In a case dealing with testimony by child victims and witnesses,[61] the Court placed significant weight on international law. First, it reiterated that section 28(2) (best interests) was no doubt inspired by international and regional instruments. The court pointed out that, in language substantially similar to section 28(2), article 3(1) of the CRC proclaims that in all actions concerning children, whether undertaken by public or private institutions, courts of law, administrative authorities or public bodies, the best interests of the child will be 'a primary consideration'. The ACRWC is similar but refers to 'the primary consideration'. The court then quoted General Comment 5 of the UN Committee on the Rights of the Child, which states that the principle was introduced because children, due to their relative immaturity, are reliant on responsible authorities to assess and represent their rights and best interests in relation to decisions and actions that affect them (para. 13).

The Court proceeded to highlight General Comment 3 of the UN Committee, which says the following about article 3:

> Every legislative, administrative and judicial body or institution is required to apply the best interests principle by systematically considering how children's rights and interests are and will be affected by their decisions and actions.

The ECOSOC Guidelines on Justice Matters involving Child Victims and Witnesses of Crime were used by the Court to gain a better understanding of the special protection and assistance children need in order to prevent the hardship and trauma that may arise from their participation in the criminal justice system. The Court concluded by setting its own guidelines, based on international law, on how the courts should deal with child victims' testimony in the future.

---

[60] *Media 24 Ltd v National Prosecuting Authority*: *In re S v Mahangu and another* 2011 (2) SACR 321.

[61] *Director of Public Prosecutions, Transvaal v Minister of Justice* 2009 (2) SACR 130 (CC).

6 Using the CRC and ACRWC Conjunctively

In some cases the courts have considered both the CRC and the ACRWC and utilised small differences in wording to the advantage of children (Skelton 2009). In the case of *Bhe*,[62] which dealt with the rule that girls and children born outside of marriage would be overlooked in intestate succession in favour of male heirs born within marriage, the wording of article 3 of the ACRWC (which includes non-discrimination on the basis of not only the child's status but also that of the parents) was pivotal to the Court's decision that the marital status of parents could not be a basis for the discrimination against children.

In *S v. M*,[63] the Court relied on article 30 of the ACRWC for its finding that the best interests of the child should be central to a determination of whether to send a primary caregiver to prison. Article 30 has no counterpart in the CRC. It provides that states shall undertake to provide special treatment to mothers who have been accused or found guilty of infringing the penal law and shall in particular ensure that a non-custodial sentence will always be the first consideration when sentencing such mothers. The Court found this clause highly persuasive.[64]

7 Conclusion

The judgments discussed in this chapter showcase the extent to which the Constitutional Court's jurisprudence has embraced the CRC, together with General Comments of the UN Committee and other soft law relating to children's rights. In addition, the courts tend to consider the CRC and ACRWC together, and at times the wording of one of them is able to fill a gap left by the other. The ability to draw on both the CRC and the ACRWC in this way, and to fill in detail through reference to soft law and general comments, gives South African child rights litigators a rich store-cupboard from which to draw. The courts have utilised foreign law, though to a lesser extent than it has international law. This may be due to the differences between foreign law and the South African Bill of Rights, with its strong emphasis on best interests of the child. The Constitutional Court shows signs of being very comfortable to chart its own jurisprudential path in child law rather than follow the lead of other jurisdictions. However, it bases its interpretation of the Bill of Rights on a close reading of international child rights law.

The work of child rights litigators is evident in the abovementioned discussion: in many instances it is their efforts which have delivered the CRC to the doors of the courts. It is gratifying that, as evidenced by the judgments, those doors have been opened wide to receive and disseminate international children's rights concepts.

---

[62] Note 23 above.

[63] Note 11 above.

[64] Para. 31.

References

Alston, P., & Tobin, J. (2005). *Laying the foundations for children's rights*. Florence: UNICEF Innocenti Research Centre.

Budlender, G. (2006). Amicus Curiae. In S. Woolman & M. Bishop (Eds.), *Constitutional law of South Africa*. Cape Town: Juta.

Du Plessis, M., & Corder, H. (1994). *Understanding South Africa's transitional bill of rights*. Cape Town: Juta.

Dugard, J. (2005). *International law: A South African perspective*. Cape Town: Juta.

Friedman, A., Pantazis, A., & Skelton, A. (2009). Children's rights. In S. Woolman, T. Roux, & M. Bishop (Eds.), *Constitutional law of South Africa* (pp. 47-1 and pp. 47-36). Cape Town: Juta.

Robertson, O. (2012). *Collateral convicts: Children of incarcerated parents*. Geneva: Quaker United Nations Office.

Rosa, S., & Dutschke, M. (2006). Child rights at the core: The use of international law in South African cases on children's socio-economic rights. *SAJHR, 22*(2), 244–260.

Skelton, A., & Courtenay, M. (2012). The impact of children's rights on criminal justice. *SAJC, 1*, 180–193.

Skelton, A. (2008). Severing the umbilical cord: A subtle jurisprudential shift regarding children and their primary caregivers. *Constitutional Court Review, 1*, 351–368.

Skelton, A. (2009). The development of a fledgling child rights jurisprudence in Eastern and Southern Africa based on international and regional instruments. *AHRLJ, 9*(2), 482–501.

Skelton, A. (2012). How far will the courts go in ensuring the right to a basic education? *Southern African Public Law, 27*, 392–408.

Skelton, A., & Proudlock, P. (2013). Interpretation, objects, application and implementation of the children's Act. In C.J. Davel & A.M. Skelton (Eds.), *Commentary on the Children's Act* (pp. 1-1 to 1-34). Cape Town: Juta.

Sloth-Nielsen, J. (2002). Children's rights in the South African courts: An overview since ratification of the UN Convention on the Rights of the Child. *International Journal of Children's Rights, 10*, 137–156.

Sloth-Nielsen, J., & Kruuse, H. (2013). A maturing manifesto: The constitutionalisation of children's rights in South African jurisprudence 2007–2012. *International Journal of Children's Rights, 21*(4), 646–678.

Sloth-Nielsen, J., & Mezmur, B. (2008). 2 + 2 = 5? Exploring the domestication of the CRC in the South African courts (2002–2006). *International Journal of Children's Rights, 16*(1), 1–28.

Spaull, N. (2013). Poverty and privilege: Primary school inequality in South Africa. *International Journal for Educational Development, 33*, 436–447.

Chapter 3
India

Children's Rights in Litigation: Use of the CRC in Indian Courts

Enakshi Ganguly Thukral and Anant Kumar Asthana

Abstract India ratified the UN Convention on the Rights of the Child (CRC) in 1992 thereby expressing its commitment to protect the human rights of all its citizens, including children. As a result, in the past 20 years the CRC has come to exert a growing influence on a range of legislative, judicial and executive decisions. This chapter attempts to highlight how the ratification of the CRC is reflected in the drafting of legislation in the country and examples of some of the cases in which the courts at different levels in India—High Courts in the States and Supreme Court—have alluded to or cited the CRC in its pronouncements.

1 Introduction

India ratified the UN Convention on the Rights of the Child (CRC) in 1992. By ratifying various international human rights instruments, among them the CRC, India has expressed its commitment to protect the human rights of all its citizens, including children. The CRC revalidates the rights guaranteed to children by the Constitution of India and the laws, policies and programmes emanating from it. The ratification of the CRC has a binding effect, and all national laws, policies, programmes and other actions must conform to or be brought into conformity with it. As a result, in the past 20 years the CRC has come to exert a growing influence on a range of legislative, judicial and executive decisions.

The Indian Constitution attaches importance to international legal obligations when, in Article 51, it exhorts the state to 'foster respect for international law and

E.G. Thukral (✉)
HAQ: Centre for Child Rights, New Delhi, India
e-mail: enakshi@haqcrc.org

A.K. Asthana
New Delhi, India
e-mail: anant.asthana@gmail.com

T. Liefaard and J.E. Doek (eds.), *Litigating the Rights of the Child*,
DOI 10.1007/978-94-017-9445-9_3

treaty obligations in the dealings of organized peoples with one another'. In turn, its Article 253 empowers the parliament to enact legislation to fulfil such international obligations.[1]

India subscribes to the dualist theory in its domestic implementation of international law.[2] International treaties do not automatically become part of national law in India, and after their ratification, the parliament has to pass legislation to implement them. With regard to the Indian judiciary, Agarwal notes that, while it is 'not empowered to make legislation', it has

> interpreted India's obligations under international law into the constitutional provisions relating to implementation of international law in pronouncing its decision in a case concerning issues of international law. Through judicial activism the Indian judiciary has played a proactive role in implementing India's international obligations under international treaties, especially in the field of human rights and environmental law (Agarwal 2010).

The case at issue was *Sheela Barse v. Secretary, Children's Aid Society*,[3] in which the Supreme Court in 1986 read an obligation on the part of Indian state to uphold the principles contained in the international treaties it has ratified (see Sect. 3.2.1 for a detailed discussion). The Indian Supreme Court's record on its insistence to uphold international consensus on issues concerning welfare is outstanding. Expounding on Article 51 of the Constitution, it has held:

> Any International Convention not inconsistent with the fundamental rights and in harmony with its spirit must be read into these provisions to enlarge the meaning and content thereof, to promote the object of the constitutional guarantee. This is implicit from Article 51 (c) and the enabling power of the Parliament to enact laws for implementing the International Conventions and norms by virtue of Article 253 read with Entry 14 of the Union List in Seventh Schedule of the Constitution.[4]

In the last decade, there have been several instances where petitioners relied on international instruments and the Courts invoked the UN Conventions, particularly the Convention on the Elimination of All Forms of Discrimination against Women (CEDAW)[5] and the CRC. For example, both of these instruments were invoked in *Sakshi v. Union of India and Others.*[6]

The Indian judicial system is one of the world's oldest legal systems, and to a large degree it is still informed by the legacy of more than 200 years of British colonial rule. However, the framework for the current legal system has been laid

---

[1] Article 253: 'Legislation for giving effect to international agreements. Notwithstanding anything in the foregoing provisions of this Chapter, Parliament has power to make any law for the whole or any part of the territory of India for implementing any treaty, agreement or convention with any other country or countries or any decision made at any international conference, association or other body'.

[2] *Jolly Jeorge versus Bank of Cochin*, AIR 1980 SC 470 (Date of Judgment: 04.02.1980).

[3] (1987) 3 SCC 50 (Date of Judgment: 20.12.1986).

[4] *Vishaka and others v. State of Rajasthan and others*. (AIR 1997 Supreme Court 3011). J.S. Verma C.J.I., Mrs. Sujata versus Manohar and B.N. Kirpal. JJ. (Date of judgment: 13 August 1997).

[5] Gita Hariharan and Vandana Shiva; Vishakha.

[6] AIR 2004 SC 3566/2004 (2) ALD Cri 504 (Date of Judgment: 26.05.2004).

down by the Indian Constitution, from which it derives its power. Although the country adopted the features of a federal system of government, the Constitution provides for a single, integrated court system to administer both Union and State laws. The Supreme Court is the apex court, followed by High Courts that function at state level. Below them are the subordinate courts, comprising of District Courts and other lower courts.[7] Cases of juveniles in conflict with law are dealt with by special courts that are known as Juvenile Justice Boards and consist of a magistrate and two social workers.

The Indian Legal System has constitutional remedies for judicial review, remedies which are enforceable in Supreme Court and High Courts. Judicial review is sought by filing a petition called a Writ Petition. The Supreme Court, using powers vested under Article 32 of the Indian Constitution, and the High Courts, using powers vested under Article 226, can hear such Writ Petitions for judicially reviewing state action or inaction. Over the years, a tradition has arisen of filing public interest litigation (class litigation). Such matters are admitted by Superior Courts (i.e. the Supreme Court and High Courts) directly; these Courts also have powers to hear appeals against orders and judgments by lower courts.

Against this backdrop, the chapter discusses a generally representative selection of Supreme and High Court cases that illustrate how the CRC has been used in framing laws and policies in India. Many of the cases that are cited were Writ Petitions filed in public interest litigation, and the discussion includes coverage of institutions such as the Humans Rights Commission, over and above those judicial bodies already mentioned.

2 Incorporation of the CRC in Domestic Legislation and Policies

The Constitution guarantees certain fundamental rights to all citizens of the country. It also provides for the creation of special legislation for women and children,[8] further to which laws have been enacted, mindful that while all children have equal rights, their circumstances are not uniform.

The first time the CRC was invoked in the formulation of any legislation was in 2000 when India enacted the Juvenile Justice (Care and Protection) Act 2000. The introduction to the Act states: 'The Government of India, having ratified the Convention, has found it expedient to re-enact the existing law relating to juveniles bearing in mind the standards prescribes in the Convention on the Rights of the Child …'[9] Since then, new legislation dealing with child sexual abuse—the Protection of Children from Sexual Offences Act, 2012—has also cited the CRC in its Statement of Objects and Reasons.

---

[7] http://www.silf.org.in/16/Indian-Judicial-System.htm. Accessed 2 December 2013.

[8] Article 15 of the Constitution of India.

[9] The Juvenile (Justice Care and Protection of Children) Act 2000.

In addition, the National Plans of Action for Children in 1992 and 2005 of the Government of India referred to the CRC. Although it had been ratified already, the Convention did not find a mention in the Eighth (1992–1997) and Ninth (1997–2002) Five Year Plans of the Government of India. It was only in the Tenth Five Year Plan (2002–2007) that it was first mentioned. The Eleventh and Twelfth Five Year Plans have not only each invoked the CRC but devoted a separate section specifically to children's rights.

The CRC's integration into the government's plans and policies is largely attributable to the role of civil society in India, particularly the rights organisations, lawyers, activists and individuals working in the area of children's rights. This shift has also come in response to the Concluding Observations made by the UN Committee on the Rights of the Child in respect of the two state reports India has submitted to date.

3 Use of the CRC in Court Proceedings

The earliest-noted instance in which the Supreme Court invoked the CRC was *M.C. Mehta v. State of Tamil Nadu*[10] in 1996. Since then it has been invoked on a number of occasions and in respect of a number of issues. A perusal of the case law shows that while the CRC has been used both by lawyers and petitioners in their arguments in cases dealing with children, there are instances where judges themselves have cited it as part of their final orders.

3.1 Child Labour

The law on child labour, the Child Labour (Prohibition and Regulation) Act, 1986, was passed after a great deal of debate and protests as it made a distinction between hazardous and non-hazardous forms of labour and did not think it necessary to prohibit all forms of labour by children. While the Act banned employment of children up to the age of 14 years in hazardous occupations and processes (as is given in the Schedules forming part of the law), it regulated the employment of children in others. In fact, in keeping with the law, the Government of India ratified the CRC with a declaration on article 32 of the CRC.[11]

[10] (1996) 6 SCC 756 (Date of Judgment: 10.12.1996).

[11] 'While fully subscribing to the objectives and purposes of the Convention, realising that certain of the rights of the child, namely those pertaining to the economic, social and cultural rights can only be progressively implemented in the developing countries, subject to the extent of available resources and within the framework of international co-operation; recognizing that the child has to be protected from exploitation of all forms including economic exploitation; nothing that for several reasons children of different ages do work in India; having prescribed minimum age for employment in hazardous occupations and in certain other areas; having made regulatory provisions regarding hours and conditions of employment; and being aware that it is not practical immediately to prescribe minimum age for admission to each and every area of employment in India-the Government of India undertook to take measures to progressively implement the provisions of Article 32, particularly paragraph 2(a), in accordance with its national legislation and relevant international instruments to which it is a State Party'.

Those who protested against the law argued that it was discriminatory and violated the right to equal opportunity for all children. Over the years, several petitions have been filed in the courts on the issue of child labour. A public-spirited lawyer, MC Mehta, pleaded that child labour violated all of the fundamental rights guaranteed to children under the Constitution of India. The case focused on the condition of child labourers in Sivakasi, Tamil Nadu, but since the problem was rampant throughout the country, the Supreme Court thought it appropriate to deal with it in a wider manner and treat it as a national problem. In its order, the Court said:

> It would be apposite to apprise themselves also about our commitment to world community. For the case at hand it would be enough to note that India has accepted the Convention on the Rights of the Child, which was concluded by the UN General Assembly on 20th November, 1989. This Convention affirms that children's right require special protection and it aims, not only to provide such protection, but also to ensure the continuous improvement in the situation of children all over the world, as well as their development and education in conditions of peace and security. Thus, the Convention not only protects the child's civil and political right, but also extends protection to child's economic, social, cultural and humanitarian rights.[12]

The Court disposed of the case after providing guidelines for the establishment of a Child Labour Rehabilitation-cum-Welfare Fund; it also ordered stiffer, and better-implemented, fines for those who employed children.

In another instance of public-interest litigation involving the CRC, a writ of Mandamus[13] was sought to direct the government to take steps to stop the employment of children in the carpet industry as well as to issue appropriate directives for ensuring the total prohibition of employment of children under 14 and for providing them with facilities such as education, health, sanitation and nutritious food. Here, the Supreme Court refers to the ratification of the CRC by the Government of India, and makes specific reference to articles 3, 27(1), 28, 31(1) and 36 of the CRC. The Court observed:

> No doubt, the Government, while ratifying the Convention with a reservation of progressive implementation of the governance, reminded itself of the obligations undertaken there under, but they do not absolve the State in its fundamental governance of the imperative of Directive Principles of the Constitution rendering socio-economic justice to the child and their empowerment, full growth of their personality—socially, educationally and culturally—with a right to leisure and opportunity for development of the spirit of reform, inquiry, humanism and scientific temper to improve excellence—individually and collectively.[14]

More recently, the non-governmental organisation Bachpan Bachao Andolan filed a case in reaction to the trafficking and serious abuse of children employed in circuses. The Supreme Court made a reference to the standards for protection of

[12] *MC Mehta versus State of Tamil Nadu* (1996) 6 SCC 756 (Date of Judgment: 10.12.1996).

[13] A writ of Mandamus is a tool of judicial review by which the Supreme Court or High Courts can order the state to perform any specific public duty mandated under any law. It includes the power to issue an order to prohibit the state from doing anything which violates the fundamental or legal rights of persons.

[14] *Bandhua Mukti Morcha versus Union of India & Ors*. 1997 (10) SCC 549 (Date of Judgment: 21.02.1997).

children contained not only in the CRC but also the UN Standard Minimum Rules for the Administration of Juvenile Justice (the Beijing Rules 1985), the UN Rules for the Protection of Juveniles Deprived of their Liberty (1990), the Hague Convention on Inter Country Adoption (1993), the Geneva Convention on Immoral Trafficking of Women and Children (1949), and the UN Protocol to Prevent, Suppress and Punish Trafficking in Persons (2000),[15] otherwise known as the PALERMO Protocol on Trafficking. In its order, the Court stated clearly:

> India has ratified the UN Convention on the Rights of the Child in 1992. The Convention inter alia prescribes standards to be adhered by all state parties in securing the best interest of the child.[16]

Despite such progressive orders from the courts, India unfortunately continues to have the largest number of working children in the world and to hold fast to its declaration on article 32 of the CRC. In a positive move, the government has drafted a new bill on child labour that regulates labour in the 14–18-year age group and—in consonance with the Right to Free and Compulsory Act, 2009—bans all child labour up to the age of 14 years.

3.2 *Juvenile Justice, Care and Protection*

International law, the CRC in particular, has been used extensively at all levels of juvenile justice in order to bring about changes in domestic law as well as to clarify it and improve its implementation.

The Juvenile Justice (Care and Protection of Children) Act, 2000, deals with two categories of children: those 'in conflict with the law' (CICL) and 'children in need of care and protection' (CNCP). The reason for including CNCP in the juvenile-justice system is that typically they are socioeconomically marginalised and vulnerable to coming into conflict with the law if there is no timely intervention. Over the years, amendments to the law have resulted in a situation in which CICL who are involved in petty offences and who have either no family or an unfit family may be treated as CNCP; in such instances, the matter is transferred from the Juvenile Justice Board (JJB)[17] to the Child Welfare Committee (CWC).[18] This ensures that they are not kept with those involved in heinous offences and are taken care of by the state until they complete 18 years of age.

---

[15] This is a Protocol supplementing the United Nations Convention against Transnational Organized Crime.

[16] *Bachpan Bachao Andolan versus Union of India and Others*. 2011 (5) SCC 1 (Date of Order: 18.04.2011).

[17] The JJB is the competent authority responsible for adjudicating and disposing cases involving children in conflict with the law. It is a bench of three persons, headed by a Judicial Magistrate of First Class and two Social Worker Members. See, too, the introduction to this chapter.

[18] The CWC is the competent authority responsible for care, protection and rehabilitation of children in difficult circumstances. It is a bench of five persons.

3.2.1 Children in Need of Care and Protection

As far back as 1986, and hence before India's ratification of the CRC, the Supreme Court, issuing directions to the State of Maharashtra in *Sheela Barse v. Secretary, Children's Aid Society*,[19] held that the conventions India had ratified, and which elucidate norms for the protection of children, placed an obligation on the state to implement their principles. Thus, in a break from its earlier judgments, the Court came to the conclusion that treaties, even if unincorporated into national law, have binding effect. It declared:

> In 1959, the Declaration of all the rights of the child adopted by the General Assembly of the United Nations and in Article 24 of the International Covenant on Civil and Political Rights 1966. India as a party to these International Charters having rectified (sic) the Declarations, it is an obligation of the Government of India as also the State machinery to implement the same in the proper way.[20]

On November 15, 1989 a public-spirited advocate, Gaurav Jain, filed a petition seeking the establishment of separate educational institutions for the children of sex-workers. Some years later, on 9 July 1997,[21] the Supreme Court made its ruling after having heard all the State Governments and Union Territories contend that 'segregating children of prostitutes by locating separate schools and providing separate hostels' would not be in the interests of the children or society at large. The Court issued several directives for creating juvenile homes for the rehabilitation of child prostitutes and neglected children.

In making their order, the judges drew extensively on a number of international declarations, treaties and conventions. Specifically, the order refers to the Declaration of the Rights of the Child, November 20, 1959; the Declaration on Social and Legal Principles relating to Protection and Welfare of the Children with Special Reference to Foster or Placement and Adoption Nationally and Internationally, December 3, 1986; and the United Nations Standard Minimum Rules for the administration of Juvenile Justice (the Beijing Rules) dated November 29, 1985. However, although the CRC had already been ratified at that point, the Court did not refer to it.

Another illustrative case dealing with children in need of care and protection is *Brindavan Sharma v. State*,[22] heard by the Delhi High Court. The children of a man jailed for murdering his wife were left destitute and virtually orphaned; while the man's daughter had to reside with a grandparent, his two sons—both of whom were nearing the age of 18—lived in an orphanage which they would have to vacate on coming of age, leaving them with nowhere else to go. The Court observed that 'the children are … victims of a system which does not provide any

---

[19] (1987) 3 SCC 50 (Date of Judgment: 20.12.1986).

[20] Ibid. '[R]ectified' is most likely a printing error and should be read as 'ratified'.

[21] *Gaurav Jain versus Union of India & Ors*. [1990 Supp. SCC 709] (Date of Judgment: 09.07.1997).

[22] Criminal Appeal No. 927 of 2002, Delhi High Court (Date of Judgment: 06.12.2006).

apparent relief to such unfortunate and totally innocent victims of a crime and its aftermath', and it took the view that it was necessary to secure some form of financial support for them.

As such, the question that exercised the Court was whether the state owes any responsibility towards such children. Declaring that it could not be a mute spectator and had to devise a procedure to assist hapless 'victims of crime and punishment', the Court in its order cited the CRC (in particular articles 2(2), 8(1), 12(1), 12(2) and 39), along with other international human rights instruments[23] and the Indian Constitution, stating that, '[a]part from the mandate of Articles 21 and 39 of the Constitution of India, this Court is duty-bound to recognize the country's obligation to its responsibilities and duties under the CRC 1989'.

Furthermore, noticing there was a void in domestic legislations on this issue, the Court relied on the CRC to bind the state towards owning responsibility for such children. It observed:

> The international conventions and norms are to be read into them in the absence of enacted domestic law occupying the field when there is no inconsistency between them. It is now an accepted rule of judicial construction that regard must be had to international conventions and norms for construing domestic law when there is no inconsistency between them and there is a void in the domestic law.

The Court also cited the CRC in directing the government to frame policies for ensuring the care and protection of children who are victims of crimes. In addition to ordering immediate support for them, the Court issued a notice directly to the Ministry of Social Justice and Empowerment, Government of India, and the Secretary, Ministry of Women and Child Development, to consider establishing and appropriately funding an assistance scheme. 'Such a welcome and socially benevolent step by the Government', it said, 'would facilitate the children who are the victims of crime, such as the three children in the present case, to escape destitution and provide avenues for becoming responsible citizens of this country'.

At the time of writing, the matter was still pending before the Delhi High Court, with the Government of Delhi having informed the latter that the views of Delhi State Legal Services Authority were obtained and that the scheme was due to go before the cabinet for approval. In a similar vein, the Supreme Court is also conducting judicial proceedings on the issue of care and protection for the children of prisoners.[24]

---

[23] It also referred to the rights of children contained in the following:

- Geneva Convention on the Rights of the Child, 1924;
- Declaration of the Rights of the Child adopted by the UN General Assembly on 20 November 1959 and recognised in the Universal Declaration of Human Rights;
- International Covenant on Civil and Political Rights (in particular articles 23 and 24);
- International Covenant on Economic, Social and Cultural Rights (in particular article 10); and
- statutes and relevant instruments of specialised agencies and international organisations concerned with children's welfare.

[24] *R.D. Upadhyay versus State of Andhra Pradesh & Others, Writ petition* (Civil) 559 of 2004.

3.2.2 Children in Conflict with the Law

The CRC has been invoked in several issues that concern children in conflict with the law, the most prominent of which was the question of the minimum age of criminal responsibility. It is also noteworthy that, in relation to these various issues, the CRC featured not only in the higher courts but even the Juvenile Justice Board (juvenile court).

The Issue of Age and Juvenility

The minimum age of criminal responsibility (MACR) has always been, and still is, a matter of controversy. The Juvenile Justice (Care and Protection of Children) Act, 2000, was ambiguous in this respect. One of the questions it raised was this: What should determine whether juveniles are subject to juvenile proceedings or to the rules applicable to adult criminals—the age at which they committed the offence, or at which they were apprehended?

In 2009 the Supreme Court dealt with the issue in *Hariram v. State of Rajasthan*[25] by giving retrospective effect to the Juvenile Justice (Care and Protection of Children) Act, 2000. It meant that those who (a) were above 16 years of age but below 18 years at the time of the commission of the offence, and (b) were treated as adults in the criminal justice system while the old Juvenile Justice Act of 1986 was in force could return to the courts and claim juvenile status, a development that saw many persons released from incarceration. The Court aligned its judgment with, inter alia, the CRC, noting that

> [i]n keeping with certain international conventions and in particular the Convention on the Rights of the Child and the United Nations' Standard Minimum Rules for the Administration of Juvenile Justice, 1985, commonly known as the Beijing Rules, the Legislature enacted the Juvenile Justice (Care and Protection of Children) Act, 2000 …

The controversy around age and juvenility reached its peak when a juvenile was involved in a gang rape in December 2012. The incident led to eight Writ Petitions in the Supreme Court, some of them demanding a reduction of the age of juvenility from 18 to 16 years, and others calling for the Juvenile Justice Act of 2000 and its provisions to be declared unconstitutional. This legislation, it was said, provided immunity to 'hardened child criminals committing heinous offences' and compromised the right to life guaranteed to citizens under Article 21 of the Indian Constitution.

All eight of the petitions were clubbed together and decided under the lead case title of *Salil Bali v. Union of India.*[26] While some of these were specific to the case

[25] Criminal Appeal No. 907 of 2009 reported as 2009 (6) SCALE 695 (Date of Judgment: 05.05.2009).

[26] (2013) 7 SCC 705 (Date of Judgment: 17.07.2013).

of the juvenile accused in the gang rape, the general request of the petitioners was that in offences such as rape and murder, juveniles should be tried under the criminal law as adults rather than under the Juvenile Justice Act. It was requested, furthermore, that the protection the Act grants to persons up to the age of 18 years should be removed, and that the investigating agency should be permitted to keep a record of the juvenile offenders so that preventative measures may be taken to detect repeat offenders and bring them to justice.

One of the interveners in this case was HAQ: Centre for Child Rights, which argued that the Juvenile Justice Act of 2000 is fairly progressive legislation largely compliant with the Constitution and the minimum standards enshrined in the CRC; that most of the problems in the administration of juvenile justice relate to gaps in the implementation of the Act; and that the age of the juvenile must not be reduced. HAQ went on to say:

> [The] Government of India on 26.04.2013 has adopted a new National Policy for Children, whereby it not only recognizes that a child is any person below the age of eighteen years but also states that this policy is to guide and inform all laws, policies, plans and programmes affecting children. All actions and initiatives of the national, state and local Government in all sectors must respect and uphold the principles and provisions of this Policy. In view of this Policy having been fairly considered at all levels and then being adopted by Government of India, it would neither be appropriate, nor possible, for Union of India to depart from its own policy and to reduce the age of child in the Juvenile Justice Act.

It further submitted that

> all these Writ Petitions appear to be based on two assumptions: (1) that age of 18 years for juvenile is set arbitrarily and (2) that by reducing the age of child in the Juvenile Justice Act, criminality among children will reduce. This approach and understanding is flawed firstly as it is not correct that age of 18 years for juvenility was set arbitrarily and secondly it fails to comprehend the causes and environment which bring children into delinquency … Setting up of age of juvenility as 18 years is a deliberate, thoughtful and consistent legislative decision which is in line with the international standard set in United Nations Convention on the Rights of the Child 1989, which India has ratified in 1992 [HAQ submitted a list of 12 pieces of Indian legislation enacted between 1872 and 2013 in which the age of the child was prescribed as 18 years].

In the case under discussion, both the petitioners and those who intervened relied heavily on the CRC, the Beijing Rules and the Riyadh Guidelines to argue their respective cases. HAQ referred as well to General Comment No. 10 of the UN Committee of the Rights of Child[27] and to the Committee's Concluding Observations on India's two state reports, submitting that, '[o]n the question of making a provision in the existing Juvenile Justice Act to allow children of a specific age group to be tried as adults, it is pertinent to take notice of the General

---

[27] Committee On the Rights Of the Child Forty-Fourth Session, Geneva, 15 January–2 February 2007. General Comment No. 10 (2007). Children's Rights in Juvenile Justice. CRC/C/GC/10. 25 April 2007.

Comment No. 10 dated 25.04.2007 made by the UN Committee on the Rights of the Child, which has specifically dealt with this aspect'.[28]

Upholding the constitutional validity of the Juvenile Justice Act, the Supreme Court dismissed all eight Writ Petitions. In doing so, it dwelt on India's international commitments:

> The Juvenile Justice (Care and Protection of Children) Act, 2000, is in tune with the provisions of the Constitution and the various Declarations and Conventions adopted by the world community represented by the United Nations. The basis of fixing of the age till when a person could be treated as a child at eighteen years in the Juvenile Justice (Care and Protection of Children) Act, 2000, was Article 1 of the Convention of the Rights of the Child, as was brought to our notice during the hearing.

The Overriding Effect of the Juvenile Justice Act

The CRC was cited in the establishment of the Over Riding Effect of Juvenile Justice Act over other Legislations—a matter of exceptional importance in the context of the stringent laws that apply where persons, including children, are involved in anti-national activities.

In 2003, *Prabakaran v. State of Tamilnadu & others*[29] was presented before the Madras High Court, a case in which prayer was made to restrain a special court from conducting a trial against a juvenile under the Prevention of Terrorism Act, 2002 (POTA). The High Court of Madras, Tamil Nadu, delivered a judgment on 18.03.2003 holding that the Juvenile Justice Act is 'monarch in all it surveys in its field' and ruling that Terror Laws shall not prevail over the Act and children shall continue to be treated as per its provisions. Explaining the genesis of juvenile justice law in India, the Court made detailed references to the CRC, stating, 'International conventions and norms were read into fundamental rights in the absence of domestic law occupying the field'.

Unfortunately, this position was altered in 2013 when the Supreme Court delivered judgment in *Mohd. Moin Faridulla Qureshi v. The State of Maharashtra*,[30] upholding a life sentence to a juvenile who—aged 17 years and two months on the date of incident—was charged along with several adults under the Terrorist and Disruptive Activities Act (TADA) for involvement in terrorist activities.

---

[28] Para. 38 of General Comment No. 10 (25.04.2007) reads: 'The Committee … recommends that those States parties which limit the applicability of their juvenile justice rules to children under the age of 16 (or lower) years, or which allow by way of exception that 16 or 17-year-old children are treated as adult criminals, change their laws with a view to achieving a non-discriminatory full application of their juvenile justice rules to all persons under the age of 18 years. The Committee notes with appreciation that some States parties allow for the application of the rules and regulations of juvenile justice to persons aged 18 and older, usually till the age of 21, either as a general rule or by way of exception.'

[29] Writ Petition No. 4511 of 2003, Kerala High Court (Date of Judgment: 18.03.2003).

[30] Criminal Appeal No. 653 and 656 of 2008, Supreme Court of India.

Decisions of the Juvenile Justice Board

The CRC's contribution is not restricted to the Supreme and High Courts. Juvenile Justice Boards, set up in each district for dealing with juveniles in conflict with the law, have also made use of CRC provisions to enforce children's rights.

An order made in 2010 by the Principal Magistrate of Juvenile Justice Board-1 of Delhi used article 40 of the CRC (which requires states to promote the establishment of laws, procedures, authorities and institutions specifically applicable to children) to institute a general rule that procedures in the Criminal Procedure Code are not suitable for children's inquiries. Further to this, the order prohibited bailable/non-bailable warrants from being issued against juveniles, holding that neither the attachment of property, under section 83 of the Criminal Procedure Code, nor the proclamation, under section 82, of a juvenile being an offender, is consonant with the CRC. The order read:

> There is no doubt that issuance of process under section 82 Cr.P.C. is a violent interference with the right of a juvenile guaranteed under the various provisions of the Delhi JJ Rules 2009 and the JJ Act 2000 including his right of privacy, dignity, confidentiality and non-stigmatization. When we talk of privacy, it definitely does not go with the provisions of section 82 Cr.P.C. which requires the public reading in conspicuous place in town or village or house/homestead of the juvenile ... This is where a need is felt to have a procedure which can look into both the aspects and brings into a harmony suited to the best interest of the juvenile.

This was the first-ever attempt by a Juvenile Justice Board to mark a clear departure from the criminal justice system for adults. With its order, the Board put to an end criminal-justice-oriented practice in Delhi, replacing it a child-friendly procedure compliant with the Juvenile Justice Act. This historic order has been incorporated in the training curriculum of the National Legal Service Authority and used to orient duty holders on juvenile justice.

3.3 The Child as Witness in Court

In 2013 the High Court of Delhi passed a crucial order regarding the competency of a child testifying in court.[31] Drawing on the CRC and the Guidelines on Justice in Matters involving Child Victims and Witnesses of Crime developed by the Economic and Social Council of the United Nations (Res. 2005/20), it said that courts are required to apply the principle of best interests by considering how the child's rights and interests are, or will be, affected by their decisions. The best interests of the child demand that children should be shielded from the trauma that may arise from giving evidence in criminal proceedings.

---

[31] *State versus Rahul*, Criminal L.P. 250 of 2012, Delhi High Court (Date of Judgment: 15.04.2013).

3.4 The Right of the Child to Protection from Sexual Abuse

Incest and sexual abuse of children have never been unknown or unrecognised phenomena in India. However, in 1994 the case of a father sexually abusing his little daughter not only shook the nation's conscience but raised debate about what constitutes rape and sexual abuse. As defined in section 375 of the Indian Penal Code (IPC), is 'rape' confined to penile penetration of the vagina? What about the penetration of a bodily orifice (vagina, anus or mouth) by a penis or other part of the body, or by an object? Would it fall within the meaning of the words 'sexual intercourse' and 'penetration' as used in this provision?

In a horrifying sequence of events, it was found that the father, working in government in the Ministry of Home Affairs, would take his six-year-old daughter to his office and from there to a hotel room along with his colleagues, two men and two women. They would consume alcohol, watch 'blue films' and revel in sexual orgies. The father would make his daughter consume alcohol, remove her clothes, and thrust his fingers in her vagina and anus. In her court testimony, the girl described how he would do the same at home after rendering his wife and two other children unconscious.

The mother filed a complaint when she became aware of the situation. However, since there had been no penile penetration, the father was not charged with rape. The mother challenged this in court,[32] but the petition was dismissed because conventional law did not regard these incidents as fitting the definition of rape. Along with Sakshi, an organisation working in the area of violence against women and children, she approached the Supreme Court with a Writ Petition[33] for a ruling that 'rape', as defined under section 375 of the IPC, include all forms of forcible penetration.[34] Sakshi claimed that the current interpretation of the law, which limited rape to forcible penile or vaginal penetration, violated the Constitution as well as India's international commitments under instruments such as the CRC and CEDAW.

In its order dated 13 January 1998, the Supreme Court directed the Law Commission to indicate its response to the Writ Petition. The Commission submitted its report on 25 March 2000, stating:

> The present Report focuses on the need to review the rape laws in the light of increased incidents of custodial rape and crime of sexual abuse against youngsters. The crime of sexual assault on a child causes lasting psychic damage to the child and as such, it is essential to prevent sexual abuse of children through stringent provisions. The UN Conventions and various constitutional provisions also underline the need for protecting the child from all forms of sexual exploitation and sexual abuse. This Report aims at the attainment of these objectives.[35]

---

[32] *Smt. Sudesh Jhaku versus K.C.J. And Others*, 62 (1996) DLT 563 (Date of Judgment: 23.05.1996).

[33] Writ Petition (Criminal) No. 33 of 1997, Supreme Court of India.

[34] *Sakshi versus Union of India* (AIR 2004 SC 3566, 2004 (2) ALD Cri 504) (Date of Judgment: 26.05.2004).

[35] Law Commission of India. *One Hundred And Seventy Second Report* On Review Of Rape Laws March 2000.

The Sakshi judgment, as it is commonly known, is one of India's landmark rulings on sexual abuse. It not only set in motion the discussion around the definition of rape, but also laid down guidelines for protecting the victim of sexual offences. The Court, however, upheld the existing definition of rape as forcible penile/vaginal penetration only, refusing to include other forms of penetration within the ambit of rape as defined under section 375 of the IPC. The Court based its decision on *stare decisis*, a legal principle that requires the courts to follow previously established decisions in the absence of exceptional circumstances and which underlines the need for criminal law to be clear and certain. Altering the established definition of rape under section 375 would lead to confusion and ambiguity, and would not be in the interests of society.

This lacuna in the law was finally corrected with the adoption of the Protection of Children from Sexual Offences Act, 2012, which makes it a sexual offence both to penetrate a child with any object or part of the body in any orifice, or to force the child to perform the same actions (section 3). Nevertheless, it is clear that the Sakshi judgment, and the issues raised therein, paved the way for this law.

3.5 The Right of the Child to Privacy and the Role of the Press

Over the last decade, the role of the press *vis-à-vis* reporting on children has become a matter of debate, one which concerns not only of issues of individual privacy but, in India's wider context, the protection of children from stigmatisation and discrimination.

In *Ajay Goswami v. Union of India*[36] the petitioner requested the Supreme Court to direct the authorities concerned to strike a reasonable balance between, on the one hand, the fundamental right of freedom of speech and expression enjoyed by the press and, on the other, the duty of the government, as a signatory to the CRC and the Universal Declaration of Human Rights, to protect the minors from abuse, exploitation and the harmful effects of such expression.[37] He also asked the Court to direct the authorities to provide for the introduction of a regulatory system to facilitate a climate of reciprocal tolerance.

Citing the CRC in its order, the Court asked '[w]hether the minors have got any independent right enforceable under Article 32 of the Constitution', and stated:

> The right of the minor flows from Article 19(1)(a), Article 21 read with Article 39(f) of the Constitution of India and United Nation Convention on the Rights of the Child. … It would be [apposite] to apprise ourselves also about our commitment to [the] world community. For the case at hand it would be enough to note that India has accepted the Convention on the Rights of the Child, which was concluded by the UN General Assembly on 20th November, 1989. This Convention affirms that children's right require

[36] AIR 2007 SC 493 (Date of Judgment: 12.12.2006).

[37] http://www.indiankanoon.org/doc/561137/.

> special protection and it aims, not only to provide such protection, but also to ensure the continuous improvement in the situation of children all over the world, as well as their development and education in conditions of peace and security. Thus, the Convention not only protects the child's civil and political right, but also extends protection to child's economic, social, cultural and humanitarian rights.

The Court nevertheless dismissed the petition, holding that the press had self-regulatory mechanisms which it followed. The Court said it was necessary that a publication be judged as a whole and that news items, advertisements or passages should not be read out of context.

However, despite self-regulation, the role of the press has remained controversial. 'Trial by the media' is a common occurrence, an issue which the Delhi High Court addressed when it admitted a letter petition as a Writ Petition following the media's role in the so-called Baby Falaak case.[38] A teenaged girl had been given charge of Baby Falaak, roughly one year old, and had then battered her and dumped her outside a Delhi hospital; the teenager herself was a victim of sexual abuse and trafficking, and had been left in charge of the baby by her abuser and 'husband'. Neither of these children was spared in the subsequent media frenzy.

In 2012, Anant K. Asthana (the co-author of this chapter) approached the Delhi High Court in a letter petition, saying that privacy and confidentiality rights had been openly flouted, that current laws and procedures were insufficient to prevent this from happening, and that, as such, the Court needed to intervene. In particular, he pointed out that while section 21 of the Juvenile Justice Act prohibits the publication of names or other details that could expose the identity of a child involved in an offence, it does not respond adequately to article 16 of the CRC and the CRC's mandate therefore remains unfulfilled under the existing law.

The Court ordered that a committee comprised of representatives of the media, the Union of India, the National Commission for Protection of Child Rights, the Government of NCT of Delhi, and NGOs working for children's welfare had to be constituted to deliberate on guidelines for regulating media reporting and disclosure of details relating to children. The Court considered the ensuing report, Guidelines for Media Reporting on Children, and, on 8 August 2012, approved them with certain modifications, ordering that they be implemented with immediate effect.

These guidelines, so approved by the High Court, place reliance on articles 16 and 40 of the CRC. The Ministry of Information and Broadcasting of the Union of India, the Press Council of India and media self-regulatory authorities have been entrusted with the responsibility of creating awareness about the guidelines, while the National and State Commissions for Protection of Child Rights have been directed to file periodic reports in the High Court about the levels of compliance with them.

---

[38] *Anant Kumar Asthana versus Union of India & Others*, Writ Petition (Civil) 787 of 2012, Delhi High Court.

3.6 Maintenance, Custody and Adoption

A case heard in 2003 clearly illustrates the impact the CRC has made on the evolution of the jurisprudence and judicial decision-making on children's rights, overriding the personal law and thereby addressing the gap left in it.

3.6.1 Maintenance

In 2003 the High Court of Kerala had to decide whether a Christian father had the obligation to maintain his minor child.[39] The father's argument was based on two pre-CRC judgments by this Court in 1952 and 1972 which held, in brief, that as a Christian he was under no legal obligation to do so; in terms of Christian personal law such an obligation was only a moral one. His contention, furthermore, was essentially that even this moral obligation did not have a bearing on the case, because the canon law—applied by ecclesiastical courts—could not be treated as the personal law governing Christians in India; in short, its provisions could not be invoked or enforced by the civil courts.

However, in opposing these arguments, one *amicus curiae* observe that 'the right of a child to be maintained is basic' and had to be recognised as an enforceable right; the second *amicus curiae* argued that

> the UN Convention on the Rights of the Child was adopted by the General Assembly on 20-11-1989. Article 18 recognises the primary responsibility of the parents to maintain their children. India had acceded to the Convention on 11-12-1992. Since the Treaties and Conventions are binding on the parties, no Indian-Christian, Hindu or Muslim, can be permitted to neglect the child.

When the father's counsel argued that, in the absence of a positive provision in the Personal Law governing Christians, the general principles of equity, justice and good conscience could not be enforced or even invoked to bind the father to maintain his child, the Court remarked, 'Is it so?' and went on to refer to articles 3, 4, 6, 9, 10, 14 and 18 of the CRC. Citing these provisions verbatim in its judgment, the Court held that:

> A perusal of the above provisions shows that the parties to the convention have recognized the child's inherent right to live. They had undertaken to ensure and make maximum possible efforts for the survival and development of the child. Various steps, which the states have to undertake, were delineated in different Articles. The Government of India had ratified the convention on 20-11-1989. Thus, it had of the faith undertaken to pass and enforce laws for the protection and maintenance of children. All the children had to be treated alike irrespective of the faith or religion professed by the parents.

Commenting on the importance of international conventions, the Court observed that these

[39] *Mathew Varghese versus Rosamma Varghese* (2003, 131 TAXMAN 646 Ker) (Date of Judgment: 09.07.2003).

> provide good guidance in the examination of vexed questions of law. The convention on the Rights of the child was adopted by the UN General Assembly on 20-11-1989. In the Preamble it was noticed that a family is the fundamental group of society and the natural environment for the growth and well-being of all its members and particularly children should be afforded the necessary protection and assistance so that it can fully assume its responsibilities within the community.

In this landmark judgment, the Court used the CRC in its reasoning to decide that a Christian father is under a legal obligation to maintain his minor child.

3.6.2 Custody

Petitioners in a custody case made use of the CRC as well as the personal law. A Bangladeshi Muslim mother filed a habeas corpus petition against her ex-husband, requesting the production of their minor daughter and restoration of custody of the child to her.[40] According to the petitioner, her ex-husband had converted to Islam and they had married under Muslim rites. The mother pleaded that the child had been placed in a boarding school and given an Indian passport through fraud and misrepresentation.

It was therefore stated in the petition that

> the Petitioner/Mother is entitled to have the custody of her female child up to the child's puberty according to Muslim Sharia and Family Laws and enforceable in Bangladesh. Even according to Indian Muslim Law, the Muslim Women is entitled for the custody of the minor child up to the age of child's puberty. Any contravention of this rule constitutes gross violation of Child Rights recognized in Convention on Child Rights (CRC).

Based on the facts of the case as they emerged before the court, the petition was disposed to maintain the *status quo ante*.

3.6.3 Adoption

In a case before the Supreme Court in 2012[41] in which the legality of the adoption of an Indian child to a foreigner was at issue, HAQ: Centre for Child Rights argued on the basis of articles 20, 21, 26 and 27 of the CRC, and pleaded that

> [i]nter-country adoption is the very last resort and should only be considered if any suitable means of foster, adoptive or residential care cannot be found in the country of origin of the child and only if it is manifestly in the best interests of the child. It must be clear that residential care comes before (inter-country) adoption, as has been prescribed in Article 21(b) of the UN Convention on the Rights of the Child.

---

[40] *Israt Jahan Tabassum versus Union of India and Ors* (W.P. (CRL) 3062/2006 and Crl. M.As. 14690/2006, 924/2008).

[41] *Stephanie Joan Becker versus State & Others*, Civil Appeal No. 1053 of 2013, Supreme Court of India (Date of Judgment: 08.02.2013).

Although the Court in this case approved the adoption, it examined the matter thoroughly in the process:

> [T]he objections raised by [HAQ: Centre for Child Rights] pertain to the legality of the practice of inter country adoption itself, besides the bona fides of the appellant in seeking to adopt the child involved in the present proceeding and the overzealous role of the different bodies involved in the process in question resulting in side-stepping of the laid down norms.

3.7 *Recommendations of the National Human Rights Commission*

The National Human Rights Commission (NHRC) of India is a statutory body set up under the Protection of Human Rights Act 1993 and enjoys powers of a civil court while conducting inquiry into allegations of human rights violations. The NHRC's mandate is to inquire, on its own initiative or on a petition presented to it by a victim or any person on his or behalf, into complaint of violation of human rights or abetment or negligence in the prevention of such violation, by a public servant. The NHRC can also intervene in any proceeding involving any allegation of violation of human rights pending before a court with the approval of such court. One of the functions of the NHRC is to study treaties and other international instruments on human rights and make recommendations for their effective implementation. The NHRC's reliance on the CRC is amongst the earliest instances of using the CRC in adjudication and inquiries.

3.7.1 The Death Penalty

The NHRC had made a recommendation for the commutation of a death sentence of a person, Ramdeo Chauhan, who claimed to be a juvenile at the time of committing the offence. This led to a key decision by the Supreme Court, wherein it reopened the case in a review petition and allowed fresh examination of the juvenility claim.[42] Conflicting interpretation of testimony and records about Chauhan's age at the time of the offence made the case extremely complicated. In spite of the uncertainty, the Court held in 2001 that he was not a juvenile and confirmed his death sentence. However, one of the judges, Justice Thomas, gave a minority dissenting judgment and raised a critical question: 'Can [the] death sentence be awarded to a person whose age is not positively established by the prosecution …?'

Prompted by Justice Thomas's dissent and an article written by Dr Ved Kumari, a well-known activist and professor at Delhi University, the NHRC inquired into the case *suo moto*. Upon the NHRC's recommendation, the Governor of Assam

[42] *Ramdeo Chauhan & Rajnath Chauhan versus Bani Kant Das & Others*. Decided by Supreme Court of India on 19 November 2010 in Review Petition (Civil) NO.1378 of 2009.

commuted Chauhan's sentence to life imprisonment. The victim's family appealed to the Supreme Court against such order of commutation and succeeded in having it set aside.

The question which came before the Supreme Court in 2009 in a review petition was whether the NHRC was right in recommending commutation of a death sentence awarded to a person who was not positively established to be an adult, this despite the fact that the Supreme Court had already confirmed the sentence. Recognising that the NHRC has a wider role to promote human rights, the Supreme Court in 2011 finally permitted the issue of the convict's juvenility to be re-adjudicated. Ramdeo Chauhan was established to have been a juvenile and released after 19 years of incarceration awaiting death sentence. Indeed, this is probably the most controversial and significant case in the history of juvenile justice litigation in India.

3.7.2 Compensation for Juvenile Victims of Torture

In July 1998 a newspaper carried story of a young boy, working in a roadside eatery, who had been tortured by two drunken police constables. The NHRC took *suo-motu* cognizance, investigated the matter and concluded that the boy was beaten with footwear and later with a walking stick by the constables. Both of them were placed under suspension and a criminal case was opened. The NHRC directed the Chief Secretary of State to pay compensation to the boy for welfare and education, and also recommended that action be taken against the eatery owner under the Child Labour (Prohibition and Regulation) Act, 1986. This case has been registered with the NHRC,[43] which observed that the CRC

> sets the standards that should prevail for the protection of children. It emphasises in particular, the rights to life, survival and development of the child. Art. 6(2) of the CRC makes it obligatory for the State to ensure the survival and development of the child to the maximum possible extent … The efforts of the Commission seek to give expression to the spirit of Art. 32 of the CRC, the provisions of Constitution of India and judicial pronouncements of the Supreme Court. These provisions recognise that the child has a right against economic exploitation and the performing of any work which is likely to be hazardous or interfere with the child's education or be harmful to the child's health or development.

In another case registered with NHRC,[44] the attention of the NHRC was drawn (as it was in 86 other such cases) to the escape of several inmates from Beggars' Homes/Juvenile Homes/Remand Homes situated in various parts of the state of Maharashtra. Taking the view that the escape of such a large number of inmates pointed to serious infrastructural or security deficiencies, the NHRC directed the Government of Maharashtra to review the functioning of these institutions in order ensure better care and bring them into conformity with acceptable standards. In doing so, the NHRC cited articles 3, 19 and 40 of the CRC.

---

[43] No. 5897/24/98–99.

[44] No. 497/13/97–98.

3.8 The CRC and the National Legal Services Authority

The National Legal Services Authority (NALSA), set up in 1995 under the Legal Services Authorities Act of 1987, is India's main body for framing schemes for legal services and determining principles and policies in this regard. Children are listed as a category of beneficiaries under Act, and NALSA's policies and schemes are rolled out nationally through a network of State and District Level Legal Services Authorities. These authorities are patronised by the Chief Justice of India and the Chief Justices of the respective High Courts.

NALSA's programme on children is extensive and influences children's right through legal processes and effective legal aid across the country. In 2011, the Supreme Court mandated NALSA to launch a nationwide training programme for police officers who deal with children. The CRC featured prominently in the curriculum it prepared.

NALSA designated 2011–2012 'the year of Rights of the Child' and released a National Plan of Action focusing on children's rights. Recognising the CRC's significance, the Plan termed it 'the Bible for all legal services institutions to take guidance from, when in doubt', saying that lawyers who handle cases of children and juveniles in conflict with law, 'require special training on juvenile psychology, child behaviour, the UN Convention on the Rights of Child and on the child-sensitive decisions of the superior Courts'.

4 Conclusion

Since its ratification by India in 1992, the CRC has contributed significantly to the growth and evolution of jurisprudence on child rights, serving in particular as a guiding force in filling gaps that existed in domestic legislation. The CRC finds explicit reference in the Juvenile Justice Act of 2000 and Protection of Children from Sexual Offences Act, 2012, as well as in several plans and policies related to children.

Moreover, it has been used both by litigants in framing their arguments as well as by courts in their judicial pronouncements. This has been so at all levels: the Supreme Court, High Courts and even sometimes the lower Courts, including the Juvenile Justice Boards in their rulings regarding children in conflict with the law. NGOs as well as statutory bodies such as the NHRC and NALSA make strong use of the CRC in training duty holders on children's rights.

So far, the treatment of, and response to, the CRC in litigation in India has been positive, and the results thereof, remarkable. However, notwithstanding this incremental growth in its use, there is still tremendous scope for identifying areas in existing laws, policies and practices where the standards set by the CRC are yet to be realised and for which judicial intervention will be required.

Reference

Agarwal, S. K. (2010). Implementation of international law in India: Role of judiciary. Hans & Tamar Oppenheimer Chair in Public International Law. http://oppenheimer.mcgill.ca/IMG/pdf/SK_Agarwal.pdf. Accessed 5 September 2013.

Chapter 4
England and Wales

Jane Williams

Abstract The United Kingdom (UK) has a dualist approach to international treaties and has not yet legislated to incorporate the Convention on the Rights of the Child (CRC) in UK domestic law. Nonetheless, there are various ways in which the CRC, like other unincorporated treaties, can influence the decisions of the courts: by means of a rule of construction, by means of developing established legal notions and by absorption into criteria for the legality of administrative decision-making. In England and Wales, which continue as a joint legal system despite devolution of legislative and executive powers to Wales, the CRC's impact can be seen in a number of areas of both substantive and procedural law. These include areas where underlying policy considerations are not traditionally inclusive of children's rights. However, judicial implementation can deliver only incremental change in response to such cases as reach the senior courts, and, in the Anglo-Welsh legal system, judicial deference to the legislature, and to executive agencies exercising statutory discretion, remains strong. Legislative incorporation is vital to deliver the necessary systemic changes. In Wales a novel legislative model is in place, using the concept of 'due regard' to require the devolved administration to think proactively about implementation. Further progress in implementation will be enhanced by a combination of such legislative measures and effective enforcement mechanisms, including but not limited to litigation and judicial enforcement.

I am indebted to my colleague Dr Simon Hoffman and to the editors for their comments. Any errors or omissions remain my own responsibility.

J. Williams (✉)
College of Law, Swansea University, Swansea, United Kingdom
e-mail: jane.m.williams@swansea.ac.uk

T. Liefaard and J.E. Doek (eds.), *Litigating the Rights of the Child*,
DOI 10.1007/978-94-017-9445-9_4

1 Status of the CRC in England and Wales

The United Kingdom[1] (UK) ratified the CRC in 1991. In the UK's legal system, ratification does not confer domestic legal effect: domestic legislation is required. Various legislative approaches may be used. For example: in respect of enforceable European Union rights, the European Communities Act 1972 confers superior effect on the international legal order of the treaties; in respect of the Hague and European child abduction and judgment recognition regimes, domestic legislation provides detailed rules to give effect to the specific international obligations; and in respect of the European Convention on Human Rights (ECHR), the Human Rights Act 1998 gives 'further effect' to the treaty provisions whilst carefully preserving UK parliamentary sovereignty in case of incompatibility of legislative provisions. Sometimes the UK as State party simply points to the existence of law generated mainly by domestic rather than international policy but which meets the treaty's requirements. The last approach has been adopted by the UK in relation to the CRC. There is no general legislative measure of implementation of the CRC at the UK level, and the only reference to the CRC in legislation passed by the UK Parliament is in connection with the role and remit of the Children's Commissioner for England.[2]

However, there are some differences between the UK level and the devolved levels in relation to the status of the CRC. The CRC is used by UK courts as an interpretative aid when applying the ECHR (Kilkelly 1999; Van Bueren 2007; Williams 2007; see further below). Accordingly, it is pertinent to note the differences between the UK and devolved levels in relation to the status of the ECHR.

The devolved parliaments[3] have no power to pass legislation which is incompatible with Convention rights under the ECHR, whereas the UK Parliament retains power to enact incompatible legislation. All public authorities (including government ministers and their officials) throughout the UK are prohibited by section 6 of the Human Rights Act 1998 from acting incompatibly with the ECHR Convention rights (except when certain exceptions apply), but the devolved governments[4] are subject to additional provisions in the respective devolution statutes[5] declaring that they have no power to act incompatibly with ECHR Convention rights.

---

[1] The United Kingdom is State Party to the CRC. However, implementation of the treaty obligations in Wales, Northern Ireland and Scotland falls to a substantial degree to the quasi-autonomous, or 'devolved', governments and parliaments for those areas. Scotland and Northern Ireland each also have their own legal systems, while the legal system of England and Wales remains joint. The process of devolution facilitated by UK legislation in 1998 is ongoing, and further, incremental change is likely.

[2] Section 2A Children Act 2004.

[3] The Scottish Parliament, the National Assembly for Wales, the Northern Ireland Assembly.

[4] The Scottish Executive, the Welsh Government, the Northern Ireland Executive, in each case comprising the Ministers and their officials.

[5] The Scotland Act 1998, the Northern Ireland Acts 1998, and the Government of Wales Acts 1998 and 2006.

ECHR compliance, and with it the influence of the CRC as an interpretative tool, is hence part of the constitutional base for devolved government and law-making. In Wales the difference in the status of the CRC is more explicitly marked by legislation passed by the devolved parliament itself, legislation which places a duty on the Welsh Ministers to have 'due regard' to the requirements of the CRC and its Optional Protocols whenever they exercise their functions.[6]

Thus, at the devolved level, especially in Wales, the requirements of the CRC are a stronger factor in determining the legality of government action than in England or in relation to non-devolved matters. In Wales, pursuant to their legal duty of due regard, Welsh Ministers routinely commission child rights impact assessments before exercising their functions; without this, many of their decisions would be open to challenge by way of judicial review. At the time of writing, no such challenge has yet been brought (no doubt in part because the legislation is still recent), and a variation on the Welsh 'due regard' approach is under legislative scrutiny in Scotland.[7]

In summary, the status of the CRC in domestic law is not the same throughout the UK State Party, and change is occurring asymmetrically, even within the fused legal system of England and Wales. The different status of the CRC in England and Wales has been noted by senior judiciary:

> The [CRC] has not been made a part of English law but the duty of the court is nonetheless to have regard to it when considering a matter relating to it. The position may now be different in Wales because the [CRC] has become part of Welsh legislation by reason of the Rights of Children and Young Persons (Wales) Measure 2011 which came into force in May 2012. The Measure will shape all future policy decisions taken by Welsh Ministers.[8]

2 The Role of Judicial Precedent

In the joint legal system of England and Wales, judicial precedent has an important role. The decisions of the senior courts (the House of Lords and Supreme Court;[9] Court of Appeal and High Court) are followed and applied in subsequent cases. The legitimacy of judicial creativity has been debated, including by the senior judiciary itself, but the view shared by 'most modern common law Judges' is that making (as opposed to merely applying) law is 'an entirely proper judicial function, provided it is exercised within certain limits' (Bingham 2000: 29). Certainly, judges can and do develop the law, both by expansion or qualification of the common law and by means of statutory interpretation.

The Human Rights Act of 1998 made important provisions affecting these functions of the courts. Section 2 requires that a court determining a question relating to

[6] Section 1 Rights of Children and Young Persons (Wales) Measure 2011.

[7] Children and Young People (Scotland) Bill, introduced to Parliament on 17 April 2013.

[8] Rt. Hon Sir Alan Ward, in *Re P-S*, 2013 (discussed further below under 'Family Law').

[9] From 1 October 2009 the Supreme Court replaced the Appellate Committee of the House of Lords as the highest court in the United Kingdom.

an ECHR Convention right must take into account the judgments, decisions, declarations or opinions of the European Court of Human Rights, the Commission and Committee of Ministers. This has the effect of incorporating the jurisprudence of the ECHR into the precedents to which the courts in England and Wales must have regard. Section 3 requires domestic legislation to be read and given effect, so far as it is possible to do so, in a way that is compatible with the ECHR Convention rights. Section 4 empowers the senior courts to make a declaration of incompatibility signalling that a provision of an Act of the UK Parliament is incompatible with an ECHR Convention right. Section 6 states that it is unlawful for a public authority—the definition of which includes courts and tribunals—to act in a way that is incompatible with a Convention right, while section 7 enables a person who is an alleged victim of a violation of a Convention right to bring a claim based on an alleged breach of section 6. The new role for the judiciary under the Human Rights Act 1998 has been described as developing a 'municipal law of human rights', a role which has been embraced with greater creativity by some senior judges than others (Masterman 2005).

In November 2009 a private Member's Bill promoting a Human Rights Act model of incorporation for the CRC was introduced in the UK Parliament.[10] This prompted the then UK Government to conduct a review of the compatibility of domestic legislation with the CRC (DCSF 2010). The Bill itself fell at an early stage, partly because of a general election in the spring of 2010. At the time of writing, no further Children's Rights Bill had been proposed at UK level.

Nonetheless, the CRC is increasingly influential in judicial decision-making. It has featured in the reasoning of the court both in its own right and through the influence it exerts when courts are considering the application of provisions of the ECHR. Apart from the interpretative requirement of section 3 of the Human Rights Act of 1998, there is a general rule of construction which privileges compliance with the international obligations of the UK in the event of ambiguity in domestic legislative expression. Furthermore, the courts have considered human rights requirements when applying or reappraising judicial precedents in key areas of law such as application of the welfare principle in family law. The CRC is also gaining prominence in judicial application of the administrative law concepts of legality, rationality, due process and proportionality.

In these ways the CRC, the comparative jurisprudence on its interpretation, and the outputs of the UN system itself, have all featured in arguments before the courts in England and Wales and in the reasoning given for judicial decisions.

3 Rule of Construction

The rule of construction is a product of the common law, not statute law. An example of its application in relation to the CRC is *Smith v. Secretary of State for Work and Pensions and Another* [2006] UKHL 35. The issue for the court was

[10] Children's Rights Bill 2009, presented by Baroness Finlay of Llandaff.

the proper construction of regulations on the calculation of child support following parental separation.

In S's case, one interpretation would have reduced by two thirds the calculation of the payer's income and thus the amount payable in child support. The majority of the Appellate Committee of the House of Lords preferred the alternative interpretation, which would result in a higher amount being payable. While there were several reasons for this, two members of the majority said that article 8 of the ECHR could generate a right to an effective system of maintenance post-separation.

One of them, Baroness Hale, noted the specific requirements of article 27(2) and 27(4) of the CRC. In an observation reflective of the classic understanding of the impact of the UK's unincorporated international obligations on the domestic law of England and Wales, she said:

> Even if an international treaty has not been incorporated into domestic law, our domestic legislation has to be construed so far as possible so as to comply with the international obligations, which we have undertaken. When two interpretations … are possible, the interpretation chosen should be that which better complies with the commitment to the welfare of children which this country made when ratifying the UNCRC.[11]

Smith is an example of the use of the CRC in conjunction with article 8 of the ECHR. By contrast, the criminal case of *R v. G and another* [2003] UKHL 50 is an example of the CRC's use as a stand-alone point of reference. The case illustrates the difficulties inherent in the relatively low age of criminal responsibility (10 years) in the law of England and Wales, which has been the subject of repeated recommendations for reform by the UN Committee on the Rights of the Child in its Concluding Observations on UK State Party reports.

At the ages of 11 and 12, the two defendants in *G and another* would not have been subject to criminal process in most other European jurisdictions. The boys had gone camping without their parents' permission and entered a yard at behind a general store. There they found bundles of newspapers, which they used to light a fire, one they did not properly extinguish when they left. The fire spread, setting light to two rubbish bins and thence to the building; the ensuing blaze caused some £1 million worth of damage. The boys were charged with arson, a serious offence under section 1 of the Criminal Damage Act 1971.

Judicial precedent had established an objective test for the requisite mental element of recklessness: no account could be taken of the personal characteristics, including the age, of the defendant. It was accepted at their trial that neither boy had any appreciation that the fire might spread in this way. Indeed, they thought it would die down on the concrete surface of the yard.

On appeal as to the correct legal test for 'recklessness', the House of Lords overruled its own precedent and substituted a subjective test capable of taking into account the age of the defendant. In reaching this conclusion, Lord Steyn quoted from article 40(1) of the CRC, in particular the clause:

[11] At para. 78, [2006] UKHL 35.

> States Parties recognise the right of every child alleged as, accused of, or recognised as having infringed the penal law to be treated in a manner … which takes into account the child's age ….

Lord Steyn noted that article 40(1) imposes both substantive and procedural obligations. It would clearly be contrary to article 40(1) to ignore, in a crime punishable by indefinite penal detention, the age of a child in judging whether the mental element for the offence was satisfied. Significantly, he added that this factor alone justified a reappraisal of the previous law, which had been settled before the UK ratified the CRC.

The next sections give further examples of judicial precedent being reappraised in the light of the CRC's requirements. The examples are drawn from family law, an area in which the CRC has been used to challenge traditional, paternalistic application of the 'welfare principle', and from administrative law, where it has been deployed to inject additional, child rights-based criteria into decision-making in a number of policy areas.

4 Family Law: Impact of the CRC on the Application of the 'Welfare Principle'

In England and Wales, where a court has to make a decision in family law cases about the upbringing of a child, section 1 of the Children Act 1989 requires the court to give paramount consideration to the welfare of the child. This 'welfare principle' dates back long before the 1989 Act and has ancient origins in the exercise of the courts' protective jurisdiction over minors lacking parental protection. It was later applied to disputes over guardianship of children, and served to enable interference with the once-unfettered power of the married father over the upbringing of his child (O'Halloran 1999: 9–34; Breen 2002: 43–45). The welfare principle has featured in successive statutes dealing with the guardianship of minors. The current formula in section 1 of the Children Act 1989 is thus, in part, a modern expression of a legal tradition reflected in both judicial precedent and statute law.

Section 1 of the 1989 Act provides that in decisions about residence, contact, prohibited steps or specific issues that concern a child, the court must pay particular regard to the 'welfare checklist' in section 1(3). The list comprises the following:

(a) the ascertainable wishes and feelings of the child concerned (considered in the light of his age and understanding);
(b) his physical, emotional and educational needs;
(c) the likely effect on him of any change in his circumstances;
(d) his age, sex, background and any characteristics of his which the court considers relevant;
(e) any harm which he has suffered or is at risk of suffering;

(f) how capable each of his parents, and any other person in relation to whom the court considers the question to be relevant, is of meeting his needs;
(g) the range of powers available to the court under this Act in the proceedings in question.

The matters specified in the welfare checklist can be seen to be compatible with aspects of the CRC and are broadly similar to the 'Elements to be taken into account when assessing the child's best interests' set out in the UN Committee's General Comment No. 14 (2013, paras. 52–57). However, the Children Act 1989 checklist does not cross-refer to the CRC, even though the Act was enacted close to the date at which the CRC was adopted. In fact, it was the fragmented state of the pre-existing domestic legislation—coupled with official reports (DHSS 1985; Law Commission 1988) and contemporaneous concerns over a succession of highly-publicised failures in state intervention in child abuse—that were the principal influences on the content of the 1989 Act, rather than the ten-year process of negotiating the terms of the CRC (Roche 2005).

What is more, nowhere in the Act is there explicit reference to the rights of the child: all is phrased in term of powers and duties of the courts, local authorities, courts and other authorities. This adheres to a tradition of legislative drafting in UK social welfare legislation, a tradition which is highly resilient. Even in Wales, where, as noted above, the devolved parliament has sought to give the CRC general effect across all Welsh Ministerial functions, contemporary legislative drafting adheres to this duty-based rather than rights-based tradition.[12]

It might be argued that the similarities between the welfare checklist and the CRC's notion of best interests justifies continuing the habit in the legal lexicon of England and Wales of equating the terms 'welfare' and 'best interests' and, likewise, 'the paramount principle', 'the welfare principle' and 'best interests test' (Fortin 2009: 291 n.1). However, it must be borne in mind that the scope of application of the Children Act's welfare checklist is very narrow compared to article 3(1) of the CRC. The court decisions to which section 1 of the 1989 Act applies are but a small (though significant) part of the range of decisions covered by the CRC provisions. In other words, the Children Act 1989 does not 'fulfill' the UK's State Party obligations under article 3. Furthermore, even where section 1 applies, differences can be discerned between the concept of the best interests of the child as developed within, on the one hand, the jurisprudence of the CRC and, on the other, the welfare tradition in Anglo-Welsh family law.

These differences have been judicially acknowledged in a number of cases. A good example is *Mabon v. Mabon* [2005] EWCA Civ 634, a case which concerned the exercise of judicial discretion to allow independent representation of children where their parents are in dispute over residence or contact. The trial judge had taken the view that to allow the children, who in this matter were mature teenagers, representation independent of the court-appointed guardian would not help the court but simply give it 'perhaps the more articulate and elegant expression

[12] For example, in the Social Services and Well-being (Wales) Bill 2013.

of what I already know'. The Court of Appeal overruled the trial judge's decision to refuse independent representation. Thorpe LJ reflected as follows on the traditional approach to children's welfare interests in family proceedings:

> In our system we have traditionally adopted the tandem model for the representation of children who are parties to family proceedings, whether public or private. First the court appoints a guardian ad litem who will almost invariably have a social work qualification and very wide experience of family proceedings. He then instructs a specialist family solicitor who, in turn, usually instructs a specialist family barrister. This is a Rolls Royce model and is the envy of many other jurisdictions. However, its overall approach is essentially paternalistic. The guardian's first priority is to advocate the welfare of the child he represents. His second priority is to put before the court the child's wishes and feelings. Those priorities can in some cases conflict.[13]

The trial judge had followed earlier judicial precedent in focusing on whether independent representation would assist the court to reach a decision on the dispute between the parents. The Court of Appeal found that this overlooked the child's agency and right to be heard as recognised in article 12 of the CRC. Thorpe LJ, again:

> The guidance given by this court in *Re S [the precedent which favored rejection of children's separate representation on 'welfare' grounds]* cited above on the construction of r 9.2A is now 12 years old. Much has happened in that time. Although the United Kingdom had ratified the UN Convention some 15 months earlier, it did not have much impact initially and it is hardly surprising that it was not mentioned by this court on the 26 February 1993. Although the tandem model has many strengths and virtues, at its heart lies the conflict between advancing the welfare of the child and upholding the child's freedom of expression and participation. Unless we in this jurisdiction are to fall out of step with similar societies as they safeguard art 12 rights, we must, in the case of articulate teenagers, accept that the right to freedom of expression and participation outweighs the paternalistic judgment of welfare.[14]

This judgment clearly demonstrated judicial acceptance that family courts in England and Wales should respect article 12 of the CRC by ensuring that the child's voice is heard in proceedings concerning the child. However, the way in which this is done in practice raises certain questions, especially in view of legislative changes pending at the time of writing.

The 'tandem model' referred to in the extract from Thorpe LJ's judgment involves a senior social worker, called the child's 'guardian', investigating, gathering evidence and reporting to the court on both the welfare question (the course of action that will best serve the child's welfare) and the wishes and views of the child. It is by these means, rather than by hearing evidence directly from the child, that the family courts 'hear' the voice of the child. Requests from children—even 'articulate teenagers'—to give evidence are invariably refused, on the grounds that it would be injurious to their welfare.

In *Re P-S (Children)* [2013] EWCA Civ 223, the Court of Appeal held this position even after detailed consideration of article 12 and the General Comment

---

[13] At para. 25.

[14] At para. 28.

Number 12 on the Right of the Child to be Heard. No-one, the Court of Appeal held, had a right to give evidence, and if the court was satisfied that it would learn nothing new by hearing directly from the child (the child's wishes and feelings having been summarised in the guardian's report), the child could not invoke the 'right to be heard' and therewith insist on being heard directly by the judge. This sits uncomfortably with both the letter and spirit of article 12 in a case such as *P-S*, where a 15-year-old is pleading to be heard in person by the decision-maker on a matter of such importance as a final care order.

In 2013/14 a number of changes to the family justice system in England and Wales were in progress, stimulated in part by the Final Report of the Family Justice Review in 2011 (Ministry of Justice 2011). No change is contemplated in the mode of representation of children in family proceedings, but some aspects of the reforms proposed to date, notably a 'presumption of involvement' following parental separation, appear to undermine a child-centred, child rights-based approach. Furthermore, it remains unclear how the 'voice of the child' will be protected in the implementation of proposals to divert potential court applications into mediation.[15] Despite the clear evidence of increased judicial acceptance of the need to apply the CRC, these issues give cause for concern. As such, family proceedings in England and Wales should be subjected to close and critical scrutiny in the course of ongoing domestic and international monitoring of CRC implementation.

5 Administrative Law: Impact of the CRC on Criteria for Administrative Decisions

An appreciation of the CRC, informed by international and comparative sources, can be seen increasingly to influence the development of principles by which to judge the legality of decisions affecting children. Just as with the development of municipal law on human rights set forth in the ECHR (Mastermann, op.cit.), this absorption of the CRC has been led by senior judges who appear to favour a creative rather than compliance approach; that is, an approach which seeks to place CRC rights in the foreground of the argument rather than treat them as a matter for compliance-checking once domestic law has been applied.

For example, the case for asserting children's rights under the ECHR was much advanced by one such judge, Munby J, in seminal judgments on the application of local authorities' duties to assess and provide services for children in prisons[16] and on the need for separate representation of babies when administrative decisions are made about segregating them from their mothers serving a term of imprisonment.[17]

---

[15] The provisions on mediation and on the presumption of involvement were enacted in sections 10 and 11 Children and Families Act 2014.

[16] *R (Howard League for Penal Reform) v Secretary of State for the Home Department* [2002] EWHC 2497.

[17] *CF v Secretary of State for the Home Department and another* [2004] EWHC 111(Fam).

In a similar vein, several judges of the higher courts in the UK[18] have given increasing prominence to children's rights under the CRC as well as, or in conjunction with, the ECHR. Often it is a matter of re-focusing on the human rights of the child where arguments had previously foregrounded those of the adults.

A case that exemplifies the need for such a shift of focus is *R (Williamson and Others) v. Secretary of State for Education and Employment and Others* [2005] UKHL 15. A group of parents argued that a statutory prohibition of corporal punishment in all schools infringed the parents' right to freedom of religion under article 9 ECHR. According to the parents' strongly-held religious beliefs, corporal punishment was not only permitted but required for the proper upbringing of children. The parents were ultimately unsuccessful, with much discussion at first instance and at two appellate levels about the nature of the article 9 ECHR rights and some discussion of the application of permissible state interference under article 9(2). For present purposes, the striking point is that throughout the litigation barely any reference was made to the rights of the children. As Baroness Hale eventually noted on the final appeal to the Supreme Court:

> [T]his is, and always has been, a case about children, their rights and the rights of their parents and teachers. Yet there has been no-one here or in the courts below to speak on behalf of the children. … The battle has been fought on ground selected by the adults.

Part of the motivation for the CRC was, and remains, the need to emphasise that children are human beings whose rights should be protected and respected just as much as adults' rights. Cases like *Williamson*, in which human rights arguments are conducted between adults without recognising the need as well to hear the case for the human rights of children, illustrate how necessary it is to advocate continually for children's rights. Despite—and, perhaps in some small way, because of—*Williamson*, re-focusing on the human rights of the child has become discernible in UK judicial decisions. This is true in several areas, not only those where decisions are overtly about children or child law. Two such areas are considered below: immigration and spatial planning.

5.1 Immigration

The overall purposes of immigration law are summarised in the extract below from statutory guidance issued by the Secretary of State to the UK Border Agency. Describing the role and functions of the Agency, the Secretary of State notes that:

---

[18] The High Court of Justice and the Court of Appeal are England and Wales courts. The Supreme Court is the highest appellate court and its jurisdiction is UK-wide. Administrative law cases in England and Wales often start in the Administrative Court, a division of the High Court. Appeal lies from there to the Court of Appeal and, ultimately, on a point of law of general significance, to the Supreme Court.

> its primary duties are to maintain a secure border, to detect and prevent border tax fraud, smuggling and immigration crime, and to ensure controlled, fair migration that protects the public and that contributes to economic growth and benefits the country.

Within this seemingly child-blind context, the rights of children to protection have gained a small but important foothold following the UK's withdrawal in 2008 of its reservation concerning immigration controls.[19] The statutory guidance cited above is issued by the Secretary of State under section 55 of the Borders, Citizenship and Immigration Act 2009. This section requires 'arrangements' to be put in place to ensure that the immigration, asylum, nationality or customs functions are discharged 'having regard to' the need to 'safeguard and promote the welfare' of children who are in the UK. It puts the UK Border Agency in a similar position to a variety of other public bodies with statutory safeguarding obligations.[20] The Agency has to implement a list of measures directed at better treatment of children and their families and at vigilance over child trafficking and other abuses. However, the guidance goes on to make a bold statement about the application of a number of international obligations, including the CRC. The Border Agency, it states, 'must fulfill the requirements of these instruments'. The mandatory language is striking, since several of the instruments listed, including the CRC, have not been given full effect in UK domestic legislation. Yet here, in statutory guidance, a mandatory duty is imposed on an administrative authority to 'fulfill' the requirements of these instruments.

A provision of this kind surely raises an expectation—a legitimate expectation, in the sense used by the courts in judicial review cases—that the requirements of these international instruments will be complied with unless it is not possible to do so and simultaneously remain compatible with UK immigration legislation. That is the position reached in Australia in *Minister for Immigration and Ethnic Affairs v. Teoh* [1995] 183 CLR 273 and *Wan v. Minister for Immigration and Multicultural Affairs* [2001] FCA 568. In those cases the Australian High Court and the Australian Federal Court, respectively, held that Australia's ratification of the CRC, even in the absence of statutory incorporation into domestic law, created a legitimate expectation that public officials would take into account the best interests of children affected by an administrative decision as a 'primary consideration' in accordance with article 3.

In *ZH (Tanzania) v. Secretary of State for the Home Department* [2012] UKSC 25, the UK Supreme Court consolidated a trend, evidenced in a number of lower

---

[19] The reservation, which was withdrawn in 2008, reserved the right of the United Kingdom to apply such legislation, insofar as it relates to the entry into, stay in, and departure from the United Kingdom, of those who do not have the right under UK law to remain in the UK, and to the acquisition and possession of citizenship, as it may deem necessary from time to time.

[20] The Children Act 2004 imposed obligations on public health bodies, police, probation and prison authorities, as well as on local authorities in England and Wales, to make arrangements to exercise their functions and deliver services having regard to the need to safeguard and promote the welfare of children.

tier immigration appeals,[21] towards explicit regard for the best interests of children. The Supreme Court also referred with approval to the Australian cases of *Teoh* and *Wan*. In *ZH*, the mother was a Tanzanian national with an 'appalling' immigration history over some 13 years. The appeal which reached the UK Supreme Court in 2010 concerned a decision to remove the mother from the UK. The deportation decision could not be criticised if one looked at the mother's immigration history alone, but she had two children born of a relationship with a British citizen and who were thus British citizens.

They were now 12 and 9 years old, and had lived all their lives in the UK, first with both parents and then, following the parents' separation, with the mother. The father visited the children regularly and enjoyed family life with them, but he had multiple problems including HIV and alcohol addiction. In practice, the removal of the mother would mean either that the children moved in with their father in the UK, a person who would not be capable of caring adequately for them, or that they went to live in Tanzania, a country foreign to them, and thereby experienced interference in their family life with the father.

In the UK Supreme Court it was held that article 3 CRC was relevant because of the elucidation it provided about the proper application of article 8 of the ECHR. The court referred both to European Court of Human Rights case law and Commonwealth precedents in reaching its conclusion that, when dealing with extradition requests or immigration, the best interests of children who will be affected by the decision was a primary consideration. This meant giving the best interests of the child *first* consideration though not *paramount* consideration (thus, not 'the trump card' status accorded to the welfare of the child in family court decisions under section 1 of the Children Act 1989). The best interests of the child should prevail unless they were outweighed by other reasons in the particular matter at hand, for example, a serious case of criminality by a non-citizen parent, which would require the parent's removal from the country irrespective of its impact on the children.

In the subsequent case of *Zoumbas v. Secretary of State for the Home Department* [2013] UKSC 74, the Supreme Court put it thus:

> Although the best interests of the child can be outweighed by the cumulative effect of other considerations, no other consideration can be treated as inherently more significant.[22]
>
> In the Australian *Teoh* case, Gaudron J in the Australian High Court had made an interesting comment linking citizenship rights with the obligation under article 3 CRC:
>
> Citizenship carries with it a common law right on the part of children and their parents to have a child's best interests taken into account, at least as a primary consideration, in all discretionary decisions by governments and government agencies which directly affect that child's individual welfare …

This dictum was not specifically referred to in *ZH*, but Lord Kerr, at paragraph 47 of the judgment, developed the thought when he stated that a child's nationality.

---

[21] The first such case was a decision of the Upper Tribunal (Immigration and Asylum Chamber): *LD (Zimbabwe) v Secretary of State for the Home Department* [2010] UKUT 278 (IAC).

[22] Lord Hodge, at para. 10 of the judgment.

> must be considered in two aspects [:]... first... as a contributor to the debate about where a child's best interests lie ... [because] to diminish a child's right to assert his or her nationality will not normally be in his or her best interests ... [second] ... if a child is a British citizen, this has an independent value, freestanding of the debate as to best interests, and this must weigh in the balance in any decision that may affect where a child will live.

In this line of cases, one can thus see recognition of the child's independent status and citizenship and support for the implementation of article 7 of the CRC (the right to birth registration, name and nationality) as well as article 3. Lord Kerr's obiter dictum has expansive potential, since it might be argued that article 7 ought to be in the foreground of a decision-maker's mind in this area as much as, or as well as, article 3 of the CRC.

An important practical implication of recognising referred to as 'the debate about where a child's best interests lie'. The Supreme Court in *ZH* expressly acknowledged that in some cases it would mean commissioning a report similar to those commissioned in the family courts when determining a question about the child's welfare. This may require dedication of both time and other resources. Concerns about these implications were raised when the courts came to consider whether the reasoning in *ZH* about the best interests of the child also applied in decisions related to the second area mentioned in this section of the chapter: spatial planning.

5.2 Planning

In England and Wales planning decisions are regarded as a matter of public policy, and local planning authorities have statutory duties to make a development plan for an area and consider individual applications for permission to use a particular area of land in a particular way. There is a statutory appeals process for decisions on individual planning decisions, and the court has jurisdiction by way of judicial review to assess the legality of decisions within that process. In exercising this jurisdiction, the courts have adhered to traditional deference to executive discretion conferred by statute and have avoided adjudicating on the merits of administrative decision-making. They have confined themselves to questions of process, including whether all material considerations have been taken into account but excluding the weight to be given to any such consideration.

However, this approach had to be adjusted to accommodate the courts' function under the Human Rights Act 1998, outlined above. As Baroness Hale stated in an appeal concerning a planning decision unrelated to children's rights:

> The role of the court in human rights adjudication is quite different from the role of the court in ordinary judicial review of administrative action. In human rights adjudication, the court is concerned with whether the human rights of the Claimant have in fact been infringed, not with whether the administrative decision-maker properly took them into account.[23]

---

[23] *Miss Behavin' Ltd v. Belfast City Council* [2007] UKHL 19, at para. 31.

Accordingly, human rights arguments may be used to challenge the substance as well as the process of planning decisions. Following the Supreme Court's decision in *ZH*, the courts have accepted that it means that article 3 CRC is engaged and applies, in conjunction with article 8 ECHR, to planning decisions that will affect a child. The court may need to consider not only whether the child's rights have been considered by the executive agency, but also whether appropriate weight has been given to those rights. A detailed examination of the rationale for and implications of this was given in the judgment of Hickinbottom J in *Stevens v. Secretary of State for Communities and Local Government and another* [2013] EWHC 792 (Admin).

Stevens was one of the latest in a line of cases involving gypsy and traveller sites in England and Wales. Discrimination against gypsies and travellers was highlighted as a concern by the UN Committee on the Rights of the Child in its Concluding Observations on the UK's third and fourth combined State party reports in 2008 (UN 2008). The Claimant Jane Stevens lived with her partner and extended family, which included several children, on a small unofficial site. She applied for a retrospective grant of permission to use this site temporarily for a period of 4 years, pending hoped-for provision by the local authority of an official site in the area. In the judicial review of the planning inspector's rejection of the Claimant's statutory appeal, one of the two grounds was that the inspector had failed to attach sufficient weight to the best interests of the children.

On this ground, Hickinbottom J held (at para. 55):

> Where action by the state affects a family, whether the action is disproportionate in its interference with their art 8 rights has to be looked at by reference to the family unit as a whole and by reference to the impact upon specific individual members of the family …. Where those family members include children, then their art 8 rights have to be interpreted in the light of general principles of international law, including obligations imposed on the state by international conventions …. In this context, the most important obligations on the United Kingdom are those derived from the UNCRC. Article 3(1) provides 'In all actions concerning children, whether undertaken by public or private social welfare institutions, courts of law, administrative authorities or legislative bodies, the best interests of the child shall be a primary consideration.' When a child's art 8 rights are engaged, they must be looked at in the context of the UNCRC or, as it has been put, 'through the prism of art 3(1)'.

Responding to the point about resource implications, Hickinbottom J rejected (at para. 58 of the judgment) the contention that a planning decision-maker would be routinely required to produce social enquiry or welfare reports on all children whose interests are or may be adversely affected by a decision. In most cases, he said, there was unlikely to be conflict between the interests and wishes of the carer and the child, so the carer would be in the best position to put forward evidence about the potentially adverse effect of any decision on the child; the planning decision-maker, or, in the event of challenge, the court, would be entitled to assume that any and all evidence of the child's best interests is put before it by the carer.

This is an important point, one which should chill premature celebration of the CRC's penetration into planning law in these cases. Although the court acknowledged that sometimes a carer could not be relied upon to ensure that the child's best interests are brought to the attention of the court, the clear assumption is that it would be rare for independent investigation of the best interests question to be required and, even less so, advocacy for the child. This approach might address the problem of resource management, but at the cost of imposing what will often be unrealistic expectations on carers in communities already on the edge of mainstream society and with people among them who are least able to access legal advice and representation.

6 Conclusion

The common law is too often overlooked as a source of human rights protection. Often, the starting point is the international obligations negotiated in the post-second world war period, from which one moves to study how they have been implemented in domestic law. Yet the same political philosophies that informed these negotiations also informed the development of the common law well before the international jurists and drafters began their work.

The UK Government sought to capture this thought, and with it the impact that the common law has had on the development of international human rights law, when the title 'Bringing Rights Home' was chosen for the White Paper proposing what became the Human Rights Act 1998. The same notion is evident in statements by some of our most eminent judges. For example, in a case in which UK law was held to be incompatible with the obligation of non-discrimination in article 14 ECHR, Lord Woolf, then Chief Justice of England and Wales, said non-discrimination was also a fundamental requirement of the rule of law, adding that

> long before the 1998 Act came into force the common law recognized the importance of not discriminating. The importance of not discriminating explains why every judge on taking office makes a vow to 'do right by all manner of people ... without fear or favour, affection or ill will'.[24]

If the traditions of the common law thus provided one of the several streams that flowed into the construction of the post-Second World War international human rights order, it must also be acknowledged that there is a distinct history—or are distinct histories—of children's rights in which different traditions (along with a number of heroic individuals) played their part.

For present purposes, the relevance of the traditions of the common law is that in England and Wales they bestowed a judicial culture in which it is possible for the CRC to be absorbed incrementally into domestic law without it (the CRC) necessarily awaiting legislative incorporation. The same process of gradual accretion of human rights principles was notable in relation to the ECHR in judicial decisions in England and Wales during the 1990s. With regard to the need to incorporate the CRC properly, it is pertinent to note that judicial decision-making contributed to conditions in which legislative incorporation of the ECHR

---

24 *A v Secretary of State for the Home Department* [2002] EWCA Civ 1502.

underwent a transformation in the eyes of senior public officials and politicians from the impossible to the inevitable and culminated in the enactment of the Human Rights Act 1998.

This chapter has focused mainly on the positive rather than the negative, demonstrating the CRC's impact on judicial decision-making and presenting evidence that municipal law is beginning to be developed on children's rights. Nevertheless, there are shortcomings. The courts are necessarily constrained to be reactive, dealing only with those issues which are brought before them and, in particular, those which crystallize as points of law for determination by the senior courts. These are inevitably but the tip of an iceberg of decisions that are made every day by governments and executive agencies and which impact on the fulfillment of the rights of children, people who are amongst the least able in society to articulate and pursue rights claims on their own behalf. In those cases that reach the courts, judicial deference to parliamentary and executive authority—especially in areas of current social policy and issues dealing with the implications of resource allocation—contributes to a generally conservative, cautious approach mindful of the proper boundaries between judicial and political responsibilities. Many judges still regard themselves, on the whole, as keepers of the law rather than creative lawmakers (Devlin 1979: 5, quoted in Bingham, op. cit.: 33).

In England and Wales, creative law reform remains largely the province of elected governments and legislatures: governments propose laws while legislatures scrutinise, improve and enact them. Although judicial creativity, conducted within its proper constitutional bounds, can be seen to be scoring small, gradual gains for children's rights in some areas, it cannot deliver the general change in legal and political culture that is required for the full implementation of the CRC. Legislation is needed, and in that regard, the Welsh legislative experiment is the most promising development so far in the UK. This chapter has not sought to examine the potential of the Welsh Measure to generate litigation, strategic or otherwise: such examination can be found elsewhere (Williams 2013). It suffices to conclude by observing that further significant change will come through a combination of such legislative reform, importing clear obligations on governments and executive authorities to implement the CRC, and the accessibility of effective enforcement mechanisms, including but not limited to litigation. The role of the senior courts in developing a municipal law of children's rights is a crucial element in this journey.

References

Bingham, T. (2000). The judge as lawmaker. In T. Bingham (Ed.), *The business of judging*. Oxford: Oxford University Press.

Breen, C. (2002). *The standard of the best interests of the child: A western tradition in international and comparative law*. The Hague: Kluwer Law International.

DCSF. (2010). *The United Nations Convention on the Rights of the Child: How legislation underpins implementation in England*. London: Department for Children, Schools and Families.

Devlin, P. (1979). *The judge*. Oxford: Oxford University Press.
DHSS. (1985). *Review of child care law: report to ministers of an interdepartmental working party*. London: Department of Health and Social Security, HMSO.
Fortin, J. (2009). *Children's rights and the developing law* (3rd ed.). Cambridge: Cambridge University Press.
Kilkelly, U. (1999). *The child and the European Convention on Human Rights*. Aldershot: Ashgate.
Law Commission (1988). *Family law review of child law guardianship and custody.* Law Com. No.172.
Masterman, R. (2005). Taking the Strasbourg jurisprudence into account: Developing a 'municipal law of human rights' under the Human Rights Act. *International and Comparative Law Quarterly, 54*, 907–932.
Ministry of Justice. (2011). *Final report of the Family Justice Review*. London: Ministry of Justice, Department for Education and the Welsh Government, HMSO.
O'Halloran, K. (1999). *The welfare of the child: the principle and the law*. Aldershot: Ashgate.
Roche, J. (2005). The 1989 Children Act and children's rights: a critical reassessment. In H. Hendrick (Ed.), *Child welfare and social policy*. Bristol: Policy Press.
Van Bueren, G. (2007). *Child rights in Europe*. Strasbourg: Council of Europe Publishing.
Williams, J. (2007). Incorporating children's rights: The divergence in law and policy. *Legal Studies, 27*, 261–287.
Williams, J. (2013). *The United Nations convention on the rights of the child in Wales*. Cardiff: University of Wales Press.

Chapter 5
United States

The Surprising Role of the CRC in a Non-state-Party

Bernardine Dohrn

'[W]hile one should always be sceptical about the law's pretensions, one should never be cynical about the law's possibilities',
—Albie Sachs (2009)

Abstract The unlikely element of success in the US campaigns challenging the juvenile death penalty and extreme sentencing of children is the express recognition, by the US Supreme Court in two germinal cases, of the standards of the Convention on the Rights of the Child (CRC), the role of international human rights law, and the practices of other nations. Strategies to abolish the juvenile death penalty in the US included coalition-building, education, legislation and litigation. This campaign culminated in the 2005 *Roper v. Simmons* decision, which held that the execution of children (persons under the age of 18 years at the time of the crime) violated the Eighth Amendment prohibition against cruel and unusual punishment. Citing article 37 of the CRC, the *Roper* opinion included an extraordinary section elucidating the US global isolation in implementing the juvenile death penalty. Subsequent Supreme Court cases address the extreme sentencing of juvenile offenders to life without the possibility of parole (JLWOP). In *Graham v. Florida* (2010), the Court concluded that sentencing a child to JLWOP for a non-homicide felony is unconstitutional and reaffirmed the role of, and global support for, the CRC. *Miller v. Alabama* (2012) held that mandatory JLWOP sentences, which do not permit consideration of the age and circumstances of child offenders, are also unconstitutional.

B. Dohrn (✉)
School of Law, Northwestern University, Chicago, IL, USA
e-mail: bernardine.dohrn@gmail.com; b-dohrn@law.northwestern.edu

B. Dohrn
Human Rights Program, University of Chicago, Chicago, IL, USA

T. Liefaard and J.E. Doek (eds.), *Litigating the Rights of the Child*,
DOI 10.1007/978-94-017-9445-9_5

1 Juvenile Justice Developments, the CRC and the USA

Undreamed-of creativity, imagination and inspired implementation have been unleashed by the CRC[1] across the globe since its adoption 25 years ago. In unpredictable ways, this dynamism has sharply revealed the ethical paradoxes, social inequalities, conflicts and rich intellectual enterprise embedded in the transformative possibilities of juvenile justice. By engaging the anguishing dilemmas of crime and punishment, youthfulness and harm, accountability and consequences, and by insisting upon meaningful second chances for the marginalised and caged children in conflict with the law, the CRC and children's international human rights law have not only reignited the promise contained in the century-old invention of the juvenile court but transcended it. Now the possibilities of realising these rights by utilising the tools of litigation are blossoming in unexpected soil—including the recalcitrant United States.

The invention in 1899 of a distinctive court for children, a legal polity described as 'one of the most important social inventions of the modern period' (Rosenheim et al. 2002), spread like a prairie fire across the US and throughout the world. It involved a radical insistence: children should neither be crushed for their transgressions nor brutalised for a lack of access and opportunity; society, in sum, should not give up on its children.

The birth of the juvenile court was part and parcel of the ferment of urban, industrialising, immigrant America at the turn of the nineteenth century, and its midwives were the militant, determined women of Hull House. The terrain of these social reformers included four decades of campaigns for compulsory education as well as the abolition of child labour, the removal of children from adult jails and poorhouses, neighbourhood democracy, women's rights, the expansion of the public space, and opposition to war. Jane Addams, Julia Lathrop and Lucy Flowers, living in an impoverished immigrant neighbourhood in Chicago in 1899, invented both the world's first juvenile court and, at the height of World War I, during the International Congress of Women in The Hague, called for an International Court of Justice that would create a code of international law. Their vision entailed local and international courthouses—linked at conception. These were citadels where justice for the child, and peace rather than warfare, would be argued and might be done.

The juvenile court, laced with tension and paradox, emerged as part of this philosophical mosaic. Ninety years later, the CRC was adopted by the United Nations General Assembly, becoming the most rapidly ratified treaty in history (Todres et al. 2006; Cohen and Davidson 1990; Cohen 1998). It was the first treaty at the end of the Cold War, and thus the first to re-integrate civil and political rights with social and economic rights in an era of global technology and massive

[1] United Nations Office of the High Commissioner for Human Rights. Convention on the Rights of the Child. http://www.ohchr.org/en/professionalinterest/pages/crc.aspx. Accessed 27 January 2014.

inequities. Twenty-five years after its adoption, the values and standards of children's human rights, as developed by the CRC, its ambitious Committee and three Optional Protocols, have encircled the world, setting down roots in unlikely soil, rock and sand, and adapting to climates, faiths, cultures and a vast range of legal traditions.

Children may not be hit in schools or at home with impunity, girls may resist early marriage and complete secondary education, children may not be recruited or deployed as soldiers in armed conflict, newborns may survive childbirth free of HIV-AIDs, female children may live their girlhoods free of genital cutting and have rights as domestic workers, and all may live the ecstasy and anguish of adolescence without fear of the death penalty.

The rights of children to be heard, to participation, to a name and nationality, to connections with family, to freedom of association, speech, thought, conscience and religion, and their right to privacy—all are secured by law.

The continuing failure of US executive and legislative bodies to ratify the CRC[2] cannot be understood without reference to the long, contested, sordid, and continuing struggle over racism. In fact, the domestic struggle over ratification of treaties was highlighted at the founding of the United Nations and the adoption of the Universal Declaration of Rights.[3] Justice for children, the recognition of children as persons, with both rights and special protection needs, has historically and intrinsically been bound to the abolition of slavery and to challenging white supremacy in the US.

Twice in the past century, the radical reframing of justice for the child closely shadowed the forward lurch of social struggle by and legal emancipation of African Americans. It was in the Reconstruction era immediately following the Emancipation, and again in the civil rights crucible of the 1960s, that US courts first addressed and then re-visited the issue of children's rights. For if an African American is a person under the Fourteenth Amendment to the US Constitution, what about immigrants, what about women, and what about the child?

At the founding of the juvenile court, property relationships in the ownership of enslaved human beings (backed by culture, tradition, religion, law, habit and practice so as to seem 'natural') were being eroded even though children had been the exclusive legal property of adult males for centuries—subject to their physical terror, torture, exploitation and sale. Agitation about the rights of incarcerated children gained momentum in the Reconstruction years, a period in which legal arguments and court opinions in Illinois closely linked abolition and anti-slavery

---

[2] In 1995 President Clinton signed the CRC on the occasion of the death of James Grant, the director of UNICEF, but never referred the treaty to the US Senate for ratification. Subsequent US Presidents have followed suit, and the CRC has never been debated or taken up by the US Senate. Numerous US legal entities, including the American Bar Association, have adopted resolutions urging US ratification. Fierce opposition to the CRC, citing phantom fears and characterizations of the Convention as diminishing the role of parents and the family, continue to hold ratification in limbo. US Department of State. Optional Protocol to the Convention on the Rights of the Child on the Involvement of Children in Armed Conflict. http://www.state.gov/j/drl/rls/c35136.htm. Accessed 27 Jan 2014. See also Cohen and Bitensky (1996).

[3] See, for example, Anderson (2003).

concepts with a lively debate on the nature of childhood. Justice for the child was rekindled in the heat of the Black Freedom Movement, when, in 1967, the US Supreme Court [*In re Gault*][4] first acknowledged children as constitutional persons and rights-bearers.

However, since the CRC came into force across the world, justice for the US child has become thoroughly racialised, in a new form of Jim Crow enslavement (W. Haywood Burns Institute 2008; The Annie E. Casey Foundation 2008a, b). Both national and state-wide data confirm that the children arrested, charged, detained, tried, transferred to adult criminal court, convicted and then incarcerated are disproportionately young people of colour: African Americans and Latinos (W. Haywood Burns Institute 2014; Annie E. Casey Foundation 2013a, b).[5] Youth of colour are arrested in and expelled from schools, seized for gang 'affiliation', stopped and frisked, disproportionately charged with drug possession or sale, and live in neighbourhoods isolated from the dominant community of resources, opportunity and wealth (The Annie E. Casey Foundation 2013b). Meanwhile white children have largely disappeared from the public juvenile justice system, directed instead to private systems of hospitalisation, mental health and drug treatment institutions, or offered restitution remedies such as financial compensation and public service rather than court prosecution, stigmatization, incarceration, punishment and pain.

Today it is global human rights law that has created a unique, comprehensive body of children's law, with powerful rights to be free from discrimination; now, sadly and ironically, international law has codified and is developing children's rights with the formal, tumultuous and elastic participation of virtually every nation in the world *except* the United States.

President Clinton signed the CRC in 1995, but the US Senate has failed even to debate or vote to ratify it. However, in 2002, during the Bush administration, the US ratified the two optional protocols to the CRC, the Optional Protocol on the Involvement of Children in Armed Conflict, and the Optional Protocol on the Sale of Children, Child Prostitution, and Child Pornography (American Civil Liberties Union 2014). These Optional Protocols provided (specifically for the US) that they might be ratified without ratification of the underlying treaty. Subsequently, the US has periodically reported to the Committee on the Rights of the Child on progress toward implementing both Protocols, sent substantial delegations to Geneva to appear before the Committee, and responded to its concluding observations. As with other treaties, domestic and international non-governmental organisations have submitted shadow reports to the CRC Committee critical of the gaps in US compliance. This relatively uncontroversial development merely highlights the unique nature of America's failure to ratify the CRC itself.

Much has been written about that failure. In part, within the US the CRC led to a highly vocal, although specifically restricted, attack on the Convention as a

---

4 *In re Gault*, 387 US 1 (1967).

5 See W. Haywood Burns Institute (2014) for an extraordinary interactive research tool that offers state-by-state statistics on racial and ethnic disparities in US juvenile justice. See also National Council on Crime and Delinquency (2007).

violation of parental and religious rights.[6] But despite substantial US participation in their drafting (Van Bueren 1998),[7] the US's continuing hostility to ratifying other treaties such as the Rome Treaty on the International Criminal Court, the Convention on the Rights of Persons with Disability, and the Convention on the Elimination of all forms of Discrimination Against Women (CEDAW), illuminates a longstanding antagonism to treaties, which are perceived as infringements on US sovereignty that present Constitutional obstacles to matters of federalism, states' rights, and issues of jurisdiction. At the most extreme, there are assertions that the CRC provisions would supersede all existing state and federal laws.

These opposition claims are not accurate. All human rights treaties ratified by the US include a 'non-self-executing' clause; that is, the treaty is not binding without specific state and federal enabling legislation. In addition, US Constitutional law states that no branch of the government can have powers conferred on it by treaty that have not been conferred by the Constitution. While it is accurate to say that significant areas of family law, education law, child protection and juvenile justice law are regulated by state law, CRC ratification would not expand federal jurisdiction. Typically, US treaty ratifications contain a set of reservations, understandings and declarations (RUDs) that include a 'federalism' clause leaving treaty implementation largely to the states.[8]

Despite the US's formal isolation on the issue of ratification, the CRC and its associated protocols and case law have flourished beyond what their drafters anticipated. The CRC embodies both the radical innovations of the juvenile-court founders and the child-rights revolution of the 1960s; added to this is the fresh notion of the full human rights of children and adolescents.

2 The *Roper v. Simmons* Judgment

Litigation addressing the human rights of children, based on the standards and values of the CRC, has accelerated across Europe, Latin American, Africa and India. Yet who would have imagined litigation involving the CRC in the United

[6] See, for example, ParentalRights.org, which singles out the CRC's disapproval of parental corporal punishment and the right of the child under the CRC to choose and practice a religion as examples that diminish 'parental rights'. ParentalRights.org. Twenty things you need to know about the United Nations Convention on the Rights of the Child. http://www.parentalrights.org/index.asp?Type=B_BASIC&SEC={550447B1-E2C1-4B55-87F1-610A9E601E45}&DE=Type=B_BASIC&SEC={550447B1-E2C1-4B55-87F1-610A9E601E45}&DE=. Accessed 27 January 2014.

[7] See also Office of the United Nations High Commissioner for Human Rights (2007). Legislative history of the Convention on the Rights of the Child, Volume 1. http://www.ohchr.org/Documents/Publications/LegislativeHistorycrc1en.pdf. Accessed 27 January 2014; Office of the United Nations High Commissioner for Human Rights (2007). Legislative history of the Convention on the Rights of the Child, Volume 2. http://www.ohchr.org/Documents/Publications/LegislativeHistorycrc2en.pdf. Accessed 27 January 2014.

[8] See a careful discussion of these issues by the US Child Rights Campaign. Questions & answers about the CRC. http://www.childrightscampaign.org/the-facts/questions-a-answers-about-the-crc. Accessed 27 January 2014.

States—one of only two nations *not* to have ratified the treaty? The story we know all too well centres on the US's global isolation in the matter of children's human rights. What is astonishing, however, are the innovative, grudging, messy and determined ways in which this aspect of US exceptionalism is cracking open, transforming itself, putting down fresh roots, and growing tendrils.

No-one could have predicted that the US Supreme Court would first write five lyrical pages about international human rights law in a case about children's rights.[9] None would have imagined that key breakthrough-decisions about children's constitutional rights would emerge in the cases of adolescents accused and convicted of murder. Few recognised that an unfunded and ragtag network of human rights advocates and youth justice litigators would abolish the juvenile death penalty in the US, move on to attack extreme sentencing of youth, and—in the process—begin to shake the cornerstones of such settled law (and notable violations of human rights law) as felony murder, transfer or waiver of children to adult criminal courts, mandatory sentencing of youth, the incarceration of children in adult prisons, and imprisonment until death without meaningful, periodic review.

That story could begin with Paula Cooper. In ninth grade at the age of fifteen, Paula led three other girls from Gary, Indiana's Lew Wallace High School into the home of a 78-year-old grandmother and bible teacher, Ruth Pelke, intending to rob an empty house. Instead, when Mrs Pelke invited them into her home, the girls hit her over the head and stabbed her dozens of times with a 12-inch knife. They stole about $10 and drove away in her car.

Although the three other girls received sentences ranging from 25 to 60 years in prison, Paula Cooper was transferred to adult criminal court, pled guilty in 1986 and was sentenced to death in Indiana's electric chair. She became the only female child on death row in the US. An international campaign to save her life garnered support in Italy and across Europe, and Pope John Paul II appealed for clemency.

In 1989, after the US Supreme Court concluded in *Thompson v. Oklahoma*[10] that executing a person under the age of 16 was unconstitutional, the Indiana Supreme Court ruled that Paula's death sentence was unconstitutional since she was 15 at the time of the crime. Her sentence was commuted to 60 years, the highest sentence then available in Indiana. It should be noted that this commutation of sentence took place in the same year the United Nations adopted the CRC.

Ten years after Cooper's death sentence, her attorney Professor Victor Streib (an academic and attorney who, amongst other things, litigated juvenile death-penalty cases in a lifelong pursuit to abolish the juvenile death penalty) and I co-chaired a workshop at the Conference on Wrongful Conviction and the Death Penalty at Northwestern University School of Law. Its convener, Professor

[9] The US Supreme Court referred to the European Court of Human Rights decision of *Dudgeon v. United Kingdom* in *Lawrence v. Texas,* 539 US 558, 573 (2003). But it is in *Roper* v. *Simmons* that the Court first develops an argument about the relevance of international law, standards and practice to the interpretation of US Constitutional law. *Roper v. Simmons*, 543 US 551 (2005).

[10] *Thompson v. Oklahoma,* 487 U.S. 815 (1988).

Lawrence Marshall, agreed to add a panel on children and the death penalty, naming it 'Another Kind of Innocence'.

Unexpectedly, 60 people attended the workshop, and an informal network to abolish the juvenile death penalty in the US was born when, months later, the Children and Family Justice Center at Northwestern University School of Law called a small invitation-only meeting. It took this tiny volunteer network[11] 6 years to organise a broad coalition, train lawyers to litigate appeals of children's death sentences, and contest every juvenile execution date with international clemency campaigns, promote legislative abolition in at least five additional states, and conduct an educational campaign about why the juvenile death penalty was barbaric, unconstitutional and a violation of human rights. The network was scrambling to prepare for a Supreme Court litigation challenge. It came—as it often does—before the network was fully prepared, in the form of *Roper v. Simmons*.[12]

Christopher Simmons was 17 years old when he and a friend broke into the home of Shirley Crook in 1983. The boys beat her, tied her with electrical cords and duct tape, put her in the trunk of a car, and threw her into the Meramec River in St. Louis County, Missouri, where she drowned. The lads bragged about their adventure the next day in school. Simmons, violently abused by his stepfather as a child, had no previous criminal record. At his trial in adult criminal court (Grisso and Schwartz 2000), his defence lawyer presented no information about his background, immaturity, or the circumstances of the crime, and the jury and judge considered his youthfulness an aggravating factor, not a mitigating one.

Because there was a story to tell which was broader than the necessarily focused, Eighth Amendment legal argument of the *Roper v. Simmons* brief, the network created an *amicus* brief strategy as a part of the litigation strategy. The team solicited briefs as *Amicus Curiae* from various coalition partners.[13] For example, there was an *amicus* brief about why children are distinct from adults, one signed by an array of educational, child welfare, health-care and family-advocacy organisations. There was, likewise, an *amicus* by the American Medical Association and the American Psychological Association elaborating on the

---

[11] The network included the (then) ABA Juvenile Defender Center led by Patricia Puritz; the Children and Family Justice Center; Steven Drizin; Stephen Harper; Anne James; Victor Streib; Randolph Stone; Connie de la Vega; Walter Long; the National Coalition to Abolish the Death Penalty; and a slew of remarkable *pro bono* attorneys.

[12] *Roper v. Simmons*, 543 U.S. 551 (2005).

[13] See *amici curiae* in support of respondent in *Roper v. Simmons*: Juvenile Law Center, Children and Family Justice Center, Center on Children and Families, Child Welfare League of America, Children's Defense Fund, Children's Law Center of Los Angeles, National Association of Counsel for Children et al., http://www.sentencingproject.org/doc/publications/sl_amicus-jdp.pdf; American Medical Association, http://www.ama-assn.org/ama1/pub/upload/mm/395/roper-v-simmons.pdf; American Psychological Association, http://www.apa.org/about/offices/ogc/amicus/roper.pdf; The Bar of England and Wales, http://www.njdc.info/njdc_members/images/pdfs/roper_amicus.pdf; Jimmy Carter, Mikhail Gorbachev, Oscar Arias, Lech Walesa, Adolfo Perez Esquivel, Dalai Lama et al., http://www.cartercenter.org/documents/nondatabase/nobel%20amicus%20brief%20on%20simmons.pdf; Murder Victims' Families for Reconciliation, http://www.njdc.info/pdf/death_penalty/mvfr.pdf. Accessed 27 January 2014.

research on behavioural and developmental differences between children and adults. There was an *amicus* brief by the Bar Associations of England and Wales, and another by Nobel Peace Prize winners, both pointing to international and human rights standards; and there was a powerful *amicus* brief by murder-victim families against the death penalty.

In the landmark 2005 *Roper v. Simmons* decision abolishing the death penalty as a criminal sentence for juvenile offenders, Justice Kennedy for the 5–4 US Supreme Court majority[14] wrestled with the question of when and whether the execution of juvenile offenders amounted to cruel and unusual punishment pursuant to the Eighth Amendment to the US Constitution.[15] (The court had previously held that this Amendment prohibited the execution of the mentally retarded in *Atkins v. Virginia.*[16]).

Using an analysis in *Roper* which recognised that children (youth under the age of 18) are different from adults, the court, citing current behavioural research, identified three areas that distinguished youth from adults:

- the inability to anticipate future consequences;
- the tendency to succumb to peer pressure; and
- the future possibility of being able to reflect on the consequences of their actions.

This common knowledge of adolescent behaviour, reinforced by contemporary behavioural and developmental research, led the *Roper* court to conclude that children are 'categorically less culpable'[17] than adults, even when their crimes were of the most serious kind. Because of this lesser culpability, and because the child has the possibility of developing into a moral person, 'the state cannot extinguish his life and his potential to attain a mature understanding of his humanity'[18]—and because 30 states had rejected that sentence for children—the death penalty for youth amounted to cruel and unusual punishment, in violation of the Eighth Amendment.

As a consequence of the *Roper* decision, 72 juvenile offenders (the majority of whom were African American and Latino men) were removed from death row and their sentences converted into life in prison without the possibility of parole.

Most astoundingly perhaps, the majority of *Roper* justices discussed the US's international isolation on the question of the juvenile death penalty, citing article

[14] Justice Kennedy delivered the opinion, in which Justices Stevens, Souter, Ginsburg and Breyer joined. Justice Stevens filed a concurring opinion in which Justice Ginsburg joined. Justice O'Conner filed a dissenting opinion. Justice Scalia filed a dissenting opinion in which Chief Justice Rehnquist and Justice Thomas joined.

[15] 'Excessive bail shall not be required, nor excessive fines imposed, nor cruel and unusual punishments inflicted.' US Constitution. Amendment 8.

[16] *Atkins v. Virginia,* 536 US 304 (2002).

[17] *Roper v. Simmons*, 543 US 551, 563 (2005).

[18] *Roper v. Simmons*, 543 US 551, 570 (2005).

37 of the CRC prohibiting the execution of children. The judgment noted that every country in the world, save the US and Somalia, had ratified the CRC and that no ratifying country entered a reservation to article 37's prohibition of the execution of juvenile offenders.[19]

Next, *Roper* cited the only seven countries other than the US that had executed juvenile offenders since 1990, noting that each had since then either abolished capital punishment for juveniles or made public disavowals of the practice: 'In sum, it is fair to say that the United States now stands alone in a world that has turned its face against the juvenile death penalty.'[20]

The *Roper* judgment discussed the Anglo-Saxon origins of the Eighth Amendment language and theory in the laws of the United Kingdom, and the historic ties between the US and the UK, noting that the UK had abolished the juvenile death penalty decades before international covenants prohibited it. 'In the 56 years that have passed since the United Kingdom abolished the juvenile death penalty,' the Court observed, 'the weight of authority against it there, and in the international community, has become well established.'[21] It added: 'It is proper that we acknowledge the overwhelming weight of international opinion against the juvenile death penalty, resting in large part on the understanding that the instability and emotional imbalance of young people may often be a factor in the crime.'[22] The Court wrote: 'The opinion of the world community, while not controlling our outcome, does provide respected and significant confirmation for our own conclusion.'[23]

Forcefully and lyrically, *Roper* concludes: 'It does not lessen our fidelity to the Constitution or our pride in its origins to acknowledge that the express affirmation of certain fundamental rights by other nations and peoples simply underscores the centrality of those same rights within our own heritage of freedom.'[24]

The opinion of the world community *does* provide respected and significant confirmation; acknowledgement of the express affirmation of certain fundamental rights by other nations and peoples *simply underscores* the centrality of those same rights within our own heritage of freedom. This germinal breakthrough in the integration of international law with US Constitutional law and criminal practice (and with our heritage of freedom), both theoretical and concrete, is a continuing accomplishment of children's rights lawyers. Its consequences and possibilities still lie before us.

---

[19] The Court also noted parallel prohibitions in other significant international covenants, citing the International Convention on Civil and Political Rights (ratified by the US), the American Convention on Human Rights (not ratified by the US), and the African Charter on the Rights and Welfare of the Child.

[20] *Roper v. Simmons,* 543 US 551, 573 (2005).

[21] *Roper v. Simmons,* 543 US 551, 574 (2005).

[22] *Roper v. Simmons,* 543 US 551, 574(2005).

[23] *Roper v. Simmons,* 543 US 551, 574 (2005).

[24] *Roper v. Simmons,* 543 US 551, 575 (2005).

3 Life Sentence Without Parole

Within months after *Roper,* the Illinois Coalition for the Fair Sentencing of Children was formed[25] and Michigan published its first state-wide report (American Civil Liberties Union 2006) on the sentence of juvenile life without possibility of parole (JLWOP). Human Rights Watch and Amnesty International, in a rare display of unity, release a joint report on the 2,500 people in jail in the US who were sentenced to JLWOP for crimes committed as children (Amnesty International and Human Rights Watch 2005). The next campaign was born.

Again virtually alone in the world, the US imprisoned over 2,500 child offenders who are *sentenced to die in prison*. No matter whom they became in prison, no matter what the family-member victims of the crime want, no matter that the prisoner now has matured and represents no threat to public safety, these juvenile offenders (now natural life prisoners) may not ever even *argue* for their release.

Again, international law prohibits this sentence for child offenders (art. 37 of the CRC). Again, human rights standards provide for meaningful, periodic reviews of youth sentences. Again, the proportion of youth of colour sentenced to JLWOP sentences is blatantly, racially and ethnically disproportionate. The national Campaign for the Fair Sentencing of Youth[26] was established to focus and coordinate state and national efforts to challenge this unconstitutional human-rights violation. Bryan Stevenson and the Equal Justice Initiative[27] began to campaign and litigate on behalf of very young children (12–15 years of age) sentenced to JLWOP.

Two years after the *Rope*r judgment, the UN Committee on the Rights of the Child published its General Comment No. 10: Children's Rights in Juvenile Justice (2007).[28] The objectives of the General Comment are to encourage States parties to develop and implement a comprehensive juvenile justice policy; to provide guidance and recommendations for implementing all the provisions in articles 37 and 40 of the CRC; and to promote the integration in national policy of international standards. In addition to clarifying that the core juvenile justice international law and standards are that incarceration should be *only* a 'last resort' and 'for the shortest appropriate period of time', the General Comment discusses the reasons for the prohibition of JLWOP sentences for crimes committed by persons under 18 years of age.

[25] The Illinois Campaign began interviewing the (then) 103 JLWOP prisoners in its state, and would write a report: The Illinois Coalition for the Fair Sentencing of Children (2008). Categorically less culpable. http://webcast-law.uchicago.edu/pdfs/00544_Juvenile_Justice_Book_3_10.pdf. Accessed 27 January 2014. See also reports on California, Connecticut, Florida, Massachusetts, Michigan, Mississippi, and Washington: The Campaign for the Fair Sentencing of Youth. State specific reports. http://fairsentencingofyouth.org/state-specific-reports-2. Accessed 27 January 2014.

[26] The Campaign for the Fair Sentencing of Youth. http://fairsentencingofyouth.org. Accessed 27 January 2014.

[27] Equal Justice Initiative. http://www.eji.org. Accessed 27 January 2014.

[28] Committee on the Rights of the Child (2007). Children's rights in juvenile justice. http://www2.ohchr.org/english/bodies/crc/docs/CRC.C.GC.10.pdf. Accessed 27 January 2014.

One of the challenges of working in a country that has more than 2,500 prisoners serving sentences of juvenile life without parole is to determine what constitutes the abolition of JLWOP. Most would agree that 60, 70 or 80 years-to-life sentences are not acceptable for a child and amount to "virtual" life without the possibility of parole. What, then, are the key elements that human rights' standards offer in the way of guidelines and clarity?

First, General Comment No. 10 states: 'The Committee wishes to emphasize that the reaction to an offense should always be proportional not only to the circumstances and the gravity of the offense, but also to the age, lesser culpability, circumstances and needs of the child, as well as to the various and particularly long-term needs of the society... In the case of children, the needs of public safety and sanctions must always be outweighed by the need to safeguard the well-being and the best interests of the child and to promote his/her reintegration.'[29]

Second, General Comment No. 10 directly addresses 'No Life imprisonment without parole', elaborating on the brief prohibition in article 37 of the CRC: 'For all sentences imposed on children the possibility of release should be realistic and regularly considered.' Further, life sentences for children are not permitted. This indicates that sentences at or beyond life expectancy are not acceptable, and that regular review (i.e. more than once or twice, and beginning within a reasonable period after incarceration) is required. The Comment points out that the child's right to 'periodic review' is provided by article 25 of the CRC, which addresses the rights of children who are placed for the purpose of care, protection or treatment. Further, those States parties that do sentence children to life imprisonment with the possibility of release must comply with the provisions of article 40(1) of the CRC, which requires that the imprisoned child must 'receive education, treatment and care aiming at his/her release, reintegration and ability to assume a constructive role in society'.

Thus, in 2006 I found myself driving to Pontiac prison to interview one of the 103 JLWOP prisoners, Mark Clements. The thin legal file explained little about the crime or the prisoner, and what it said was disquieting. Mr Clements, then incarcerated for 26 years and described as retarded, was convicted of quadruple homicides at the age of 16 and given a mandatory sentence of JLWOP.

We entered the attorney/client visiting room fully unprepared for Mark, an all-too typical underestimation of the fierce determination, self-education and humanity of prisoners. He had a stack of papers and files that rose above his head. Mark knew everything about the Illinois Coalition and its goals, ran a weekly radio show in the prison, and was deeply knowledgeable about his case and his circumstances. He was an astonishing advocate for his own freedom. There were no witnesses and no material evidence against him—just his own 16-year-old confession, extracted under police interrogation and torture during the scandalous Area Two Chicago police torture cases, in which at least 120 African American men were tortured by police over a twenty-year period on Chicago's Southside (Taylor 2012).

[29] Committee on the Rights of the Child (2007). Children's rights in juvenile justice, p. 20. http://www2.ohchr.org/english/bodies/crc/docs/CRC.C.GC.10.pdf. Accessed 27 January 2014.

This 16-year-old was convicted of starting an arson fire in which four people died. No-one else was charged in the crime, and there was no forensic or testimonial evidence, except his own confession. Mark was automatically tried as an adult in criminal court. He repudiated his confession at his trial, but was sentenced to four life sentences plus 30 years in the state penitentiary.

Driving back to our office at record speed, we called an attorney at the law firm of Skadden Arps, Tim Nelson, who agreed to take Mark's case; he worked with Mark and undertook an extensive (and costly) investigation of the 26-year-old crime. Ultimately, because the Cook County state's attorneys' office was unwilling to dismiss all the charges against him, and despite the lack of any credible evidence, Mark accepted a plea to a single homicide in exchange for time served. He stipulated to the facts that were in evidence, admitting to no crime in the plea agreement.

Mark Clements was released from prison on August 18, 2009, an example of how children incarcerated with no hope of freedom do grow, mature and come into their own full humanity and grace. His case raises urgent Constitutional and human rights issues of competent counsel, trying children in adult criminal courts, police interrogation of youth and false confessions (Drizin and Leo 2004; Tepfer et al. 2010), and mandatory sentencing of children, the latter to be taken up by the U.S Supreme Court after his release.

Just months after Mark was freed, two JLWOP cases were granted *certiorari* by the US Supreme Court, the first such JLWOP-sentenced cases to be reviewed by the US's highest court. Both concerned *non-homicide* juvenile offenders in Florida.[30] *Graham v. Florida*[31] involved a 16-year-old convicted of armed burglary who had accepted a plea agreement with probation. When Terrance Graham subsequently violated his probation by committing another armed burglary, the trial judge revoked his probation and sentenced him to life without parole. In *Graham*, the US Supreme Court again clarified, strengthened and expanded the boundaries of the Eighth Amendment regarding the sentencing of children, this time in non-homicide cases (Levick et al. 2012). Again, the Court reaffirmed the link between the CRC and international law and the Eight Amendment: 'An offender's age is relevant to the Eighth Amendment and criminal procedure laws that fail to take defendants' youthfulness into account at all would be flawed.'

The Supreme Court, moreover, goes deeply into the nature of childhood:

> The juvenile should not be deprived of the opportunity to achieve maturity of judgment and self-recognition of human worth and potential… life in prison without the possibility of parole gives no chance for fulfillment outside prison walls, no chance for reconciliation with society, no hope… maturity can lead to that considered reflection which is the foundation for remorse, renewal, and rehabilitation.[32]

---

[30] The second Florida case granted *certiorari* was subsequently dismissed on procedural grounds. *Sullivan v. Florida*, No. 08-7621, slip opinion (US 2010). http://www.supremecourt.gov/opinions/09pdf/08-7621.pdf. Accessed 27 January 2014.

[31] *Graham v. Florida,* No. 08-7412, slip opinion at p. 22 (US 2010). http://www.supremecourt.gov/opinions/09pdf/08-7412modified.pdf. Accessed 27 January 2014.

[32] *Graham v. Florida*, No. 08-7412, slip opinion at p. 28 (US 2010). http://www.supremecourt.gov/opinions/09pdf/08-7412modified.pdf. Accessed 27 January 2014.

Age is relevant. In the US this raises vital questions about the legality of prosecutorial waiver of children to adult criminal courts, mandatory (statutory) waiver or transfer, and mandatory sentencing (the latter becomes clear in the third child criminal sentencing case decided in this decade, *Miller v. Alabama*, discussed below).

The *Graham* court concluded that neither a judge nor jury can make final judgment *at the time of sentencing* about what kind of a person this youth will become as an adult. '[F]rom a moral standpoint,' the Court observed, 'it would be misguided to equate the failings of a minor with those of an adult, for a greater possibility exists that a minor's character deficiencies will be reformed.' Since maturation could take some years of reflection and character development, it is necessary to have meaningful sentencing reviews in order to assess what kind of person that child offender has become.

In *Graham,* the Kennedy majority discussed the differences between those who *themselves* kill another and all others who may also be charged (in the US) with felony murder. In fact, *Graham* shifts the line by describing youth who are convicted of felony murder as having a 'twice-diminished culpability' due to their age as children and lesser role as non-shooters (Keller 2012). This freshly-opened window on the constitutionality of felony murder sentences for children—a murder crime almost unique to the US—could have an enormous impact on the lengthy prison terms of those convicted in the US. For example, approximately one-quarter of the 2,500 youth serving JLWOP sentences were convicted of felony murder.

Significantly, *Graham* forcefully reiterates the role of international law and standards articulated in the *Roper* judgment: 'The United States adheres to a sentencing practice rejected the world over.' While the judgments of other nations and international opinion are neither controlling nor dispositive to the meaning of the Eighth Amendment,

> the climate of international opinion concerning the acceptability of a particular punishment is also 'not irrelevant'.... The Court has looked beyond our Nation's borders for support for its independent conclusion that a punishment is cruel and unusual ... Today we continue that longstanding practice in noting the global consensus against the sentencing practice in question.[33]

Note that this reaffirmation of the *Roper* analysis takes place after sustained, explicit criticism of Justice Kennedy, personally, for citing 'the law of other countries' in *Roper.*[34] Yet, here in *Graham* 5 years later, the judgment directly refutes that criticism: 'The question before us is not whether international law prohibits the United States from imposing the sentence at issue in this case. The question is whether that punishment is cruel and unusual.' In that inquiry, 'the overwhelming weight of international opinion against [life without parole for non-homicide offenses committed by juveniles] provide[s] respected and significant confirmation

[33] *Graham v. Florida,* No. 08-7412, slip opinion at p. 30 (US 2010). http://www.supremecourt.gov/opinions/09pdf/08-7412modified.pdf. Accessed 27 January 2014.

[34] *Roper v. Simmons*, 543 US 551, 571 (2005).

for our own conclusions' (De le Vega and Leighton 2008).[35] The legal standard being cited is not enforceable, the behaviour not 'prohibited'; but the standard is noted with approval by the six justice majority in *Graham*, and followed.

Providing further clarification, the Court notes that it 'has treated the laws and practices of other nations and international agreements as relevant to the Eighth Amendment not because those norms are binding or controlling but because the judgment of the world's nations that a particular sentencing practice is *inconsistent with basic principles of decency* demonstrates that the Court's rationale has respected reasoning to support it.'

Not prohibiting, not binding, not controlling, not dispositive … however, it is worth looking to the climate of international opinion, the global consensus, the judgment of the world's nations, to basic principles of decency, as support for our own independent conclusions, to confirm our own Eight Amendment jurisprudence.

This is an artful, dizzying process of harmonising international standards and US Eighth Amendment jurisprudence regarding children.

***

So, let us return to a different aspect of the case of Paula Cooper. You will remember that she murdered Ruth Pelke in 1984 at the age of 15. The victims' grandson, Bill Pelke, originally supported the death penalty for Paula Cooper. A Vietnam veteran and a Gary, Indiana, steelworker for two decades, he rethought his position after realising his grandmother herself would have forgiven Paula. He began corresponding with her, then visiting her, then campaigning for her life, and then, for the next 22 years, her release. He has created a non-profit organisation called *Journey of Hope: From Violence to Healing*.[36] 'Paula has changed,' he says. 'She's not the same person that committed that terrible crime in 1985.' In July 2013 Paula Cooper walked out of prison and into the arms of family and friends, and Bill Pelke welcomed her to the free world on the day of her release.

4 Some Concluding Remarks

These transformative US Supreme Court judgments—along with an important third case which does not refer to the CRC or international human rights law, *Miller v. Alabama*[37]—came about through a complex and multifaceted strategy of

[35] See also The Center for Law and Global Justice. http://www.usfca.edu/law/jlwop/other_nations. Accessed 27 January 2014.

[36] Journey of Hope. http://www.journeyofhope.org. Accessed 27 January 2014.

[37] See also, *Miller v. Alabama*, No. 10-9646, slip opinion (US 2012). http://www.supremecourt.gov/opinions/11pdf/10-9646.pdf. Accessed 27 January 2014. *Miller* extends the *Roper* and *Graham* reasoning to JLWOP defendants convicted of homicide. *Miller* holds that mandatory sentencing of youth to JLWOP (80 % of JLWOP sentences) violates the Eighth Amendment because such sentencing fails to take into account the youthfulness of the defendant, his potential for growth and development, and the circumstances of the crime.

education, coalition-building, communication and legislative campaigns that included, and ultimately relied upon, litigation.

Litigation alone would not have taught the coalitions how to reframe the issues (for example, by describing JLWOP as 'children sentenced to die in prison'), how to locate extreme sentencing of children in an historical context, and how to engender broad support for the remedy. But preparation for litigation remedies was fundamental to and enhanced by every stage of the overall strategy.

The integration of international standards into national policy and law, and the adoption of human rights law, principles and values into a nation's legal and constitutional framework is neither a mechanical act nor a drafting matter that can be left to the technicians.

In the realm of youth sentencing, bringing human rights standards and law into a constitutional and common law regime requires an imaginative, interpretive and creative series of gestures; it demands some of the growth, chaos, luck, conflict, inspiration, accident, and transcendent mutuality of any dynamic relationship.

Implementing children's international legal rights through litigation is a dynamic work in progress, not a frozen idea limited forever by the constraints, biases and perspectives of the CRC drafters. The three Optional Protocols of the CRC, over a period of 25 years, correct a major fault (the lower age of children in armed conflict) and add new specificity. The Third Optional Protocol opens a door for administrative litigation filled with creative possibility. Children's human rights law is a set of norms already undergoing growth and modification, adapting to fresh challenges, emerging realities, and resolving sometimes contending rights.

In this landscape of law reform—in coordination with education, coalition-building, communication, and legislation—litigation uniquely provides an explicit set of facts on behalf of a specific petitioner or class. Imagine, for example, litigation that benefits children with disabilities, or children crossing borders who are separated from their families, or children carrying out the worst forms of child labour. This chapter illustrates the unlikely progress that has been made in litigating for the human rights of children in conflict with the law in the very country that has most conspicuously failed to ratify the CRC.

Litigation demands choices, nuance and resolution; litigation invites us to revisit core ethical values, standards and principles in the tumultuous and messy world of courtroom trials, appeals, post-conviction remedies, and class action lawsuits involving real children and families. Litigation may compel a nation or private entity to act on behalf of a child's rights or to cease behaviours that violate them; it may also set us back. But it is a powerful instrument for illuminating issues and for specific justice, as part of an expansive and multifaceted campaign to bring tangible rights and resources home to children.

References

American Civil Liberties Union. (2006). Second chances. https://www.aclu.org/human-rights-racial-justice/second-chances-juveniles-serving-life-without-parole-michigan-prisons. Accessed 27 January 2014.

American Civil Liberties Union. (2014). Frequently asked questions about the convention on the rights of the child and its optional protocols. https://www.aclu.org/files/assets/crc_faqs_20091001.pdf. Accessed 27 January 2014.

Amnesty International & Human Rights Watch. (2005). The rest of their lives. http://fairsentencingofyouth.org/wp-content/uploads/2010/02/The-rest-of-their-lives.pdf. Accessed 27 January 2014.

Anderson, C. (2003). *Eyes off the prize*. Cambridge: Cambridge University Press.

Cohen, C. P. (1998). Role of the United States in drafting the convention on the rights of the child. *Loyola Poverty Law Journal, 4*(9), 25–26.

Cohen, C. P., & Bitensky, S. H. (1996). *Answers to 50 Questions.* Child Rights International Research Institute.

Cohen, C. P., & Davidson, H. A. (Eds.). (1990). *Children's rights in America.* Chicago: American Bar Association.

De la Vega, C., & Leighton, M. (2008). Sentencing our children to die in prison. *University of San Francisco Law Review, 42*(4), 983–1044.

Drizin, S. A., & Leo, R. A. (2004). The problem of confessions in the post DNA world. *N.C.L.Rev.,82*, 891–1007.

Drizin, S. A., & Warden, R. (Eds.). (2009). *True stories of false confessions*. Chicago: Northwestern University Press.

Grisso, T., & Schwartz, R. (2000). *Youth on trial: A developmental perspective on juvenile justice*. Chicago: University of Chicago Press.

Keller, E. C. (2012). Constitutional sentences for juveniles convicted of Felony murder in the wake of Roper, Graham & J.D.B. *Connecticut Public Interest Law Journal*, 11(2), 297–326.

Levick, M., Feierman, J., Messenheimer Kelley, S., & Goldstein, N. (2012). The eighth amendment evolves: defining cruel and unusual punishment through the lens of childhood and adolescence. *University of Pennsylvania Journal of Law and Social Policy, 42*(2), 286–321.

National Council on Crime and Delinquency. (2007). *And justice for some. Differential Treatment of Youth of Color in the Justice System.* http://www.nccdglobal.org/sites/default/files/publication_pdf/justice-for-some.pdf. Accessed 27 January 2014.

Rosenheim, M. K., Zimring, F. E., Tanenhaus, D. S., & Dohrn, B. (Eds.). (2002). *A century of juvenile justice*. Chicago: University of Chicago Press.

Sachs, A. (2009). *The strange alchemy of life and law*. New York: Oxford University Press.

The Annie E. Casey Foundation. (2008a). Road Map to Juvenile Justice Reform. Baltimore. http://www.aecf.org/m/resourcedoc/AECF-KidsCountDataBook-2008.pdf#page=8. Accessed 15 July 2014.

The Annie E. Casey Foundation. (2008b). Kids Count Data Book, Juvenile Justice Focus. Baltimore. http://www.aecf.org/resources/the-2008-kids-count-data-book/ Accessed 15 July 2014.

The Annie E. Casey Foundation. (2013a). Reducing Youth Incarceration in the United States. Baltimore. http://www.aecf.org/resources/reducing-youth-incarceration-in-the-united-states/. Accessed 15 July 2014.

The Annie E. Casey Foundation. (2013b). Infographic: Youth incarceration in the United States. Baltimore. http://www.aecf.org/KnowledgeCenter/Publications.aspx?pubguid=%7BEC9F363E-43A6-45F9-B0B8-2709D084C412%7D. Accessed 27 January 2014.

Taylor, F. (2012). The Long and Winding Road: The Struggle For Justice in the Police Torture Cases. *Loyola Law School Public Interest Law Reporter, 17*(3), 178–203.

Tepfer, J., Nirider, L., & Tricarico, L. (2010). Arresting development: Convictions of innocent youth. *Rutgers Law Review, 62*(4), 891–941.

Todres, J., Wojcik, M. E., & Revaz, C. R. (Eds.). (2006). *The UN convention on the rights of the child.* Ardsley: Transnational Publishers.

Van Bueren, G. (1998). *The international law on the rights of the child.* The Hague: Martinus Nijhoff Publishers.
W. Haywood Burns Institute. (2008). Adoration of the question. http://burnsinstitute.org/article.php?id=83. Accessed 27 January 2014.
W. Haywood Burns Institute. (2010). The keeper and the kept. http://burnsinstitute.org/article.php?id=161. Accessed 27 January 2014.
W. Haywood Burns Institute. (2014). Mapping the youth incarceration problem. http://www.burnsinstitute.org/blog/our-new-data-map-is-live/. Accessed 15 July 2014.

Chapter 6
The Netherlands

Two Decades of the CRC in Dutch Case Law

Manuela Limbeek and Mariëlle Bruning

Abstract This chapter addresses the influence of the Convention of the Rights of the Child (CRC) on Dutch case law in the past two decades. What impact has the CRC had on the practice of the Dutch judiciary since its ratification? Has it had any effect on legal proceedings in the Netherlands? If so, what does this tell us about the functions, challenges and limitations of the CRC as a legal instrument in such a context? While the CRC's influence has grown, that influence has followed divergent paths in different fields of Dutch law and among different courts and judges. In the Dutch courts the CRC has led to a special interpretation of both national and international law, but has also given rise to the duty transparently to balance the child's best interests in decision-making. Children's rights are taken more seriously in the Dutch courtroom. Future challenges include deploying the CRC in substantive, meaningful ways instead of as a piece of abstract magic, and preventing it from being used to over-protect children.

1 Introduction

Almost two decades ago, on 5 February 1995, the Netherlands ratified the CRC.[1] The Dutch government considered it as an important step towards the recognition of children's human dignity. Nevertheless, given its assumption that national legislation and policy were already in conformity with the CRC,[2] the government did not expect that ratification would have a large impact in the Netherlands.

[1] The CRC entered into force in the Netherlands on 8 March 1995.

[2] *Kamerstukken II* 1993/94, 22 855 (R1451), nr. 6, p. 7 (parliamentary documents). See also Doek (1995).

M. Limbeek (✉) · M. Bruning
Department of Child Law, Leiden Law School, Leiden University, Leiden, The Netherlands
e-mail: m.m.c.limbeek@law.leidenuniv.nl

M. Bruning
e-mail: m.r.bruning@law.leidenuniv.nl

T. Liefaard and J.E. Doek (eds.), *Litigating the Rights of the Child*,
DOI 10.1007/978-94-017-9445-9_6

After ratification, the CRC took immediate domestic effect in the Netherlands; no further legal action was required to incorporate it into national law,[3] and the Dutch legislature, executive and judiciary have been bound by its provisions since the time of its ratification.

This automatic domestic effect does not imply that all CRC provisions can successfully be invoked before a Dutch court. Doing so depends on the *direct effect* of a CRC provision, which is determined by national courts. However, the Dutch government was of the opinion that articles 7(1), 9(2), 9(3), 9(4), 10(1), 12(2), 13, 14, 15, 16, 30, 37 and 40(2) of the CRC should have direct effect, either for reasons to do with the wording of the articles or because the articles include rights distilled from existing human rights treaties of which the direct effect had been already recognised.[4] In addition, the government emphasised that articles 5, 8 and 12(1) would possibly have direct effect. It did not examine the horizontal effects of the treaty, as this was—and is still—a topic 'in development'.[5] Furthermore, the government did not make any observations or suggestions about those provisions which, so it held, would not have direct effect.

What, therefore, has been the impact of the CRC on Dutch case law since ratification? Has it had any effect on legal proceedings in the Netherlands? What do the answers tell us about the functions, challenges and limitations of the CRC as a legal instrument in this context?

The chapter examines the influence of the CRC on Dutch case law over the past two decades, beginning with an account of the constitutional framework of the direct-effect doctrine. Several questions are raised: How can national judges decide whether a treaty provision has direct effect or not? What is the importance of this doctrine? What is the relevance of provisions that have no direct effect?

The chapter then provides information about the Dutch court system and how children can have access to it, after which the CRC's implementation in Dutch case law is analysed; in this regard, particular reference is made to the fields of family, administrative and criminal law. The conclusion assesses whether the CRC has had any impact on legal proceedings in the Netherlands, with the focus placed on the functions, challenges and limitations of the CRC.

---

[3] Under customary constitutional law, all binding international law has domestic effect.

[4] *Kamerstukken II* 1993/94, 22 855 (R1451), nr. 3, p. 8 (explanatory memorandum on the Act of Approval CRC).

[5] *Kamerstukken II* 1993/94, 22 855 (R1451), nr. 3, p. 10 (explanatory memorandum on the Act of Approval CRC). Recently, the horizontal effect of article 3 of the CRC was discussed for the first time in Dutch case law; see District Court 10 January 2013, ECLI:NL:RBAMS:2013:BY8619.

2 Direct or No Direct Effect? A Constitutional Framework

Articles 93 and 94 of the Dutch Constitution set the rules for a direct effect of international law:

- provisions of treaties which by nature of their content can be binding for everybody have binding power (art. 93); and
- national law provisions will not be applied if this application is not compatible with a provision of treaties binding for everybody (art. 94).

These rules obviously only apply to treaties ratified by the Netherlands. Courts can decide whether an invoked provision of international law has direct effect within the definition of article 93 of the Dutch Constitution, using criteria established in case law. According to the existing case law of the Dutch Supreme Court, the *content* of the provision is decisive:[6] 'Does the provision oblige the lawmaker to implement a national law with a certain essence, or is the nature of the provision that it can function as objective law in the national legal order?'[7] The invoked treaty provisions should be sufficiently detailed to enable the court to apply these norms. In this regard, the court can take into account different aspects of the provision: its nature, content, meaning, wording and context. In addition, the intention of the legislator and that of the States parties to a particular treaty may be used as guidance, for example, by referring to the *travaux preparatoires* related to the instrument.

In practice, this constitutional framework (art. 93–94) implies that the CRC provision, judicially labeled with direct effect, can override the national law provision.[8] While CRC provisions with direct effect thus have important implications, those without it are also of significance. In the Netherlands a national norm may never be interpreted in a manner that will lead to a breach of treaty obligations. This is a long-established rule in Dutch case law.[9] Correct application of the rule leads to the conclusion that the need to examine the direct effect of an article is required only if the application of national law is not sufficient to meet a specific obligation under the CRC. This means that in principle a judge has to apply national law in the light of the CRC. The principle derives from the presumption that the Netherlands, by ratifying a treaty, intends to fulfill its treaty obligations.

---

[6] Except in the cases where the States Parties to a particular treaty agreed on the fact that the provisions have no direct effect. In case of the CRC, the States parties did not make any agreements in relation to the direct effect of CRC provisions in national jurisdictions.

[7] Supreme Court of the Netherlands 30 May 1986, *NJ* 1986, 688 (Railway Strike Judgment).

[8] It should be noted that on 6 September 2012 a Bill was introduced concerning the amendment of the articles 93 and 94 of the Dutch Constitution, intended to prevent the judicial review of Acts of Parliaments: *Kamerstukken II* 2011/12, 33 559 (R 1986), nr. 3.

[9] Supreme Court of the Netherlands 3 March 1919, *NJ* 1919, 371 (Border Treaty Aken).

3 Dutch Court System

The Dutch court system consists of 11 District Courts (*Rechtbanken*), four Courts of Appeal (*Gerechtshoven*), one Supreme Court of the Netherlands in civil, tax and criminal matters (*Hoge Raad der Nederlanden*), and three special supreme courts in specific administrative matters: for general administrative matters, the Administrative Jurisdiction Division of the Council of State (*Afdeling Bestuursrechtspraak van de Raad van State*); for public service and social security matters, the Central Appeals Tribunal (*Centrale Raad van Beroep*); and for economic public law matters, the Trade and Industry Appeals Tribunal (*College van Beroep voor het bedrijfsleven*). National judges are not allowed to examine national legislation or international treaties for compatibility with the Constitution (article 120 of the Dutch Constitution); there is no Constitutional Court in the Netherlands.

4 Children's Access to Justice

In the Netherlands, the question of whether a child can represent his or her own (legal) interests independently before a court depends on which field of law—civil, administrative or criminal—is applicable in a particular case.

In civil law, the rule is that children are legally incompetent unless an exception is regulated by law (Ter Haar 2012; Mink 2012).[10] The bearers of parental responsibility (parents or guardians) are responsible for the child's legal representation in civil matters (art. 1:245, paragraph 4, Dutch Civil Code). In situations of 'conflicting interests' between the parent(s) or guardian(s) and the child, the court can appoint a guardian *ad litem* (*bijzondere curator*) to represent the child (art. 1:250 Dutch Civil Code).

Nevertheless, current case law does not provide a clear definition of 'conflicting interests'; as such, the appointment of a special guardian ad litem is, in practice, a complex issue (Limbeek 2013). Thanks to the interpretative differences between judges and courts about when to appoint such a guardian, the process is so unpredictable in outcome that the Dutch Children's Ombudsperson has likened it to 'a ticket in the lottery' (Kinderombudsman 2012). In some family law issues (contact between a child and a parent, custody after divorce), children can contact the judge on their own behalf informally and without legal representation by letter, e-mail or telephone to ask for a specific decision. Judges have discretion as to how they deal with these requests and whether they make a decision or not.

However, children in closed youth care who are either 12 years or older, and children younger than 12 who are deemed to have a reasonable understanding of their interests, are assumed to be competent to perform procedural actions on their own behalf (art. 29(a), paragraph 2, Youth Care Act). Furthermore, article 809 of the Code of Civil Procedure provides the child with the right to express his or her

---

[10] For an overview and discussion of the so-called 'patchwork of exceptions', see Doek and Vlaardingerbroek (2009), Leuven and de Klerk (2013) and Van Teeffelen (2013).

views in civil law matters. According to this article, the court is obliged to invite (in writing) children who are 12 years or older to be heard in relation to matters affecting them, unless it decides it is a matter of minor importance or an urgent situation.[11] The court has discretionary power to hear younger children below the age of 12 years in a manner decided by it.

In administrative law, the child has a stronger legal position. Children who are deemed to have a reasonable understanding of their interests can perform procedural actions on their own behalf. Nevertheless, the incompetent child must be represented by his or her legal representative (parents or guardians) under civil law (art. 8:21, paragraph 1 and 2, General Administrative Law Act). In urgent matters where no legal guardian is present or available, a judge can appoint a special guardian. The appointment expires as soon as the legal guardian under civil law is available.

In criminal law, a juvenile suspect participates independently in legal proceedings, that is, without representation by a legal guardian but with the representation of a court-appointed lawyer. Children from the age of 12 years and older are held responsible for criminal behavior, which implies legal competence in criminal procedures. Special rules regarding the formal position of a juvenile suspect (from the age of 12) are laid down in the Code of Criminal Procedure (art. 486ff). A juvenile suspect has the right to legal representation by a lawyer and cannot waive this right. Lawyers who represent children younger than 16 years can exercise the child's rights independently (that is, without the child's instruction; art. 503 Code of Criminal Procedure). Depending on the severity of the offence, arrested children have the right to legal assistance prior to and during questioning by the police (De Jonge and Van der Linden 2013).

5 Implementation of the CRC in Dutch Case Law

5.1 The CRC in the First Decade After Ratification

Ruitenberg (2003) published the first report on the implementation of the CRC in Dutch case law. The report provides an overview of 75 (mainly published) cases in which the CRC played a role in the years 1995–2001, concluding that, in general, reliance on the CRC was not seen as successful or as having had a bearing on the final outcome of the majority of cases. On the other hand, there were many cases in which the court applied the CRC *ex officio*. Articles 3, 7, 9, 10 and 37 of the CRC were applied most frequently. Courts explicitly recognised the direct effect of CRC provisions in only a few cases (articles 3, 9(3), 23 and 40(1)), but Ruitenberg concludes that in several cases the courts do in addition seem to give implicit recognition to the direct effect of articles 7(1), 23, 37 and 40(3).

---

[11] These two exceptions are explicitly regulated in article 809 Code of Civil Procedure. For more exceptions formulated in case law, see Supreme Court of the Netherlands 11 November 2013, ECLI:NL:HR:2013:1084.

In the thematic-review section of Ruitenberg's report, it becomes apparent that the CRC is invoked relatively often in immigration law cases. Although in some such cases the CRC had a positive effect in influencing or having a bearing on the outcomes, immigration cases on the whole have displayed a cautious attitude towards the application of CRC provisions. The CRC has also played a role in family law matters and, to a more marginal degree, in criminal law cases. Extrapolating from her findings, Ruitenberg predicted that the direct effect of articles 3, 7(1), 9(3), 37 and 40(1) would (also) be recognised in the future.

Two years after Ruitenberg's report, Van Emmerik (2005) explored the implementation of the CRC in case law during the years 2002–2005. He concluded that the CRC is frequently invoked in different types of cases, especially in immigration ones but also relatively often in family law cases. He noted that reliance on the CRC was rather unsuccessful in influencing or having a bearing on the final outcome of proceedings, but was nevertheless more successful in the period after 2002 than before. According to Van Emmerik, this could be attributed to a stricter immigration policy: arguably, judges applied the CRC to cut off the 'sharp edges' of a policy that did not give room to balance the best interests of the child or the position of the child against the public interests of immigration policy. Van Emmerik welcomed the fact that the CRC was becoming better-known in legal practice and consequently being used more frequently in proceedings.

5.2 The CRC in the Previous Decade

It took a considerable time before further research appeared on the CRC's implementation in case law. In 2012 such a report was published, covering the period 2002–2011 and dealing with 1,028 (mainly published) cases in which the CRC was mentioned either by the parties to proceedings and/or by the court (De Graaf et al. 2012).

As in the work by Ruitenberg and Van Emmerik, the report shows that the CRC is most often mentioned in immigration law cases (430), relatively often in family and civil child law cases (324), and much less so in juvenile justice cases (102). But De Graaf et al. also find that other fields of law were influenced by the CRC, which was mentioned in court decisions pertaining to social security (113) as well as a variety of cases in administrative (32) and civil law (26). In every field, the number of cases referring to the CRC rose each year. This upward trend indicates clearly that the CRC is receiving mounting attention from practitioners in court proceedings, and that increasingly they see it as relevant to the task of making a case across a range of legal disciplines.

De Graaf et al. found that in the period in question District Courts were less reluctant in applying provisions of the CRC than the Courts of Appeal and the Supreme Courts. Furthermore, courts which mentioned the CRC in their decisions—mostly District Courts—preferred to apply it by interpreting national law and principles in the light of the CRC rather than by stating that a certain CRC provision should be understood as having 'direct effect'. In some exceptional cases in which the Supreme Courts had used this technique (interpretation in the light of the CRC), it led not only to a higher level of legal protection for the children in these cases but occasionally to policy change and law reform.[12] De Graaf et al. emphasised the importance of the CRC's function as an interpretive tool, noting that by utilising it in this way the courts could learn more about a fairly unknown technique capable of producing positive outcomes for children's rights. Courts are often reluctant to mention that a provision of the CRC has direct effect, preferring instead to use the CRC as a tool for the interpretation of national law.

The various Dutch courts hold different views about the direct effect of CRC provisions. On the one hand, they have recognised in case law the direct effect of articles 2, 3, 6, 7, 8, 9, 10(2), 12, 16, 18, 19, 20, 23, 27(3), 31, 37 and 40 of the CRC; on the other, the courts have explicitly denied the direct effect of articles 2, 3, 4, 5, 6, 7, 9, 18, 19, 20, 22, 23, 24, 26, 27, 28, 31, 37 and 40(1). These inconsistent views have created legal uncertainty in the Netherlands about the direct effect of almost all CRC provisions.[13]

De Graaf et al. argue that, when using the CRC in court proceedings, legal practitioners very often deploy it as an abstract tool to bolster an argument in favour of a decision in conformity with the rights of the child as set out in the CRC. The authors stress that practitioners should focus instead on advancing arguments that make it clear why the CRC is pertinent to the case's circumstances and what consequences this should have for a decision relating to the individual child.

6 The Impact of the CRC in Different Fields of Law

6.1 Family Law

In the field of family law, the District Courts have been those most active in implementing the CRC. Many of its provisions have been applied directly or used to interpret national law (De Graaf et al. 2012). Direct application has occasionally resulted in national law being excluded from application, situations which in turn have led to law reform.[14] The concept of the best interests of the child is incorporated in Dutch family legislation. However, its exact meaning remains

[12] This occurred in particular in the fields of family, immigration and social security law. See, for example, de Graaf et al. (2012).

[13] See also Pulles (2011) and Pulles (2012).

[14] For example, article 36(2) of the Passport Act was reviewed after a relocation conflict: District Court Maastricht 5 August 2005, ECLI:NL:RBMAA:2005:AU1654. All judgments with ECLI-number can be found on www.rechtspraak.nl.

unclear as no further definition or clarification is provided in national legislation.[15] Family court judges of District Courts and Courts of Appeal have thus used the CRC regularly as an interpretive tool. For example, articles 3 and 20 have been of influence in instances where not all of the legal conditions for an adoption have been fulfilled but where adoption would nevertheless be in the best interests of the child.[16]

Article 20 of the CRC has also played a role in several judgments to do with long-term foster care,[17] one example of which is the decision of the Court of Appeal of Arnhem 16 February 2010. The Court ruled that, based on article 3 of the CRC in conjunction with article 8 of the European Convention on Human Rights (ECHR),[18] a juvenile judge has the power to decide that a child should be cared for by a particular foster family (in this instance, the child's grandparents). The decision was contrary to legislation (the Youth Care Act), according to which the administrative body supervising the child had the discretionary power to decide on foster care placements.

In several decisions regarding children in secure treatment institutions (closed youth care), articles 3 and 37 of the CRC have proven to be influential in legal proceedings, sometimes in conjunction with article 5(4) of the ECHR.[19] This has led to groundbreaking court decisions in which requests that young people of 18 years or older be placed in secure treatment institutions for their own protection were refused on the grounds that it would violate article 5(4) of the ECHR. By law youngsters of 18 years or older can legitimately be placed in a secure treatment setting, but as a result of these decisions this element of the Youth Care Act was hardly ever used again (and then only for an interim transition period).

The rulings demonstrate that, in order to make successful use of the CRC in proceedings, it is important that it be combined with other human rights treaties. To date, the Dutch Supreme Court has not given much attention to the possible role and significance of the CRC in family law cases. Nevertheless, in November 2013 the Supreme Court underlined the importance of the right of the child to be heard by referencing article 12 of the CRC.[20] In this case the social worker in charge of implementing a child protection order argued that it was in the child's best interests that he not be heard in court, even though the law requires (under article 809 of the Code of Civil Procedure) that, unless it is clear that one of the

[15] Until the CRC Committee published its General Comment on the best interests of the child under the CRC in 2013, no definition existed as such at international law of the concept of the best interests of the child.

[16] For example, Court of Appeal Leeuwarden 2 December 2010, ECLI:NL:GHLEE:2010:BP0604; District Court Zutphen, 19 December 2007, ECLI:NL:RBZUT:2007:BC0797.

[17] For example, Court of Appeal Den Haag 12 April 2011, ECLI:NL:GHSGR:2011:BQ1391.

[18] Court of Appeal Arnhem 16 February 2010, ECLI:NL:GHARN:2010:BL6961.

[19] For example, Court of Appeal Den Haag 4 November 2009, ECLI:NL:GHSGR:2009:BK3510; District Court Groningen 20 December 2006, ECLI:NL:RBGRO:2006:AZ5794, ECLI:NL:RBGRO:2006:AZ5807.

[20] Supreme Court of the Netherlands 11 November 2013, ECLI:NL:HR:2013:1084.

exceptions is applicable, the child be provided with the opportunity to express her or his views.[21] The Supreme Court was not convinced, and referred to article 12 of the CRC to emphasise the right of the child to be heard. The Court formulated this right as a duty to provide children with the opportunity to express their own views in matters affecting them, and it noted, too, that there is an explicit obligation for the judge to justify any exception to this rule.

6.2 Immigration Law

In immigration law, the highest Dutch court, the Administrative Jurisdiction Division of the Council of State (hereafter Council of State), has shown great reluctance to recognise the direct effect of CRC articles,[22] with the result that lawyers relying on the CRC have frequently been unsuccessful. The Council of State has usually been of the opinion that, due to their wording, various provisions of the CRC were not directly applicable because they required specific legislative measures for their implementation.

While the administrative District Courts have generally followed the Council of State in this regard, it is important to note at the same time that lower courts have been quite active in applying article 3 of the CRC through open standards and principles of administrative law (Limbeek 2012), for example, to substantiate the justification principle[23] in cases where an administrative body did not give justifiable reasons for deciding that a specific decision was contrary to article 3(1) of the CRC. In this way, the (indirect) application of article 3(1) of the CRC can be seen as having an influence on the decisions of administrative bodies.

A high number of cases reliant on the CRC have also failed in the Dutch courts for reasons other than a lack of direct effect. In these instances, the arguments that were made in relation to CRC rights did not have proper and adequate factual substantiation. As noted earlier, it is clear from the case law that reliance on the CRC should be well-substantiated with relevant facts and set out in detailed terms with

---

[21] Exceptions are: (1) the child does not want to be heard; (2) the child cannot give his or her opinion because of a physical or psychological disorder; (3) it is an urgent situation; (4) it is a matter of minor importance; (5) damage to the health of the child is a possibility. See also *NJ* 2014/24 with commentary from S.F.M. Wortmann. Wortmann pleads for a stricter formulation regarding the damage-criterion. Wortmann thinks it is better that the judge should be able to decide not to send an invitation to the child concerning his or her right to be heard only in cases where *severe* damage to the health of the child is a possibility. Wortmann is of the view that the lower threshold makes it too easy to decide not to hear a child.

[22] In the period 2002–2011 the Council of State only implicitly recognised the direct effect of article 12 of the CRC.

[23] This is a general principle of proper administration, which holds that an administrative body should give proper reasons for its decisions.

reference to specific CRC provisions applicable in the specific situation.[24] Making a lone, general complaint that the CRC has been violated is not enough to win the day. In this regard, lawyers can and should strengthen their reasoning and argumentation in order to bring the CRC better to bear in legal proceedings.

In the field of immigration law, courts have been reluctant in giving due weight to the rights of the child. The Council of State, however, has gradually developed a somewhat more amenable attitude towards the rights of immigrant children resident in the Netherlands. For many years, it was of the view that children of parents with illegal residence cannot rely on the CRC. The first, small change came in 2005 when the Council ruled that even if CRC provisions have direct effect, this has no further meaning other than that the interests of the children should be considered in decision-making, a ruling which was frequently repeated in later decisions. In February 2012, it made another—and important—change by ruling that article 3(1) of the CRC has direct effect to the extent that, in all actions concerning children, the interests of the children involved should be considered.[25]

According to the Council of State, this implies that the best interests of the child should be taken into account in every decision but that the decision-makers have discretionary powers with regard to the way in which they balance the best interests of the child against other interests (for example, the public interest). What it means in practice is that decision-makers enjoy a wide margin of appreciation; judges should, according to the Council, exercise restraint with regard to the test of whether the best interests of the child are sufficiently taken into account.

Although the ruling was welcomed as an important step in realising children's rights and implementing the CRC (Van Os and Rodrigues 2013), the Council of State declared only 15 days later that article 3 of the CRC does not have direct effect.[26] Therefore, the approach of the Council of State towards the influence of article 3 of the CRC in administrative procedures cannot, at this point in time, be said to be clear (Spijkerboer 2013).

In a milestone ruling of 15 August 2012, the Council of State decided that article 3 of the CRC obliges administrative decision-makers to take into account the best interests of the child even when this is not in line with specific legislation.[27] The impossibility of balancing these interests is sometimes apparent, such as when applying the Youth Care Regulation. The Regulation prescribes a parental allowance in case of a foster care placement by supervision order without any exceptions, but

[24] Administrative Jurisdiction Division of the Council of State 30 August 2002, 200203697/1; Administrative Jurisdiction Division of the Council of State 8 November 2004, *JV* 2005/21; Administrative Jurisdiction Division of the Council of State 19 October 2005, *JV* 2005/462; Administrative Jurisdiction Division of the Council of State 5 March 2010, ECLI:NL:RVS:2010:BL7404.

[25] Administrative Jurisdiction Division of the Council of State 7 February 2012, ECLI:NL:RVS:2012:BV3716.

[26] Administrative Jurisdiction Division of the Council of State 22 February 2012, ECLI:NL:RVS:2012:BV6578 (*JV* 2012/200).

[27] Administrative Jurisdiction Division of the Council of State 15 August 2012, ECLI:RVS:2012:BX4660.

according to the Council of State it does not prevent a decision-making body from fulfilling its duty to balance the child's best interests.

In this case, the father claimed that a parental allowance would mean that he could not pay the travel expenses to make regular visits to his three children who had been placed in foster care several hours away from him. He argued that the obligatory financial contribution to the foster care placement was in violation of articles 3 and 9 of the CRC. The Council of State decided that article 3 does indeed imply that administrative bodies must balance the child's best interests in every decision, even when legislation does not give room for the best interests of the child.

Meanwhile, it appears from consistent case law that the Council of State recognises the direct effect of article 3(1) of the CRC to the extent that, in all actions concerning children, the interests of the children involved should be considered.[28] This means children can rely on article 3(1) of the CRC.

The cautious, positive trend towards the application of the rights of children in immigration law is most likely due to way in which the ECHR and Charter of Fundamental Rights of the European Union (the EU Charter) have served to make children's rights matters of increasing prominence and have thereby improved the position of children (Reneman 2011).[29] In a key judgment by the Dutch Supreme Court on 21 September 2012, the impact of children's rights also becomes apparent in the implementation of several relevant international and regional (human) rights documents.[30] This ruling emphasises the right of the child to adequate shelter, even when parents who are responsible for their child do not cooperate with immigration policies. The state has a duty to take measures to protect the rights of vulnerable children whose parents resist expulsion; that duty can be distilled from the case law of the European Court of Human Rights (ECtHR), which mentions article 3 of the CRC as well as European immigration legislation and principles, the European Social Charter, and the opinions of the European Committee of Social Rights.

6.3 Social Security

In the field of social security, the courts have demonstrated a highly reticent attitude towards the acknowledgement of the direct effect of CRC provisions. Only article 2(1) of the CRC was explicitly considered as a directly applicable norm. Nevertheless, the case law of the Central Appeals Tribunal shows that

---

[28] See, for example, Administrative Jurisdiction Division of the Council of State 20 February 2012, 201105996/1/V1; Administrative Jurisdiction Division of the Council of State 15 August 2012, 201109886/1/A2; Administrative Jurisdiction Division of the Council of State 23 August 2012, 201100449/1 A/1; Administrative Jurisdiction Division of the Council of State 8 July 2013, 201207411/1/V4, Administrative Jurisdiction Division of the Council of State 20 January 2014, 201308853/1/V3.

[29] For an extensive overview of international and regional standard regarding children's rights in the field of immigration law, see Van Os and Beltman (2012).

[30] Supreme Court of the Netherlands 21 September 2012, ECLI:NL:PHR:2012:BW5328.

CRC provisions, taken independently of the direct-effect principle, can be of added value.

This is illustrated by several court decisions in which the Tribunal applied articles 3(1), 3(2) and 27(3) of the CRC to interpret the concept 'very pressing reasons' in article 16(1) of the Work and Social Assistance Act. By using such an interpretation, the Tribunal created a right for minors with Dutch nationality to receive social assistance independently of their parents in emergency cases.[31] In 2006, the Tribunal widened the circle of rights-holders to minor foreign national with legal residence not (yet) permitted entry to the Netherlands, doing so by means of the direct application of article 2(1) CRC, in the light of articles 2(2), 3 and 27 of the CRC.[32] The Tribunal held that the exclusion (and hence the application of article 16(2) of the Work and Social Assistance Act) of this group was inconsistent and therefore in violation of article 2(1) of the CRC.[33]

In some other cases, the Tribunal took the CRC into consideration in determining whether a refusal of social services to a minor foreign national was in violation of article 8 of the ECHR. The Tribunal used the CRC to interpret this article, something which has resulted occasionally in exceptions to policy and legislation being exercised for the benefit of the child.[34] However, it should be noted that the Tribunal's reasoning has not always been accepted by the Supreme Court.[35]

6.4 Juvenile Justice

In the field of juvenile justice, the impact of the CRC has been rather marginal. District Courts have applied some CRC provisions[36] directly or as an interpretive tool, but their judgments have quite often been brushed aside by the Supreme Court.

In 2008 it ruled that article 40 of the CRC does not imply a positive obligation to interpret legislation concerning the use of DNA samples of suspects of crimes in a national database differently for minors. Although the Supreme Court heard the argument that the obligatory use of DNA from minor suspects would lead to unnecessary stigmatization and should be decided on a case-by-case basis depending on the specific circumstances, it stated that the legislature had taken this element into account and had decided that no change of policy was needed for minors.[37]

---

[31] See, for example, Central Appeals Tribunal 29 March 2005, ECLI:NL:CRVB:2005:AT3468.

[32] Central Appeals Tribunal 24 January 2006, ECLI:NL:CRVB:2006:AV0197.

[33] In addition, the Tribunal underlined that the exclusion of minor foreign nationals with no legal residence was still justified, also in the light of the CRC.

[34] See, for example, Central Appeals Tribunal 20 October 2010, ECLI:NL:CRVB:2011:BR1905.

[35] Supreme Court of the Netherlands 23 November 2012, ECLI:NL:HR:2012:BW7740 (child allowance case); in continuation of: Central Appeals Tribunal 15 July 2011, ECLI:NL:CRVB:2011:BR1905.

[36] Most often articles 3 and 40 of the CRC.

[37] Supreme Court of the Netherlands 13 May 2008, ECLI:NL:HR:2008:BC8231.

Concerning the right to a fair and public hearing within a reasonable time, the Supreme Court denied that article 40 of the CRC should lead to the conclusion that stricter sanctions are prescribed when deciding that a hearing did not take place within a 'reasonable time' (namely, that it should result in the dismissal of the case instead of a reduction in penalty).[38] Nonetheless, recently several District Court rulings point out that article 40 implies that a procedure which did not meet the standards of 'within a reasonable time' can lead to stricter sanctioning where child, rather than adult, criminal suspects are concerned.[39]

The Supreme Court seems to be more receptive to the views of the ECtHR concerning the rights of minors during pre-trial police interrogation. Influenced by the Salduz and Panovits case law of the ECtHR,[40] it has decided that minors need special and extra legal assistance during police interrogation.[41]

It is crucial to realise that children's rights are found not only in the CRC but can be distilled from other human rights treaties and bodies as well. Strategic children's rights litigation should therefore focus on more than the CRC alone and make use of all human rights treaties and case law of human rights bodies, invoking the CRC provisions in conjunction with them. While this holds true for all legal domains, in the field of juvenile justice in particular, other human rights treaties—such as articles 5 and 6 of the ECHR and the relevant case law of the ECtHR—provide important opportunities for implementing children's rights. Remarkably, the ECtHR judgments in the field of juvenile justice show less influence by CRC provisions than those in the fields of immigration, child protection and family law; but, with that being said, articles 37 and 40 of the CRC could offer a useful interpretative tool when the rights of child suspects are at stake (Mijnarends et al. 2013).

7 Limitations, Challenges and Caveats

As mentioned, the influence of the CRC in the Netherlands varies between fields of law and between courts. An important implication is that the possibilities for, and limitations on, using the CRC successfully in litigation depend partly on the applicable field of law.

In family law, the best interests of the child are incorporated in Dutch legislation, and in many of the situations and conflicts that ignite family law proceedings, the Dutch Civil Code obliges family court judges to take the best interests of the child into account. These cases entail a conflict between two parents or between parent

---

38 Supreme Court of the Netherlands 16 December 2003, ECLI:NL:PHR:2003:AL9062; Supreme Court of the Netherlands 17 June 2008, ECLI:NL:HR:2008:BD2578.

39 See, for example, District Court Amsterdam 7 October 2013, ECLI:NL:RBAMS:2013:6632; District Court Amsterdam 19 March 2013, ECLI:NL:RBAMS:2013:BZ7798; District Court Amsterdam 29 November 2011, ECLI:NL:RBAMS:2011:BV2784.

40 ECtHR 27 November 2008, no. 36391/02 (*Salduz v. Turkey*) and ECtHR 11 December 2008, no. 4268/04 (*Panovits v. Cyprus*).

41 Supreme Court of the Netherlands 30 June 2009, ECLI:NL:HR:2009:BH3079.

and child. The state has the duty to protect the child who is in need of care when parents or caregivers fail to provide it, but in juvenile justice and immigration proceedings, it will often have strong public interest considerations that conflict with the child's best interests (for example, combating crime, ensuring public safety, and protecting and developing economic interests). In the field of juvenile justice, the rights of the child suspect are also incorporated in legislation that regulates special protection orders for juvenile justice proceedings (for example, the minor has the right to a criminal hearing behind closed doors, to legal counsel and to special child-friendly sanctions). Although the interests of the minor suspect and the state differ, the rights of the child are taken into account in criminal-procedure settings.

Furthermore, in family law, child protection and juvenile justice cases, the judge is informed by a child expert (working for the Child Care and Protection Board) about the best interests of a specific child. In immigration law, by contrast, the best interests of the child are not incorporated in statutory law. Moreover, administrative judges are normally not informed by a child expert and have a duty to consider only whether the decision-making bodies have, within their margin of appreciation, decided reasonably in the specific circumstances of the case. Administrative judges do not have the power to balance the best interests of the child, only to review the decision marginally (Beltman and Zijlstra 2013). This explains why, on the one hand, the CRC is often invoked in immigration cases, but, on the other, has not always led to the desired result for the affected children. However, the CRC can still be of influence in such cases. The extent to which this is true in practice also depends, of course, on the willingness of a judge to incorporate the CRC actively into decision-making, even when the boundaries of actively reviewing decisions are clear and legislative or policymaking bodies resist (further) implementation of the CRC.

Last but not least, it is important to be aware of the risk of using and interpreting the CRC in litigation in an unsubstantiated way. Forder (2013) has pointed out that several judges have used the best interests of the child principle (article 3, CRC) to reason that children needed protection even in instances where granting such protection would be in violation of other human rights. Article 3 of the CRC, for example, was used for the placement of a child in a police station[42] or a youth detention institution despite the fact that this violated article 5 of the ECHR. The child only needed protection, had not committed a crime, and was not a suspect.[43] Bakker (2013) rejects this use of the CRC as a so-called 'magic wand' in court proceedings, while Forder (2013) argues that article 3 of the CRC should not be used when doing so would lead to the violation of the child's other human rights. Judges, that is to say, should be wary of over-protecting children at the cost of putting their rights in jeopardy.

Furthermore, they should not limit the implementation of children's rights to the use of the CRC alone, but should broaden their horizons to encompass other

[42] District Court Utrecht 12 August 2009, ECLI:NL:RBUTR:2009:BJ5287.

[43] District Court Roermond 21 January 2009, ECLI:NL:RBROE:2009:BH0359; District Court Maastricht 21 February 2008, ECLI:NL:RBMAA:2008:BC6106

human rights instruments and relevant case law. Such tools will sometimes offer both a broader context and more detailed standards for the protection of children's rights than that in the CRC. In the meantime, further explanation and guidance is necessary to facilitate adequate interpretation of the CRC provisions and their application in the domestic setting. The General Comments of the Committee on the Rights of the Child, the case law of other human rights bodies, and, arguably, the Committee's future decisions in relation to the third Optional Protocol are key resources for advancing the in-depth development of children's rights.

8 Conclusion

In Dutch litigation the CRC is used as a tool for interpreting national standards (open standards, concepts and principles) as well as international ones (for example, article 8 of the ECHR); in the course of being so used, it has influenced different legal fields, courts and judges in different ways. Some articles of the CRC have been implemented directly, whereas, in most of the case law, it has been of indirect influence, namely, as a tool of interpretation. In both ways, the CRC has been useful in promoting the rights of the child and ensuring that children's rights are considered and taken seriously in the courtroom.

Education and training seem to be critical. It is a challenge to educate all legal practitioners in all fields of law and at all levels of the judiciary in order to make them aware of the different implementation techniques of the CRC; it is a challenge, likewise, to educate them so as to encourage them to use the CRC provisions in factually substantiated lines of legal reasoning and in conjunction with other human rights instruments and case law that could sometimes offer a more detailed approach to the implementation of children's rights.

In the Dutch courts the CRC has led not only to a special interpretation of national legislation and norms but also to a duty to balance the child's best interests transparently in decision-making. Furthermore, in some instances the CRC has seen judges refrain from applying a specific rule because of an alleged inconsistency with, and therefore violation of, the CRC. In order to prevent the CRC from being used in strategic litigation as a piece of abstract magic lacking further substantiation or meaning, and to prevent it from being used to over-protect children in instances where invoking it would lead to violation of other human rights, ongoing debate and discourse on future approaches are both desirable and necessary.

References

Bakker, R. (2013). Rechterlijke creativiteit in kinderbeschermingszaken. In C. Forder (Ed.), *Rechterlijke creativiteit en de rechten van het kind* (pp. 11–33). Den Haag: Boom Juridische Uitgevers.

Beltman, D., & Zijlstra, E. (2013). De doorwerking van 'het belang van het kind' ex artikel 3 VRK in het migratierecht: Vanuit een bottom-up benadering op weg naar een top-down toepassing. *Journaal Vreemdelingenrecht, 12*(4), 286–306.

De Graaf, J. H., et al. (2012). De toepassing van het Internationaal Verdrag inzake de Rechten van het Kind in de Nederlandse rechtspraak. Nijmegen: Ars Aequi Libri.

De Jonge, G., & van der Linden, A. P. (2013). Jeugd en strafrecht. Deventer: Kluwer.

Doek, J. E. (1995). De ratificatie van het verdrag voor de rechten van het kind. Enige beschouwingen over de mogelijke gevolgen voor de Nederlandse rechtspraktijk. *NJCM-Bulletin, 20–1*, 10–21.

Doek, J. E., & Vlaardingerbroek, P. (2009). *Jeugdrecht en jeugdzorg*. Amsterdam: Elsevier Juridisch.

Forder, C. (2013). Rechterlijke creativiteit en de rechten van het kind. In C. Forder (Ed.), *Rechterlijke creativiteit en de rechten van het kind* (pp. 33–39). Den Haag: Boom Juridische Uitgevers.

Kinderombudsman. (2012). De bijzondere curator, een lot uit de loterij? Adviesrapport over waarborging van de stem en de belangen van kinderen in de praktijk. KOM2A/2012. http://www.dekinderombudsman.nl/92/ouders-professionals/publicaties/rapport-bijzondere-curator-een-lot-uit-de-loterij/?id=178.

Leuven, C. A. R. M., & Klerk, M. J. (2013) Formele en informele rechtsingang(en) minderjarige. EB 2013/32.

Limbeek, M. M. C. (2013). De bijzondere curator: Een volwaardig sluitstuk van rechtsbescherming? In J. H. de Graaf, et al. (Eds.), *Rechten van het kind en waardigheid* (pp. 199–217). Nijmegen: Ars Aequi Libri.

Mijnarends, E. M., Liefaard, T., & Bruning, M. R. (2013). De doorwerking van het IVRK in het Nederlandse jeugdstrafrecht. *NJCM-Bulletin, 38*(4), 532–544.

Mink, E. A. (2012). De procespositie van de minderjarige in de civiele procedure. EB 2012/41.

Pulles, G. J. (2011). Onduidelijkheid over de rechtstreekse werking van de kernbepalingen van het VN Kinderrechtenverdrag. *NJB, 4*, 231–234.

Pulles, G. J. (2012). Doorwerking van het IVRK: de wetgever geeft het voorbeeld. FJR 2012/64.

Reneman, M. (2011). Het Kinderrechtenverdrag krijgt tanden: Over hoe het VN Verdrag inzake de Rechten van het Kind via het EU-recht en het EVRM binnendringt in het Nederlandse vreemdelingenrecht (pp. 354–358). A&MR.

Ruitenberg, G. C. A. M. (2003). *Het Internationaal Kinderrechtenverdrag in de Nederlandse rechtspraak*. Amsterdam: Uitgeverij SWP Amsterdam.

Spijkerboer, T. (2013). De Afdeling bestuursrechtspraak van de Raad van State en kinderrechten in het vreemdelingenrecht. In C. Forder (Ed.), *Rechterlijke creativiteit en de rechten van het kind* (pp. 67–81). Den Haag: Boom Juridische Uitgevers.

Ter Haar (2012). Art. 245, aant. 4. In M. J. C. Koens, A. P. M. J. (Ed.), *Tekst & Commentaar Personen- en familierecht*. Deventer: Kluwer.

Van Emmerik, M. L. (2005). Toepassing van het Kinderrechtenverdrag in de Nederlandse rechtspraak. *NJCM-Bulletin, 30*(6), 700–716.

Van Os, C., & Beltman, D. (2012). Kinderrechten in het migratierecht. In M. Blaak, et al. (Ed.) Handboek internationaal jeugdrecht (pp. 648–818). Leiden: Defence for Children 2012.

Van Os, C., & Rodrigues, P. (2013). Op de hurken: Naar een kinderrechtenperspectief in het vreemdelingenrecht. *NJCM-Bulletin, 38*(4), 545–560.

Van Teeffelen, P. A. J. Th. (2013). Formele en informele rechtsingang(en) minderjarige. EB 2013/62.

Chapter 7
Belgium

The Convention of the Rights of the Child in Belgian Case Law

Wouter Vandenhole

Abstract Since the entry into force in Belgium of the Convention on the Rights of the Child (CRC), its provisions have been invoked by tribunals and courts in about 250–300 judicial decisions. A major obstacle in Belgian doctrine is the denial of direct effect to a number of CRC provisions. The CRC has played a gap-filling role in the absence of domestic legislation, particularly in regard to the right of children to express their views and have access to court. In the area of migration, it has performed a strong corrective role towards the legislator and a legitimising one towards the judicial bodies. The CRC often plays a subsidiary role in the absence of domestic legislation or relevant provisions in the European Convention on Human Rights. The CRC is certainly not the only legal reference text on children's rights; nonetheless, the full potential of the CRC and the interpretative work of the CRC Committee has not yet been fully capitalised upon by Belgian judicial bodies.

1 Introduction to the Belgian Legal System

The CRC was signed by Belgium on 26 January 1990, and ratified on 16 December 1991. It entered into force on 15 January 1992. The Optional Protocol on the Involvement of Children in Armed Conflict (OPAC) was signed on 6 September 2000, and ratified on 6 May 2002. It entered into force on 6 June 2002. On 6 September 2000, Belgium also signed the Optional Protocol on the Sale of Children,

The UNICEF Chair in Children's Rights is a joint-venture of the University of Antwerp and UNICEF Belgium. UNICEF respects the academic freedom of the chair-holder. Opinions expressed by the chair-holder do not commit UNICEF. I would like to thank Steven Van Raemdonck for offering research assistance.

W. Vandenhole (✉)
Faculty of Law, Law and Development Research Group, University of Antwerp, Antwerp, Belgium
e-mail: wouter.vandenhole@uantwerp.be

T. Liefaard and J.E. Doek (eds.), *Litigating the Rights of the Child*,
DOI 10.1007/978-94-017-9445-9_7

Child Prostitution and Pornography (OPSC), which was ratified on 17 March 2006, entering into force on 17 April 2006. The Optional Protocol to the Convention on the Rights of the Child on a communications procedure (OPIC) was signed on 28 February 2012, ratified on 30 May 2014 and entered into force on 30 August 2014.

1.1 The Question of Direct Effect

The Belgian legal order is a civil law system.[1] The relationship between the CRC and its Protocols, as international treaties, and national law is closest to monism (Cassese 2001: 164–165): that is, international treaties like the CRC are an integral part of the Belgian legal order. They are directly applicable without any need to transform or incorporate the international rules into domestic law.

However, the CRC's direct applicability does not mean its provisions are directly invokable by individuals before Belgian judges, which raises the question of direct effect, often also referred to as the self-executing character of a treaty or treaty provisions (Alen and Pas 1996). This question is assessed at the level of each treaty provision individually, or even at the level of paragraphs of a provision, but assuredly not at the level of the treaty as a whole. For each CRC provision or paragraph thereof, it needs to be established whether it has direct effect or not, that is, whether individuals can invoke it directly before Belgian judicial bodies.

Whether a treaty provision has direct effect in the Belgian domestic order is determined by the domestic judge. Each judge is free to take a stance on this matter, so that it is perfectly possible that one judge could decide that a certain CRC provision has direct effect while another opines that it does not. There is a general tendency with the Council of State (*Conseil d'état*), the highest administrative court, to deny direct effect to CRC provisions. The Court of Cassation, Belgium's main court of last resort, has become rather restrictive on this since 1999 and accepts any direct effect only for a selected number of CRC provisions. Lower courts and tribunals tend to be more open, as will be discussed in detail in section 3.

In the literature, the restrictive approach to the direct effect of the CRC (and to that of other human rights treaties, with the exception of those which, like the European Convention on Human Rights (ECHR) and International Covenant on Civil and Political Rights (ICCPR), deal with civil and political rights) has been deplored. Even the most cautious authors in this regard have argued that while they believe it is unthinkable to extend direct effect to all CRC provisions, the provisions that guarantee civil and political rights similar to those in the ECHR or ICCPR must be given direct effect, as the latter treaty provisions have been given direct effect (Senaeve and Arnoeyts 2004: 111–113).[2] Others argue in favour of a

[1] Belgium is a federal state with six main federated entities: the Flemish Community and the Flemish Region; the French Community; the Walloon Region; the German-speaking Community; and the Brussels Capital Region.

[2] Senaeve rejects direct effect for a number of provisions on the basis of their wording, that is, when in his view they are only imposing obligations on States parties (art. 4, art. 11 and 26 CRC).

more evolutive interpretation of the direct effect of the CRC provisions. Alen and Pas have suggested a gradual concept, comparable with Scheinin's more-or-less scale (1994: 75–78), whereby the degree of direct effect depends on the normative power of a provision as well as on the policy space left to the state (Alen and Pas 1996: 173). Claes and Vandaele (2001) have proposed the introduction of an assumption of direct effect. They endorse a gradual approach in which, inter alia, the core content of a right plays a guiding role.

Clearly, then, the CRC Committee was too optimistic and too generalizing in welcoming, in 1995, 'the fact that the Convention is self-executing [in Belgium] and that its provisions may be, and in practice have been in several instances, invoked before the court'.[3]

Once a treaty provision has been accorded direct effect, it prevails over conflicting domestic norms. CRC provisions with direct effect are, in other words, superior in the hierarchy of norms to domestic provisions. However, the absence of direct effect of a CRC provision does not deprive it from all meaning in the Belgian legal order. Such a provision may play an indirect role, for example, by being supportive of judicial reasoning even if it does not give direct legal grounding to a court's decision (Senaeve and Arnoeyts 2004: 106), or by contributing to the interpretation of a norm.[4]

1.2 Children's Rights in the Belgian Constitution

Belgium's constitution has a separate section, Title II, on fundamental rights and freedoms, while a provision on children's rights, article 22bis, was introduced in two stages. Following the horrendous cases of sexual abuse of children that came to light in the 1990s, the right of each child to respect for his or her moral, physical, mental and sexual integrity was codified in 2000. In 2008 this constitutional provision concerning children's rights was broadened into a more comprehensive guarantee. Article 22bis now reads:

> Each child is entitled to have his or her moral, physical, mental and sexual integrity respected.
> Each child has the right to express his or her views in all matters affecting him or her, the views of the child being given due weight in accordance with his or her age and maturity.
> Each child has the right to benefit from measures and facilities, which promote his or her development.
> In all decisions concerning children, the interest of the child is a primary consideration.
> The law, federate law or rule referred to in Article 134 ensures these rights of the child.

[3] CRC Committee (1995). Concluding Observations of the Committee on the Rights of the Child: Belgium, para. 5.

[4] Court of Cassation 4 November 1999. Judgments are available in German, French and Dutch on http://www.const-court.be/ (last accessed 27 August 2013). Summaries in English of the Constitutional Court's case law can be found on http://www.const-court.be/en/common/home.html. Accessed 27 August 2013.

Article 22bis contains an explicit integrity guarantee, as well as three of the four general principles of the CRC. The general principle of non-discrimination and equality was not included because the Constitution already has two general provisions on the matter (arts. 10 and 11 Belgian Constitution). Article 22bis thus captures the spirit of the CRC well without repeating it verbatim.

The wording of this article's final paragraph, possibly somewhat opaque to those unfamiliar with the Belgian Constitution, is borrowed from article 23 of the Constitution, the provisions of which contain social and economic rights. The paragraph is intended to mean that the constitutionally guaranteed children's rights provision has no direct effect, i.e. that it cannot be directly invoked in litigation. In a recent judgment, the Council of State confirmed the absence of direct effect of the fourth paragraph of article 22bis (on the best interests of the child).[5]

2 Access to Justice

Broadly speaking, Belgium has three types of judicial bodies: the Constitutional Court (known until 2007 as the Court of Arbitration), administrative judges (with the Council of State as supreme administrative judge), and the ordinary judicial branch of tribunals and courts (with the Court of Cassation as supreme court).

In principle, children have no standing and claims have to be brought to court by their legal representatives. However, children with sufficient maturity (the capacity of discernment) may be given legal standing, mainly when it comes to (highly) personal issues such as marriage or affiliation, but so too if their legal representatives fail to act and/or if the issue is pressing, for example, where a claim for damages is introduced against an assaulter,[6] if a claim is made against the Public Social Assistance Centre, that is, the local administration in charge of social assistance,[7] or where proceedings are instituted with regard to education[8] or in the context of migration procedures.

These exceptions are not guaranteed in law, though, and depend on the proclivities of the judge concerned.[9] Judges have divergent practices—and the literature, differences of opinion—on the question of whether article 12 of the CRC can serve as a legal basis for allowing minors to intervene at their own initiative in procedures among their parents.[10] The *Cour de Cassation* has held that the provisions

---

[5] Council of State 29 May 2013, Judgments of the Council of State can be found on http://www.raadvst-consetat.be. Accessed 27 August 2013.

[6] Criminal Tribunal Liège 1 March 1994, *Journal du droit des jeunes* (hereafter *JDJ*) 1994, no. 136, 46.

[7] Labour tribunal Brussels 22 June 1994, *JDJ* 1996, no. 155, 230–234.

[8] Council of State 19 March 1997, http://www.raadvst-consetat.be.

[9] For an in-depth discussion, see Robert (2006) as far as civil procedures are concerned, and Veny and De Vos (2006) with regard to administrative procedures.

[10] Not granted: Civil Tribunal (Summary Proceedings) Liège 7 March 2003, *Revue trimestrielle de droit familial* (hereafter *RTDF*) 2005, 1175–1177. Granted: Summary Proceedings Leuven 16 September 2010, *NieuwJuridischWeekblad* (hereafter *NJW*) 2011, 236.

guaranteeing a right to be heard (inter alia, art. 12 CRC) do not give minors the right to intervene voluntarily in legal proceedings which do not directly affect their interests, such as the criminal prosecution of one of the parents in the case of non-observance of contact-rights arrangements.[11] Sometimes, voluntary intervention is accepted (for example, on the basis of article 9 of the CRC), but it is limited to the right to express one's views in the procedure and does not extend to material claims such as limiting a parent's right to personal contact.[12]

For more than a decade, attempts have been made to guarantee in legislation that children have subsidiary standing in instances such as when legal representatives fail to take action or have conflicting interests, but so far all have failed. In view of the ratification of OPIC by Belgium, the discussion might be revived.

An important institution is the public prosecutor, who plays a role not only in criminal but also civil procedures. As protector of public order and society's more vulnerable members (including minors), he or she has the power to institute legal action in a number of instances defined by law, particularly in the area of youth protection.[13]

As far as the Constitutional Court is concerned, litigation on behalf of children by advocacy groups is possible. Every legal person with a justifiable interest can institute annulment proceedings against a statute. The Human Rights League and Defence for Children have done so repeatedly in matters affecting children. In addition to the annulment procedure, there is a procedure whereby a judicial body can ask the Court's guidance in the interpretation of a constitutional provision that is at stake (referral for preliminary ruling).

3 An Overview of Case Law on the CRC

The following analysis of Belgian case law focuses on the CRC and its Optional Protocols; it does not include case law in which the CRC is not referenced by the judicial body.[14] It should be borne in mind nonetheless that the Belgian case law on children's rights is more elaborate than that alone on the CRC and its Optional Protocols, given that children's rights are also guaranteed in general human rights treaties, in the Belgian Constitution and possibly through the general principle of the best interests of the child.

---

[11] Court of Cassation 15 September 2010, *RechtskundigWeekblad* (hereafter *RW*) 2011–12, 1085–86; Court of Cassation 26 May 2010.

[12] Court of Appeal Ghent 20 June 2005, *Tijdschrift voor Jeugdrecht en Kinderrechten* (hereafter *TJK*) 2007, 35–36.

[13] For an extensive analysis, see Swennen and Caluwé (2006).

[14] We therefore did not include cases in which children's rights, but not the CRC itself, were referenced by the judicial body. Similarly, we excluded cases in which only (one of) the litigating parties invoked the CRC. We did, however, include cases in which the judicial body cited another judgment in which the CRC had been referenced, even though the judicial body directly concerned did not itself reference the CRC.

In 2004, Senaeve published an extensive, and allegedly exhaustive, review of the Belgian case law for the 1992–2002 period. His review built on more than 130 cases in which the CRC had been referenced (Senaeve and Arnoeyts 2004). For the purpose of this chapter, we undertook a review of the 2003–2013 period, the second decade of CRC litigation in Belgium, and identified about 140 published cases in which the CRC was referred to by the tribunal or court itself. The number of cases thus seems to have remained stable between 1992 and 2013. In what follows, we flag the major tendencies that emerged during those years, and, where appropriate, important shifts that took place in the second decade of CRC litigation.

Regarding the highest courts in Belgium, it is mainly the Constitutional Court that engages with the substance of the CRC. The Court cannot directly assess if a statute (i.e. a formal law) is in conformity with the CRC. It only has the power to assess the *constitutionality* of a statute, which means that it tests it in the light of constitutional provisions rather than those of international treaties. That being said, the constitutional provisions themselves are sometimes explicitly interpreted with reference to the CRC. A key reason why the Constitutional Court has been able to engage with the CRC is that it has dismissed the relevance of the direct-effect doctrine for its work, precisely because it cannot directly assess the compatibility of statutes with the CRC or any other human rights treaty.[15] As such, the CRC has played an important role in cases of migration, family law (paternal affiliation and adoption, parental rights), juvenile justice and education.

3.1 Direct Effect

The supreme administrative court, the *Conseil d'état*, has been dismissive of the direct effect of CRC provisions (Senaeve and Arnoeyts 2004: 114),[16] and consequently has hardly engaged with them. Lemmens, a Council of State judge until September 2012, explained that this is due to the nature of the cases it hears, that is, ones involving migration issues. In migration cases, a substantive assessment of administrative acts is seldom made, and the reasoning remains basic (Lemmens 2008). However, the Council of State has accepted, at least implicitly, the direct effect of some CRC provisions in other areas of litigation (Senaeve and Arnoeyts 2004: 151, 156; Lemmens 2008: 52), albeit that so far it has never found a violation of them.

The Aliens Appeal Board (*Raad voor Vreemdelingenbetwistingen, Conseil du Contentieux des Etrangers*), an administrative judicial body in the field of migration established in 2006 to ease the caseload of the Council of State, systematically

[15] Constitutional Court 22 July 2003, no. 106/2003, B.4.2.

[16] See, for example, Council of State 29 May 2013 with regard to articles 3, 8 and 20 of the CRC; Council of State 30 March 2005; Council of State 28 June 2001 with regard to article 9(1) of the CRC.

denies article 3 of the CRC any direct effect.[17] It recognises, nevertheless, that this article is a useful interpretative tool.[18] Moreover, in a recent case on family reunion, the Board accepted that article 24 of the EU Charter of Fundamental Rights was applicable, and that, to better understand it, article 3 of the CRC had to be studied, along with the interpretative work of the CRC Committee.[19] The Aliens Appeal Board does recognise that article 12 of the CRC has direct effect.[20]

Turning to the judicial branch, the Court of Cassation—after an initial period of openness to the direct effect of the CRC—has since 1999 grown far more restrictive.[21] In its case law, it has generally said that article 3 of the CRC has no direct effect. Nonetheless, in some cases the Court has included this article in its reasoning, which appears to suggest an implicit recognition that it does indeed have direct effect.[22] The underlying logic as to when article 3 is considered to have direct effect is hard to deduce, for it has been used in both civil and criminal cases; Senaeve's position that the 1999 judgment is to be interpreted in a very restrictive way (i.e. only applicable to a specific penal law provision) is therefore hardly tenable. The *Cour de Cassation* has explicitly rejected the direct effect of articles 2,[23] 7[24] and 26[25] of the CRC. It accepts, though, that the European Convention on Human Rights (ECHR) needs to be applied in conformity with the principles of international law such as the CRC.[26]

Lower courts and tribunals tend to be unanimous in recognising the direct effect of article 12 of the CRC.[27] Following the introduction of specific legal provisions in Belgian legislation on the right to be heard, some tribunals and courts have built on this article in a complementary or even corrective way, mainly so in order to grant access to court (see section 2).

Where the greatest divergence of opinion is found, however, is in respect of article 3 of the CRC, which concerns the best interests of the child. For some judges, it has no direct effect[28] or none, at any rate, according to a certain

---

[17] Aliens Appeal Board 4 May 2009, www.rvv-cce.be. Accessed 27 August 2013.

[18] Aliens Appeal Board 18 May 2010, *JDJ* 2011, no. 307, 39–41.

[19] Aliens Appeal Board 21 February 2013. Drawing on the CRC Committee's General Comment No. 5, it concluded that article 3(1) of the CRC and article 24 of EU Charter also apply to measures that affect children indirectly, such as requests for family reunification by adults.

[20] Aliens Appeal Board 29 May 2008, *TJK* 2009, 66–68.

[21] Court of Cassation 4 November 1999. Judgments of the Court of Cassation can be found on http://jure.juridat.just.fgov.be. Accessed 27 August 2013.

[22] At least implicit recognition of direct effect article 3 in the Court of Cassation 16 January 2009 (personal contact); Cass 31 October 2006; 14 October 2003 (trial by adult court).

[23] Court of Cassation 26 May 2008.

[24] Court of Cassation 11 June 2010.

[25] Court of Cassation 26 May 2008.

[26] Court of Cassation 30 September 2011.

[27] See, for example, Summary Proceedings Leuven 16 September 2010, *NJW* 2011, 236.

[28] Court of Appeal Ghent 30 May 2005, *Revue de droit judiciaire et de la preuve* 2005, 313–315.

reading[29]; for others, it has direct effect if it is joined in combination with other provisions[30] or viewed in its negative-obligations dimension.[31] Other judges, yet again, seem to accept its direct effect unconditionally.[32] It has been argued, too, that it has some direct effect as a binding interpretative framework for other CRC provisions[33] or when examining the compatibility of legislation with article 8 of the ECHR.[34]

The discussion about the direct effect of article 3 of the CRC is, nevertheless, not particularly relevant in practice, given that the consideration of the child's best interests is recognised as a general principle of law and is, as such, frequently invoked by parties and used by judges without any reference to a formal source of law, be this article 3 of the CRC or article 22bis of the Constitution.

With regard to a significant number of CRC provisions, the direct effect has been recognised by some judges (that is, for articles 2(2)[35]; 7[36]; 8[37]; 9,[38] 16,[39]20[40];21[41]; 26,[42] 27[43] and 28[44]). Other judges have denied the direct effect, in particular in litigation on social assistance to undocumented foreign children, to articles 2, 3, 6, 26 and 27,[45] and 37.[46] However, such denial of direct effect does

[29] The view is that the article does not have direct effect if it is read so as to create a right to social assistance; it does have direct effect, however, in the sense that the judge has to take into consideration as a matter of priority the best interests of the child whenever he or she has a certain margin of appreciation. Labour Tribunal Brussels 9 December 2004, *JDJ* 2005, no. 244, 33–40 and *SocialeKronieken* (hereafter *Soc.Kron.*) 2005, 135–141.

[30] In combination with art. 28 CRC, see CRC President Brussels 7 December 2004.

[31] By negative-obligations dimensions I refer to those obligations that require a state to abstain from certain action, as opposed to positive obligations which do require a state to take action. See Labour Tribunal Huy 19 January 2005, *JDJ* 2005, no. 242, 29–35: the CRC prohibits a rule that allows parents and children to be separated without the possibility of invoking the best interests of the child.

[32] Summary Proceedings Brussels 1 July 2005, *JDJ* 2007, no. 262, 37–40.

[33] Labour Tribunal Bruges 12 November 2003, *NJW* 2004, 168–170.

[34] Labour Tribunal Brussels 19 May 2005, *JDJ* 2005, no. 246, 24–39.

[35] Summary Proceedings Brussels 1 July 2005, *JDJ* 2007, no. 262, 37–40.

[36] Court of Appeal Brussels 28 March 2006, *Jurisprudence de Liège, Mons et Bruxelles* (hereafter *JLMB*) 2007, 513–516.

[37] Id.

[38] Summary Proceedings Brussels 1 July 2005, *JDJ* 2007, no. 262, 37–40.

[39] Labour Tribunal Brussels 7 October 2004, *Soc.Kron.* 2005, 160–163.

[40] Labour Court Mons 3 September 2009, unpublished (implicitly).

[41] Youth Tribunal Antwerp 29 April 2003, *NJW* 2003, 1376–1377.

[42] Tribunal of First Instance Antwerp 24 May 2004, *Tijdschrift voor Vreemdelingenrecht*(hereafter *T.Vreemd.*) 2004, 365–368.

[43] Tribunal of First Instance Antwerp 24 May 2004, *T.Vreemd.* 2004, 365–368.

[44] Labour Tribunal Brussels 3 September 2007, *Soc.Kron.* 2010, 101–105.

[45] Labour Tribunal Namur 28 April 2006, *Soc.Kron.* 2008, 233–235; Labour Court Antwerp 26 January 2005, *Soc.Kron.* 2005, 125–128.

[46] President Brussels 17 November 2003, *JDJ* 2003, no. 230, 36–41.

not always deprive the CRC of all meaning. Sometimes a so-called standstill-effect[47] or minimum core[48] is nevertheless recognised, or CRC provisions without direct effect are mentioned in combination with constitutional provisions and other CRC provisions; it is also the case that judges draw on the Constitutional Court's case law, which in turn has been inspired in part by the CRC.[49]

3.2 *Areas of Law*

The fields of law in which judicial bodies use the CRC have shown fairly consistent trends in the past two decades. The CRC features most prominently in immigration law, particularly in regard to social assistance for undocumented children. In family law, questions of affiliation, adoption and parental authority have been raised. Somewhat remarkably, the CRC has not been especially prominent in the fields of education, youth protection and juvenile justice, although some cases have arisen. As the 1992–2002 period has been discussed extensively elsewhere, the focus here is on the second decade of CRC litigation in Belgium.

3.2.1 Migration

The bulk of CRC litigation in 2003–2013 dealt with migration, particularly social assistance to children who were in the territory illegally. Key provisions included articles 2, 3, 26 and 27 of the CRC.

Early case law addressed the question of whether undocumented children fell under the jurisdiction of the state[50] and what scope of social assistance was due to them.[51] In a landmark judgment of 2003, the Constitutional Court held that it could not be limited to urgent medical care as it was for adults (discussed in more detail in section 4).[52] Subsequent cases examined whether and how this could be given practical effect under the restrictive conditions outlined by the Court, inter alia, without indirectly encouraging parents with illegal status not to leave the country.

---

47 Judge of the Peace Roeselare 5 July 2005, *RW* 2006–07, 693–695: with regard to art. 3 and 19 CRC; Labour Tribunal Antwerp 5 January 2005, *Soc.Kron.* 2005, 176–177 (standstill and minimum core).

48 Labour Tribunal Bruges 12 November 2003, *NJW* 2004, 168–170.

49 Labour Court Liège 26 October 2004, *JDJ* 2005, no. 241, 35–39.

50 Affirmative case law: Labour Tribunal Ghent 24 July 2003, *OCMW-visies* 2003, 61–67.

51 Labour Tribunal Antwerp 6 January 2003, *T.Vreemd.* 2003, 366–370. Contra: no direct effect, hence no subjective right to guaranteed family benefit: Labour Tribunal Ghent 24 July 2003, *OCMW-visies* 2003, 61–67.

52 Constitutional Court 22 July 2003, no. 106/2003.

The CRC was often used pending the applicability of the new legislation[53]—or to challenge that new legislation, which provided that only material aid in kind could be given to children in a reception centre.[54] It was feared that this approach would separate children from their parents.[55] The CRC was also invoked to justify judicial orders to Public Social Assistance Centres to grant social assistance pending the allocation of a place in a reception centre[56] or awaiting the outcome of a regularisation request to be allowed to reside in Belgium due to exceptional circumstances.[57] While a majority of judges still ordered social assistance under the common system,[58] others pointed out that the new legislation was in line with the CRC[59] and that the situation of these children was the responsibility of their parents.[60] Following an acute shortage of places in reception centres, it was argued that the Public Social Assistance Centres had the obligation to provide social assistance.[61]

In addition, cases arose in which parents were in Belgium illegally but their Belgian children were not.[62] An order to leave the country served on the parents of a child who is entitled to stay (due to his or her Belgian nationality) has been held to equate to the de facto removal of that child from the territory and found in violation of articles 2, 3 and 9 of the CRC.[63]

Likewise, the expulsion of unaccompanied children without a concrete, sustainable solution in their country of origin has been considered a violation of the best interests of the child and articles 3 and 20. The children were said to be under the care of the Belgian state, not of their parents, with the implication that the latter could not be blamed for the situation and the former not absolve itself of its responsibility.[64]

The right to education has played an important role in migration litigation. Re-assigning a family to a reception centre in another language-area of Belgium has been held to violate the CRC, in particular articles 3 and 28.[65] Likewise, expulsion during the schooling period has been held to be in violation of art. 3 *juncto* 28

53 Labour Tribunal Antwerp 22 November 2004, 157–159.

54 For an attempt to operationalise the system such that only children would benefit from it, see Labour Tribunal Kortrijk 4 February 2004, *OCMW-visies* 2004, 73–77.

55 Labour Tribunal Brussels 19 May 2005, *JDJ* 2005, no. 246, 24–39.

56 Labour Tribunal Brussels 1 July 2010, vreemdelingenrecht.be.

57 Labour Tribunal Antwerp 5 January 2005, *Soc.Kron.* 2005, 176–177.

58 Labour Tribunal Brussels 29 October 2007, *JDJ* 2008, no. 275, 34–37.

59 Labour Court Ghent 24 June 2005, *Journal des tribunaux de travail* (hereafter *JTT*) 2005, 435–438.

60 Labour Court Antwerp 26 January 2005, *Soc.Kron.* 2005, 125–128.

61 Summary proceedings Labour Tribunal Charleroi 20 January 2012, *JDJ* 2012, no. 314, 40–41. This line of reasoning has been criticised.

62 Court of Arbitration 15 March 2006, no. 43/2006, B.5; Court of Arbitration 1 March 2006, no. 35/2006, B.4.

63 President Brussels 16 November 2005, *JDJ* 2006, no. 255, 49–52.

64 Tribunal of First Instance (Civil) Brussels 7 September 2009, unpublished.

65 Labour Tribunal Brussels 3 September 2007, *Soc.Kron.* 2010, 101–105.

CRC.[66] Judges have ordered that a minor had to be offered a temporary residence permit until he finished suitable training[67]; alternatively, they suspended the removal order to guarantee continuity in schooling.[68] Other judges have argued, however, that responsibility for any threat to the continuity of education due to expulsion is to be attributed exclusively to the parents, who refuse to leave the country.[69]

Prohibiting minors from participating in sports competitions on account of their illegal status was held to be in violation of the Constitution's non-discrimination provisions, which were said to apply as well to the rights guaranteed in the CRC, particularly articles 28, 29 and 31.[70]

Where the CRC has proven less powerful has been in challenging the deprivation of liberty of non-accompanied foreign minors. Some judges maintained that this practice is not prohibited as such by article 37 of the CRC, provided that any deprivation of such children's liberty remains an ultimate measure, is for the shortest period possible, and has taken the child's best interests into account.[71]

However, the detention of children in an *adult* reception centre has been held to violate articles 3 and 37 of CRC (as well as 3 and 8 ECHR) because the housing and living conditions were deemed wholly inadequate for children's well-being and development.[72] Other judges have argued that when parents are detained with a view to their being expelled, the children who accompany them are not themselves deprived of liberty; indeed, the rather cynical argument went, according to articles 3, 9 and 10 of the CRC the state was not allowed to separate them from their parents and was thus obliged to ensure their residence in these closed reception centres.[73]

The federal legislator and migration authorities have been reminded that the requirements to give children the opportunity to express their views and have their best interests taken into account cannot be ignored or denied, even if these requirements are not explicitly provided for in the migration bill.[74]

3.2.2 Affiliation

In family law, the CRC, and in particular the best interests provision, has played a significant role in litigation on paternal affiliation. The establishment of paternal affiliation tends to be considered as in the best interests of the child.[75]

---

66 President Brussels 7 December 2004, unpublished.

67 Tribunal of First Instance (Civil) Brussels 7 September 2009, unpublished.

68 Summary proceedings Bruges 28 March 2007, *T.Vreemd.* 2007, 212–214.

69 Court of Appeal Ghent 21 June 2007, unpublished.

70 Court of Appeal Mons 16 December 2009, vreemdelingenrecht.be.

71 Investigation Chamber Brussels 6 October 2005, *T.Vreemd.* 2006, 40.

72 Council Chamber Liège 22 February 2007, *JDJ* 2007, no. 263, 41.

73 Investigation Chamber Brussels 13 August 2007, unpublished.

74 Constitutional Court 18 July 2013, no. 106/2013.

75 Tribunal of First Instance (Civil) Brussels 15 February 2011, unpublished.

With regard to genetic testing to establish who the biological father is, it has been held that physical integrity (invoked to bar genetic testing) has to be balanced with the right of the child to know his or her parents and to be raised by them; the interests of the child thereby prevail (art. 7 CRC).[76] Likewise, the right to know one's parents was considered more important than the fact that the alleged biological father had a criminal record (including for sex offences). The latter was not considered serious enough to be overtly inimical to the child's best interests, and hence the request to establish paternal affiliation could not be refused.[77] Furthermore, in view of the right to have one's full identity established as soon as possible after birth, it was ordered with regard to a child that had been left behind, to include place and date of birth as fundamental elements of identity in the birth registration system.[78]

The Constitutional Court has made it clear that in the various procedures for establishing paternal affiliation, judicial supervision of the best interests of the child must be possible, thereby entailing that the child's views and interests can be taken into account by a judge.[79]

Cases on parental authority also drew heavily on the best interests of the child as per article 3 of the CRC: alimony arrangements[80] or forced contacts between father and child[81] were held to be contrary to the best interests of the child by civil (juvenile) courts. Penal judges who dealt with the crime of non-observance of contact arrangements (*niet-afgifte kind, non-représentation d'enfants*) sometimes argued that article 3 of the CRC does not prevent forced contacts rights with a parent, as it in the best interests of the child to develop an emotional bond with both parents[82]; others held that this article is not directly applicable in such cases.[83] However, if an applicant shows an affective bond with a child but that bond is not or no longer mutual, the juvenile court cannot automatically deny contact rights: it has to examine whether granting the right to personal contact is in the best interests of the child.[84]

Still in regard to issues of parental authority, the best-interests principle has also been used to deal with the dispensation of the minimum age limit for marriage[85] and to establish the procedure to follow in order to have the main place of residence of children be given to the grandparents.[86] In an exceptional instance,

---

[76] Court of Appeal Brussels 22 December 2008, *JLMB* 2009, 1074–1080.

[77] Tribunal of First Instance (Civil) Liège 16 May 2008, *RTDF* 2009, 214–216.

[78] Court of Appeal Brussels 28 March 2006, *JLMB* 2007, 513–516.

[79] Constitutional Court 9 August 2012, no. 103/201; 23 May 2012, no. 2012/61; 16 December 2010, no. 2010/144; 14 May 2003, no. 66/2003, B.4.3–B8.

[80] Court of Appeal Ghent 1 March 2004, *RechtspraakAntwerpen, Brussel, Gent* 2004, 1233–1236.

[81] Court of Appeal Ghent 20 June 2005, *TJK* 2007, 35–36.

[82] Tribunal of First Instance (Criminal) Brussels 30 June 2011.

[83] Court of Cassation 4 March 2008.

[84] Court of Cassation 16 January 2009 (personal contact).

[85] Youth Tribunal Antwerp 13 February 2004, *Revue générale de droit civilbelge*2006, 480–482.

[86] Court of Appeal Brussels 2 March 2009, *TJK* 2009, 339–344.

the judge relied on article 12 of the CRC to ensure that the views of the child were taken into account in residential arrangements.[87]

The particular relevance of the CRC (inter alia, art. 21) to adoption has been acknowledged, and article 8 of the ECHR has to be read in the light of the CRC.[88] In one matter, a man who had formerly been in a stable relationship with a woman was allowed to adopt their biological child on the grounds that it was in the child's best interests[89]; in another, an adoption which the intended mother sought for the purpose of concealing commercial surrogacy was found in violation of children's rights, in particular article 35 of the CRC and articles 1–3 of the OPSC.[90] It was held that not granting an adoption allowance in the case of kafala (that is, the practice under Islamic law of taking care of a child who has been left behind) does not contravene article 20 of the CRC, given the fundamental differences between *kafala* and adoption.[91]

3.2.3 Juvenile Justice

The CRC has not been relied upon very often in juvenile justice matters. A contentious matter remains the possibility of trying minors older than 16 years in adult courts under the procedure of *uithandengeving* or *dessaisisement*, one whereby the judge in the juvenile court hands over the minor to an adult criminal court. The CRC Committee has asked Belgium to eliminate this procedure.[92] The right to appeal as guaranteed in article 40(2)(b)(v) of the CRC has been held not to be applicable because of the reservation made by Belgium. In instances in which a judge has been willing to make a substantive assessment, he or she has not found a violation: article 3 of the CRC does not prevent judges in the adult courts from (re)qualifying the facts after a minor has been handed over to them.[93] Neither article 37 nor 40 of the CRC is believed to impose an obligation on the judge who deals with the deprivation of liberty of a minor to examine the precise detention situation of the minor.[94] The Constitutional Court has given more transformative power to the CRC in some of its judgments on juvenile justice matters (see section 4).

---

87 Court of Appeal Brussels 17 November 2008, *RW* 2011–12, 1852–1857.

88 Court of Cassation 30 September 2011.

89 Youth Tribunal Antwerp 29 April 2003, *NJW* 2003, 1376–1377.

90 Court of Appeal Ghent 30 April 2012, *TJK* 2012, 261–263.

91 Constitutional Court 19 June 2013, no. 92/2013, B.5.2.

92 CRC Committee (2010). Concluding Observations Belgium of 18 June 2010, UN Doc. CRC/C/BEL/CO/3-4, para. 83(a).

93 Court of Cassation 31 October 2006.

94 Court of Cassation 22 March 2005.

3.2.4 Social Security

Social security arrangements have been held to be in violation of the CRC. In Belgium, guaranteed family benefits (*gewaarborgde gezinsbijslag, prestations familiales garanties*) have been established under a residual, non-contributory regime for those with a sufficient link with Belgium. However, although there were some exceptions to this, it was not enough that a foreign applicant's child be of Belgian nationality and resident in the country; to be eligible, the applicant also had to prove 5 years of actual and uninterrupted residence in Belgium. This was considered disproportionate to the objective being pursued, namely to expand the residual regime where prospective beneficiaries had a sufficient link with the Belgian state. The Constitutional Court explicitly used the CRC to develop an a fortiori argument to its constitutional non-discrimination analysis.[95] Contrariwise, similar legislation with regard to a *non-Belgian* child was held not to be in violation of the CRC.[96]

The CRC was also believed to reinforce the finding of constitutional discrimination in a case challenging the differential treatment of fully unemployed persons, some of whom were entitled to unemployment benefits while others were not. The children of the former were entitled to a higher level of child benefits than those of the latter. Here again, the Constitutional Court pointed out in particular that article 2 of the CRC also prohibits unequal treatment on the basis of the status of children's parents.[97] In a number of other constitutional cases on child benefits and equal treatment, the CRC did not play a role.

4 Notable Cases

A cross-section of notable cases will show how the CRC has helped to facilitate legal reform. These cases were heard by different judicial bodies, relate to different legal fields, and draw on diverse CRC provisions, but a commonality underlying them is that the CRC tended to function as a set of meta-norms enabling the judicial bodies to go beyond existing domestic legislation or challenge problematic legislative arrangements.

The Constitutional Court has used article 3 of the CRC in a series of judgments relating to paternal affiliation to underline that judicial bodies need to be able to take the child's best interests into account. The Court held that a legislative arrangement according to which a judge can only marginally assess the best interests of the child and take them into account only if they are seriously damaged is

95 Constitutional Court 25 March 2009, no. 62/2009, B7.

96 Constitutional Court 21 February 2013, no. 12/2013.

97 Constitutional Court 30 October 2008, no. 145/2008, B.7.2.

in violation of article 22bis of the Belgian Constitution and article 3(1) of the CRC. In its view, both of these provisions necessitate that the best interests of the child should be prioritised even though they are not to be granted an absolute character.[98] Here, the Court broke with its earlier case law and, for the first time, emphasised the *prioritisation* of the child's best interests in any exercise of balancing of interests.

In the field of juvenile justice, the Constitutional Court has been unwilling to challenge the practice per se of trying minors in an adult court. It has argued, though, that when minors are handed over by a juvenile judge to a Court of Assize, the latter has to take into account the best interests of the child. In view of the specific nature of the administration of juvenile justice, a separate system of criminal administration of justice is required. With regard to the Court of Assize, this means that its composition needs to be adapted so that at least a majority of the bench of three has received special training in youth law and criminal law.[99]

Quite remarkably, the Constitutional Court relied less on the CRC than on general human rights treaties (namely, article 14(4) of the ICCPR and article 6 of the ECHR). Similarly, it relied heavily on the ICCPR and the ECHR, in addition to article 40(2)(b)(i) and (iv) of the CRC, in its ruling that in case of diversion, the requirement to give up the presumption of innocence in order to be eligible for a restorative justice procedure is unconstitutional.[100]

With respect to the right to education, the Constitutional Court has made it clear that the child's right to education prevails over the educational freedom of parents.[101] Historically, educational freedom has been strongly protected under Belgian constitutional law, as is reflected in article 24 of the Constitution. The Court has held that the freedom of choice of parents in the field of education is to be interpreted in such a way that it takes into account both the observance of compulsory education as well as, crucially, the best interests of the child and his or her fundamental right to education.[102] The parents' freedom of choice is therefore not absolute; the child's right to education may limit it.[103] Hence, the state can introduce control mechanisms for home schooling. Likewise, it can impose final objectives, basic skills and development targets on all educational institutions that receive subsidies—though not on home schooling[104]—without violating constitutional provisions, article 28 of the CRC or article 13(3) of the International Covenant on Economic, Social and Cultural Rights.[105]

---

[98] Constitutional Court 7 March 2013, no. 30/2013, B.10–B11.

[99] Constitutional Court 22 December 2010, no. 154/2010, B.10–B.12; Constitutional Court 13 March 2008, no. 49/2008, B.30.7.

[100] Constitutional Court 13 March 2008, no. 50/2008, in particular B.15.6–B.15.18.

[101] Constitutional Court 29 October 2009, no. 168/2009, B.5.2 and B.6.2 and following.

[102] Constitutional Court 11 March 2009, no. 50/2009, B.16.2.

[103] Ibid., B.17.2.

[104] Constitutional Court 29 October 2009, no. 168/2009, B.10.1–10.2.

[105] Court of Arbitration 18 February 1998, no. 19/98, B.11.1.

In the field of migration, the Court of Arbitration handed down a landmark judgment in 2003 concerning the treatment of undocumented children. It found that the governmental objective of abstaining from measures that would encourage illegal adult residents to stay on in the country (an objective which was meant to be served by restricting social assistance to urgent medical care) could not justify denying social assistance to a child entirely and under all circumstances if that denial would force the child to live in conditions detrimental to his or her health and development. The Court drew explicitly and elaborately on articles 2, 3, 24(1), 26 and 27 of the CRC. It held in particular that the state had the obligation to guarantee that children are protected from discrimination based on the status of their parents. The judgment was a watershed development in entitling undocumented children to full social assistance as a matter of principle.

5 Conclusion

Since it entered into force in Belgium, the CRC and its provisions have been invoked in about 250–300 published or publicly available judicial decisions and judgments. Although this might seem a significant figure, not all of these cases engaged with the CRC in a meaningful way. A major obstacle in Belgian doctrine is the denial—in particular by some of the higher courts—of direct effect to various CRC provisions, with the result that this often precludes substantive analysis of a matter in relation to the CRC. Denial of direct effect does not necessarily render a CRC provision irrelevant, given that it might be accepted as having an interpretative or 'standstill' minimum-threshold function. Nonetheless, the recognition of direct effect allows a party to a case to invoke the CRC directly in the absence of comparable domestic legal provisions, thus giving the CRC provisions greater strength.

In cases in which the direct effect of CRC provisions was accepted, or in which that question is considered irrelevant (i.e. in the case law of the Constitutional Court), the CRC has sometimes played a gap-filling role in the absence of domestic legislation. For example, prior to the introduction of legal measures specifically on the right of children to express their opinions, tribunals and courts often used article 12 of the CRC in order to hear children in court proceedings (Senaeve and Arnoeyts 2004: 141–143).

In performing this gap-filling role, the CRC also served to raise awareness about the need for legislation which could both clarify modalities and complete the implementation of article 12 in the domestic legal order (Poelemans 1997: 57–58). Some judicial bodies have used the CRC, in particular article 12, to trigger new legal developments, doing so by allowing children to intervene voluntarily in proceedings that concerned them and thereby granting them standing.

Among the supreme courts in Belgium, the Constitutional Court, liberated from the doctrine of direct effect, has engaged the most actively and substantively with the CRC provisions. The CRC has been instrumental in annulling migration legislation with regard to social assistance for undocumented children. It has likewise helped lower courts and tribunals refrain from applying restrictive legislation in that area. Here, the CRC has played a strong corrective role towards the legislator and a legitimising one towards judicial bodies.

Nevertheless, judges tend to resort to open concepts such as non-discrimination[106] and best interests. The CRC provisions dealing with more specific rights have been used rather rarely, albeit that there are exceptions to this trend (namely, articles 12, 26–27, and 28). Moreover, judicial bodies seem to prefer constitutional norms, general principles in the domestic legal order (in particular the best interests of the child principle), or the ECHR over the CRC as their main reference norms. In that sense, the CRC often plays a subsidiary role in the absence of domestic or ECHR provisions; when the latter are available, they are often more specific or have been interpreted and developed by the European Court of Human Rights.

In sum, it is important to remember that the CRC is not the only legal reference text on children's rights. At the same time, the full potential of the CRC and the interpretative work of the CRC Committee has not yet been fully capitalised upon by Belgian judicial bodies.

References

Alen, A., & Pas, W. (1996). The UN convention on the rights of the child's self-executing character. In E. Verhellen (Ed.), *Monitoring children's rights* (pp. 165–186). Den Haag: Martinus Nijhoff.

Cassese, A. (2001). *International law*. Oxford: Oxford University Press.

Claes, E., & Vandaele, A. (2001). L'effet direct des traités internationaux. Une analyse en droit positif et en théorie du droit axée sur les droits de l'homme. *Revue belge de droit International, 36*(2), 411–491.

Lemmens, P. (2008). De rechten van het kind als grondrechten in de Belgische rechtsorde. In W. Vandenhole (Ed.), *Kinderrechten in België* (pp. 37–58). Antwerp: Intersentia.

Poelemans, B. (1997). Het hoorrecht van minderjarigen. In P. Senaeve & W. Pintens (Eds.), *De hervorming van de echtscheidingsprocedure en het hoorrecht van minderjarigen. Commentaar op de wetten van 30 juni 1994, 27 december 1994 en 20 mei 1997* (pp. 53–123). Antwerpen/Apeldoorn: Maklu.

Robert, T. (2006). De burgerrechtelijke procesbekwaamheid van de minderjarige. In CBR (Ed.), *De procesbekwaamheid van minderjarigen* (pp. 37–73). Antwerp: Intersentia.

Scheinin, M. (1994). Direct applicability of economic, social and cultural rights: A critique of the doctrine of self-executing treaties. In K. Drzewicki, C. Krause, & A. Rosas (Eds.), *Social rights as human rights: A European challenge* (pp. 75–78). Åbo: Åbo Akademi University.

Senaeve, P., & Sara Arnoeyts, S. (2004). Tien jaar belgische rechtspraak inzake de Aanwending van het Ivrk. In P. Lemmens & P. Senaeve (Eds.), *De betekenis van de mensenrechten voor het personen- en familierecht*. Antwerp: Intersentia.

[106] The distinctive characteristic of art. 2 CRC—that it also prohibits discrimination on the basis of the status of the parents—has been used in particular in migration cases where the irregular status of the parents was at stake.

Swennen, F., & Caluwé, N. (2006). De (vorderings)rechten van het Openbaar Ministerie in burgerlijke zaken. In CBR (Ed.), *De procesbekwaamheid van minderjarigen* (pp. 75–101). Antwerp: Intersentia.

Veny, L. M., & De Vos, N. (2006). Procesbekwaamheid van minderjarigen in bestuurlijke (beroeps) procedures. In CBR (Ed.), *De procesbekwaamheid van minderjarigen* (pp. 103–162). Antwerp: Intersentia.

Chapter 8
France

Meda Couzens

Abstract This chapter provides a brief account of the application of the Convention on the Rights of the Child (CRC) by the French courts. It identifies the direct application of the CRC as a central aspect of the courts' jurisprudence, and explores the position of the judicial and administrative courts in this regard. A notable feature of the courts' application of the CRC is the frequent use of the principle of the best interests of the child. Selected decisions of the Constitutional Council illustrate the shortcomings of not having explicit constitutional protection for children's rights and of not utilising the CRC in controlling the constitutionality of laws. A discussion of secret or anonymous births highlights the complex interaction between the CRC and the French legal system.

1 Introduction

This chapter outlines how the CRC is applied by the Court of Cassation and the Council of State, the two supreme courts of France. They exercise judicial control over the CRC's application by the lower courts and thus have the final word in this regard. Brief attention is also given to the Constitutional Council; although it is not part of the judicial system, describing some of its child-related decisions helps to paint a fuller picture of how the CRC operates in France.

The analysis that follows is limited to decisions where the courts engaged with the CRC, and does not include cases in which the courts could have engaged with the CRC but did not. The chapter begins with an introduction to the French legal system, followed by an overview of children's rights and the CRC in France. Sections 4 and 5 discuss the jurisprudence of the Court of Cassation and Council of State, while Sect. 6 deals with that of the Constitutional Council. Section 7 examines *accouchement sous X* (secret or anonymous birth) to illustrate the CRC's complex interaction with the French legal system.

M. Couzens (✉)
University of KwaZulu-Natal, Durban, South Africa
e-mail: couzensm@ukzn.ac.za

T. Liefaard and J.E. Doek (eds.), *Litigating the Rights of the Child*,
DOI 10.1007/978-94-017-9445-9_8

2 Introduction to the French Legal System

France is a civil law country where the judicial system is divided into two main branches: the judicial jurisdiction, the apex of which is the Court of Cassation (*Cour de cassation*), and the administrative jurisdiction, the apex of which is the Council of State (*Conseil d'Etat*).

Only the Constitutional Council may decide on the constitutionality of laws (Constantinesco and Stéphane Pierré-Caps 2010). It functions outside the court system and cannot be approached directly by interested parties. Traditionally, the Council engaged only in *a priori* control of constitutionality, but the constitutional law of 23 July 2008 (effective 1 March 2010) introduced the possibility for litigants to raise a '*question prioritaire de constitutionalité*' (QPC) during litigation, in which they may challenge the compatibility of statutes with the constitutional provisions protecting human rights and freedoms (article 61(1) of the 1958 Constitution).[1] Such a question is then referred to the Constitutional Council by the relevant court.

France is a monist state, and therefore international treaties may be applied directly. They do not supersede constitutional norms, but enjoy supra-legislative status (article 55 of the 1958 Constitution). A treaty is directly applicable if it has been ratified by France and published in the *Journal officiel*, and if it creates individual rights rather than imposing obligations on the state. The rights created by the treaty must have a sufficiently clear content that further national legislation is not necessary for their application (Monéger 2006). If the international treaty is formulated too generally, is vague or conditional, or if the relevant treaty contains only recommendations or directives to the state, the direct application is decided on an article-by-article basis by analysing the content of the articles concerned (Zani 2008).

International treaties duly ratified form part of the rule of law and thus may provide the independent legal basis for the invalidation of administrative acts, even when the acts were performed according to national law (Rivero and Waline 2002).

3 Children's Rights and the CRC in France

The 1958 French Constitution does not contain child-specific rights.[2] Some child-relevant norms—such as the Preamble to the 1946 Constitution and the fundamental principles recognised by the national law—are included in a group of norms called '*bloc de constitutionnalité*' ('constitutional block') against which the Constitutional Council decides on the constitutionality of laws.[3]

The 1946 Preamble contains the only legal provisions with constitutional status which refer explicitly to children. It contains a commitment by the state to guarantee

[1] The cases and laws referred to in this chapter have been accessed from the online database *Le service public de la diffusion de droit* http://www.legifrance.gouv.fr/.

[2] In France a child is a person below the age of 18 (article 388 of the Civil code).

[3] See Constantinesco and Pierré-Caps 2010.

health services, material security, and rest and leisure to children amongst others (para. 11), as well as to guarantee equal access to education, professional training and culture to children and adults (para. 13). In addition, in its jurisprudence the Constitutional Council has recognised the specialised system of juvenile justice as one of the fundamental principles of the national law.[4]

Certain mechanisms exist to compensate for the absence of comprehensive constitutional protection for the rights of children, such as various statutes that deal with the legal protection of these rights (Bonfils and Gouttenoire 2008) and the fact that the CRC may be applied directly by courts and the administration. The CRC prevails over statutes, although not over constitutional provisions. The direct application by the courts, however, has been one of the most contentious issues in the jurisprudence of the French courts, as discussed below.

The CRC came into effect for France on 6 September 1990 (Bonfils and Gouttenoire 2008). France has not adopted a consolidated children's rights statute following the ratification of the CRC, but has taken a gradual approach to reforming national laws affecting children.

The Committee on the Rights of the Child considers French law largely compliant with the CRC, although the Committee (2009) has flagged a few areas of concern. These include: the low number of CRC provisions recognised by the courts as having direct effect (para. 11); the institution of *accouchement sous X* (anonymous birth), which in its view deprives the child of his or her rights (para. 43); and the fact that *kafala* is not taken into consideration for the purposes of family reunification (para. 90). The repressive tendencies in juvenile justice, discussed in Sect. 6 below, are also an area of concern for the Committee (para. 94).

Adjudication on children's rights and connected matters falls under the jurisdiction of both judicial and administrative courts. In the judicial courts, most of the civil and criminal cases pertaining to children are dealt with by specialised judges for children (*juges des enfants*) and judges assigned to deal with family law matters.

Much of the litigation concerning children in civil and administrative matters is initiated by parents. When administrative decisions with general impact are challenged, litigation has also been promoted by non-governmental organisations. In a 2014 decision, the Council of State decided that although, generally, an un-emancipated minor cannot approach an administrative court independently, in urgent situations, when fundamental rights may be infringed upon by a body exercising public power, an un-emancipated child has standing to seek the judicial review of an administrative decision.[5] In this particular case, the Council of State recognised standing to an unaccompanied Nigerian minor, who challenged the failure of an administrative body to comply with a judicial decision ordering that the child be provided with emergency accommodation as provided by the child protection legislation.[6] This ruling opens the opportunity for children to be recognised standing

[4] Decision 2002-461 of 29 August 2002.

[5] No. 375956 of 12 March 2014.

[6] No. 375956 of 12 March 2014 para. 3.

in a wide variety of cases where their rights are under threat from those entrusted with the exercise of public power. In child protection and family matters, the law allows children to approach the courts independently in certain cases,[7] and has generous rules regarding hearing the voice of the children concerned, even in matters where the children are not parties to the procedures.[8]

In January 2008 the National Conference of the Bars adopted the *Charte nationale de l'avocat d'enfant* (National Charter of the Advocate of the Child) which requires the creation of a group of lawyers specialised in representing children in each bar in the country. So far, 70 % of all bars have created such groups (Attias 2012). These offer legal services to children in criminal and civil matters, with the services being provided to children themselves rather than their parents or legal representatives (para. 2 of the Charter).

4 The Court of Cassation

The issue which marked the jurisprudence of the Court prior to May 2005 was its reluctance to apply the CRC directly. The tone was set in *Lejeune*, where the appellant argued that a lower court disregarded articles 1, 3, 9 and 12 of the CRC in that the court could not have decided what was in the best interests of the child without listening directly to him or her; the appellant was concerned that the position expressed by the child during interviews with the psychologist might have been influenced by the mother. The Court decided[9] that the CRC in its entirety was not directly applicable because it created obligations only for the state (and not individual rights). In a subsequent decision, the Court elaborated on its reasoning by stressing that the CRC cannot be applied directly because article 4 requires the intervention of the legislator.[10]

This jurisprudence has been widely criticised,[11] especially in the light of the position of the Council of State, which did not rule out the direct application of certain CRC articles. Concerned with the potentially destabilising effect of the direct application of the CRC on various areas of law, the Court decided to leave it mainly to the legislature to ensure compliance with the CRC (Bonnet 2010). In the process, it distorted the application of the established legal principles that govern the application of international conventions in the national legal order (Bonnet 2010; Bureau 2005; Monéger 2006).

A radical change occurred in May 2005, when in two decisions the Court applied directly the best interest of the child (article 3(1) of the CRC) and the right

[7] Article 375 Civil code, for example, provides that a child may request a children's court to take protective measures concerning him or her (*assistance educative*).

[8] Article 388-1 Civil code.

[9] No. 91-11.310 of 19 March 1993.

[10] No. 91-18735 of 15 July 1993.

[11] See the literature referred to by Monéger 2006.

to be heard in judicial and administrative proceedings (12(2)). In one case, the Court decided[12] that by not considering the request of a child to be listened to during litigation between parents regarding the child's residence, the lower court breached the two articles of the CRC above, read together with the relevant articles of the French law.[13]

The second case concerned a child born to a lesbian couple through artificial insemination. After separation, one of the partners changed her sex and recognised the paternity of the child. The recognition was contested by the mother of the child for being contrary to the biological reality. The case reached the Court, which indicated, *inter alia*, that although the court of appeal invalidated the recognition of paternity, it has nonetheless considered the best interests of the child and established visitation rights for the transsexual parent.[14]

A number of factors seem to have influenced the shift made by the Court in 2005, in its approach to the direct application of the CRC. A certain role was played by the desire to unify the approach of the judicial and administrative courts to the direct application of the CRC (Bureau 2005). The dominant factor, though, appears to have been the change of the Court's approach to article 4 of the CRC. The Court decided that the legal content of article 4 does not determine the legal nature of all the CRC provisions; and that while some articles create obligations for the state, others create individual rights which are not conditional on legislative intervention (ibid). Thus, the Court embarked on an article-by-article approach, similar with that embraced by the Council of State.

It is also possible that the jurisprudence of the Council had a persuasive effect on the Court, which realised at the same time that the feared cataclysmic effects did not materialise following the direct application of the CRC by the Council.

The sparsely-worded 2005 decisions and their implications are rather complex. No doubt they have had a positive impact on the courts' engagement with the CRC, but they have also raised concerns that the Court might have been either too conservative or too ambitious in its approach.

For example, the revolutionary character of the Court's direct application of article 12(2) of the CRC in case no. 02-20613 of 18 May 2005 (discussed above) was somewhat overshadowed by the fact that the courts already had an obligation established by statutes to listen to a child affected by court procedures. On the other hand, although it could have disposed of the matter by relying exclusively on the national law, the Court invoked the CRC *ex officio* and directly applied article 12(2) (Ancel 2011; Bureau 2005).

Furthermore, in the same decision, although article 12(2) of the CRC was the directly relevant provision, the Court also applied article 3(1) (Bureau 2005). The approach it took regarding the direct application of article 3(1) is surprising in that it departs from the Court's own jurisprudence pertaining to the direct application of

[12] No. 02-20613 of 18 May 2005.

[13] Articles 388-1 Civil code, and 338-1 and 338-2 Code of civil procedure.

[14] No. 02-16336 18 May 2005.

international conventions (Bureau 2005). Article 3(1) is not formulated as an individual right, and, as previously indicated, this is a point that would normally disqualify an international provision from being applied directly by the French courts. The Court, like the Council of State, did not question the nature of article 3(1) and simply decided to grant it direct effect. This suggests a Court intent on breaking with its old jurisprudence and keen to find a place for the CRC in its adjudication process.

Since 2005, the Court applied directly the right to know one's parents (article 7(1); no. 05-11285 of 7 April 2006, *Benjamin*); the right to preserve one's identity (article 8; no. 08-18871 of 6 January 2010); and the right to maintain regular contact with one's parents (article 9(3); no. 06-12687 of 22 May 2007). Notable is the decision in *Benjamin*, where the Court approached the CRC as a direct source of rights not explicitly recognised in the French law. In this case, the Court decided that the recognition by the father of a child born *sous X*,[15] prior to the child's birth, led to the establishment of the filiation with the father from the moment of the child's birth. Although French law does not explicitly recognise the right of a child to know his or her parents (Bonfils and Gouttenoire 2008), the Court, relying on article 7(1) of the CRC, decided that the child has the right to know the person who recognised him or her as his child and that the father has the right to consent or withhold consent to the adoption.

The Court's post-2005 jurisprudence is dominated by the application of article 3(1) (Ancel 2011). This is significant, especially considering that national law refers most often to 'the interest of the child' rather than to 'the best interests of the child' (ibid). The Court expects a consistent application of article 3(1) by the lower courts (Bonfils and Gouttenoire 2008), and sets aside decisions in matters concerning children where the lower courts have not inquired into the best interests of the child. For example, relying on article 3(1), the Court criticised a lower court for deciding that children with double nationality—French and Luxembourg—residing in Luxembourg were to attend a francophone school in order to satisfy the interests of the father (i.e. being able to communicate with the children), but without inquiring into the best interests of the children themselves.[16] In another decision, the Court criticised the appeal court, which, deciding on contact between a child and his father, did not inquire into what was in the best interests of the child when expert evidence, although not flawless, revealed that the contact between the child and the father could destabilise the child.[17]

Some reservation was expressed about the potentially far-reaching effects of the use of article 3(1) to challenge family law, civil law and even private international law provisions (Bureau 2005). Bonfils and Gouttenoire (2008) warned that using the best interests of the child to invalidate laws may lead to legal chaos since this principle is best suited for application in individual cases. Although article 3(1)

---

[15] *Accouchement sous X* is an old practice endorsed by the law, which allows the mother to keep the birth of her child as well as her identity secret. No filiation can be established between the mother (and her family) and the child.

[16] No. 02-18.360 of 8 November 2005.

[17] No. 06-12655 of 13 March 2007.

has been turned by the Court into a powerful legal tool, this did not result in the provision trumping all other legal norms whose application may lead to an outcome, which is less favourable to a child. This is reflected in decisions pertaining to *kafala* children and the registration of birth documents of children born through surrogacy, as briefly discussed below.

Article 370-3 of the Civil code prohibits the adoption of a child whose national law does not allow an adoption. When children whose national law prohibits adoption are placed by foreign courts in *kafala*[18] with French parents, these parents find it impossible to adopt the children. This may affect the parents' ability to bring the children to live with them in France, since, with some exceptions, the law allows family reunification only with biological or adopted children (Monéger 2006). Nevertheless, the Court decided that French adoption law is not contrary to article 3(1) of the CRC because article 20(3) of the same Convention explicitly recognises *kafala* as a means to secure the best interests of the child.[19]

In relation to surrogacy, according to article 16-7 read with article 16-9 of the Civil code, all surrogacy agreements are void for being contrary to the public order. French residents, however, travel overseas and enter surrogacy agreements, which raises challenges as to the legal status of the children so born. Some courts have refused to authorise the registration into the French official registers of children born through surrogacy, a position endorsed by the Court. In a recent case, it was argued that 'by refusing to take into consideration the interest of the child and to inquire, as it ought to, into whether the refusal to register the act of birth in the French civil register … would result in a breach of the best interest of the child, the court of appeal violated, by refusing to apply [it], article 3–1 of the international Convention on the rights of the child …'.[20] The applicant argued for an *in concreto* application of the best interests of the child, requesting the Court to enquire and establish what is in the best interests of the individual child concerned in the dispute. The Court rejected these arguments, stating that a legal norm of public order cannot be superseded by article 3(1) of the CRC. It is very likely that this jurisprudence will be re-evaluated in light of two very recent ECtHR decisions, in which the French law that prohibits the legal recognition of the parent-child relationship between the child born to a surrogate mother and the French commissioning parents was found to be inconsistent with children's rights to private life, as protected by article 8 of the ECHR.[21] The legal uncertainty created by the failure of the law to recognise such parent-child relationships raised concerns about the compatibility of the law with children's best interests. When one of the

[18] An institution of Islamic law which allows for the care of a child to be transferred to another person without creating a filiation link (Ancel 2011).

[19] No. 08-11033 of 25 February 2009; no. 09-10439 of 15 December 2010.

[20] No. 12-18315 of 13 September 2013; translation by MC.

[21] *Mennesson v. France* (Application no. 65192/11) of 26 June 2014; *Labassee v. France* (Application no. 65941/11) of 26 June 2014, It is of great significance for the rights of children that the Court found no violation of the commissioning parents' rights under article 8 of the ECtHR, but instead decided that children's article 8 rights were infringed upon by France.

commissioning parents was also the biological parent of the child born through surrogacy, France overstepped the acceptable margin of appreciation, and was in breach of article 8 of the ECtHR, by preventing the recognition and the establishment of a legal tie between the child and the biological parent.

5 The Council of State

Unlike the Court of Cassation, the Council engaged from the start with the direct application of the CRC on an article-by-article basis. The Council stayed clear of the 'political-legal controversy surrounding the direct effect' of the CRC in the national law (Bonnet 2010; translation by MC). It strictly applied the standard legal principles pertaining to the application of international law, without questioning the impact of the CRC on areas of law concerning children (ibid).

In 1995 the Council found no violation of a child's right to privacy (article 16) in the refusal of an administrative body to issue a residence permit for the applicant.[22] Since then, it has applied directly various other provisions. In 1997 the Council decided that article 3(1) of the CRC can be relied on to invalidate an individual administrative decision.[23] It set aside a decision denying a residence permit to a Turkish child brought into France illegally by his mother, who was residing legally in France. The Council decided that despite the illegal entry of the child, a separation of the child from the mother in the circumstances (the father was unknown and the child had no family members able to receive him in Turkey), even on a temporary basis, was contrary to article 3(1) of the CRC. This decision brought the jurisprudence of the Council into direct conflict with that of the Court of Cassation at the time, as seen above.

Articles 2(1) (the right to equal protection), 7(1)[24] and 10 (rights pertaining to family reunification)[25] have also been applied directly by the Council. After initial reluctance,[26] article 12(2) was also found to be of direct application.[27]

The Council of State also decided that a significant number of articles are not of direct application because they create obligations for the state rather than individual rights. These provisions include articles 2(2), 18, 20, 28 and 29 (Meininger-Bothorel 2007); 3(2) (no. 291561 of 27 June 2008; no. 293785 of 31 October 2008) and 3(3) (no. 293785 of 31 October 2008); 8 (no. 155096 of 1 April 1998); 9 (no. 143866 of 29 July 1994; no. 240238 and 240239 of 21 June 2002); 12 and 14(1) (no. 140872 of 3 July 1996);[28] and 24(1), 26(1) and 27(1) (no. 163043 of 23 April 1997 *Groupe d'information et de soutien des travailleurs immigrés (GISTI)*).

---

[22] No. 12-18315 of 13 September 2013; translation by MC.

[23] No. 161364 of 22 September 1997 (*Cinar*).

[24] No. 300721 of 8 April 2009.

[25] No. 155096 of 1 April 1998.

[26] No. 140872 of 3 July 1996.

[27] No. 291561 of 27 June 2008.

[28] Later, the Council decided that art. 12(2) can be applied directly. See above.

A positive aspect of the administrative jurisprudence is that the CRC is relied on for invalidating administrative decisions affecting individuals as well as for controlling the legality of administrative decisions with normative value (Gouttenoire 2012). In 1997 the Council declared that articles which are not of direct application cannot be invoked against administrative decisions concerning individuals or against administrative decisions of general application (such as a ministerial decree). In *GISTI* above, the applicants requested the invalidation of a government decree that made access to social security conditional on proof of legal residence in the French territory. The applicants invoked, amongst others, articles 24(1) (the right to the highest attainable standard of health), 26(1) (the right to benefit from social security) and 27(1) (the right to an adequate standard of living) of the CRC. The Council refused to apply these articles, indicating that they do not produce effects regarding individuals, and as a consequence cannot be invoked as a basis for the invalidation of a decision concerning individuals or of a decision with general effect.

This position has been criticised by French writers. Gouttenoire (2012) argues that while it is necessary for the norms applied to control decisions affecting individuals to create individual rights, the same is not applicable if the CRC norms are used to control the legality of normative decisions. The simple fact that some CRC provisions do not create individual rights does not mean that they have no coercive power (Bonnet 2010). To decide otherwise would deprive duly ratified international conventions of their role as sources of law in the national legal order, a position that contravenes article 55 of the 1958 Constitution (ibid).

On a positive note, article 3(1) seems to have gathered momentum in the jurisprudence of the Council. An interesting decision rendered in 2011 pertains to two children suspected to have been born as a result of a surrogacy agreement between a French national (the father) and an Indian mother residing in India.[29] A request addressed by the father to the French Embassy in India, for the issuing of travel documents for the two children, was rejected because the French authorities suspected that the children had been born as a result of surrogacy. The ensuing litigation reached the Council, which applied article 3(1) of the CRC to conclude that, despite the agreement between the Indian mother and French father being potentially invalid, the administration remained bound to give primary consideration to the best interests of the children concerned.[30]

This puts the position of the Council at odds with that of the Court of Cassation, whose view is that it cannot be in children's best interests to be born to surrogate mothers (Gouttenoire 2012). Thus, in issues of surrogacy, the Court favours an abstract application of the best interests of the child, whereas the Council prefers an *in concreto* application that responds to the needs of the individual children concerned (ibid).

As in *Cinar*, the Council showed concern for children whose legal status is tainted by some form of illegality for which the parents may be responsible. Using

[29] No. 348778 of 4 May 2011.

[30] The Council pointed out, however, that the decisions pertaining to the registration of birth in France and the recognition of French nationality for the concerned children falls under the jurisdiction of judicial courts.

the principle of the best interests of the child, it asserted the independence of the rights of children, which should be considered, where appropriate, independently of the connected rights or the faults of their parents. Unfortunately, this approach is not applied consistently. For example, in some cases pertaining to the deportation of parents (but not their children) the Council inquires very little into the best interests of the affected children. There is no comprehensive discussion of the impact on the children of the removal of their parents from the country where the parents reside illegally,[31] nor is there evidence of an inquiry into the effect on the children of an immigration decision pertaining to the parent. No separate legal representation is provided for the affected children;[32] no indication exists either that children are given an opportunity to be heard at any stage in the process. Despite the Council's recitals of the provisions of article 3(1), the article cannot be applied effectively in the absence of sufficient information about what is in the best interests of the affected children.

A trend in the administrative jurisprudence seems to be that article 3(1) is applied to protect the substance of other CRC provisions, notably those which have not yet been declared as having direct application. In immigration decisions with an impact on the child's family life, the Council applies article 3(1) but protects the substance of provisions whose direct application has been previously rejected (Monéger 1998).[33] In 2006 (*L'Association Aides* above), the Council adjudicated on a statute that made access to state medical care by illegal immigrants (both children and adults) conditional on three months' uninterrupted residence in France, declaring that it and the decrees which implemented it were incompatible with the CRC. The effect of the decrees was that, prior to fulfilling the residence requirement, children living in France illegally could have access only to emergency medical care. This disregarded articles 3(1) and 1, which require that the state not limit children's access to medical services that are necessary to protect their health.

Thus, although the Council claimed to be applying article 3(1), it actually gave effect to article 24 (Gay 2006), which in the past had been declared not directly applicable. Reluctant to reconsider its earlier jurisprudence on article 24, and, more generally, its approach to the application of international socio-economic rights instruments (Gay 2006), the Council took shelter under its uncontroversial application of article 3(1).

Although the application of article 3(1) in cases such as these might obscure some CRC rights, certain rights benefit from their association with the article, in that they have been recognised as having direct effect even though they would not

[31] In decisions no. 258031 of 24 March 2004 and 248478 of 28 February 2003, where article 3(1) was applied, most of the aspects relied on by the Council related to the situation of the defaulting parent rather that to the situation of the children.

[32] Article L7 of the Code of administrative justice does provide that a public rapporteur (who is a member of the administrative jurisdiction) presents an independent view on the matter and the solutions which it requires.

[33] The author mentions articles 9 and 10. In the meantime, the Council has declared article 10 as being of direct application.

be good candidates for direct application if they were regarded on their own. For example, in 2008 the Council invalidated a ministerial decree on solitary confinement to the extent that this regulation applied to children, maintaining that articles 3(1) and 37 (which contain rights pertaining to juvenile justice) require 'the adaptation of a detention regime of minors in all its aspects in order to respond to their age, and imposes on the administrative authority an obligation to give a primary consideration to the best interest of children in all the decisions which concern them'.[34] Because the decree did not offer sufficient guarantees in this respect, the Council invalidated the disputed provisions in as far as they applied to children.

Interestingly, in both *L'Association Aides* and *L'Observatoire* the Council of State invalidated the normative acts only to the extent of their application to children; moreover, in both it did so on the strength of article 3(1). Two important consequences arise from this. First, the rights of children must be considered independently, in the light of the special law which governs their protection, *in casu* the CRC. Second, normative acts that apply to children must respond to their specific needs in order to pass the control of legality. These are strong premises for developing a jurisprudence which would ensure that children do not fall between the cracks when general administrative decisions affecting them are challenged.

6 The Constitutional Council

As discussed in Sect. 3 above, the scope of constitutionality control on child-specific grounds is relatively limited. This is compounded both by the fact that the CRC does not enjoy constitutional status and by the Constitutional Council's reluctance to assess national law against international instruments. According to the Council, article 55 of the Constitution enables it to assess statutes against the Constitution but not against international treaties (Rivero and Waline 2002), and as a result the CRC does not feature in its jurisprudence. Arguably, the spirit of the CRC is nonetheless reflected in some of its decisions; by the same token, that spirit is conspicuously absent in others. A few examples illustrate these points.

In 2002 the Council ruled that a specialised system of juvenile justice (specialised courts applying special procedures) is one of the fundamental principles of the French law,[35] and thus forms part of the constitutional block, as defined in Sect. 3 above. The Council justified its position by referring to the consistency with which the principle was reflected in the French law. It made clear, however, that this was not an absolute principle but one which operates within strict boundaries (para. 26) that allow the legislature sufficient room to adopt more repressive legislation when it is deemed necessary (Darsonville 2012). Although France's

[34] No. 293785 of 31 October 2008 (*Section Francaise de l'Observatoire International des Prisons*); translation by MC.

[35] Decision 2002-461DC of 29 August 2002, para. 26.

legal tradition regarding juvenile justice has clearly influenced this development, the decision nevertheless results in an inconsistent approach to protecting children, which suggests that their special protection has constitutional value only in the context of juvenile justice.

One could speculate on the likelihood of the Council recognising the best interests of the child as one of the fundamental principles of the French law. The consolidation of the best-interests jurisprudence by both the Court of Cassation and Council of State, and the consistent reference to the interest of the child or the best interest of the child in the national law (Bonfils and Gouttenoire 2008), are factors to consider should such an argument be made before the Constitutional Council. A constitutional status for this cross-cutting principle would provide a unifying factor for the legal protection of children because of the principle's possible application in all matters concerning children, regardless of the area of law. This would dramatically extend the constitutional block and conceivably make the CRC an instrument the Council relies on for the interpretation of the Constitution.

The Council is, however, reluctant to extend this category of principles (Constantinesco and Pierré-Caps 2002). What is more, in view of its current approach to juvenile justice, the Council's child-centredness is open to question. In 2007 the Council found consistent with the fundamental principles on juvenile justice the provisions of a law which introduced minimum sentencing for juvenile offenders and provided the conditions under which certain categories of juvenile offenders may be subjected to criminal sanctions applicable to adults.[36] In 2011, a decision of the Council confirmed the constitutionality of a law creating new courts (correctional tribunals) for certain categories of child offenders.[37] Of the three judges who sit on these correctional tribunals, only the judge presiding is a judge specialised in juvenile justice. For some, this is a breach of the fundamental constitutional principle that children are to be dealt with by a specialised jurisdiction (Darsonville 2012). In 2011 the Council also decided that the fact that specialised judges cumulatively exercised the functions of instruction and adjudication resulted in a breach of the principle of impartiality and was thus unconstitutional.[38]

This cumulative exercise of functions—which had been one of the hallmarks of the French juvenile justice system—aimed to ensure that the judge had a good understanding of the child and hence could take the most effective measures to contribute to his or her re-education. In 2012 a law providing for speedy prosecution of juvenile offenders was declared constitutional (Decision 2012-272 QPC of 21 September 2012) even though such a procedure creates the risk that judges would have insufficient information about the personality of the child concerned to be able to impose measures suitable for his or her re-education. The limitations of the fundamental principle developed by the Council in 2002 are evident in these cases.

---

[36] Decision 2007-554 DC of 9 August 2007, paras. 22–26.

[37] Decision 2011-635 DC of 4 August 2011.

[38] Decision 2011-147 QPC of 8 July 2011.

As the Council does not assess laws against the CRC, situations may arise where laws declared consistent with the Constitution are declared inconsistent with the CRC by the judicial or administrative jurisdiction. This situation occurred in *L'Association Aides* above, where the Constitutional Council confirmed the constitutionality of legal provisions later found inconsistent with the CRC by the Council of State (Gay 2006). It is perhaps telling that although the Constitutional Council decided the matter on one of the few provisions with constitutional status explicitly mentioning children (para. 11 of the Preamble of the 1946 Constitution), at no point did it consider the situation of children independently, as a distinct category amongst those affected by the law (Gay 2006). Nevertheless, relying on article 3(1) of the CRC, the Council of State 'zoomed in' on children, recognising that they have different needs from other persons affected by the law and that the state has a special obligation to consider such needs when making decisions with general impact.

7 *Accouchement Sous X*: A Test for the CRC?

A brief discussion of this practice will illustrate the multitude of factors which potentially influence the application of the CRC in France. *Inter alia*, legal tradition, social practices, multiple national jurisdictions and the influence of the regional system of human rights protection make the application of the CRC in France a complex exercise.

Accouchement sous X (anonymous birth, birth in secret or birth by an unidentified person) is an old and controversial practice protected by law.[39] It allows a mother to require that her identity and act of having given birth be kept secret[40] and that her child be given up for adoption (Vasseur-Lambry 2012). The law recognises no filiation between the mother and the child or between the mother's family and the child.

This is problematic under article 7 of the CRC (the child's right to know his or her parents), and raises issues pertaining to a potential conflict between this article and the mother's right to a private life. The Committee on the Rights of the Child (2009, para. 43) found the practice contrary to the rights of children, but did not recommend its abolition. For the European Court of Human Rights, the practice does not exceed the boundaries of the state's margin of appreciation, and, so the Court held, there are sufficient guarantees that children can access information about their filiation on reaching the age of majority (*Odièvre,* para. 49).

---

[39] The institution was maintained by Law 2002-93 of 22 January 2002 on the access to information about personal origins by adopted persons and wards of the state (Monéger 2006).

[40] The mother has two possibilities: not to disclose her name (anonymous birth); or to disclose her name to the institution provided by the law, requesting that the name be kept secret, and disclosed only to the child on reaching the age of 18 (secret birth). See Vasseur-Lambry (2012). For a brief history of the practice, its reasons and its successive legal regulations, see *Odièvre v France* 13 February 2013 (Application no 42326/98) (*Odièvre)* paras. 15–18.

The Constitutional Council joined the debate in dealing with a QPC raised by an applicant who argued that creating a legislative framework which allows a woman to give birth anonymously, and makes the disclosure of information about the mother and her identity conditional on the mother's agreement, amounts to a violation of private and family life.[41] The Constitutional Council found no violation of constitutional norms. It reasoned that by preserving the confidentiality of the mother's identity and leaving medical expenses incurred during a birth *sous X* in the charge of the state, 'the legislator intended to avoid pregnancies and births susceptible of creating a danger for the health of both the mother and the child, and to prevent infanticide or child abandonment; [the legislator] also pursued the constitutional objective to protect [their] health' (para. 6; translation by MC). The Council deferred to the legislature for achieving a balance between the interests of the mother and those of the child (para. 8).

Predictably, the Constitutional Council did not refer to the CRC in its decision. The intricacies of births *sous X* came face to face with the CRC instead in the *Benjamin* case, discussed in Sect. 4 above. The direct application of article 7(1) of the CRC in that case resulted in the filiation with the father being established, whilst the maternal filiation remained unknown. Arguably, this approach provides a truncated compliance with article 7 of the CRC by allowing the child to establish filiation with only one of the parents. In defence of the *status quo*, however, it was argued that article 7(1) of the CRC contains an internal limitation, in that the right to know and be raised by one's parents is guaranteed only 'as far as possible'; the mother's desire not to have a relationship with the child creates an impossibility of fulfilling article 7 rights in relation to the mother (Vasseur-Lambry 2012).

Although the CRC did not emerge unscathed from such a complex network of jurisdictions and legal instruments, its application in this delicate and controversial legal issue shows its versatility as a legal instrument. While the ECtHR and the Constitutional Council deferred to the state, the reliance of the Court of Cassation on article 7(1) of the CRC enabled the Court to secure an opportunity for child to establish, however partially, his or her biological origins.

8 Conclusion

The discussion above indicates that French courts are conversant with the application of the CRC, and currently both supreme jurisdictions apply directly certain of its provisions. The number of provisions so applied is not high, but the jurisprudence is evolving and seemingly in a positive direction. Significantly, the Court of Cassation has used the CRC as a direct source of rights that are not otherwise explicitly protected in the French law. The courts, however, seldom find national law inconsistent with the CRC, and the position of the Council of State—that the CRC norms applied to control the legality of administrative normative acts be of direct application—is too restrictive.

[41] Decision 2012-248 QPC of 16 May 2012 para. 3.

The jurisprudence of the two supreme courts is dominated by the application of article 3(1) of the CRC. The direct application of this article by the courts, although surprising, has set the French courts on the same path as that of the Committee on the Rights of the Child (General Comment No 14 of 2013)—namely, approaching this article as a direct source of legal entitlements and obligations. Significant, too, is the fact that the use of article 3(1) has secured a child-centred outcome when reliance on other legal instruments such as the Constitution or the European Convention on Human Rights and Fundamental Freedoms has failed to do so.

There are concerns, though, that over-reliance on article 3(1) will lead to the jurisprudential underdevelopment of other CRC rights (Gouttenoire 2012), a prospect that in turn may have a negative impact on the recognition of direct effect to certain CRC provisions. With the jurisprudence of the Court of Cassation and Council of State having reciprocal persuasive effect,[42] it is desirable that the courts engage with all the CRC provisions relevant in specific disputes. This, it is hoped, will contribute to movement in the direction recommended by the Committee on the Rights of the Child—that of increasing the number of CRC provisions with direct effect.

Despite its direct application, the CRC was not able to mobilise radical legal change in controversial issues such as births under X or adoption of *kafala* children, nor could it secure a child-centred approach to the legal status of children born to surrogate mothers overseas. The CRC was also ineffective in stopping the legislative trend towards imposing a more severe criminal law regime on children in conflict with the law. Part of this weakness may come from the sub-constitutional status of the CRC, which does not give it sufficient clout to dislocate existing legal practices. This points to a need to explore ways to introduce the CRC into the Constitutional Council's jurisprudence, possibly by persuading the Council that the principle of the best interests of the child is now a fundamental principle recognised by the national law, or by encouraging the Council to make use of the CRC when interpreting the Constitution.

References

Ancel, J.-P. (2011). La Convention de New York relative aux droits de l'enfant devant la Cour de cassation. *Justice & Cassation*, 13–22.

Attias, D. (2012). Les nouveaux droits de l'enfant sont-ils compatibles avec sa protection et ne mettert-ils pas en danger l'authorite parentale? *Petites affiches, 50*, 51–53.

Bonfils, P., & Gouttenoire, A. (2008). *Droit des mineurs*. Paris: Editions Dalloz.

Bonnet, B. (2010). Le Conseil d'Etat et la Convention internationale des droits de l'enfant à l'heure du bilan: De l'art du pragmatism. *Dalloz, 17*, 1031–1037.

Bureau, D. (2005). De l'application directe en France de la Convention de New York du 26 janvier 1990 sur les droits de l'enfant. *Revue critique de droit international privé,* 679–697.

[42] For example, the Court followed on the steps of the Council in embracing an article-by-article approach to the direct application of the CRC. The Council followed the Court in directly applying article 12(2) of the CRC.

Commission Droit des Mineurs de la Conférence des Bâtonniers. (2008). Charte nationale de l'avocat d'enfant. http://www.barreau-bordeaux.avocat.fr/article.php?idr=92&idssr=113&ida=139&PHPSESSID=aa3756dbd6b85dae3c12aa99c0308d18#paragraphe_1. Accessed 22 June 2013.
Committee on the Rights of the Child. (2009). Concluding observations of the Committee on the rights of the child: France CRC/C/FRA/CO/4. http://www2.ohchr.org/english/bodies/crc/docs/co/CRC-C-FRA-CO-4.pdf. Accessed 23 June 2013.
Constantinesco, V., & Stéphane Pierré-Caps, S. (2010). *Droit constitutionnel français*. Paris: Presses Universitaires de France.
Darsonville, D. (2012). QPC du 21 septembre 2012: la poursuite de la désagrégation du droit pénal de mineurs. *Constitutions: droit constitutionnel appliqué*, *4*, 609–615.
Gay, L. (2006). L'affirmation d'un droit aux soins du mineur étranger ou l'inconventionnalité partielle d'une loi jugée conforme à la Constitution. *Revue de droit sanitaire et social, 11*(6), 1047–1059.
Gouttenoire, A. (2012). L'application de la Convention internationale des droits de l'enfant. *Petites affiches, 50*, 17–20.
Meininger-Bothorel, C. (2007). Les apports de la Convention international des droits de l'enfant. *Gazette du Palais* (18–20 November), 4–9.
Monéger, F. (1998). Le Conseil d'Etat met en avant l'intérêt supérieur de l'enfant contenu dans la Convention des Nations Unies sur les droits de l'enfant. *Revue de droit sanitaire et social, 3*(1), 174–180.
Monéger, F. (January 2006). Enfant (droits de l'). *Répertoire international Dalloz,* 1–13.
République Française. (2013). Le service public de la diffusion de droit. http://www.legifrance.gouv.fr/. Last accessed November 7, 2013.
Rivero, J., & Waline, J. (2002). *Droit administrative*. Paris: Dalloz.
Vasseur-Lambry, F. (2012). Les message troublants du juge de la filiation: L'accouchement sous X en question. *Pettites affiches, 137*, 13–17.
Zani, M. (2008). La mise on oeuvre de la Convention international des droits de l'enfant. *Revue de droit international de sciences diplomatiques et politiques, 86*(2), 195–219.

Chapter 9
Serbia

Strategic Litigation on the Rights of the Child in Serbia

Nevena Vučković Šahović and Ivana Savić

Abstract Serbia belongs to the civil law system, namely, its legal system does not recognize judgments of domestic courts as sources of law and does not treat them as precedents. Still, there are some avenues that can be used for strategic litigation, such as, for example, administrative decisions and recommendations of the National Human Rights Institutions. This article presents, describes and analyzes challenges and opportunities for the strategic litigation for the rights of the child in Serbia. It also presents some administrative decisions and judgments that were used to initiate social changes. The article deals with the legal understanding of the rights of the child in Serbia: it provides analysis of the main characteristics of the legal system, including analysis of the civil, criminal, administrative, constitutional protection mechanisms and their procedural tools. The authors underline the role of the National Human Rights Institutions and civil society as potential champions for the strategic litigation in Serbia. Special attention was given to the actions related to the rights of the child, questions such as who can have a stand before the court and the role of judges and judgments in the law and public policy creation. Case studies present administrative decisions and judgments of the courts in Serbia. The article offers recommendations for changes of law and in particular the procedural rules, which will create an enabling environment for the use of litigation as a tool for advancement of the rights of the child.

N.V. Šahović (✉)
Faculty of Law, UNION University, Belgrade, Serbia
e-mail: vnevena17@gmail.com

I. Savić
Centre for Human Rights and Development Studies (CHRDS), Belgrade, Serbia
e-mail: ivana.savich@gmail.com

T. Liefaard and J.E. Doek (eds.), *Litigating the Rights of the Child*,
DOI 10.1007/978-94-017-9445-9_9

1 Introduction

The Republic of Serbia is one of the 'new' states on the world map. Serbia became an independent state in 2006, after almost 90 years of having been incorporated in broader state unions. The Serbian legal system is based on the civil law tradition; it does not recognise decisions of domestic courts as sources of law (even subsidiary) and thus does not treat them as precedents, which is a factor impeding the use of strategic litigation in general.

So far, the implementation of international law on the rights of the child, principally the Convention on the Rights of the Child (CRC), has been improved upon in Serbia through political, legislative and practice reforms. The fine web that can be spun around jurisprudence to enhance the exercise of the rights of the child is still missing, though: there are no public debates on particular cases, advocacy is scattered and there is no research on the usefulness (or influence, if any) of existing court or administrative decisions.

Nonetheless, avenues are available for using the CRC and other relevant international law for strategic litigation. Some courts, as well as administrative decisions and recommendations by the National Human Rights Institutions in Serbia, hold strategic potential for the protection and promotion of human rights in general and the rights of the child in particular. Even though strategic litigation, as a method of achieving wider social changes and advancement of human rights, is still in its infancy in Serbia, the number of judicial and other procedures to which a *strategic potential* can be attributed is gradually increasing. However, there is a long way to go before, as in some other countries, the use of the CRC for strategic litigation becomes a reality in Serbia.

In the deliberations on strategic litigation that are aimed at advancing the rights of the child and achieving social justice, the overall country situation as well as the state of the judicial system must be taken into consideration. Some of those considerations in the case of Serbia are: the unsatisfactory extent of the rule of law[1]; the long average length of trials[2]; high levels of corruption[3]; and lack of judicial independence.[4] Access to justice for children is a problem: a child-friendly justice system is still not in place. Furthermore, civil proceedings need improvement: some provisions lack clarity, are vague, contradictory and confusing, and thus do not

[1] For more information, see Agrast et al. (2012): p. 136.

[2] Ibid.

[3] For more information, see Transparency International (2012). Corruption Perceptions Index 2012. http://issuu.com/transparencyinternational/docs/cpi_2012_report/3?e=0 Accessed 15 October 2013.

[4] For more information, see: High Representative of the European Union for Foreign Affairs and Security Policy. (2013). *Joint Report to the European Parliament and the Council* on Serbia's progress in achieving the necessary degree of compliance with the membership criteria, and notably the key priority of taking steps towards a visible and sustainable improvement of relations with Kosovo. Brussels: European Commission. .

correspond to material law. There are legal limitations regarding the child's capacity to protect her or his rights and express her or his opinion independently before the court and administrative bodies, as well as to have capacity to be a party in judicial and administrative proceedings. All of these factors are obstacles in implementing the CRC, including the use of this treaty for the initiation of strategic litigation. Furthermore, laws more often than not provide a more or less appropriate framework for the exercise of the rights; it is the implementation that is the missing link.

Thus, this chapter is about opportunities rather than achievements: it describes and analyses challenges and opportunities for the strategic litigation for the rights of the child in Serbia. The chapter begins with an introduction to the Serbian legal system and an overview of the human rights framework, including the protection of the human rights. Thereafter, it describes the state of the rights of the child in Serbia and analyses the child rights framework and access that children have to justice; in addition, it presents three court decisions that have strong potential to be used to initiate necessary changes. Finally, the authors recommend steps that should be taken to advance the implementation of the CRC, in particular the introduction of effective remedies to redress the violation of rights.

2 The Serbian Legal System

According to the Constitution of the Republic of Serbia, generally accepted rules of international law and ratified international treaties are considered to be an integral part of national law, while the human rights guaranteed by the Constitution, generally accepted rules, ratified international treaties and laws are directly implemented.[5] Serbia is a State party to all relevant human rights treaties adopted under the auspice of the United Nations, with the exception of the Convention on the Rights of Migrant Workers,[6] which it signed in 2004 but still has not ratified. Serbia is a State party to a number of regional instruments for the protection of human rights: in 2003 it ratified the European Convention for the Protection of Human Rights and Fundamental Freedoms[7] as well as all the protocols to this Convention. The CRC was ratified by the Socialist Federal Republic of Serbia[8] in 1991,[9] which meant that Serbia was also bound by this ratification as a federal unit of the country. As of 2006, Serbia is a State party to the CRC.

---

[5] Constitution of the Republic of Serbia (Official Gazette of Republic of Serbia, No. 83/06), art. 18.

[6] UN Doc A/RES/45/158.

[7] Council of Europe ETS 5.

[8] Hereafter SFRY.

[9] The Law on Ratification of the Convention on the Rights of the Child (Official Gazette of SFRY—International contracts No. 15/90 and Official Gazette of FRY—International Contracts No. 4/96 and 2/97).

The Constitution of Serbia[10] contains comprehensive provisions on human rights. Article 18, paragraph 3 of the Constitution stipulates that omissions and ambiguities regarding human rights are to be overcome by the interpretation of those rights.[11] Article 22 guarantees the right to judicial protection and the right to redress violations of human right, as well as the right to address international institutions for the protection of human rights.

The Serbian Constitution envisages five mechanisms for the protection of human rights, including the rights of the child: constitutional,[12] judicial,[13] administrative,[14] protection through bodies that specialise in human rights protection,[15] and international protection of human rights.[16]

According to the Constitution, the primary mechanism is judicial protection.[17] It is provided within the court system and is initiated by the lawsuit[18] or criminal offence report[19] initiated or submitted by a person who believes that her or his right was denied or violated. The courts resolve two types of disputes—civil disputes, for which civil law courts are competent, and criminal cases, for which competence lies with criminal courts. Courts also resolve administrative disputes about the legality of acts; the Administrative Court is the competent authority in this regard. Administrative litigation is provided before public administrative bodies according to the Law on General Administrative Procedure.[20]

Courts in Serbia are entitled not to create legal norms but to apply them; hence, case law is not regarded as a source of law.[21] However, this does not mean that courts, especially the Supreme Court of Cassation, do not have some law-creating

---

[10] Arts. 23–81.

[11] Article 18, paragraph 3 foresees that provisions on human and minority rights are 'interpreted to the benefit of promoting values of a democratic society, pursuant to valid international standards in human and minority rights, as well as the practice of international institutions which supervise their implementation'. This means that during the interpretation of human rights provisions, the viewpoints of international human rights bodies must be taken into account (i.e. the European Court for Human Rights or other contract bodies established by the international contracts on human rights under the auspice of UN), a requirement which stands in the favour of advancing human rights in Serbia.

[12] Art. 166.

[13] Art. 22.

[14] Art. 36.

[15] Art. 138.

[16] Art. 22.

[17] Art. 22.

[18] Code of Civil Procedure (Official Gazette of Republic of Serbia, No. 72/2011, 49/2013–Constitutional Court Decision and 74/2013–Constitutional Court Decision), art. 191.

[19] Criminal Procedure Code (Official Gazette of Republic of Serbia, No. 72/2011, 101/2011, 121/2012, 32/2013 and 45/2013), art. 280.

[20] Law on General Administrative Procedure (Official Gazette the Federal Republic of Yugoslavia No. 33/97 and 31/01 and Official Gazette of Republic of Serbia, No. 30/2010).

[21] Constitution, art. 142.

role.[22] The latter is the highest authority for interpreting the law, which it does by adopting general legal opinions and reviewing the work of the courts and the application of laws and other regulations.[23] In fact, these competencies provide the potential for the Supreme Court of Cassation to initiate social change and promote human rights, including the rights of the child.

Similarly, the Constitutional Court could also be regarded as having a strategic legal role in this respect. By way of a constitutional appeal, protection can be sought for the human rights guaranteed by the Constitution or any other international instruments that are binding for the Republic of Serbia.[24] All natural or legal, domestic or foreign persons, among them children (not explicitly mentioned but included by virtue of the term 'everyone'), who are holders of the human rights guaranteed by the Constitution are entitled to file a constitutional appeal.[25] Such appeals could be filed only by one who believes his or her rights have been violated.[26]

Furthermore, Serbia has National Human Rights Institutions (NHRIs) which are specialised, independent bodies with the mandate to control the work of the government and its agencies, and to promote and protect human rights.[27] In cases of violations, the NHRIs make recommendations on how to rectify government omissions. The courts are not obliged, however, to takes the opinions and recommendations of NHRIs into consideration.

3 Rights of the Child in Serbia

3.1 State of the Rights of the Child in Serbia

The CRC's implementation has been affected by the transition from a socialist to market economy as well as the long-term consequences of regional wars in the 1990s. The current political situation in Serbia is characterised by a struggling coalition government, inadequate rule of law, high degrees of corruption, a mismanaged economy and a slow decentralisation process. Needless to say, all of this impacts on the realisation of the rights of the child, with the result that large numbers of children still live in poverty (Government of the Republic of Serbia 2011); moreover, persistent political

[22] Law on organisation of courts (Official Gazette of Republic of Serbia, No. 116/2008, 104/2009, 101/2010, 31/2011– other law, 78/2011– other law and 101/2011), art. 12.

[23] Ibid., art. 31.

[24] Constitution, art. 170.

[25] However, as the child does not have *locus standi* to act in her or his own name, only the child's legal guardian could file a constitutional appeal, not the child him- or herself.

[26] Law on Constitutional Court, (Official Gazette of Republic of Serbia, No.109/2007, 99/2011 and 18/2013-Constitutional Court Decision) art. 83.

[27] NHRIs in Serbia are the Protector of Citizens and the Commissioner for Protection of Equality. For more information on NHRIs, see International Coordinating Committee of National Institutions for the Promotion and Protection of Human Rights (ICC). http://nhri.ohchr.org. Accessed 15 October 2013.

problems stall reform and shift focus from economic issues, the major ones of which are unemployment and a low level of productivity (World Bank 2012).

In Serbia, it is an ongoing struggle to address the negative attitudes towards children's rights found in every stratum of society, from teachers and social workers to the judiciary, health professionals, members of parliament, government officials and many others.[28] Often, efforts to implement the CRC or claim the rights of the child involve not only legal but social and moral action to overcome obstacles imposed by the dominant social discourse. Conservative ideologies make certain areas of children's rights more difficult to engage than others. For example, violence against children, especially in schools and families, is a big problem in the country. In this regard, corporal punishment is still seen as an acceptable means of disciplining children in families, and is often used in educational and social welfare institutions as well as residential care settings even though it is prohibited. Of particular concern is the increase in, and change in the nature of, peer violence (Petrović et al. 2013: 17).

In Serbia, numerous challenges and tasks thus need to be addressed in order to improve the implementation of the CRC. These include, but are not limited to:

- advancing legal reform through, for example, the adoption of a Child Rights Law;
- eradicating poverty among children;
- increasing and specifying budget allocations for children;
- securing greater political interest in, knowledge of and attention to children;
- fundamentally reforming the education system in accordance with international standards;
- improving health care for children, including adolescent health;
- providing a better of quality of education and information dissemination about child rights, and to as broad a spectrum of beneficiaries as possible, especially children, parents, teachers and health workers;
- facilitating an efficient child protection system covering all forms of abuse and exploitation, including those linked to trafficking, those occurring in the media, and those concerning harmful content on the internet; and
- improving legal and practical conditions to enable the child's access to justice.[29]

3.2 Legal Framework

Since the ratification of the CRC, Serbia has significantly improved its legal framework for the rights of the child; however, it is still not enough. Within the Serbian legal system, more than 80 laws are relevant to the realisation of the CRC and its Optional Protocols. Over the years the Republic of Serbia has taken important

[28] See The Children's Coalition (2008).

[29] See: UN Doc. CRC/C/SRB/CO/1.

steps to harmonise national legislation with the CRC and adopt numerous laws that advance the rights of the child in the country. Among the key laws are: the Family Law (2005),[30] the Law for Prevention of Discrimination against Persons with Disabilities (2006),[31] the Law on Juvenile Criminal Offenders and Criminal Protection of Juveniles (2006),[32] the Law on the Foundations of the Education System (2009),[33] the Law on the Prohibition of Discrimination (2009),[34] the Law on Registry Books (2009),[35] the Public Information Law (2009),[36] the Law on Associations (2009)[37] and the Law on Social Protection (2011).[38]

Of particular importance is that the 2006 Constitution of Serbia for the first time guaranteed the rights of the child, especially the right to a name and entry in the registry of births, the right to learn about her or his origins, the right to preserve her or his own identity, and the right to protection from psychological, physical, economic or other forms of exploitation or abuse; the child born out of wedlock also has the same rights as the one born in wedlock.[39] Additionally, the Constitution guarantees child rights[40] and their protection by law. Such a constitutional provision is a guarantee of the codification of the rights of the child, namely through the adoption of a *lex specialis* for the rights of the child, a Child Rights Law.[41] However, no such law yet exists.

3.3 The Child's Legal Protection and Access to Justice

Serbia lacks a child-friendly justice system in accordance with international standards. There are no children's or family courts, although it is the case that the Law on Juvenile Criminal Offenders and Criminal Protection of Juveniles introduces

---

30 Family Law (Official Gazette of Republic of Serbia, No. 18/2005 and 72/2011).

31 Law for Prevention of Discrimination against Persons with Disabilities (Official Gazette of Republic of Serbia, No. 33/2006).

32 Law on Juvenile Criminal Offenders and Criminal Protection of Juveniles (Official Gazette of Republic of Serbia, No. 85/2005).

33 Law on the Foundations of the Education System (Official Gazette of Republic of Serbia, No. 72/2009 and 52/2011).

34 Law on the Prohibition of Discrimination (Official Gazette of Republic of Serbia, No. 22/2009).

35 Law on Registry Books (Official Gazette of Republic of Serbia, No. 20/2009).

36 Public Information Law (Official Gazette of Republic of Serbia, No. 43/2003, 61/2005, 71/2009, 89/2010—Constitutional Court Decision and 41/2011– Constitutional Court Decision).

37 Law on Associations (Official Gazette of Republic of Serbia, No. 51/2009 and 99/2011—other laws).

38 Law on Social Protection (Official Gazette of Republic of Serbia, No. 24/2011).

39 Constitution, art. 64.

40 Ibid.

41 In a similar vein, see UN Doc. CRC/C/SRB/CO/1.

juvenile judges and a juvenile court bench in courts of first and second instance.[42] The notion of having a separate court for children in criminal matters (for offenders as well as victims of crimes) is not new in Serbia, but previous reforms to the judiciary failed to properly establish a juvenile justice system. For example, most of the courts lack premises adequately equipped for children's hearings, which would otherwise help to ensure that hearings are not traumatic for children. Similarly, courts do not have staff appointed to prepare and inform children about proceedings.[43]

The law requires that juvenile judges acquire special skills and undergo advanced, continuing professional education.[44] However, such education is limited in content, and is short and a once-off event. It is no surprise, then, that it took years before judges began referring to the CRC in decisions. Other parts of the justice system, including civil law courts, administrative courts and those involved in administrative procedures, particularly centres for social work, do not have an obligation to acquire any knowledge on the rights of the child.

Currently, strategic litigation the rights of the child is limited by various factors (discussed in detail further below). First, as noted, court decisions are not formally and legally considered to be a source of law. Secondly, children's access to courts is limited. Thirdly, interested parties, for example, NGOs, have limited access to the judiciary. In this respect, the legal system does not allow for the concept of *amicus curiae* or a similar institution which would enable civil society organisations and NHRIs to contribute further to strategic litigation. Moreover, professionals, civil society, media and the general public in Serbia do not have a culture of monitoring court and administrative decisions with a view to using them as tools in their work for the rights of the child. This is reflective of a situation in which there is a lack of confidence in the courts; trials do not commence within the time limitations specified by law; judicial expertise, transparency and independence are lacking; and there are no mechanisms for monitoring, inter alia, the execution of judgments.[45]

Most of the rights of the child are protected in the civil and administrative proceedings, to which the child (mainly through representatives) may be a party as a plaintiff, complainant, intervener or witness. The Civil Procedure Code foresees extraordinary legal remedies[46] in addition to the ordinary legal remedies.[47] Any natural person or legal entity may be a party to the proceedings.[48] Situations in which the child rights are protected in the court are numerous, and usually are related to family law protection, education, health and social protection.

---

[42] Arts. 42–43.

[43] For more information, see Centar za prava deteta (2013).

[44] Law on Juvenile Criminal Offenders and Criminal Protection of Juveniles, arts. 44 and 165.

[45] For more information, see Petrović and Joksimović (2013).

[46] Arts. 403, 421 and 426. Extraordinary legal remedies are: review, request for examining of final judgment and repeated trial.

[47] Arts. 367 and 399. The Code foresees appeal as an ordinary legal remedy, appeal against judgment and a court's decision.

[48] Code of Civil Procedure, art. 74.

Initiation of the procedure for the protection of the rights of the child requires undertaking a range of legal actions, including providing information on legal remedies, legal capacity, legal skills and knowledge. According to the Family Law, parent(s) represent the child in all legal operations and in all proceedings exceeding the limits of the child's legal capacity and capacity to be a party in the proceedings,[49] except in a situation when a temporary guardian is appointed by the guardianship authority due to a conflict of interests between the child and parent.[50] This means that children cannot initiate the procedure for the protection of their rights, as they do not have *locus standi* to act in their own name. The only exception to the rule is the action to establish maternity or paternity. The Family Law foresees this as the only instance in which children themselves may initiate proceedings.

In spite of its complex procedures and the high level of skill and knowledge these require, the legal system provides neither specialised legal aid for children nor attorneys specialised in the rights of the child who can represent the child's rights and interests in an adequate, impartial and objective manner in civil and administrative proceedings.[51] However, according to the Family Law, the public prosecutor and guardianship authority[52] may be a party to the proceedings for the protection of rights of the child, including to the initiation thereof.[53] Similarly, in cases involving the protection of the child's right to non-discrimination, the Equality Commissioner could be a party to the proceedings.[54] In terms of existing legal norms, civil society organisations in the field of children's rights, as well as human rights defenders[55] and NHRIs (with the exception of the Equality Commissioner), may not be a party to such proceedings. Civil society organisations may nevertheless offer legal expertise in such cases and act as attorneys of the plaintiffs;[56] in other words, they can initiate strategic litigation on behalf of the party to the proceeding.

In all proceedings concerning the protection of the rights of the child, with the exception mentioned above, a child does not have the status of a party due to lack of *locus standi*; even so, he or she has the status of intervener, because the proceedings in question are of the child's concern. Where the child is not satisfied with a judgment, he or she does not have a right to appeal independently. In the cases where the child's parents or guardians are not willing to file an appeal on the judgment and where the child is at the age of 10 or older, the child has an opportunity to notify the guardianship

---

[49] Art. 72.

[50] Art. 132.

[51] *Pravosuđe po meri deteta u Republici Srbiji*, p. 4.

[52] According to the Family Law, public prosecutor and guardianship authorities are *ex officio* parties and could also be interveners in proceedings concerning the rights of the child.

[53] Family Law, art. 263, para. 2.

[54] Law on Prohibition of Discrimination, art. 33, para. 3.

[55] Such as human rights organisations and human rights lawyers.

[56] Code of Civil Procedure, art. 85 and Law on Obligations (Official Gazette of SFRY, No. 29/78, 39/85, 45/89—Constitutional Court of Yugoslavia Decision and 57/89, Official Gazette of SRY, No. 31/93 and Official Gazette of Serbia and Montenegro, No. 1/2003—Constitutional Chapter), art. 89, para. 3.

authority about the unwillingness of his or her representative to file an appeal and to request that appropriate action be taken. However, this rarely happens in practice.

The child is in the same situation as the Protector of Citizens and the Equality Commissioner when he or she files a complaint to the NHRIs, given that the child cannot be a party to the proceeding for the protection of rights; furthermore, he or she cannot be provided with legal aid or independent representation in such proceedings.

Judicial procedures, particularly in civil law, have other shortcomings, too. First, civil law procedures are very expensive. In cases involving members of marginalised groups—persons who are most commonly exposed to human rights violations—financial obstacles such as court fees and the cost of witnesses, expert witnesses, on-site inspections, court notices and so on,[57] indirectly prevent the protection of rights. Similarly, the state has not provided measures to support the initiation of litigation for the rights of the child.

Secondly, the process for the protection of rights is not fast enough. According to the data of the Ministry of Justice, until 2011 the average duration of civil law proceedings was 7 years.[58] Even though the Family Law recognises the principle of urgency in proceedings for the protection of the rights of the child,[59] in complicated cases application of the urgency principle cannot be guaranteed.

Thirdly, because a civil law proceeding is initiated only by the right holder,[60] including a child, it assumes awareness of the rights, which is a particular obstacle for children (Petrović et al. 2013). When deciding whether to embark on litigation holding strategic opportunities, one should thus consider its likely duration, as well as the possibility of the child's exposure to secondary and tertiary victimisation.

Certain of the child's rights are protected in criminal proceedings. The Law on Juvenile Criminal Offenders and Criminal Protection of Juveniles encompasses children in conflict with the law as well as child victims, which explains the increased interest in protecting children's rights in criminal proceedings. Every child in the juvenile justice system has to have defence counselling; if not, counsel is appointed *ex officio* by the juvenile judge, a matter of great importance for children and families affected by poverty. The counsel must be an attorney with a qualification in children's rights.[61] A criminal proceeding against a juvenile is instituted only at the motion of the Juvenile Public Prosecutor, who has specialist qualifications in the field of children's rights and juvenile delinquency.[62] Additionally, the child who is a victim of the crime(s) is guaranteed an attorney in the proceedings.[63]

---

57 See Law on Court's Fees (Official Gazette of Republic of Serbia, No. 28/94, 53/95, 16/97, 34/2001—other law, 9/2002, 29/2004, 61/2005, 116/2008—other law, 31/2009, 101/2011 i 93/2012).

58 See Ministry of Justice (2008).

59 Family Law, art. 269.

60 Code of Civil Procedure, art. 194.

61 Law on Juvenile Criminal Offenders and Criminal Protection of Juveniles, art. 49.

62 Ibid., art. 57.

63 Ibid., art. 15.

4 Selected Case Law

There have been several significant child-rights cases in domestic courts with the potential to promote the use of the CRC and bring it to public attention. Thanks to extensive awareness-raising campaigns on human rights in general and, more particularly, the European Court for Human Rights, Serbia's citizens and legal professionals[64] are reasonably aware of the Court's jurisprudence, especially its decisions in cases against Serbia,[65] some which specifically concerned violations of children's rights.[66] This growing recognition of the importance of human rights and their protection is a result of two decades of training and awareness-raising about the value of international human rights treaties and the usefulness of their procedures. Effort of equal magnitude should be go into building people's capacity to understand and use Serbia's domestic jurisprudence.

Monitoring court cases related to the rights of the child—be they routine or ones with a strategic dimension—is rendered difficult by the fact that the decisions are published only selectively and are not always publicly accessible. This applies as well to monitoring the use of the CRC and other international law in domestic procedures, particularly when these instruments have been invoked in court decisions. Nevertheless, even when decisions are published, they are not classified according to the nature of the dispute or the right at issue. Proper mechanisms for informing the public of decisions have yet to be established in the Serbian judiciary.[67] The situation certainly poses challenges to researchers and all those initiating strategic litigation.

This section presents two instances of such litigation undertaken by the Commissioner for Protection of Equality as well as one decision of the Supreme Court of Cassation. Even though their decisions make no explicit reference to the CRC, the three cases are based on domestic laws that reflect international standards binding upon Serbia. The selection of cases is inspired by their importance in advancing the rights of the child in Serbia and their value as models for future litigation seeking to use the CRC to this end.

---

[64] In the period January–July 2013, 3,567 applications concerning Serbia were allocated to a judicial formation.

[65] For more information, visit Council of Europe, European Court for Human Rights. http://www.echr.coe.int/Documents/CP_Serbia_ENG.pdf. Accessed 20 October 2013.

[66] For example, see: *Krivošej v. Serbia*, 13 April 2010: 'Access rights of a divorced mother with respect to her child, in Serbia', *Zorica Jovanović v. Serbia*, 26 March 2013: 'Missing babies from hospitals, in Serbia' and *Jevremović v. Serbia*, 17 July 2007: 'Establishment of paternity and child maintenance in Serbia'.

[67] To make matters stranger, the Law on Prohibition of Discrimination, art. 43, para. 5, prescribes the obligation to publish the verdict as one of the measures that may be required for claims for violations of the rights guaranteed by the Law.

4.1 Commissioner for Protection of Equality

The following two cases brought by the Commissioner for Protection of Equality[68] concerned violations of the Law on the Prohibition of Discrimination.[69] They are critically important because the Commissioner has a strategic position per se and can institute litigation when children's rights are violated. The Commissioner uses these and other similar cases as models of good practice by the courts and as a message to those who would treat children differently based on their personal characteristics. In addition, the Commissioner regularly publishes reports on inequalities, including a report to the parliament, thanks to which different forms of discrimination are brought into the open as problems that society at large should address.

4.1.1 Case 1: Discrimination Against Children and Youth with Disability in Provision of Public Services (29 P no. 19199/12)[70]

A café owner from Niš, the third largest city in Serbia, refused to provide service to a group of deaf children and youth who came to the café for a birthday celebration. While seated, they were communicating in sign language. When the café's workers noticed this, they asked the group to leave, offering the explanation that the table they occupied, as well as all other tables in the café, were not 'available for deaf people'.

The group filed a complaint to the Commissioner, who brought an action under the Anti-discrimination Law against the café owner before the First Basic Court in Belgrade. In her claim, the Commissioner invoked violation of the Constitution of the Republic of Serbia, the Anti-discrimination Law, the Law on Prevention of Discrimination against Persons with Disabilities, and the Convention on the Rights of Persons with Disabilities (CRPD). In its decision the Court found that the defendant committed 'discrimination against persons with disability which constitutes direct discrimination in provision of public services'.

By bringing this case before the court, the Commissioner aimed both to contribute to the advancement of the position of children and youth with a disability as well as to ensure their access to public services.

4.1.2 Case 2: Discrimination Against Minority Children and Denial of Access to Education (11 P no. 8484/13)[71]

A secondary vocational school in the village of Bela Palanka, Serbia, contracted a local bakery shop to provide its students with an apprenticeship programme. When the student I.L. entered the programme, the owner of the bakery told her that she 'smells

[68] Hereafter Commissioner.

[69] Hereafter Anti-discrimination Law.

[70] Judgment of the First Basic Court in Belgrade from 2011.

[71] First Basic Court in Belgrade.

… that she is [a] Gypsy, that she should go home and have a bath and not show up in the shop again, because the shop loses customers because of her'. Humiliated and insulted, I.L. told her father what had happened. He then notified the police[72] and the school. Shortly afterwards, the school terminated its contract with the bakery shop.

With the victim's consent, the Commissioner initiated a lawsuit before the First Basic Court in Belgrade against the owner of the bakery shop. The claim of the Commissioner referred to the owner's act of denying access to the programme and acts of insulting and humiliating a child based on her membership of an ethnic minority, acts which constitute direct discrimination against children on the basis of ethnicity. The Commissioner invoked violation of the Constitutional Equality provision and violation of the Anti-Discrimination Law.

In its ruling, the Court pointed out two important aspects. First, it established that the bakery shop owner treated I.L. in a discriminatory manner and found that the owner, by 'denying the access to undergo the apprenticeship programme, insulting and humiliating the student directly discriminated against the student on the basis of belonging to national minority and thus openly show[ed a] discriminatory attitude towards Roma people'. Secondly, the Court found that the owner, by 'denying the access to undergo the apprenticeship programme had shown [a] discriminatory attitude in providing job and professional development opportunities', and confirmed the protection of the right to equal access to education.

***

In both cases, the Commissioner invoked the CRPD (but not the CRC). Although the cases are significant, they reflect society's relatively weak reaction to discrimination. This is visible primarily in the attitudes toward compensation demands for the pecuniary and non-pecuniary damages, in this case compensation for the victims. First, in both lawsuits compensation for such damages was not demanded.[73] Secondly, the Court did not dispense monetary sanction for discrimination[74]; it ordered only that its decision be published in a major newspaper and that discrimination should be discontinued.

Furthermore, the Commissioner and Court alike could have taken a more assertive approach to alleviating the imperfections of the Law on the Prohibition of Discrimination. The fact that the latter stipulates as measures (inter alia) 'imposing a ban on an activity that poses the threat of discrimination, a ban on proceeding with a discriminatory activity, or a ban on repeating a discriminatory activity'[75] is almost laughably vacuous and highlights the need for legislative change. One may wonder how it is possible to order merely that the decision be published in a major newspaper and that discrimination be discontinued.

---

[72] The father contacted the police as he believed that, by discriminating against his child, the bakery owner had perpetrated violence against children based on the child's belonging to a minority.

[73] Law on Prohibition of discrimination, art. 43, para. 4.

[74] Between 50 (100) and (5,000) 10,000 Euro (approximately).

[75] Art. 43, para. 1.

The meaningless character of that measure is especially evident in the second case, in which the court ordered the defendant to refrain from discriminating against an individual person, declaring, '[I]n the future, the defendant is prohibited to give statements that [are] aimed at violating [the] dignity of I.L. based either on her national belonging or any other personal characteristic'. Here, the implication is that discrimination is otherwise and elsewhere tacitly permitted but that the Court had felt moved to step in and ban it on this particular occasion. In view of the Court's tepid reaction in both of the cases, it is unsurprising that the defendants did not appeal against the decisions.

These and similar challenges limit the Commissioner's initiatives for strategic litigation, challenges that could be overcome were the Commissioner to issue stronger claims, including compensation for material and immaterial damages, and make broader resort to international law. This might lead the courts to adopt a stronger position against discrimination. All of it could in turn serve to generate social change by advancing both the implementation of international and domestic law and the effectuation of legislative reform.

4.2 *The Supreme Court of Cassation*

Unlike the basic courts and the courts of appeal, the Supreme Court of Cassation, according to its mandate, is in a position to influence changes in the area of the rights of the child through its judicial activities. In addition, it is assumed that the judges of the Supreme Court have extensive legal knowledge and experience and are appointed in a rigorous selection process.[76] The Supreme Court's mandate is to examine legal gaps and fill them by means of judicial decisions reached by interpreting the law in each particular case. Although it is not so in this instance, the Court has invoked the CRC on several occasions—a promising sign of the potential the treaty has in future deliberations of this court. Even though there were several cases relevant to this section, the one which has been selected sets an even higher standard than that by the CRC.

4.2.1 Case 1: The Rights of the Child to Habitation (Rev 3036/10)[77]

The plaintiff (mother) and the defendant (father) were married and had two children. After the divorce, and based on the court decision, the plaintiff received custody of the children, while the defendant was allowed regular contact with them and was obliged to provide maintenance. The plaintiff and children lived in a rented apartment; the defendant had an apartment which had been bought during the marriage, but he was renting it out rather than living in it himself.

[76] Constitution, art. 147.

[77] Supreme Court of Cassation.

The plaintiff filed a lawsuit against the defendant for the protection of the right of the child to habitation as a part of the right to housing. The lower courts concluded that the children have the right to live with the plaintiff in the apartment owned by the defendant until they reach the age of majority. Subsequently, the defendant was obliged to hand over the unfurnished apartment to the plaintiff, as the plaintiff was the legal guardian of the children. The defendant filed a revision against the final decision of the second instance court, which the Supreme Court of Cassation rejected as unfounded. In its decision the Court concluded that

> the right of the child to habitation is not protected by the special procedure, and it is placed under the section concerning property rights. Therefore, under the authority of article 263, paragraph 2 of the Family Law, protection of such right is under the regime of the protection of the rights of the child stipulated by the Family Law.

In addition, the Court held that the right of habitation is constituted in order to ensure the protection of the children's wellbeing; this right belongs to the *corpus juris* of the rights of the child, and it is in the interest of the parent that independently exercises the parental rights. Furthermore, contrary to the allegations stated in the revision, such ruling neither threatens the defendant's right of habitation nor manifests injustice due to the fact established by the lower courts that the apartment is not used for the habitation of the defendant. The Court also concluded that 'all other interests must be subordinated to the best interest of the children'.

***

In this decision the Supreme Court of Cassation recognised the right of the child to habitation as part of the right of the child to housing. Secondly, the Court concluded that there is a lack of special proceedings for the protection of the right of the child to habitation, and that the general family law regime for the protection of the rights of the child should be applied.

The case could encourage further strategic litigation on children's rights relating to housing and an adequate standard of living, as provided, for example, in article 27 of the CRC (even though the provision was not mentioned here). Furthermore, this decision and others like it could be used as an argument supporting advocacy aimed at the adoption of the Child Rights Law that would encompass the child's right to habitation and establish a special procedure for the protection of rights. The Court refers to the best interests of the child, which is of primary consideration when resolving conflicts between rights (see also article 3 CRC).[78]

In overall terms, this case can provide inspiration for future strategic litigation and has the potential to play a role in initiating and supporting legislative and social change.

---

[78] Regarding the interpretation of the concept and role of the best interests of the child, see General Comment No. 14 (2013) of the CRC Committee on the right of the child to have his or her best interests taken as a primary consideration (art. 3, para. 1).

5 Conclusion

As noted in the CRC Committee's General Comment No. 5, 'for rights to have meaning, effective remedies must be available to redress violations'.[79] The major recommendation to States parties is that they

> need to give particular attention to ensuring that there are effective, child-sensitive procedures available to children and their representatives. These should include the provision of child-friendly information, advice, advocacy, including support for self-advocacy, and access to independent complaints procedures and to the courts with necessary legal and other assistance.

All of this is exactly what Serbia has yet to achieve. Despite legislative reforms, despite the incorporation of most of the rights of the CRC into domestic legislation, and despite the establishment of parliamentary and administrative bodies to oversee the rights of the child, Serbia's realisation of the CRC continues to be weakest in the area of the implementation of law, the ensurance of access to justice, and the provision of judicial safeguards. This chapter, in the course of identifying positive cases with the strategic potential to enhance protection of children's rights, has highlighted how far the country is from enjoying a system in which violations of children's rights could be redressed as a matter of routine. For the time being, one cannot speak of the existence of effective and child-sensitive procedures in Serbia.

One of the biggest challenges in this respect is that the current procedural law does not work in complementarity with the substantive law. Furthermore, the existing rules of procedure do not provide the requirements necessary for the application of substantive law. Children lack autonomous access to independent complaints procedures and to the courts. Essential legal and other assistance is provided in some cases (in criminal justice matters) but not in others (administrative and civil law issues); even when the law guarantees legal or other assistance to children, there is little or no independent monitoring of the standard of this assistance.

With regard to the CRC Committee's request to States that 'where rights are found to have been breached, there should be appropriate reparation, including compensation, and, where needed, measures to promote physical and psychological recovery, rehabilitation and reintegration, as required by article 39,'[80] it remains the situation that in Serbia the victims of child-rights violations do not benefit from such compensation and care. As noted in the discussion of the first two cases presented in this chapter, reparation or compensation was not even requested in the lawsuit.

Ensuring the justiciability of child rights will require numerous changes over a long period of time. The key changes for developing effective remedies where rights are violated have to be made on the structural and political level, and must include all aspects of good governance in the country; in other words, even if such remedies are permitted by the legal system, it is well-nigh impossible to undertake

---

[79] Committee on the Rights of the Child, General Comment No. 5, General Measures of Implementation of the Convention on the Rights of the Child, CRC/GC/2003/5 (2003), para. 24.

[80] Ibid.

strategic litigation successfully if the rule of law is weak, corruption is high and the judiciary, inefficient.

Nevertheless, in an imperfect system one has to be imaginative, to improvise and to look into all the possibilities. The CRC is a very good tool to use in litigation that seeks redress of the violation of child rights; it is a tool, moreover, which it is possible to use in Serbia. Therefore, some general as well as particular steps that Serbia needs to undertake in order to promote, accept and respect strategic litigation are:

- to introduce a child-friendly justice system as a legal and political concept necessary for the realisation, advancement and protection of the rights of the child;
- to carry out legislative reform so as to enable:
  - improvement of procedural laws so that they effectively serve the substantive laws;
  - effective and independent access to justice for children;
  - advancement of the role and position of defenders of human rights;
  - the introduction of *amicus curiae* in the Serbian justice system; and
  - the introduction of a lawsuit for the protection of the rights of the child that would have the character of the *actio popularis*;
- to adopt a comprehensive child rights act (as organic law);
- to introduce an independent state body for the protection of the rights of the child with the mandate to protect and promote the rights of the child;
- to provide ongoing training and education on the CRC to the judiciary and other professionals working with and for children (this includes the production and distribution of manuals and other educational material);
- to support NHRIs in their strategic work with children and use of the CRC, in particular where they can receive children's complaints and represent them in a court or administrative case;
- to support civil society organisations dealing with human rights and the rights of the child through budgeting and enabling a legal and social environment in which those organisations can address child-rights violations as well as assist and represent children; and
- to undertake ongoing activities to raise awareness about the CRC and other relevant international law in Parliament, all government departments, health and education systems, and among all professionals, media, parents, children and society as a whole.

References

Agrast, M. D., Botero, J. C., Ponce, A., Martinez, J., & S. Pratt, C. (2012). *The rule of law index 2012–2013 report*. Washington, DC: The World Justice Project.

Centar za prava deteta. (2013). *Pravosuđe po meri deteta u Republici Srbiji*. Beograd: Centar za prava deteta.

Committee on the Rights of the Child, General Comment No. 5. *General measures of implementation of the Convention on the Rights of the Child*, CRC/GC/2003/5 (2003).

Government of the Republic of Serbia. (2011). *First national report on social inclusion and poverty reduction in the Republic of Serbia: The status of social exclusion and poverty trends in the period 2008–2010 and future priorities*. Belgrade.

High Representative of the European Union for Foreign Affairs and Security Policy. (2013). *Joint report to the European parliament and the council on Serbia's progress in achieving the necessary degree of compliance with the membership criteria and notably the key priority of taking steps towards a visible and sustainable improvement of relations with Kosovo*. Brussels: European Commission.

Ministry of Justice, Republic of Serbia. (2008). http://arhiva.mpravde.gov.rs/en/articles/ministry. Accessed 8 October 2013.

Petrović, M., et al. (2013). *Izveštaj o ostvarivanju opštih mera primene Konvencije o pravima deteta U Republici Srbiji*. Beograd: Centar za prava deteta.

Petrović, V., & Joksimović, V. (Eds.). (2013). *Ljudska prava u Srbiji: pravo, praksa i međunarodni standardi ljudskih prava*. Beogradski centar za ljudska prava: Beograd.

The Children's Coalition for Reporting on Child Rights in Serbia. (2008). *Alternative report: Child rights in Serbia—the children's perspective*. The Children's Coalition for Reporting on Child Rights in Serbia.

Transparency International. (2012). Corruption perceptions index 2012. http://www.transparency.org/cpi2012/results . Accessed 3 September 2014.

World Bank Europe and Central Asia region Poverty Reduction and Economic Management Department (ECA PREM). (2012). *South East Europe Regular Economic Report No. 3: From double-dip recession to accelerated reforms*. http://www.worldbank.org/content/dam/Worldbank/document/SEERER_3_Report_FINAL_eng.pdf. Accessed 3 September 2014.

Chapter 10
Algeria

Experiences in Algeria with the Use of the CRC in Legal Proceedings

Kamel Filali

Abstract Algeria ratified the UN Convention on the Rights of the Child (CRC) in December 1992 and took steps to facilitate its implementation by publishing the text of this landmark document in the Official Gazette as required by the constitution. These developments can be taken as a sign of the state's commitment to see the status of Algerian children change and become compatible with the standards envisaged by the CRC. In particular, publishing the text was an important step in facilitating implementation of the new norms, since Algeria's constitution and constitutional jurisprudence provide for the superiority of this instrument after its ratification and publication. This chapter presents an example of a State party to the Convention in which the Sharia law system is juxtaposed with the civil law system and in which the former has supremacy in family matters: Sharia law prevails over any other given legal norm that would contradict its text and spirit. In such circumstances, then, what would be the faith of the ratified Convention? Can lawyers and magistrates invoke its provisions as a legal basis in litigation and implement the rights of the child as expressed by the Convention within the framework of state obligations? It is submitted that the CRC is either not utilised or is of a limited application as a legal instrument in Algeria's domestic litigation.

1 Introduction

This chapter focuses on the difficulties, not to say obstacles, that limit the efforts made to enhance children's rights in Algeria; more generally, these difficulties can explain the lack of implementation of the CRC in many African and Arab states. Some of the problems arise because the CRC has not been integrated into national legislation, or because, where it has, either the political will is lacking or there is

K. Filali (✉)
Law School, University of Constantine, Constantine, Algéria
e-mail: kamelzim.82@gmail.com

T. Liefaard and J.E. Doek (eds.), *Litigating the Rights of the Child*,
DOI 10.1007/978-94-017-9445-9_10

misinterpretation and insufficient knowledge of its content by administrative and judicial authorities. In Islamic states, it is also the case that Islamic law has irreversible superiority over other laws, particularly in family affairs.[1]

The insufficiency of knowledge about the CRC and treaty law, notably the obligation to abide by the terms of treaties after their ratification, must be emphasised. This is not understood by Algerian judges, who give priority and exclusivity to the application of national law even when the fundamental law of Algeria declares unambiguously that treaties, including the CRC, which have been ratified in conformity with the law are superior to domestic law.

In delineating the national jurisdiction's scope of implementation of the international norms in the CRC, this chapter refers to multiple sources, mainly provisions of the Algerian Family Code and family case law; the latter are convergent as they are by their nature Sharia law.[2] The first section addresses the problem of integrating international norms into the internal legislation of Algeria; the second deals with the CRC's application by the judiciary; and the third covers the sensitive issue of child neglect and abuse as a penal or criminal offence.

A question that emerges is why a convention that Algeria ratified as long ago as 1992 has not become more deeply embedded in the country's domestic jurisprudence. It is important to stress that searching in Algeria for case law in regard to children's rights, or any other human rights jurisprudence, is no easy task. The researcher does not have access to judicial documents, and those which are located in magistrates' libraries are reserved for use by magistrates—to the exclusion of others with an interest in studying the jurisprudence of the courts, such as law lecturers, students, attorneys at laws, experts and researchers who would like to work on these valuable documents and contribute to the advancement of internal law and its conformity with international norms, particularly in the area of children's rights.

In this regard, it should be noted that information in this chapter stems from the author's own experience in tribunals and courts as well as similar experience gleaned from lawyers and magistrates. Reference is also made to jurisprudence dated before (as well as after) Algeria's ratification of the CRC; this fact should not be seen as contradicting the analysis undertaken in this chapter, given that, both before and after, Sharia law has been relied upon as a source of law. The strict application of the norms in Sharia law is constant, and the impact is the same on children whether the cases took place before or after ratification of the CRC.

This international treaty has permitted to children to move from a situation in which they were regarded as objects to one in which they have their own rights. This is visible, real and immense progress for the benefit of all children, in

[1] Belhadj, Larbi, (2010). Manual on the explanation of the Family Code of Algeria. University. Printing Office, Part I, p. 30. See also Hamoudiin (2001) The place of Sharia Law in the sources of Algerian legislation. p. 123; Supreme Court of Algeria, Supreme Court Review. July 1995. Family Affairs Chamber. Case no. 123051; Supreme Court of Algeria. Supreme Court Review no. 2. 10 September, 2008. Family Affairs Chamber. Caseno. 457038.

[2] Sharia law is the body of Islamic law. Sharia deals with all aspects of day-to-day life.

keeping with the fact that the Committee on the Rights of the Child[3] has always emphasised that a child should be considered as an active subject of rights.

Algeria ratified the CRC on 19 December 1992[4] and presented its joint third and fourth report in June 2012[5]; its next such periodic report is due in November 2018.[6] After ratification, Algeria published the CRC in the National Official Gazette, or *Journal Officiel de la République Algérienne Démocratique et Populaire* (JORADP). This could be interpreted as an official engagement from the State party to acknowledge the new vision of the child proposed by the Convention; moreover, it could be held that this strategic reaction by Algeria indicates that children should be reared in the spirit of the United Nations Charter and raised in preparation for leading lives as individuals in society.

Algeria's practice emphasises that an international treaty will be part of national law if it has been ratified according to national legislation and published in JORADP and that the citizen can use the norms of the international convention before all the jurisdictions of Algeria.[7] Moreover, according to article 132 of the Constitution, treaties prevail over national law.

In one of its conclusions in 1999, and thus 7 years after the ratification of the CRC, the Supreme Court explained in a decision[8] that 'the breach of constitutional provisions and of [i]nternational human rights conventions on which the appeal has been based should be rejected'. It continues by stating that 'consequently the legal construction based on the fact that there was a violation of article 47[9] of the Algerian Constitution and article 1/9[10] of the international Covenant on civil and Political rights is rejected'.

In this rather bizarre judgment by the country's highest court, there is no ambiguity in understanding that the Human Rights Conventions are not a legal basis for the defense of legitimate rights. In other words, an individual cannot rely on International Human Rights Conventions, including the CRC.

The case had not been published until 23 February 2011. This judicial approach explains why the present chapter makes reference interchangeably to case law

---

[3] Article 43 of the CRC.

[4] Presidential Decree (23 December 1992. no. 92/461).

[5] UNCRC, 60th Session, 29 May–15 June 2012.

[6] Ibid., Concluding Observations No. 89.

[7] Decision of 20 August 1989 no. 1 Constitutional Council. Electoral code. JORADP 1989, p. 872.

[8] Supreme Court of Algeria. Penal Chamber, Case no. 190666. Dated 26 July 1999. Unpublished until 2011 in Algerian Procedural penal code by Hassene, Bouskia, Berti Edition, 23 February 2011.

[9] Article 47 of the Algerian Constitution: 'None can be pursued, arrested or detained unless within the cases … defined by the law and in accordance with the forms prescribed.'

[10] Article 9/1 of the Covenant on Civil and Political Rights: 'Everyone has the right to liberty and security of …. person. No one shall be subjected to arbitrary arrest or detention. No one shall be deprived of his liberty … except on such grounds and in accordance with such procedure as are established by law.'

issued before as well as after the CRC came into existence and was ratified by the State of Algeria: the attitude of magistrates is not affected by the ratification of international human rights documents because of the nature of the rights that are covered by intangible Islamic law.

2 The Legal Status of the CRC

The Constitution is the supreme law to which all other laws must comply.[11] This fundamental principle means that treaties do not affect domestic law unless they have been incorporated into it by various legislative acts.

The dualist doctrine is based on the notion that there are two distinct systems of law operating separately and that, before any rule or principle of international law can have effect in the domestic jurisdiction, it must be expressly and specifically 'transformed' into national law. By '*transformation*' is meant the amendment of existing laws or the adoption of new domestic legislation in line with a ratified treaty. The process of incorporation entails the wholesale inclusion of an international instrument in national law. It follows, then, that when new obligations are created by treaty, legislation is needed for them to become rules of national law. According to the Algerian Civil Code (ACC),[12] an international norm will have a binding effect only after its integration in the national legislation. In a decision dated 20 August 1989, the Constitutional Council reaffirmed the constitutional principle according to which duly ratified international treaties prevail over domestic law.[13]

Article 26 of the Vienna Convention on the law of treaties imposes an obligation on States parties that have ratified a convention or treaty to take all legislative and other pertinent measures to seek the full implementation of its provisions.[14] In Algeria, in order for a convention to enter into force, it must be published in the JORADP. The date of publication determines the date of entry into force and creates a presumption of awareness of the treaty towards everyone. Unfortunately, judges are known to have denied the applicability of ratified treaties if these have not been published.[15]

As mentioned above, the Constitution, as well as the decision by the Constitutional Council of 20 August 1989 in relation to the Electoral Code, authorises all those on the territory of Algeria to use in their litigation only the provisions of those ratified conventions that have been duly published.

[11] See article 70 and 72 of the Algerian Constitution, dated 8 December 1996; modified in 2002 and 2008, ... JORAPD no. 63, dated 16 November 2008.

[12] Algerian Civil Code, article 4, Law no. 07-05, 13 May 2007, modifying and completing Ordinance no. 75–58 of 26 September, 1975 related to the Algerian civil code.

[13] Decision no. 1 Constitutional Council, 20 August 1989 related to the Electoral code, JORADP 1989, p. 872.

[14] Vienna Convention on the Laws of Treaties.

[15] This is based on the author's experience as an attorney at law before the Supreme Court of Algeria and the State Council.

The Constitution determines the function of a judge, which is applying the law—meaning the national legislation that is found in the official gazette of the state—but judges are not using the CRC's articles as a legal support for their decisions, preferring to rely only on national legislation.

The Algerian legal system is governed by *dualité de Juridiction* (dual jurisdiction system). The judiciary is organised into three levels.[16] This means that in principle matters should be referred to ordinary tribunals dealing with civil matters, commercial matters, labour matters, family affairs, penal cases and juvenile matters; if it is a matter of an administrative nature, it is referred to the tribunal dealing exclusively with administrative cases.[17] Litigation is governed by various codes that deal either with the procedural aspects of different kinds of cases (for example, the Penal Procedure Code,[18] the Civil and Administrative Procedure Code[19]) or with the substance of the matter (for example, the Civil Code,[20] Commercial Code,[21] Labour Code,[22] and Custom Code[23]). No code on the rights of the child has yet been enacted.

The Constitutional Council of Algeria has the competence to interpret the constitution and monitor the constitutionality of laws and the conformity of international treaties with the constitution. However, the Council's limited mandate and its lack of accessibility prevent it from becoming a genuine protector of human rights. The option of referring a case to the Constitutional Council is not open to all litigators,[24] a situation which does not respond adequately to the demand for fruitful human rights litigation.

Litigating human rights at the domestic level requires the creation of appropriate judicial bodies capable of dealing with human rights violations. Algeria and other Maghreb Arab States do not have a specialised human rights court able to deal such violations, including violations of children's rights. Algeria has indeed established a national institution of human rights.[25] However, it does not have the right to receive human rights complaints and conduct investigations; furthermore, it is not in conformity with the Paris Principles on national human rights institutions.[26] Calls from experts, nongovernmental organisations and associations for the protection of the rights of the child have been made for the establishment of an ombudsman on children's rights, but so far they have been ignored by the government.

---

[16] http://www.mjustice.dz/.

[17] Ibid.

[18] Ibid.

[19] Ibid.

[20] Ibid.

[21] Ibid.

[22] Ibid.

[23] Ibid.

[24] Ibid.

[25] Presidential Decree (25 March 2001, no. 01–71) establishes the Commission and defines its mandate and mission.

[26] Principles relating to the Status of National Institutions (The Paris Principles).

As such, there is a need to establish a judicial body competent to undertake matters pertaining to human rights violations. It is therefore important to create such a judicial structure or to broaden the existing one. This could enhance the protection and promotion of human rights in the Algerian context, one which in recent years has been marked by numerous human rights violations, particularly of children's rights.[27]

In the Algerian legal tradition, international norms are not applied directly. One of the problems is that tribunals and courts do not argue their cases based on international law.[28] This is due mostly the nationalistic legacy of the Algerian War of Independence, which after the recovery of full sovereignty in 1962 drove the authorities, including the judiciary, to consider only Algerian law, as found in the Official Gazette, in settling litigation before the courts.

The limited use of international human rights law, particularly the CRC, by national courts in Algeria stems from other reasons, too. These include limited access to relevant international documents; lack of adequate case reporting both at the national and international level; the attitudes of judicial officers and their lack of exposure to international human rights law; and poorly drafted pleadings that do not bring out the relevant issues.

2.1 Human Rights Treaties and Conventions

Algeria has participated actively in adopting most of the human rights treaties, particularly the CRC, and has ratified almost all of the United Nations and African Union human rights treaties. However, when it comes to giving those treaties which the country has accepted at the international level force of law in local jurisdiction,[29] the state's attitude is ambiguous.

Although Algeria has ratified the CRC, this was not followed up at home with appropriate enactments to give it force of law. More than 20 years after ratification, Algeria does not have a specific code for children in which one would be able to find all provisions concerning the rights of the child in conformity with the Convention.

In its examination of the joint Third and Fourth Report of the State Party of Algeria, the Committee on the Rights of the Child expressed concern at the non-existence of specific legislation on children's rights and requested

> the State party to speed up the adoption process of the Child Protection [Code] … to ensure that the Child Protection Code be fully in compliance with the principles and provisions of the Convention and that, once enacted, it supersedes all legislation that is not in conformity with the Convention. The Committee further urges the State party to promptly

---

[27] Abductions, sexual abuse and murder of children increased significantly from 2009 to 2013.

[28] Supreme Court of Algeria, Penal Chamber, Case no. 190666. Dated 26 July 1999. Unpublished until 2011 in Algerian Procedural penal code by Hassene, Bouskia, Berti Edition, 23 February 2011.

[29] 19 December, 2012, lecture on the implementation of UNCRC Final Observations following the examination of the Third and Fourth Joint Report of Algeria. Hotel Hilton, Algiers, Algeria.

repeal from the Family Code all other provisions that discriminate against girls and women and negatively impact on all children, such as legal provisions concerning child custody, inheritance, divorce, polygamy and repudiation.

In its Concluding Observations and Recommendations, the Committee has frequently called for Algeria to apply the international human rights provisions contained in the CRC, especially given that article 4 provides that 'States Parties shall undertake all appropriate legislative, administrative and other measures for implementation of the rights recognized in the present convention'.

It is to be noted that Algerian legislation emphasises some of the Convention's fundamental principles, such as non-discrimination and the principle of the best interests of the child.[30] Practice shows that discrimination between girls and boys, against disabled children, and against children born out of wedlock remains a reality; that is to say, measures are not taken to implement the CRC. It is worthwhile to recall that the law of treaties presupposes that international standards ratified by states will be observed in good faith.[31]

2.2 *Interpretative Declarations*

Algeria ratified the CRC in 1992 with the following Interpretative Declarations: to Article 14(1) and (2) on children's freedom of conscience and religion, as Algerian law stipulates that a child's education is determined by the religion of the father; and to articles 13, 16 and 17 on children's freedom of expression, right to privacy, and access to information, on grounds relating to particular provisions of the Algerian penal and information codes and the interpretation of the provisions of the CRC in the light of possible breaches of public order and incitement of minors.

The latter Declaration also cites article 26 of the Information Code, which states that 'national and foreign periodicals and specialized publications must not contain any illustration, narrative, information or insertion contrary to Islamic morality, national values or human rights or advocate racism, fanaticism and treason'.[32]

Like various other states with which it shares Islamic religious principles, Algeria's approach to certain rights in the CRC is affected by the following considerations:

- Article 2 of the Constitution provides that Islam is the religion of the state, while its article 35 stipulates the inviolability of freedom of conscience and freedom of opinion.
- Law number 84/11 of 9 June 1984 related to the Family Code declares expressly that the education of the child occurs within the framework of the religion of the father.

---

[30] Article 66 Algerian Family Code, Law no. 84-11, dated 9 June 1984; related to the Family Code completed and modified by Ordinance no. 05-01, dated 27 February 2005.

[31] Vienna Convention on the Law of Treaties.

[32] Law no. 90-70 dated 3 April 1990, relating to the media, JORADP no. 014 dated 04 April 1990.

The Interpretative Declaration emphasises that article 13 of the CRC (concerning freedom of expression) as well as articles 16 and 17 (relating to the right to a private life and the right to receive information) should be taken into consideration only when the best interests of the child and his or her physical and moral integrity allow that.

This is why it is permitted to say that the formulation made by Algeria in its Interpretative Declaration, mainly when it says that 'Algeria interpretation of these articles is made in conformity with its judicial order meaning its constitution and its Family Code is in fact a concrete and real obstacle to any attempt for freedom of religion'.

In scrutinising these Interpretative Declarations, it is obvious that there is *prima facie* violation of the principle of the hierarchy of norms, because:

- the principle of the prevalence of treaty over internal legislation, as provided for in article 132 of the Constitution, is not applied;
- the reference to the internal legal order, particularly to the Family Code of 1984 and including the amendment made by Law 02/05 of 27 February 2005, will limit the adhesion of the State Party to the Convention.

From a legislative point of view, the Family Code has a fundamental role and can, in the author's view, be interpreted as a legal text with the same value as the Constitution itself.

2.3 The Publication of the Ratified Convention in the JORADP

Questioned as to why the CRC is not used as a legal basis in judicial decisions even though it has been ratified and is in conformity with the Constitution, a number of judges answered that they have their own methodology, in terms of which they use the CRC's principles and rights in their decisions; for unexplained reasons, they avoid relying on specific articles. However, from his long experience with Algerian case law, the author can attest that it is difficult to find cases using or defining these principles, especially the principles concerning the best interests of the child, non-discrimination and the right of the child to be heard. Furthermore, the problem of sovereignty cannot be invoked to justify non-compliance with the CRC, since implementation is a logical effect of ratification, which in turn is an act of sovereignty.

3 The Implementation of the CRC

3.1 Implementation of the Rights of the Child by the Judiciary

It is impossible to advance any truly authoritative empirical analysis of the extent to which the terms and provisions of the CRC are deployed in Algerian Tribunal and Courts. There will be limited instances when judges and practitioners refer to the provisions of the Convention in exchanges that do not find their way into any written judgment. There will also be many occasions when practitioners deploy the underlying concepts of the Convention without making express reference to a particular provision of the UNCRC itself.

In a direct but informal conversation with a magistrate in charge of the Penal Juvenile Section cases in the city of Constantine (Eastern Algeria), he was asked how he and other juvenile magistrates apply the provisions of the CRC, bearing in mind that they have received training on the use of the Convention at the Superior School of Magistrates and that the training was conducted by recognised experts in juvenile justice from Algeria and abroad.[33] The answer was that there is no need to apply it directly and make reference to international norms on the right of the child as long as nothing in the national law obliges the magistrates to do so. According to the magistrate, it is enough that the courts apply the international principles embodied in Algerian legislation that addresses the problems faced by Algerian children.

The problem which this raises that the interpretation of the international principles will be made in conformity with the country's culture, thereby applying its cultural specificities to the principles rather than a universal interpretation mindful of conventional norms.

It is appropriate, nevertheless, to recall that Algeria does not have a juvenile code. The Algerian authorities declared during the presentation of the Second State Party Report in May–June 2004 that the process of enacting a code on the rights of the child was being finalised. The same declaration was made eight years later in 2012 during the examination of the Third and Fourth State Party Report, presented jointly.

The lack of political will is evident; however, civil society has revived debate on the urgent need for legislation on children's rights. This took place in February 2013, after incidents of child abduction, sexual abuse and murder spread across the territory of Algeria (Filali 2013).

Analysis of the reported written judgments of the tribunals and courts may, therefore, provide an uncertain guide to the extent to which the spirit (and, at times, the letter) of the CRC permeates certain aspects of legal practice in Algeria. Seeing as the CRC features in such a relatively small number of judgments reported from the Algerian jurisdiction, this should lead to the conclusion that it is an instrument of limited relevance to litigation in Algerian juvenile justice.

3.2 Statute of the Child in the Algerian Family Code

To assess the impact of the CRC's ratification and the degree to which the Algerian judiciary respects the rights of the child, it is useful to check if the country's adoption of other human rights instruments relevant to children were accompanied

[33] The experts include Jean Zermatten (former Chair of the UNCRC); Kamel Filali (former Vice-Chair of the UNCRC); and Hatem Kotrane (former Vice-Chair of the UNCRC).

by a drive to respect children's rights. These instruments include the International Covenant on Civil and Political Rights (ICCPR), the International Covenant on Economic, Social and Cultural Rights (ICESCR), the Convention against Torture and Other Cruel, Inhuman, Degrading Treatment or Punishment, and the Convention on the Elimination of all Forms of Discrimination against Women (CEDAW).

In the following discussion, reference is made to jurisprudence that has taken place before the CRC entered into force in Algeria to see if its main principles—such as the child's right to life, the right to express opinions freely and to be heard, the right not to be subject to discrimination, violence or abuse—are part of the Algerian judicial culture. In addition, the discussion refers to juvenile justice and the child's right to education and to be reintegrated into society free of stigmatization.

It is of paramount importance to note that the jurisprudence issued before the CRC's ratification continues to serve as a legal basis for today's decisions, given that this jurisprudence is taken from Sharia law which cannot be reviewed. As previously mentioned, the Family Code of Algeria is Sharia law, and in certain areas, such as the status of the child, his or her identity, succession and custody, it carries the same authority as the Constitution.

It is also pertinent to note that, in order to protect public order, the amendment made to the Family Code in 2005 involves the public prosecutor as a party in all litigation in family affairs. The state representative can appeal decisions even when the two parties in a conflict accept it. This shows again that there is a reinforcement of applying what is perceived as public order in conformity with the sources of law referred to above.[34]

3.3 Foster Family in the Algerian Family Code and Case Law

The status of the child differs from one situation to another. The Family Code considers the enlarged family based on traditional organisation and based on ties of family blood. Article 2 of the Algerian Family Code (AFC) views the family as the basic unit of Algerian society. The ties referred to above are set by marriage and parenthood. These elements of the family are also found in the articles 32 and 34 of the Algerian Civil Code (ACC).[35]

This situation is not applicable to all Algerian children, which is why one should look at the case of those children born out of wedlock. They are regarded as illegitimate children, are accorded an inferior status, and are discriminated against. By contrast, legitimacy is held as the norm since it is in conformity with Algerian law.

[34] Supreme Court Decision (11 October 2006. Review of the Supreme Court 2007. no. 2 Court Family Affairs Chamber, Case no. 401317). The State representative will make sure that religious, social and historical values will be respected and that no other views will be tolerated.

[35] Algerian Civil Code, articles 32 and 34, Law no. 07-05, 13 May, 2007, modifying and completing Ordinance no. 75-58 of 26 September, 1975, related to the Algerian Civil Code.

The majority of children, in fact, are legitimate because they were born within a legal union of their parents. Legitimacy is proven by marriage[36] since it (marriage) will introduce a child in a pre-constituted group, namely the family. Legitimacy confers a privileged status on the child, who will have filiation even if it is not the father who declares the birth registration to the civil or administrative authorities.

The Supreme Court of Algeria declared that a child is illegitimate if he or she is born 64 days, or 2 months and 4 days, after the act of marriage registration. The Court added:

> There is no contradiction in the judgment that considers the marriage valid but refuses to recognize the paternity of the spouse of the mother of the child since the child is born six months after the official marriage and sexual intercourses anterior to the official marriage do not constitute marriage fact.[37]

In another case related to evidence of the child's legal filiation, the Supreme Court considered that giving birth to a child in a period less than 6 months after marriage is contrary to article 42 of the AFC, which can be interpreted only within the context of Sharia law. The Court declared that 'the Tribunal and then the Court of Appeal have violated the law when they attributed to the child the name of the spouse of the child's mother'. The case was to be retransferred for re-examination by the same regional court and according to the legal instructions given by the Supreme Court and in conformity with article 38 of the Algerian Civil Procedure Code (ACPC).[38] Here, the Supreme Court breached the principle of non-discrimination, which is a fundamental principle in human rights common to all human rights conventions, particularly the CRC.

In conformity with Sharia law and the Family Code, a religious marriage can be validated in Algeria by a judgment issued by the Family Affairs Section of the Tribunal. Such a judgment will recognise the *Fatiha*,[39] but even in the case of a validation of a marriage by *Fatiha*, the judge can withhold recognition of the child as legitimate if he concludes on the basis of appropriate evidence that the date of sexual intercourse precedes the date of marriage. It is evident that there is no space for other interpretations; the Supreme Court is extremely rigorous in its application of the AFC, based as the latter is on Sharia law.

In a decision in 1987 concerning child maintenance, the Supreme Court decided that the Tribunal and then the Court violated the law when they decided to allocate alimony (*nafaka*) to children without first establishing that the parents

[36] Supreme Court decision (7/02/1989. File no. 47915. Algerian legal Review 1990, no. 3, p 69).

[37] Supreme Court Decision (1984. Supreme Court Review. 19 November 1984, Case no. 34791).

[38] Supreme Court of Algeria (1990. Law journal of the Supreme Court 1992, no. 2. Case no. 57756 dated January 1990). Ibid., (Case no. 168408 dated 8 July 1997). Ibid., (Case no. 296020 dated 25 December 2002. Review of the Supreme Court 2004 no. 1). Ibid., (Case no. 355180 dated 5 March 2006, Review of the Supreme Court 2006 no. 1).

[39] Article 6 of the Algerian Family Code. The *Fatiha* is the opening *sura* of the Koran, the sacred book of Muslims, consisting of seven verses; it emphasises the sovereignty and mercy of Allah. Marriage by *Fatiha* consists of a lecture of a simple '*Fatiha*'; whereas in some countries it does not require a preliminary civil ceremony, in Algeria one is required by law to have a civil ceremony.

were married.[40] This is a very strong indication that, after the ratification of the CRC and until today, the Family Code of 1984 is applicable and that the case law supports the principles of Sharia law which are integrated therein. The positive law in the domain of family affairs is strict: the 'illegitimate' child is discriminated against, and, over and above suffering from stigmatization, will encounter birth-registration difficulties that impact on school registration and access to health care.

A large number of children find themselves in this situation as a result of having been born in the 'black decade', a period between 1992 and 2002 when Algeria experienced instability due to militant Islamist opposition. Armed groups used terrorism to destabilise the state, and in these action numerous women were abducted, raped and taken as war prizes by the terrorists. Many victims of rape were minor girls who became pregnant and gave birth to children that do not have birth registration. Such children, who today are about 10 years old, live in particular hardship because they have been stigmatized and registered administratively on a document establishing only the name of the mother and under *kafala* law; this has been so even where the biological father is known and not opposed to the registration.

Tribunals and courts have rejected cases made by victimised mothers to obtain ordinary birth certificates stating the name of their child's known father. This was particularly evident after the National Reconciliation Policy came into effect 2005,[41] a piece of exceptional legislation granting amnesty to those who were in armed groups and did not commit serious offences. The irony is that rapists live in impunity in the same towns as their victims, whereas the women and their children are stigmatized, with most of their cases having gone unreported.

3.4 The Civil Rights of the Child

A child can be placed in a foster family undertaking to provide for his or her needs, education and protection.[42] In Islamic law, adoption—which creates family bonds comparable to those formed by biological filiation—is prohibited[43]; instead it provides for a form of guardianship called *kafala.*[44] *Kafala* resembles adoption, but there are major differences between them.

---

[40] Supreme Court of Algeria (7 February 1987. Family Affairs Chamber. Case no. 47915).

[41] The Charter on Peace and National Reconciliation was approved by referendum on 29 September, 2005, and published in the JORAPD, no. 11, 28 February 2006.

[42] Article 116 of AFC, Law no. 84-11 dated 9 June 1984, related to the Family Code completed and modified by Ordinance no. 05-01 dated 27 February 2005.

[43] Article 116 of AFC, Law no. 84-11 dated 9 June 1984, related to the Family Code completed and modified by Ordinance no. 05-01 dated 27 February 2005. Also, Supreme Court (21 November 2000. Review of the Supreme Court 2001. No. 2. Chamber of Family Affairs, case no. 246924).

[44] Article 125 of the AFC.

The *kafala* was introduced in Algerian positive law in 1976 by the Code of Public Health and held as a substitute to adoption.[45] Foster families are those in which at least one of the parents has no biological ties with the child; the foster father or mother is known as the *kafil*. In 1984 a ministerial decree, relating to the possibility of a change of names, authorised the *kafil* to give his family name to the *makfoul*, or foster child. In practice the *kafala* is instituted before a judge or under the scrutiny of a public notary. When the *kafil* gives his family name to the *makfoul*, it does not imply that the *makfoul* will be registered in the family registration book; the child will have a separate judicial or quasi-judicial document which will always remind him that legally he or she is not a member of the family and, as such, does not enjoy all the family rights, particularly succession rights.

When the *kafil* dies, the right to keep the *makfoul* child is transferred to his heirs. With regard to the legitimate child, when the father of this child dies the tutorial rights will belong to the mother; but the mother does not have automatic tutorial rights over the *makfoul* child—she is among the group of heirs who together have authority over such a child.

This rather bizarre arrangement complicates the life of the *makfoul* administratively and emotionally due to discrimination and the fragility of his legal status compared to that of his brother or of other children. As mentioned, the mother in this instance is among the heirs, but the right to take care of the *makfoul* and become a *kafil* is not automatic. It is the juvenile judge who will decide upon this at the end, further to which he should take into consideration the best interests of the child.[46]

3.4.1 The Right to an Identity

According to article 28 of the Algerian Civil Code, every child has the right to a name and identity, fundamental rights which are proclaimed by articles 7 and 8 of the CRC.

Every child born on the soil of Algeria has to be declared to the administrative authority within 5 days of his or her delivery.[47] The family name is always the father's name, except in cases where the born child is born out of wedlock or abandoned: if born out of wedlock, the child is given the name of the mother, and if abandoned, the administrative authority will attribute a name and first name. A child who is recognised by neither the father nor the mother is considered a child born to unknown parents and is put under public protection until placed in a foster family within the framework of *kafala* law.

The Algerian Tribunal and Court make a restrictive interpretation of the Family Code, the Civil Code and the Ordinance on the Status of Persons. The judiciary is

[45] Algerian code of Public Health, Law no. 85-05 dated 16 February 1985, on the protection and promotion of health.

[46] Supreme Court of Algeria (1990. Supreme Court Review 1991 no. 4 case no. 59013 dated 19 February 1991).

[47] Ordinance on Civil Status of Persons no. 70/20 dated 19 July 1970, article 61.

bound to justify its decision explicitly by expressly citing the articles of the Family Code or other Algerian legislation in terms of which the decision has been made, but has cited the CRC only on very rare occasions. As previously stated, in a Conference in Algiers on the implementation of the Concluding Observations of the Committee on the Rights of the Child, the juvenile administrative department of the Ministry of Justice declared that there were seven juvenile judgments that reported the articles of the Convention as a legal basis. The evaluation is that 20 years after its ratification by Algeria, the CRC is still not used as a legal basis for judicial decisions.

3.4.2 The Right of the Child to Maintenance

According to article 75 of the AFC, the father is under an obligation to provide materially for his children's needs. For the boy child, he is obliged to provide maintenance until the child reaches the age of majority; for the girl child, he should provide for her until she marries—in this case, the maintenance ceases on the day her marriage is consummated.[48]

In a decision by the Supreme Court in 1989, it was decided that attributing alimony to an adult male whose age is 21 years old was a violation of the law.[49]

Article 75 of the AFC extends maintenance after majority to the disabled child; in the event that the child is left without care and maintenance, the father can be prosecuted before a penal jurisdiction under the charge of family abandonment.[50]

A Supreme Court judgment confirmed that child alimony can be decided by the Tribunal of Interim Measures, thus reinforcing the requirement that the child's maintenance cannot be delayed.[51] In practice, divorced women to whom custody has been attributed have difficulties in alimony recovery. It is only after a penal proceeding on the basis of family abandonment and child neglect that the author of the abuse will be sanctioned and deprived of his liberty if evidence of non-payment of the alimony is presented to the penal judge. The Tribunal of Interim Measures can order a sampling of the father's wages.

3.4.3 Child Custody

The selection of cases mentioned below demonstrate that the Supreme Court is strict in its application of the AFC; since the latter derives from Sharia law, this is a constant judicial stand and it is thus immaterial that the cases pre-date Algeria's

---

48 Articles 36, 74, 77, 78, 79 and 80 of the AFC. Supreme Court Decision (14 June 1994. Review of the Supreme Court no. 2. Case no. 110607). Supreme Court Decision (13 July 2005. Review of the Supreme Court 2005 no. 2. Case no. 337343).

49 Supreme Court of Algeria (25 December 1989, Family Affairs Chamber, Case no. 57227).

50 Article 331 of the CPA. Supreme Court Decision (15 February 2000. Family Affairs Chamber. Case no. 253111).

51 Supreme Court of Algeria (7 February 1987. Family Affairs Chamber. Case no. 47915).

ratification of the CRC. What is important to stress is the fact that the child's opinion is not heard and that no interpretation other than Sharia law is possible.

According to article 38 of the ACC, the domicile of a minor is that of his legal representative. This is applied in normal situations when the child lives with his two parents, but the problem is different in a divorce where the parents are each claiming custody of the child. Article 62 of the AFC provides that 'custody means maintenance, schooling and education (moral and intellectual) within the framework of the religion of the father'. The main school of thought in Algeria would like to keep child custody aligned with the precepts of Sharia law, which provides that the mother is responsible for custody until the child becomes a grown-up (at about 10 years of age).

The judge in a case of divorce is always required to take the principle of the child's best interests into account in determining which parent has custody of the child.[52]

In a case relating to the custody of four children, the Supreme Court declared that the Tribunal and then the Court of Appeal of Family Affairs of the city of Constantine—which rendered their decision based on the wishes of two of the children who wanted to remain and reside with their paternal grandmother—violated article 42 of the AFC because *hadana* (custody) is indivisible and the four children should remain under the custody of the mother, as ordered by Sharia law.[53]

Numerous custody cases involve parents of different nationality. Children born out of a mixed marriage are Algerians since they are born from an Algerian ascendance. In the many cases before the judiciary, the decision regarding *hadana* is always in favour of the father even when the foreign mother is Muslim. Fathers are rarely sued for child abduction when they bring their children from abroad for a so-called 'vacation' in Algeria or a 'visit to parents' but then oblige the children to remain in this, the father's own national home.

In a case involving litigation on the custody of children, the Supreme Court declared that the Tribunal of Hussein Dey (Algiers) and then the Court of Appeal of Algiers made a wrongful application and violated the law when they attributed custody to a mother living in a foreign country.[54]

In a case before the Family Affairs Section of the Tribunal of Ain Beida (Eastern Algeria) in 2010, the Tribunal refused to attribute the custody of three girls to their Muslim Australian mother. The children, girls born in Australia, were abducted by the father, who had married and lived in Australia.

In principle, in all actions concerning children the best interests of the child shall be 'a primary consideration'. What this means in practice is that the child shall remain with the mother and that the father pays for alimony when both parents are Algerian. In cases of mixed marriage, and even where the mother is Muslim, the father will obtain custody in accordance with the principle that the child should grow up within the religion of the father.

---

[52] Article 64 of the AFC.

[53] Supreme Court of Algeria (2 April 1984. Supreme Court Review no. 1 Case no. 32594).

[54] Supreme Court of Algeria (case no. 59013, dated 19 February 1990, Supreme Court Journal 1991 no. 4).

The AFC mentions the principle of the best interest of the child in its article 66, but no definition or interpretation of the principle has been made by the courts. The Supreme Court declared in a decision that the *hadana* attributed to a father is not in conformity with article 66 of the AFC since the Tribunal and then the Court confirmed a judgment which gives custody to the father after the renunciation of her priority right to custody by the mother. The girl child was ill, and the Supreme Court declared that it is in the best interests of the child that she remain with the mother, an arrangement which is in alignment with Sharia law.[55] A mother can renounce custody only if she finds a person capable of insuring custody by substitution; if not, her renunciation will not be accepted. Should the child be left without due care, the mother can be prosecuted on the penal ground of child abandonment.

In this case, the father accepted custody after the mother's renunciation of it, but since the girl child was ill, the Supreme Court rejected attribution of custody to the father on the basis of Sharia law, in terms of which the best interests of the child are interpreted differently according to the sex of the child. The mother's renunciation was refused, a decision which confirms that the CRC is not applicable and that the Sharia-based Family Code prevails over certain constitutional principles such as equality and non-discrimination.

It is also appropriate to mention that a mother perceived by the community as unfit to bring up a child will lose her right to custody according to article 62 of the AFC, which will be applied literally by the judiciary.[56] In terms of the last such reported case, it is not only so that the mother loses custody—her own mother in turn becomes ineligible for custody, on the basis of an extended lack of trust.[57] The interpretation of what constitutes an unfit mother is made strictly on cultural grounds.

4 Child Neglect and Abuse as a Penal or Criminal Offence

Child neglect and abuse is a penal or criminal offence and is severely sanctioned. Article 19 of the CRC deals with maltreatment in all its forms: physical and psychological violence, as well as neglect and negligent treatment and exploitation, including sexual abuse. Many cases of maltreatment are unreported and thus remain unknown to the police and others with the authority to intervene.

An investigation into children's maltreatment, conducted by the Ministry of Solidarity in charge of family and children's affairs, revealed that physical maltreatment is the most prevalent crime against children, followed by psychological violence associated with sexual violence and neglect.

---

[55] Supreme Court of Algeria (3 July 1989. Supreme Court. Review 1992, no. 1. Case no. 54353).

[56] Supreme Court of Algeria (22 May 1989. Supreme Court. Review 1991, no. 4. Case no. 53578).

[57] Supreme Court of Algeria (9 January 1984. Supreme Court Review 1985 no. 1. Case no. 31997).

4.1 Crimes Related to the Life and Health of the Child

The Algerian Penal Code refers to such crimes against the child as infanticide, voluntary assault and battery, and voluntary food deprivation and willful neglect to the point of jeopardising the health and life of the child. Offenders are subject to confinement for one to five years. These sanctions are aggravated in cases when the author of the crime is a parent, a legal representative or the guardian. The penalty can extend to capital punishment.

Child neglect in public places is also punishable by severe penalties, taking into consideration the child's level of suffering and his or her social proximity to the author of the crime; if the latter is the mother or father, he or she can lose parental authority over the child victim.

It should be noted that numerous cases remain unreported and go unpunished due to lack of sufficient evidence or lack of prosecution.

4.2 Protection Measures

The judicialisation of the protection of children is a theoretical reality. To put an end to threats to the child's life and security, the juvenile judge can be called upon to intervene as the institution with the jurisdiction to provide assistance to children in moral threat. He will intervene following a request by the father or mother, the legal representative or the child, the Wali (the top administrative representative of the state in the region), the prosecutor or the president of the municipality (i.e. the mayor).

According to Article 453 of the Algerian Penal Procedural Code (APPC), the juvenile judge—after a thorough examination of the personality of the juvenile based on a serious social investigation, a medical and psychological report—can order on a provisional basis the placement of the child in a foster centre or a unit with the duty to provide assistance to children in an educative or professional training centre. The judge has to decide within 1 month after the date of the request.

It is the author's opinion that the judge does not intervene in all cases because of a lack of will or lack of sufficient centres. When a placement decision is made, the child can be sent to remote centres, which deprives him or her of the right to keep in direct contact with the family. Placement in a remote centre also weakens the likelihood of there being adequate judicial follow-up of the child's file, given that these centres can sometimes be as far as 200 km away from the juvenile section of the tribunal.

The judge can either decide that the child should remain with the family, or choose which of the parents is fit to exercise custody of the child, taking into consideration all binding norms of the AFC. He may also decide, in conformity with the AFC, that custody should be exercised by another person who shows an interest in this and meets the material and moral conditions. Alternatively, the judge could rule that the child be assisted, protected and guided by a state department in charge of monitoring, educating or re-educating children in an open regime.

4.3 Child Offenders

In terms of article 40 of the CRC, every child alleged as, accused of, or recognised as having infringed the penal law is entitled to treatment that is likely to foster a sense of dignity and self-worth and thereby facilitate his or her reintegration into society as a constructive role-player within it.

Juvenile delinquency is not a new phenomenon, and it not for the author to attempt to explain it in terms of criminal sociology or psychology and the like; the task instead is to take it as a fact and determine what Algeria's judicial response to child offenders should be in view of the applicability of international norms and standards.

To enable children to avoid coming into conflict with the law and hence to prevent juvenile delinquency, Algeria has provided for a special penal system. The placement of the child offender is its main measure, and this can be done in either a closed or open environment (article 455 of the APPC). The tribunal may appoint an institution specialised in vocational education and training or designate a public or private care setting to assist the child offender. Offenders under 13 years of age may not be placed, even temporarily, in a penitentiary due to the presumption that such children lack criminal responsibility.

In practice the juvenile section of the tribunal has difficulties when it comes to implementing the CRC, because the child-friendly approach this necessitates would provoke dire criticism by the public: 'the street' today reacts violently if the serious punishments required by Sharia law fail to be applied, as, for instance, in a situation where a minor of 16 years commits a grave offence such as assassination.

5 Conclusion

Algeria's legislative compliance with the CRC is evident in several laws, and the state's interest in children's rights is visible in the official texts that give them recognition. However, there is no basis as yet on which to launch a code on the rights of the child in Algeria and to strengthen these rights within an independent jurisdiction; at present, the juvenile court has jurisdiction in all cases involving child offenders. Legislation has certainly allowed for the management of children but it is insufficient, given that protection of the child requires a framework of laws, regulations and mechanisms which is geared towards enhancing such protection, especially in the case of the offender or child in conflict with the law.

Should one conclude, then, that Algeria's legislation on children's rights is compliant with the CRC and that these rights are respected and implemented? Given what this chapter has presented, the answer cannot be in the affirmative.

Ratification of the CRC has not been followed by implementation, and fundamental rights—the best interests of the child, non-discrimination, the right to be heard, and the right to life and to growth in an environment favourable to health, education and psychological balance—are neither protected nor respected, especially by the judiciary. Algeria needs a specific code for children's rights, and it needs judiciary dedicated to, and engaged in, defending the rights of the child set out in the CRC.

The chapter covered several important questions on the rights of the child in Algeria and their implementation by the judiciary. As has been noted repeatedly, there are no judicial decisions that demonstrate judicial compliance with the CRC. Sharia law, the primary and prioritised source of law, constitutes a major legal and cultural limit to the application of the children's rights in the CRC. This is why it is imperative to adopt a child-friendly approach capable of creating an environment that promotes children's dignity and supports their education, health and psychological stability. Children in conflict with the law should not be regarded, as is the case today, as criminals to be stigmatized. Culture must change, because changing the laws alone is not enough.

Reference

Filali, K. (2013, March 19). SOS enfants en danger. *Le Soir D'Algérie.*

Chapter 11
The CRC in Litigation Under the ICCPR and CEDAW

Litigating the Rights of the Child Through the Individual Complaints Procedures of the Human Rights Committee and the Committee on the Elimination of Discrimination Against Women

Alfred de Zayas

Abstract The Third Optional Protocol to the Convention on the Rights of the Child has entered into force in April 2014. Petitions concerning violations of the rights of the child were hitherto justiciable before the Human Rights Committee and the Committee on the Elimination of Discrimination against Women, both of which have produced useful jurisprudence. While these Committees will continue to have jurisdiction over such cases, it is to be expected that henceforth petitioners will turn to the Committee on the Rights of the Child as the most specialised body in the field.

1 Introduction

All nine core United Nations human rights treaties impact in one way or another on the rights of the child. State reporting procedures under the treaties are useful and necessary, but the individual complaints procedures offer advantages, such as enhancing visibility and education. The system of petitions is a crucial tool, because it empowers individuals to submit complaints to domestic and international instances, judicial and quasi-judicial, enabling a case-by-case analysis of situations so as to determine whether a violation of a treaty provision has occurred and, if so, to formulate specific remedies.

Alfred de Zayas is an UN Independent Expert on the Promotion of a Democratic and Equitable International Order

---

A. de Zayas (✉)
Former Chief of the Petitions Section, Retired Lawyer Office of the UN High Commissioner for Human Rights, Geneva, Switzerland
e-mail: alfreddezayas@gmail.com

T. Liefaard and J.E. Doek (eds.), *Litigating the Rights of the Child*,
DOI 10.1007/978-94-017-9445-9_11

The League of Nations already knew human-rights petitions procedures under the mandate and minority protection systems (Walters 1952; Von Truhardt 1931). The United Nations Charter, under Chapters XI and XII, subsequently provided for petitions procedures concerning the rights of persons living in non-self-governing territories or placed under Trusteeship in the context of UN mandates.

Regional human-rights petition systems emerged quickly after the Second World War, notably the Inter-American Commission and Court on Human Rights and the European Commission and Court of Human Rights. In the United Nations system it took longer to recognise human rights complaints procedures, notably by virtue of Resolutions 728F, 1235 and 1503 of the Economic and Social Council and by the procedures established under article 14 of the Convention on the Elimination of All Forms of Racial Discrimination (in force in 1969); article 22 of the Convention Against Torture (in force in 1987); article 31 of the Convention on Enforced Disappearances (in force in 2010); and the Optional Protocols to the International Covenant on Civil and Political Rights (ICCPR, in force in 1976); to the Convention on the Elimination of Discrimination Against Women (CEDAW, in force in 2000), to the Convention on the Rights of Persons with Disabilities (in force in 2008), and to the International Covenant on Economic, Social and Cultural Rights (ICESCR, in force 2013). A petitions procedure is foreseen pursuant to article 77 of the Convention on the Rights of All Migrant Workers and Members of their Families (not yet in force) and the Third Optional Protocol to the Convention on the Rights of the Child (in force in 2014).

Prior to the entry into force of the Optional Protocol to the Convention on the Rights of the Child establishing a Communications Procedure, the two principal petition procedures pertinent to the defence of child rights have been those of the Human Rights Committee (pursuant to articles 10(3), 17, 23 and 24 of the ICCPR)[1] and of the Committee on the Elimination of Discrimination Against Women, particularly concerning issues such as rape, abortion and female genital mutilation. By the summer of 2013, a rich jurisprudence has emerged which will be of guidance to the Committee on the Rights of the Child when it begins its petitions work.

Victims of violations of child rights have the choice of various procedures to which they may address their complaints. Following the entry into force of the Third OP to CRC, victims will continue to have the opportunity to engage the communications procedures of the Human Rights Committee, the Committee on the Elimination of Discrimination against Women, the Committee on the Elimination of Racial Discrimination, the Committee against Torture, the Committee on Disappeared Persons, and the Committee on Persons with Disabilities, if they believe that these bodies would adjudicate their claims faster or with greater authority. In order to ensure coherence and consistency in the case law and avoid conflicting or competing holdings on similar situations, all UN treaty bodies and their petitions procedures are serviced by the same United Nations Secretariat at the Office of the UN High Commissioner for Human Rights.

---

[1] See Möller and De Zayas (2009), Nowak (2005). A useful link to the jurisprudence is http://sim.law.uu.nl/sim/caselaw/tribunalen.nsf.

Whereas each Committee can examine cases only on the basis of its own treaty or convention and may not interpret or apply the provisions of other conventions, the members of each Committee regularly inform themselves about relevant jurisprudence in the other UN Committees as well as before the International Court of Justice[2] and in regional human rights courts and tribunals, including the African Committee of Experts on the Rights and Welfare of the Child,[3] and on the pronouncements of specialised UN agencies such as UNICEF, UNESCO and the International Labour Organization, which has adopted several conventions of relevance to child rights, notably Convention 138 on the minimum age for admission to employment (1973) and Convention 182 on the prohibition and immediate action for the elimination of the worst forms of child labour (1999).

What are also pertinent are the reports of the Human Rights Council's Special Procedures mandate holders, including the Special Rapporteur on trafficking in persons, especially women and children, Joy Ngozi Ezeilo,[4] the Special Rapporteur on the sale of children, child prostitution and child pornography, Najat Maalla M'jid,[5] the Special Rapporteur on Violence against Women, Rashida Manjoo, and the Special Rapporteur on the Right to Education, Kishore Singh. The United Nations Special Representative of the Secretary-General (SRSG) on Violence against Children (a Secretariat post at the Assistant Secretary–General (ASG) level), Marta Santos Pais, advises the Secretary General and issues relevant reports that also provide further guidance to Committee experts.

It bears repeating that case law is living law that gives a human face to abstract norms, interprets them in concrete situations and exemplifies how they should be applied. Case law is not merely curative, but in a very real sense preventive, of human rights violations, because once a decision, opinion or judgment has become public, governments and individuals know that in similar cases the norms should be applied in a prescribed way. Case law is thus eminently educational.

The paramount consideration under article 24 of the ICCPR and under the CRC is the best interests of the child and the obligation of the state to ensure special protection of children. Existing jurisprudence elucidates multiple areas where the rights of minors have been protected, including the prohibition of child labour; military recruitment of minors; child prostitution and child pornography; trafficking; paedophilia; female genital mutilation;[6] child marriage; indefinite detention[7] in the context of asylum and deportation procedures; family reunification; ill-treatment; domestic violence; custody and visiting rights, in particular the right of the child to

---

[2] http://www.icj-cij.org/docket/index.php?p1=3&p2=4&k=5a&case=131&code=mwp&p3=4.

[3] http://www.ihrda.org/515-2/.

[4] Statement to the General Assembly on the special workshop of 13 May 2013. http://www.ohchr.org/Documents/Issues/Trafficking/SRontraffickingHL13May2013.pdf

[5] http://daccess-dds-ny.un.org/doc/UNDOC/GEN/G10/178/28/PDF/G1017828.pdf?OpenElement.

[6] See CEDAW General Recommendation 14 (1990). http://www.un.org/womenwatch/daw/cedaw/recommendations/recomm.htm#recom14.

[7] http://www.icrc.org/eng/assets/files/other/irrc_857_zayas.pdf.

have continued contact with both parents; disappeared persons; and the right, inter alia, to a nationality, child-care facilities and education.

The Human Rights Committee's General Comment No. 17 on the rights of the child (adopted 1994) provides guidance:

> Article 24 … recognizes the right of every child, without any discrimination, to receive from his family, society and the State the protection required by his status as a minor. Consequently, the implementation of this provision entails the adoption of special measures to protect children, in addition to the measures that States are required to take under article 2 to ensure that everyone enjoys the rights provided for in the Covenant. … Responsibility for guaranteeing children the necessary protection lies with the family, society and the State. Although the Covenant does not indicate how such responsibility is to be apportioned, it is primarily incumbent on the family … and particularly on the parents, to create conditions to promote the harmonious development of the child's personality and his enjoyment of the rights recognized in the Covenant.

Important Human Rights Committee case law has interpreted and applied, inter alia, articles 10, 17, 23 and 24 of the ICCPR.[8] The Committee on the Elimination of Discrimination against Women has interpreted and applied, inter alia, articles 5, 11, and 16. Examples of this case law will be presented in the next paragraphs, focusing first on procedural issues, then on substantive issues. The selection of these issues is linked to provisions of the CRC. I address the fundamental right of the child to proper registration and preservation of identity (art. 7 and 8 CRC), before turning to cases on the child's right to maintain contact with both parents (art. 9(3) CRC). A few decisions concerning children of immigrant or asylum-seeking parents are outlined. The right of the child to protection is primarily the domain of the CRC (art. 19, 32–38). Examples of decisions regarding the right to protection are given, inter alia, on the protection from abuse as well as harmful traditional practices and female genital mutilation. Finally, examples are given of decisions about the detention of children and their treatment (art. 37 and 39 CRC).

The following section presents decisions of the Human Rights Committee (HRC) and Committee on the Elimination of Discrimination Against Women concerning the interpretation of provisions of the ICCPR and CEDAW, decisions which can be considered as relevant, too, for the interpretation of articles of the CRC.

2 Selected Jurisprudence of the HRC and CEDAW

2.1 Procedural Issues

The rules of procedure of the Committees with communications or petitions procedures have fairly standard admissibility criteria. Among the classical

[8] Article 24: 1. Every child shall have, without any discrimination as to race, colour, sex, language, religion, national or social origin, property or birth, the right to such measures of protection as are required by his status as a minor, on the part of his family, society and the State. 2. Every child shall be registered immediately after birth and shall have a name. 3. Every child has the right to acquire a nationality.'

preconditions of admissibility are the requirement that the claim be submitted by or on behalf of the victim of a specific violation of a treaty provision in a concrete situation (no *in abstracto* examination of State legislation or *actio popularis*), the exhaustion of domestic remedies, and the preclusion of simultaneous submission to other instances of examination or settlement.

Particularly relevant in the context of child rights is the standing of the person submitting the communication. Who has authority to present petitions? Whereas in some countries only the custodial parent has authority to act on behalf of a minor, the Human Rights Committee has stated that a non-custodial parent can submit a case on behalf of his or her minor child.

This issue arose in case No. 397/1990 (*P.S. v. Denmark*), where a non-custodial parent submitted a case on his own behalf and on behalf of his minor son. While the case was declared inadmissible for non-exhaustion of domestic remedies, it is important to note that the Committee did not take the narrow view that the non-custodial parent lacked standing, but recognised the father's legitimate right under the Optional Protocol to represent before the Committee the Covenant rights of his minor son:

> The Committee has taken notice of the State party's contention that the author has no standing to act on behalf of his son, as Danish law limits this right to the custodial parent. The Committee observes that standing under the Optional Protocol may be determined independently of national regulations and legislation governing an individual's standing before a domestic court of law. In the present case, it is clear that T.S. cannot himself submit a complaint to the Committee; the relationship between father and son and the nature of the allegations must be deemed sufficient to justify representation of T.S. before the Committee by his father.[9]

However, in a subsequent case the Committee did *marche arrière,* and held in case No. 1012/2001 (*Burgess v. Australia*) that the author, a British citizen who had been expelled from Australia, whereas his Australian wife and three children born in Australia had remained behind, submitted the case on behalf of himself, his wife and his children. The Committee did not recognise Mr Burgess' right to represent his wife and children. His authority to do so was challenged by the State party, and the Committee decided that, in the absence of a power of attorney from the wife and children, Mr Burgess had no standing to represent them before the Committee.

This anomalous decision may be explained by the rather 'conservative' approach that some Committee members manifest in matters of expulsion and deportation. I consider that to demand the father or mother of a child to submit a power of attorney is unreasonable. The Committee can very well examine the claim and find no violation, if the factual submissions are insufficient to substantiate a violation. Happily, subsequent jurisprudence has allowed parents to submit cases on behalf of their offspring without power of attorney.

It is not clear under what circumstances children themselves would be deemed to possess standing before the Human Rights Committee and the Committee on

---

[9] HRC 1992 Report, Annex X, Sect. R., para. 5.2.

the Elimination of Discrimination against Women. The Optional Protocol to the Convention on the Rights of the Child does allow children to submit communications themselves. See also the OPIC rules of procedure, pursuant to which representation is also allowed and, in cases where consent is not possible, the Committee may accept the communication if it considers it in the best interests of the child (CRC/C/62/3 rule 13).

2.2 Substantive Issues

2.2.1 The Right of the Child to Proper Registration and Preservation of Identity (Art. 24 ICCPR)

In the context of the 'dirty war' in Argentina of the 1980s, some 30,000 persons disappeared and their children were frequently given up for adoption. In an early case before the Human Rights Committee, the issue was the identity of a girl child who had been given in adoption to another family and whose grandmother succeeded in locating. In finding a violation of article 24 by Argentina, the Committee held in case No. 400/1990 (*Darwina Rosa Monaco de Gallicchio and Ximena Vicario v. Argentina*):

> While the Committee appreciates the seriousness with which the Argentine courts endeavoured to redress the wrongs done to Ms. Vicario and her grandmother, it observes that the duration of the various judicial proceedings extended for over 10 years, and that some of the proceedings have not yet been completed. The Committee notes that in the meantime Ms. Vicario, who was 7 years of age when found, reached the age of maturity (18 years) in 1994, and that it was not until 1993 that her legal identity as Ximena Vicario was officially recognized. In the specific circumstances of this case, the Committee finds that the protection of children stipulated in article 24 of the Covenant required the State party to take affirmative action to grant Ms. Vicario prompt and effective relief from her predicament.... Bearing in mind the suffering already endured by Ms. Vicario, who lost both of her parents under tragic circumstances imputable to the State party, the Committee finds that the special measures required under article 24, paragraph 1, of the Covenant were not expeditiously applied by Argentina, and that the failure to recognize the standing of Mrs. Mónaco in the guardianship and visitation proceedings and the delay in legally establishing Ms. Vicario's real name and issuing identity papers also entailed a violation of article 24, paragraph 2, of the Covenant, which is designed to promote recognition of the child's legal personality.[10]

It should be noted that the disappearances of children in Argentina and their adoption were the reasons for the inclusion of article 8 in the CRC, which requires States parties to respect the right of the child to preserve her or his identity and to provide the child illegally deprived of some or all elements of her or his identity appropriate assistance and protection with a view to re-establishing speedily her or his identity (Detrick 1992).

---

[10] http://www1.umn.edu/humanrts/undocs/html/vws400.htm.

2.2.2 The Right of the Child to Maintain Contact with Both Parents (Art. 17 ICCPR)

This right, which can be seen as an element of the right to respect family life, is particularly relevant in case the parents of the child separate or in case the parent is denied custody and the child is placed in alternative care. Some examples of decisions of the Human Rights Committee follow.

In case No. 946/2000 (*L.P. v. the Czech Republic*) the author was a divorced parent whose rights to family visits with his children had been recognised in various orders by the competent Czech courts. In practice, however, these orders had not been implemented. In finding a violation of article 17, *juncto* article 2 of the Covenant, the Committee observed

> that article 17 generally includes effective protection to the right of a parent to regular contact with his or her minor children. While there may be exceptional circumstances in which denying contact is required in the interests of the child and cannot be deemed unlawful or arbitrary, in the present case the domestic courts of the State party have ruled that such contact should be maintained. Consequently, the issue before the Committee is whether the State party has afforded effective protection in the author's right to meet his son.... Although the courts repeatedly fined the author's wife for failure to respect their preliminary orders, these fines were neither fully enforced nor replaced with other measures aimed at ensuring the author's rights. In these circumstances and taking into account the considerable delays at various stages of the proceedings, the Committee takes the view that the author's rights under article 17 of the Covenant, in conjunction with article 2, paragraphs 1 and 2 of the Covenant, did not receive effective protection.[11]

This holding manifests a pragmatic approach in the Committee's jurisprudence and imposes an obligation on the State party to take the necessary measures so as to ensure that its own court decisions are enforced. In case No. 1407/2005 (*Juan Asensi Martinez on his own behalf and on behalf of his children v. Paraguay*), the Committee followed the L.P. precedent. In holding that articles 23 and 24 had been violated, the Committee noted:

> that the author and his ex-wife were married in August 1997 and that his daughters were born in 1997 and 1999 respectively. The family first lived in Paraguay and in September 1999 moved to Spain, where the author was working. Starting in January 2001, when his ex-wife left Spain for good with their daughters, the author made numerous attempts to keep in contact with the children, obtain their return and meet their material and emotional needs. On the legal front, his efforts took the form of administrative and judicial action of various kinds, both in Spain, the last place the family lived, and in the State party [Paraguay]. The remedies invoked in the Spanish courts gave rise to a separation order in November 2002 granting the author care and custody of the girls. In addition, the Spanish authorities made approaches to the State party with a view to protecting the author's rights under the Hague Convention on the Civil Aspects of International Child Abduction, to which both States are party.
>
> With regard to the measures taken in the State party [Paraguay], the Committee notes that the author applied to the courts in proceedings of two kinds: (a) to obtain the return of the children and (b) to obtain effective access to his children and assert his right of custody.

[11] HRC 2002 Report, Vol. II, Annex IX, Sect. HH, para. 7.2–7.4.

> The former gave rise to judgements in three courts, of which the Appeal Court and Supreme Court rulings found against the return of the children. Both the Appeal Court and the Supreme Court state that they have taken account of the children's best interests and that taking them to Spain would in their view have put them at psychological risk given their young age. Yet the judgements do not explain what either court understands by 'best interests' and 'psychological risk' or what evidence was considered in reaching the conclusion that there was in fact such a risk. There is also nothing to show that the author's complaints concerning the children's unsafe living conditions in Paraguay were duly examined.[12]

It is axiomatic that contact between parents and their children is important for the proper development of the children, except in extraordinary situations. In case No. 1052/2002 (*Natalya Tcholatch on her own behalf and on behalf of her daughter, Julia Tcholatch v. Canada*), the Canadian Court had taken custody away from the mother, who challenged the fairness of the hearings. In finding violations of articles 23 and 24 of the ICCPR, the Committee recalled:

> its jurisprudence that the national courts are generally competent to evaluate the circumstances of individual cases. However, the law should establish certain criteria so as to enable the courts to apply the full provisions of article 23 of the Covenant. 'It seems essential, except in exceptional circumstances, that these criteria should include the maintenance of personal relations and direct and regular contact between the child and parents.'[13] In the absence of such special circumstances, the Committee recalls that it cannot be deemed to be in the best interest of a child to eliminate altogether a parent's access to him or her.[14] In the present case, the judge, during the child protection trial of 2000, considered that 'there were no special circumstances demonstrated which would justify the continuation of access in these circumstances', instead of examining the issue whether there were exceptional circumstances justifying terminating access, thereby reversing the perspective under which such issues should be considered.[15]

2.2.3 The Right of the Child to Respect for Family Life

Children of Immigrants

Case No. 930/2000 (*Winata* et al. *v. Australia*) concerned Indonesian parents who had irregularly stayed in Australia and had a son who, after 10 years, was entitled to Australian citizenship. The Human Rights Committee found that the deportation of the parents, if implemented, would entail violations of articles 17, 23 and 24 of the ICCPR. The Committee observed:

> that a decision of the State party to deport two parents and to compel the family to choose whether a 13-year-old child, who has attained citizenship of the State party after living

---

[12] http://sim.law.uu.nl/SIM/CaseLaw/CCPRcase.nsf/4efdbe13073fc6b7c12567b70044cc04/31291719bec69457c12576400054800c?OpenDocument, paras. 7.2–7.4.

[13] Communication No.201/1985, *Hendriks v. The Netherlands*, Views adopted on 27 July 1988, paragraph 10.4.

[14] Communication No.514/1992, Fei v. Colombia, Views adopted on 4 April 1995, paragraph 8.10.

[15] http://www.unhchr.ch/tbs/doc.nsf/(Symbol)/c7fdc9eeec70029fc12572cd00480d76?Opendocument, paras. 8(7), 8(8).

> there 10 years, either remains alone in the State party or accompanies his parents is to be considered 'interference' with the family, at least in circumstances where, as here, substantial changes to long-settled family life would follow in either case.... It is certainly unobjectionable under the Covenant that a State party may require, under its laws, the departure of persons who remain in its territory beyond limited duration permits. Nor is the fact that a child is born, or that by operation of law such a child receives citizenship either at birth or at a later time, sufficient of itself to make a proposed deportation of one or both parents arbitrary. Accordingly, there is significant scope for States parties to enforce their immigration policy and to require departure of unlawfully present persons. That discretion is, however, not unlimited and may come to be exercised arbitrarily in certain circumstances. In the present case, both authors have been in Australia for over fourteen years. The authors' son has grown in Australia from his birth 13 years ago, attending Australian schools as an ordinary child would and developing the social relationships inherent in that. In view of this duration of time, it is incumbent on the State party to demonstrate additional factors justifying the removal of both parents that go beyond a simple enforcement of its immigration law in order to avoid a characterisation of arbitrariness. In the particular circumstances, therefore, the Committee considers that the removal by the State party of the authors would constitute, if implemented, arbitrary interference with the family, contrary to article 17, paragraph 1, in conjunction with article 23, of the Covenant in respect of all of the alleged victims, and, additionally, a violation of article 24, paragraph 1, in relation to Barry Winata due to a failure to provide him with the necessary measures of protection as a minor.[16]

Case No. 1011/2011 (*Francesco and Ana Madaferi and their children v. Australia*) concerned the threatened deportation of a family and its impact on family life. In holding that the deportation would entail violations of the Covenant, the Committee observed:

> that a decision by the State party to deport the father of a family with four ... children and to compel the family to choose whether they should accompany him or stay in the State party is to be considered 'interference' with the family. ... The issue thus arises whether or not such interference would be arbitrary and thus contrary to article 17 of the Covenant. The Committee observes that in cases of imminent deportation the material point in time for assessing this issue must be that of its consideration of the case. It further observes that in cases where one part of a family must leave the territory of the State party while the other part would be entitled to remain, the relevant criteria for assessing whether or not the specific interference with family life can be objectively justified must be considered, on the one hand, in light of the significance of the State party's reasons for the removal of the person concerned and, on the other, the degree of hardship the family and its members would encounter as a consequence of such removal. In the present case, the Committee notes that the State party justifies the removal of Mr. Madafferi by his illegal presence in Australia, his alleged dishonesty in his relations with the Department of Immigration and Multicultural Affairs, and his 'bad character' stemming from criminal acts committed in Italy twenty years ago. ... [T]he Committee considers that the removal by the State party of Mr. Madafferi would, if implemented, constitute arbitrary interference with the family, contrary to article 17, paragraph 1, in conjunction with article 23, of the Covenant in respect of all of the authors, and additionally, a violation of article 24, paragraph 1, in relation to the four minor children due to a failure to provide them with the necessary measures of protection as minors.[17]

[16] http://www1.umn.edu/humanrts/undocs/930-2000.html, paras. 7.2–7.3.

[17] http://www1.umn.edu/humanrts/undocs/html/1011-2001.html, para. 9.8.

Family Reunification

In case No. 1143/2002 (*Farag El Dernawi v. Libyan Arab Jamahiriya*) the author had obtained asylum in Switzerland and sought family reunification in Switzerland with his six children. The Libyan government, however, refused to allow the children to leave the country to join him in Switzerland. In finding a violation of article 17 of the ICCPR, the Committee stated:

> that the interference with family life was arbitrary in terms of article 17 with respect to the author, his wife and six children, and that the State party failed to discharge its obligation under article 23 to respect the family unit in respect of each member of the family. On the same basis, and in view of the advantage to a child's development in living with both parents absent persuasive countervailing reasons, the Committee concludes that the State party's action has failed to respect the special status of the children, and finds a violation of the rights of the children up to the age of eighteen years under article 24 of the Covenant.[18]

2.2.4 The Right of the Child to Protection (Art. 24 ICCPR)

Protection from Domestic Violence and Molestation

Case No. 31/2011 (*S.V.P. v. Bulgaria*) before the Committee on the Elimination of Discrimination against Women concerned a 7-year-old child who had been sexually molested by a man who was subsequently given a suspended sentence and ordered to pay civil compensation, which remained unenforced. In finding a violation by the State party of articles 2 and 15 of CEDAW, the Committee observed:

> that article 15 of the Convention embodies the principle of equality before the law, and that under this article, the Convention seeks to protect women's status before the law, be it as a claimant, a witness or a victim, and that the above includes the right to adequate compensation in cases of violence including sexual violence. The Committee observes that the State party has not provided a reliable system for effective compensation of the victims of sexual violence, including for moral damages and that no legal aid scheme exists for the execution procedure, even for victims who are disabled as a result of the sexual violence experienced, such as the author's daughter.[19]

Case No. 32/2011 (*Isatou Jallow v. Bulgaria*) concerned a Gambian woman who had a daughter by a Bulgarian man who subsequently became violent, sexually molested their daughter, and took the child away. In finding a violation of articles 5 and 16 of CEDAW, because of lack of adequate protection to the mother and her daughter, the Committee observed

> that the author and her daughter have suffered serious moral and pecuniary damage and prejudice. The author had to continue a relationship with a violent husband since she was in a vulnerable position and did not receive adequate protection. For a considerable

---

[18] http://www.worldcourts.com/hrc/eng/decisions/2007.07.20_El_Dernawi_v_Libya.htm, para. 6.3.

[19] http://www2.ohchr.org/english/law/docs/CEDAW/CEDAW-C-53-D-31-2011_en.pdf, para. 9.11.

period, the author and her daughter were forcibly separated. Furthermore, the Committee has taken note of the author's statement that she had to accept disadvantageous terms for a divorce by mutual consent in order to obtain custody of her daughter.[20]

Protection in the Context of Child Pregnancies and Abortion

In case No. 1153/2003 (*Karen Noelia Llantoy Huamán v. Peru*), the Human Rights Committee found violations of articles 2, 7, 17 and 24 of the ICCPR, given that the State party refused to allow the child mother to have an abortion. In so doing the Committee noted

> that a public-sector doctor told the author that she could either continue with the pregnancy or terminate it in accordance with domestic legislation allowing abortions in cases of risk to the life of the mother. … In the circumstances of the case, the refusal to act in accordance with the author's decision to terminate her pregnancy was not justified and amounted to a violation of article 17 of the Covenant. … The Committee notes the special vulnerability of the author as a minor girl. … It further notes that, in the absence of any information from the State party, due weight must be given to the author's claim that she did not receive, during and after her pregnancy, the medical and psychological support necessary in the specific circumstances of her case. Consequently, the Committee considers that the facts before it reveal a violation of article 24 of the Covenant.[21]

Case No. 22/2009 (*T.P.F. v. Peru*), before the Committee on the Elimination of Discrimination against Women, concerned a 13-year-old girl who was raped, became pregnant, attempted suicide and became a paraplegic. Urgent spinal surgery to prevent permanent paralysis was cancelled because of her pregnancy, although she had requested an immediate therapeutic abortion. It was alleged that the refusal by the doctors at the hospital to perform the therapeutic abortion in view of the Peruvian anti-abortion law, along with the delay in performing spinal surgery, violated the girl's rights to health, a life of dignity and to be free from discrimination in access to such care. In holding that articles 2, 3, 5 and 12 of CEDAW had been violated, the Committee observed

> that the failure of the State party to protect women's reproductive rights and establish legislation to recognize abortion on the grounds of sexual abuse and rape are facts that contributed to L.C.'s situation. The Committee also notes that the State party bears responsibility for the failure to recognize the risk of permanent disability for L.C., coupled with her pregnancy, as a serious physical and mental health risk, and to provide her with appropriate medical services, namely a timely spinal surgery and a therapeutic abortion allowed in such cases under the Penal Code. … The Committee notes that L.C, a young girl of 16 (at the time of submission of the communication) is paralyzed from the neck down save for some partial movement in her hands. She is in a wheelchair and needs constant care. She cannot pursue her education and her family is also living in precarious conditions. Her mother (the author) who has to provide L.C. with constant care, cannot work. The cost of medicines and equipment required by L.C. has also placed a heavy undue financial burden on the family.[22]

---

[20] http://www2.ohchr.org/english/law/docs/CEDAW-C-52-D-32-2011_en.pdf.

[21] http://www1.umn.edu/humanrts/undocs/1153-2003.html.

[22] http://www2.ohchr.org/english/law/docs/CEDAW.C.50.D.22.2009_en.pdf, para. 8.18.

Protection from Female Genital Mutilation

Case No. 1465/2006 (*Diene Kaba v. Canada*) before the Human Rights Committee concerned the threatened expulsion by Canada of a minor to a country where she might be exposed to female genital mutilation. In warning about a potential violation of articles 7 and 24 of the ICCPR, the Human Rights Committee observed:

> that in Guinea female genital mutilation is prohibited by law. However, this legal prohibition is not complied with. The following points should be noted: (a) genital mutilation is a common and widespread practice in the country, particularly among women of the Malinke ethnic group; (b) those who practise female genital mutilation do so with impunity; (c) in the case of Fatoumata Kaba, her mother appears to be the only person opposed to this practice being carried out, unlike the family of Fatoumata's father, given the context of a strictly patriarchal society; (d) the documentation presented by the author, which has not been disputed by the State party, reveals a high incidence of female genital mutilation in Guinea; (e) the girl is only 15 years old at the time the Committee is making its decision. Although the risk of excision decreases with age, the Committee is of the view that the context and particular circumstances of the case at hand demonstrate a real risk of Fatoumata Kaba being subjected to genital mutilation if she was returned to Guinea. Consequently … the Committee is of the view that Fatoumata Kaba's deportation to Guinea would constitute a violation of article 7 and article 24, paragraph 1, of the Covenant, read in conjunction.[23]

2.2.5 Deprivation of Liberty (Art. 9 and 24 ICCPR)

The Human Rights Committee has received an increasing number of complaints concerning indefinite detention of children, particularly in the context of immigration detention. In its views on case No. 1069/2002 (*Ali Aqsar Bakhtiyari* et al. *v. Australia*), the Committee held that articles 9 and 24 of the ICCPR had been violated, observing:

> that until the decision of the Full Bench of the Family Court on 19 June 2003, which held that it had jurisdiction under child welfare legislation to order the release of children from immigration detention, the children were in the same position as their mother, and suffered a violation of their rights under article 9, paragraph 4, up to that moment on the same basis. Concerning the claim under article 24, the Committee considers that the principle that in all decisions affecting a child, its best interests shall be a primary consideration, forms an integral part of every child's right to such measures of protection as required by his or her status as a minor, on the part of his or her family, society and the State, as required by article 24, paragraph 1, of the Covenant. The Committee observes that in this case children have suffered demonstrable, documented and on-going adverse effects of detention suffered by the children. … [T]he Committee considers that the measures taken by the State party had not, until the Full Bench of the Family Court determined it had welfare jurisdiction with respect to the children, been guided by the best interests of the children, and thus revealed a violation of article 24, paragraph 1, of the Covenant.[24]

---

23 http://sim.law.uu.nl/SIM/CaseLaw/fulltextccpr.nsf/160f6e7f0fb318e8c1256d410033e0a1/01a7e0fbfd5aa1adc1257768004f7ceb.

24 http://www1.umn.edu/humanrts/undocs/1069-2002.html, paras. 9.5–9.7.

The most recent 'Views' in this context were issued in case No. 2136/2012 (*M.M.M.* et al. *v. Australia*), in which the Committee held that article 9 had been violated, noting:

> that the authors have been kept in immigration detention since 2009–2010, first under mandatory detention upon arrival and then as a result of adverse security assessments. Whatever justification there may have been for an initial detention, for instance for purposes of ascertaining identity and other issues, the State party has not, in the Committee's opinion, demonstrated on an individual basis that their continuous indefinite detention is justified. The State party has not demonstrated that other, less intrusive, measures could not have achieved the same end of compliance with the State party's need to respond to the security risk that the adult authors are said to represent. Furthermore, the authors are kept in detention in circumstances where they are not informed of the specific risk attributed to each of them and of the efforts undertaken by the Australian authorities to find solutions which would allow them to obtain their liberty. They are also deprived of legal safeguards allowing them to challenge their indefinite detention. For all these reasons, the Committee concludes that the detention of authors M.M.M., R.R., K.P., I.M. F., N.V., M.S. and A.A.K. B.B.A. is arbitrary and contrary to article 9, paragraph 1, of the Covenant. This conclusion extends to authors M.J. and her minor son R. J., in connection with the period of time prior to their release.[25]

Detention of Indigenous Children and their Treatment

Case no. 1184/2003 (*Corey Brough v. Australia*) concerns the claims of an aboriginal man that while he was a minor, he was detained and not treated according to his status as a minor. In holding that articles 10, paragraphs 1 and 3 of the Covenant had been violated, the Committee noted:

> The State party has not advanced that the author received any medical or psychological treatment, apart from the prescription of anti-psychotic medication, despite his repeated instances of self-harm, including a suicide attempt. ... Moreover, it remains unclear whether the requirements not to use confinement to a safe cell as a sanction for breaches of correctional centre discipline or for segregation purposes, or to ensure that such confinement does not exceed 48 h unless expressly authorized, were complied with in the author's case. The Committee further observes that the State party has not demonstrated that by allowing the author's association with other prisoners of his age, their security or that of the correctional facility would have been jeopardized. Such contact could have been supervised appropriately by prison staff. Even assuming that the author's confinement to a safe or dry cell was intended to maintain prison order or to protect him from further self-harm, as well as other prisoners, the Committee considers that the measure incompatible with the requirements of article 10. The State party was required by article 10, paragraph 3, read together with article 24, paragraph 1, of the Covenant to accord the author treatment appropriate to his age and legal status. In the circumstances, the author's extended confinement to an isolated cell without any possibility of communication, combined with his exposure to artificial light for prolonged periods and the removal of his clothes and blanket, was not commensurate with his status as a juvenile person in a particularly vulnerable position because of his disability and his status as an Aboriginal. As a consequence, the hardship of the imprisonment was manifestly incompatible with his condition, as demonstrated by his inclination to inflict self-harm and his suicide attempt.[26]

---

[25] Views adopted 25 July 2013.

[26] http://www1.umn.edu/humanrts/undocs/1184-2003.html, para. 9.3–9.4.

3 Third Optional Protocol to the CRC: Potential Jurisprudential Development

Although child rights have been justiciable before UN treaty-bodies for decades, many aspects remain to be tested. The new petitions procedure under the Third Optional Protocol to the CRC possesses ample potential to further define and advance the rights of children. When the CRC Committee consider complaints, it should take into account the jurisprudence of the other human rights treaty bodies.

Many problems must yet be placed before the competent committees for examination and adjudication. Test cases could be brought, for instance, on issues of the destruction of the identity of indigenous or aboriginal children by transferring them to state educational or religious institutions, a practice that has left psychological scars. Even if violations occurred before the entry into force of the various complaints procedures, there may be 'continuing effects' that in themselves may constitute violations of human rights. Nor is the State party *ratione temporis* off the hook, merely because the children have become adults. These human beings carry the traumata with them and pass them on to their children. The children of disappeared persons also need affirmative action. In some countries the ongoing indoctrination of children for war, and their recruitment into various military activities, must cease, and the children should be given assistance to 'unlearn war'.

The right of children to grow up in an environment conducive to a harmonious, balanced development, one aimed at allowing them to achieve their potential and become free human beings capable of functioning in society and establishing their own families, must be more clearly defined and reflected in the jurisprudence.

In this regard, the issue of adoption is particularly thorny. Ideally, all children should have the opportunity of being brought up in stable families, have a caring mother and a responsible father as role models—but this is not always the case. Orphans and children given up for adoption require special protection. It is the responsibility of the state to ensure that the environment provided by adoptive parents is psychologically safe for the development of the adopted children, and that the adopted children are not exposed to complex identity situations, ambiguities and tensions, which as children and adolescents they are not equipped to handle.

As such, there is ongoing debate about the pros and cons of allowing children to be adopted by same-sex parents. Bearing in mind that the paramount interest is the best interests of the child, it is extremely problematic to expose children to the psychological tension of having two male or two female adoptive parents while all of their friends in school have a father and a mother. The psychological damage done to children growing up in anomalous situations may be devastating for life.

Other important areas where case law is necessary include the right of privacy of children, which is *terra incognita* in the jurisprudence of the Committees. Suitable cases will no doubt be submitted and enable the Committees to expand the existing jurisprudence.

4 Enforcement

Because the Human Rights Committee and the Committee on the Elimination of Racial Discrimination are not courts but quasi-judicial instances whose decisions are not legally binding, the enforcement of their Views on the merits of individual cases depends on the political will of the Parties.

While the rate of enforcement of Committee decisions is less than fifty percent, experience shows that the failure to implement Committee decisions often is not attributable to the refusal of the state concerned to do so, or its rejection of the Committee's rationale, but is explainable by the absence of enabling legislation granting Committee decisions enforceable status in the domestic legal order. No national judge can give effect to Committee decisions unless they are transformed into domestically executable orders. Some countries like Colombia have chosen a 'half-way house' arrangement, whereby a standing ministerial committee examines decisions to determine which Ministry will implement them—finance, justice or education (see Law 288 of 1996).

As far as the Third Optional Protocol to the CRC is concerned, it would be desirable to persuade those that have already ratified it and all future States parties to adopt the necessary enabling legislation. The Office of the High Commissioner for Human Rights could draft model legislation and propose it to States parties and potential States parties with an offer to provide advisory services and technical assistance for its adjustment and adoption.

References

Detrick, S. (1992). *The United Nations convention on the rights of the child: a guide to the 'tavaux preparatoires'*. Dordrecht/Boston/London: Martinus Nijhoff Publishers.

Möller, J Th, & De Zayas, A. (2009). *United Nations Human Rights Committee Case Law*. Kehl am Rhein: N.P. Engel Verlag.

Nowak, M. (2005). *CCPR Commentary* (2nd ed.). Kehl am Rhein: N.P. Engel Verlag.

Von Truhardt, H. (1931). *Völkerbund und Minderheiten-Petitionen*. Leipzig.

Walters, F. P. (1952). *A history of the league of nations* (Vol. 2). Oxford: Oxford University Press.

Chapter 12
The CRC in Litigation Under the ECHR

The CRC and the ECHR: The Contribution of the European Court of Human Rights to the Implementation of Article 12 of the CRC

Ursula Kilkelly

Abstract The European Convention on Human Rights (ECHR), formally the Convention for the Protection of Human Rights and Fundamental Freedoms, is a uniquely successful system for enforcing human rights, but it contains few references to children's rights. The case law of the European Court of Human Rights is a rich source of human rights, which, at the same time, has been interpreted in a way that advances children's rights. This chapter aims to explore the contribution of the European Court's jurisprudence in this area; in particular, it considers the use of article 12 of the Convention on the Rights of the Child (CRC) to interpret the ECHR in the two areas of child access/custody and juvenile justice.

1 Introduction

The Council of Europe is Europe's leading human rights organisation, promoting human rights through a variety of activities that include standard-setting and international treaty monitoring and enforcement. Although the Council has focused recently on children's rights,[1] its two main human rights treaties are general in nature. The ECHR, which focuses mainly on civil and political rights, was adopted in 1953, while the European Social Charter, focusing on economic, social and cultural rights, was adopted in 1961 and revised in 1996. Both treaties provide for children's rights to differing degrees and employ different mechanisms for monitoring and enforcing their implementation.

[1] See the work of the Children Programme ('Building a Europe for and with Children') at http://www.coe.int/children.

U. Kilkelly (✉)
School of Law, University College Cork, Cork, Ireland
e-mail: U.kilkelly@ucc.ie

T. Liefaard and J.E. Doek (eds.), *Litigating the Rights of the Child*,
DOI 10.1007/978-94-017-9445-9_12

The Social Charter makes provision for children's rights in two main provisions, namely article 7, which provides for the right of children and young people to protection from economic exploitation, and article 17, which provides for children's right to care, assistance and education and to the protection from violence and negligence. The European Committee of Social Rights, the body set up to monitor and receive collective complaints on the Charter's implementation, has considered the application of these provisions in numerous cases, issuing decisions on diverse matters such as services for children with disabilities,[2] the rights of a foreign nationals illegally resident,[3] non-discrimination in education[4] and a series of cases concerning corporal punishment.[5] The decisions of the Committee are fully informed by more specific children's rights standards, including the CRC.

There is little doubt, however, that even though it contains fewer references to children's rights, it is the ECHR, through its system of individual petition, that has made the more substantial contribution to their advancement; for this reason it is the focus of this chapter. Despite its scant references to children, the European Court of Human Rights (ECtHR) has applied various interpretive approaches to develop the potential of the ECHR to protect children's rights. One such approach—and arguably that with the most potential to advance children's rights—is its use of the CRC to inform the interpretation of general human rights standards to children.

The aim of this chapter is to explore this approach to the interpretation of the ECHR. Rather than attempting to review the use of the CRC as a whole, the chapter considers the ECtHR's approach with respect to article 12 of the CRC, the right of the child to be heard. It examines the Court's approach to this right in the areas of family law and juvenile justice, and considers what this case law tells us about the application of the CRC in international children's rights litigation.

2 Brief Introduction to the ECHR

The European Convention on Human Rights is a treaty of its time. Enacted in the light of the 1948 Universal Declaration of Human Rights, the ECHR is limited mainly to traditional civil and political rights such as the right to freedom from

---

[2] 13/2002—*Autism-Europe v. France*, 41/2007–*Mental Disability Advocacy Center (MDAC) v. Bulgaria.*

[3] 14/2003—*International Federation of Human Rights Leagues (FIDH) v. France concerning access to medical services* and 47/2008—*Defence for Children international (DCI) v. The Netherlands* concerning the right to shelter and protection.

[4] 45/2007—*INTERIGHTS v. Croatia.*

[5] 17/2003—*World Organisation against Torture (OMCT) v. Greece*, 18/2003—*World Organisation against Torture (OMCT) v. Ireland*, 19/2003–*World Organisation against Torture (OMCT) v. Italy*, 20/2003–*World Organisation against Torture (OMCT) v. Portugal*, 21/2003—*World Organisation Against Torture (OMCT) v. Belgium*. A further challenge in this area is currently pending before the Committee.

torture, the right to liberty and fair trial, and freedom of expression, religion and association. Its explicit references to children are limited to two articles: article 5 provides for the detention of a minor 'for the purpose of educational supervision and to bring a minor before the competent legal authority'; and article 6 places limits on the right to a public hearing 'where the interests of juveniles so require' (Kilkelly 2000).

Moreover, rights relevant to children are phrased in adult terms. For instance, the right to education in the First Protocol to the ECHR recognises the right of parents to ensure that their children's education conforms with their convictions, rather than recognising education as a right of the child. Neither article 8 (which provides for the right to respect for private and family life, home and correspondence), nor article 3 (which prohibits inhuman and degrading treatment), makes explicit provision for the rights or interests of children. Nonetheless, these two provisions have been shown, through the case law of the ECtHR, to have significant potential to advance children's rights; either unwittingly or by design, the provisions—predominantly article 8, the most litigated provision in children's cases—are the source of the Court's extensive jurisprudence on children's issues (Kilkelly 1999).

The Court has used a number of approaches in this regard, including the development of procedural rights and a focus on positive obligations. Neither approach is exclusive to children's cases, but their use—including their combination on occasion—has strengthened the potential of the ECHR to protect children's rights across a range of areas (Kilkelly 2010).

The procedural approach, which emphasises the safeguards that states must put in place to support the protection of substantive rights, has played a particularly important role in the area of alternative care and child protection. For instance, where decisions may interfere with family relationships, such as placing children in the care of the state, the Court has found certain procedural safeguards to be implicit in respect for family life. In particular, it requires that the entire decision-making process (administrative and judicial proceedings) be fair and respect the interests protected by article 8.[6] According to the Court, parents have a right to be involved in the decision-making process to a degree sufficient to provide them with requisite protection of their interests.[7] However, the Court has not, as yet, developed procedural rights for children, although it has addressed the weight to be attributed to children's views, as discussed below.

The positive-obligations approach has been even more instrumental in effective application of the ECHR to children's cases. Analysis has shown that this approach has been particularly crucial in the areas of family ties, abduction and reunification, and custody and access under article 8; it has also been important in areas like child protection and abuse covered by article 3, where it has genuinely pushed the boundaries of the state's duty to protect children from harm. The

[6] *W v. UK*, no. 9749/82, Series A, No. 120, 10 EHRR 95; *McMichael v. UK*, no. 16424/90, Series A no. 307-B, 20 EHRR 205, para. 87.

[7] *W v. UK*, no. 9749/82, Series A, no. 120, 10 EHRR 95 para. 64.

result is, according to this author writing elsewhere, that the positive-obligations approach has not just ensured the relevance of the ECHR to children's rights but enabled the Court to make its own unique contribution to children's rights through the development of an entirely new set of legal requirements and rules (Kilkelly 2010). At the same time, reliance on the procedural-rules and positive-obligations approaches has its drawbacks: they are interpretive tools whose outcome is difficult to predict, and as such they lack the certainty of other methods.

One such approach used by the Court—the one to be examined here in more detail—involves taking into account the more specific children's rights instruments—notably, but not exclusively, the CRC—in its application of the more generally-worded ECHR to children's cases. This approach was first identified in 2001, where it was proposed as an approach that would combine the child-specific provisions of the CRC with the ECHR's effective system of individual petition in order to maximise the potential of both instruments to advance children's rights (Kilkelly 2001). The approach recognises that the CRC is the world's leading children's rights treaty, detailed and comprehensive in scope, and that, through its ratification by all member states of the Council of Europe, it binds all states party to the ECHR.

As is clear even from the brief discussion above, the Court uses a variety of approaches to interpret and apply the ECHR in the circumstances of individual cases. These are necessitated by the broad nature of the ECHR's provisions and the Court's clear acceptance that the ECHR is a 'living instrument that must evolve so as to maintain relevance to current legal and social conditions'.[8] The commitment to ensure that the ECHR keeps pace with modern social conditions is vital to its continued relevance and legitimacy. The duty to keep pace with legal conditions also creates an onerous duty on the Court, particularly given the increasing complexity, variety and amount of international law that now exists at national, regional and international levels. In the children's area alone, the last decade has seen a veritable explosion of legal instruments and standards in Europe emanating from the European Union (Stalford 2012) and the Council of Europe itself. The value of these standards is that they represent consensus on the rights to which children are entitled and provide a specific and detailed account of the measures states must take to protect and promote the rights of children.

3 Case Law

3.1 Setting the Standard: Article 12 of the CRC

The purpose of this chapter is not simply to examine the potential of an approach which applies the use of the CRC as an interpretive tool; its aim is to examine the ECtHR's use of the CRC and to reflect on what that says about the CRC itself.

[8] *Tyrer v. UK*, A 26 (1978); 2 EHRR 1.

Because a comprehensive audit of ECHR case law from the perspective of the CRC is beyond the scope of this chapter, it is proposed instead to focus on a single provision of the CRC in this regard.

A case might be made for an analysis in ECHR law of article 3 of the CRC, which requires that the best interests of the child be considered a 'primary consideration' in all actions concerning the child. This principle is not explicitly referenced in article 8 of the ECHR which requires respect for family life.[9] However, it has been read into the provision by the ECtHR in numerous cases of private and public family law in which the Court has stressed that compliance with article 8(2) requires a fair balance to be achieved between competing interests—of children, parents and society.[10] Moreover, in certain cases notably concerning child custody, the Court has articulated that children's interests may indeed be the paramount consideration, arguably going beyond the standard set out article 3 of the CRC.[11]

Although the ECtHR's case law has increasingly engaged with article 3 of the CRC and now benefits from the Committee on the Rights of the Child's General Comment on this provision (UN Committee 2013), the nebulous nature of the best interests principle makes its coherent application difficult, at best (Choudhry and Fenwick 2005; Choudry 2009). What is emerging, to some extent, is a reliance on article 9 of the CRC, which provides that children shall not be separated from their parents against their will unless the competent authorities decide it is in the best interests of the child. While this provision is more precise than article 3 in its content and purpose, engagement with it arguably holds the greater potential to influence ECHR law, even though the question of when it is or is not legitimate to deny contact with parents on the grounds of the child's best interests is also not without difficulty (Kaganas 2013).

For a variety of reasons, therefore, article 12—the right of the child to be heard—was chosen for the purpose of this ECHR/CRC analysis.[12] Article 12 of

---

9 Article 8(2) provides that '[t]here shall be no interference by a public authority with the exercise of this right (to respect for family life) except such as is in accordance with the law and is necessary in a democratic society in the interests of national security, public safety or the economic well-being of the country, for the prevention of disorder or crime, for the protection of health or morals, or for the protection of the rights and freedoms of others.'.

10 See, for example, *Maumousseau and Washington v. France*, 6 December 2007, a case concerning child abduction. This is also relevant in cases of positive obligation under article 8(1). See *Hokkanen v. Finland* (1994) 19 EHRR 139 and above.

11 See, most controversially, *Neulinger and Shuluk v. Switzerland no. 41615/07*, Grand Chamber, 6 July 2010.

12 Article 12 provides as follows: '1. States Parties shall assure to the child who is capable of forming his or her own views the right to express those views freely in all matters affecting the child, the views of the child being given due weight in accordance with the age and maturity of the child. 2. For this purpose, the child shall in particular be provided the opportunity to be heard in any judicial and administrative proceedings affecting the child, either directly, or through a representative or an appropriate body, in a manner consistent with the procedural rules of national law.'.

the CRC is a hugely important provision that provides for both a substantive and a procedural right (Parkes 2013). It has been identified by the Committee on the Rights of the Child as one of the four general principles of the CRC (UN Committee 2009), and so its importance extends beyond the provision itself as it guides the application of the entire Convention. According to the Committee, the right to be heard 'imposes a clear legal obligation on States parties to recognize this right and ensure its implementation by listening to the views of the child and according them due weight' (UN Committee 2009: para. 15). With respect to article 12(2), the obligation requires that 'States parties, with respect to their particular judicial system, either directly guarantee this right, or adopt or revise laws so that this right can be fully enjoyed by the child' (UN Committee 2009: para. 15).

In many respects, article 12 is an iconic and symbolic provision whose demand to ensure that children are heard reflects children's inherent right to dignity and respect. The provision makes clear that although children might struggle to be heard for a variety of reasons, it is adults' duty to listen and respond. Moreover, article 12 makes clear that the duty on the state is to 'assure' the right to the child, a legal term of 'special strength' which, according to the Committee on the Rights of the Child, 'leaves no leeway for State parties' discretion' (UN Committee 2009: 19). Accordingly, the Committee has stipulated that states are

> under strict obligation to undertake appropriate measures to fully implement this right for all children. This obligation contains two elements in order to ensure that mechanisms are in place to solicit the views of the child in all matters affecting her or him <u>and</u> to give due weight to those views.[13]

The right of the child set out in article 12(1) has application to 'all matters that affect the child', while article 12(2) places specific obligations on states to ensure that children are heard in judicial and administrative proceedings. According to the Committee on the Rights of the Child, states have particular duties to ensure children are heard in family and criminal law proceedings (UN Committee 2009: para. 51–61). With respect to divorce and separation, the Committee recommends that all legislation include the right of the child to be 'heard by decision makers and in mediation processes' (UN Committee 2009: 52). In juvenile justice, the Committee has made clear that effective participation requires that the child be

> informed promptly and directly about the charges against her or him in a language she or he understands, and also about the juvenile justice process and possible measures taken by the court. The proceedings should be conducted in an atmosphere enabling the child to participate and to express her/himself freely.[14]

In order to consider the extent to which article 12 has influenced ECHR case law, it is now proposed to examine the ECtHR's case law in these two areas.

[13] UN Committee (2009), para. 19. Emphasis added.

[14] UN Committee (2009), para. 60.

3.2 Custody and Access

As noted above, article 12(2) provides that the child has 'the opportunity to be heard in any judicial and administrative proceedings affecting the child', directly or indirectly, in accordance with the rules of national law. This clearly applies to proceedings affecting the child's family, where parents separate or divorce, or where arrangements are being made for the child's residence or contact with parents (Parkes 2009).

Under the ECHR, disputes in this area fall squarely under article 8, which guarantees the right to respect for family life; it is significant, as noted above, that the ECtHR has developed both a positive obligation to protect family life and a procedural duty to ensure that parents are involved in decision-making to protect their interests under that provision. Applications before the ECtHR in this area are normally taken by parents aggrieved about a decision made at national level and seeking to challenge how that decision was made. It is rare for a child to make such an application, and even rarer still for the complaint to come from the child alone (Kilkelly 1999).

As such, the application is usually examined by the ECtHR from the parents' perspective, and while the Court has been guided increasingly by the national authorities' regard for what is in the best interests of the child (Kilkelly 2002), this is not a substitute for a child-centred, decision-making process. For this reason, the Court has never been asked by a child applicant as to whether article 8 requires that he or she be heard in judicial or administrative proceedings at national level to satisfy article 8 of the ECHR. It has considered, however, the question of the child's participation in judicial proceedings in a number of cases concerning the custody/access rights of unmarried fathers.[15]

In *Sahin v. Germany,*[16] the applicant complained that the national court had failed to hear his child or to consider expert evidence evaluating her wishes, with the result that he was not sufficiently involved in the judicial proceedings to protect his interests under article 8. The Chamber found a violation of article 8, concluding, in particular, that the failure to hear the child in court had entailed insufficient protection of the applicant's interests in the access proceedings.[17] In doing so, the Chamber showed support for the applicant's contention that a decision concerning his right of access had to be made with reference to all the relevant information, including the views of the child. In particular, it concluded that it is 'essential that the competent courts give careful consideration to what is in the best interests of the child after having had direct contact with the child'.[18]

---

[15] *Elsholz v. Germany*, no. 25735/94, Reports 2000-VIII; *Sahin v. Germany* no. 30943/96; *Sommerfeld v. Germany* no. 31871/96 and *Hoffmann v. Germany,* no. 34045/96, judgments of 11 October 2001, (2003) 36 EHRR 565.

[16] *Sahin v. Germany* no. 30943/96, judgment of 11 October 2001.

[17] Paras. 45–48.

[18] Para. 47.

However, the Grand Chamber of the ECtHR disagreed, finding that even without directly hearing the views of the child, the German courts had relevant reasons in the child's best interests to justify refusing access, namely the serious tensions between the parents and the risk that visits would affect her development.[19] Moreover, when the Court looked at the father's involvement in the proceedings, it noted that he both enjoyed access to all relevant information relied on by the courts and had been able to put arguments forward in favour of obtaining access. In relation to hearing the child in court, the Court observed that 'as a general rule it is for the national courts to assess the evidence before them, including the means used to ascertain the relevant facts'. Furthermore, it considered '[i]t would be going too far to say that domestic courts are always required to hear a child in court on the issue of access to a parent not having custody, but this issue depends on the specific circumstances of each case, having due regard to the age and maturity of the child concerned'.[20]

In this case, the Court noted that the child was between 3 and 5 years old at the time of the domestic proceedings; that the expert reached her conclusion that contact was not in the child's interests after several meetings with the child, the mother and the father; and that she had plausibly explained in testimony that hearing the child in court entailed a risk for the child which could not be avoided.[21] Accordingly, the Court concluded that the German authorities' approach was reasonable and provided sufficient material to reach a reasoned decision on the question of access in the particular case.[22]

Therefore, it was within the margin of appreciation, and no violation of article 8 took place.

Notwithstanding that no violation of article 8 was found to have occurred, the Grand Chamber put down some markers about the way national courts should determine custody and access issues.[23] Clearly, the judgment recognises that children of a sufficient age and maturity should be heard by the courts engaged in such disputes (of what age and maturity, however, is not clear); it also signals to national courts the importance of seeking expert advice when taking such decisions. In this regard, the judgment would appear to be consistent with the terms of article 12, which presents a choice as to whether children's views should be put before a court either directly by the children themselves or indirectly by a representative (Raitt 2004). That the child in this case was very young—barely three when the proceedings began—and had been spoken to by a professional whose considered view was that it was not appropriate for the child to speak

---

[19] *Sahin v. Germany* [GC] no. 30943/96, judgment of 8 July 2003, para. 67.

[20] Para. 73.

[21] Para. 74.

[22] Para. 77.

[23] However, the Court went on to find a violation of article 14 together with article 8, in respect of the discrimination against the unmarried father caused by the German civil code; at the time, the latter placed the divorced father in a more favourable position with respect to the right to contact. Ibid., para. 94.

directly to the court, were clearly influential factors not out of line with the requirements of article 12 (UN Committee 2009: 16).

The case of *Sommerfeld v. Germany* also involved a father's complaint as to the manner in which his child's views had been handled in proceedings concerning custody and access rights.[24] However, in this case the child, who was 13 years old, had expressed a clear wish not to see her father. The Chamber of the ECtHR had upheld the father's complaint, finding that the domestic courts 'should not have been satisfied with hearing only the child as to her wishes on the matter without having at its disposal psychological expert evidence in order to evaluate the child's seemingly firm wishes'.[25] The question of whether the child's views were sufficient basis for the decision made was the key issue before the Grand Chamber.

Along the same basis as in *Sahin*—that it was mainly for the domestic courts to assess the evidence before them including the means to ascertain the relevant facts—it held that the German courts were, in this instance, within the margin of appreciation in handling the case as they did.[26] In particular, the decision not to order a psychological opinion and to instead to take the views of the applicant's teenage daughter at face value was one it was entitled to take in the circumstances. Significantly, what was persuasive before the Grand Chamber was that the domestic court had heard the girl at age 10 and 11, meaning that it had benefited from direct contact with her over time and so was 'well placed to evaluate her statements and to establish whether or not she was able to make up her own mind'.[27]

This conclusion—that there had been no violation of article 8—was reached by a majority of ten to three. The three dissenting judges considered that in cases where access is disputed, the wishes of a child should always be analysed by a psychological expert to ensure that the child has not been subjected to undue influence by the other parent. In their view, '[t]he procedural requirement to have up-to-date psychological expert evidence in order to obtain correct and complete information on the child's relationship with the applicant as the parent seeking access to the child' (a requirement set out in the *Elsholz* judgment[28]) was an 'indispensable prerequisite for establishing a child's true wishes'.[29]

The Court's conclusion in *Sommerfeld* is consistent with article 12 to the extent that it supports judicial decision-making informed by the views of a child expressed directly to the court on a matter of clear importance to the child. At the same time, the concerns of the dissenting judges in *Sommerfeld* raise a question as to whether a child can express his or her views 'freely', as article 12(1) requires, where the relationships between the adults at least are acrimonious.

---

[24] *Sommerfeld v. Germany* [GC], no. 31871/96, 8 July 2003.

[25] Para. 43 in the Chamber judgment.

[26] *Sommerfeld v. Germany* [GC], no. 31871/96, 8 July 2003, para. 71.

[27] Para. 72.

[28] *Elsholz v. Germany* [GC], no. 25735/94, ECHR 2000-VIII, para. 49.

[29] Partly Dissenting Opinion of Mr Ress joined by Mr Pastor Ridruejo and Mr Türmen.

According to the Committee on the Rights of the Child, the child's right to 'free' expression means that the child must be able to express his or her views 'without pressure' and 'without undue influence' (UN Committee 2009: para. 22). Moreover, the requirement in article 12 to take the child's views into account in line with the child's age and maturity is also relevant here. According to the Committee, 'the views of the child have to be assessed on a case-by-case basis' (UN Committee 2009: para. 29). This appears to leave open when such 'assessment' of the child's views will need to be undertaken, and what form any such assessment might take.

Against such a backdrop, the approach of the Court—which in the main defers these matters to the discretion of the courts, which have direct contact with the parties—appears both sensible and legitimate. In this regard, article 12 does not demand a rigorous, professional analysis be undertaken in respect of the merits of every child's views. The dominant principle is that it is important to hear what children have to say, with flexibility being offered as to how those views find their way into the decision-making process and, once they get there, the role they play in line with the twin criteria of the age and maturity (Parkes 2013).

The extent to which the views expressed by children against parental contact were made 'freely' and 'without undue influence' arose again in the case of *C v. Finland*.[30] Here, the father of two children, who lived with the now-deceased mother's female partner, L, complained that too much weight had been attached to the children's preference not to have contact with him. The domestic court had awarded custody to L on the basis of a Finnish law that prevented enforcement of such arrangements against the will of children over 12 years.

On the matter of the weight to be attached to the children's views, the ECtHR noted that 'it is generally accepted that courts must take into account the wishes of children in such proceedings'.[31] Indeed, it went on to say, 'On a practical basis, there may also come a stage where it becomes pointless, if not counter-productive and harmful, to attempt to force a child to conform to a situation which, for whatever reasons, he or she resists.'[32] On the facts of the case, it noted that all of the domestic courts which considered the matter 'essentially agreed as to the consistency and strength of the children's views'.[33]

Nevertheless, the ECtHR was critical of the fact that the decision of the lower courts—which awarded custody to the father—had been overturned by a process which, without oral hearing, placed exclusive weight on the children's views. In this respect, the Court's difficulty was not solely with the extent to which the children's views were considered final by the domestic court, but also with its failure to take other factors into account in its decision-making process: the result was that the applicant's article 8 rights were violated.

---

[30] *C v. Finland*, no. 18249/02, 9 May 2006.

[31] Para. 57.

[32] Ibid.

[33] Ibid.

There is little doubt that article 12 does not require that the views of children determine the final outcome of a decision-making process. Instead, it requires a more nuanced process that takes into consideration the child's views, freely expressed, bearing in mind the twin elements of age and maturity (Parkes 2013). The above comments from the Committee on the Rights of the Child—that children's views have to be assessed on a case-by-case basis—combined with the principle of evolving capacity inherent in article 12 (and set out in article 5 of the CRC), indicate that this is a dynamic process which changes as the child's develops.

A further noteworthy element, evident in all three of the cases outlined above, is the tension between what is in the child's best interests and what the child him- or herself wants. This was arguably at its most obvious in *C v. Finland*, but it is evident throughout the case law that the purpose of the decision-making process in the domestic courts is to determine what is best for the child concerned. As the Committee on the Rights of the Child has made clear, hearing the views of the child is an essential part of the process. It is important that, as outlined above, the ECtHR has now expressed a similar view in *C v. Finland*.

3.3 Juvenile Justice

Given its focus on civil and political rights—including the right to liberty and fair trial—it is perhaps to be expected that the ECHR has been applied with some effect to the treatment of young offenders. Moreover, the ECtHR has contributed to the interpretation and application of article 12 of the CRC in the area of juvenile justice, notably in the relationship between effective participation in criminal proceedings and the right to fair trial.

In 1999 the ECtHR decided two high-profile cases against the United Kingdom concerning the trial of two 11-year-old boys convicted of the murder of two-year-old James Bulger.[34] The two applicants challenged the compatibility of their trial in adult court with their article 6 rights, relying especially on the case of *Stanford v. UK* in which the ECtHR had held that the accused has a right to be present and to participate effectively in his or her trial.[35] This was the ECtHR's first opportunity to consider the application of this article 6 principle to children and, in particular, to consider 'whether procedures which are generally considered to safeguard the rights of adults on trial, such as publicity, should be abrogated in respect of children in order to promote their understanding and participation'.[36]

[34] *T v. UK*, no. 24724/94, 16 December 1999 and *V v. UK*, no. 24888/94, 16 December 1999.

[35] *Stanford v. the United Kingdom* judgment of 23 February 1994, Series A no. 282-A.

[36] *T v. UK*, para. 83.

Although the ECtHR was clear that it was not contrary to article 6 per se to put a child as young as 11 years on trial, it agreed with the (former) European Commission of Human Rights that

> it is essential that a child charged with an offence is dealt with in a manner which takes full account of his age, level of maturity and intellectual and emotional capacities, and that steps are taken to promote his ability to understand and participate in the proceedings.[37]
>
> This principle reflects international standards—such as articles 3, 37 and 40 of the CRC, and Rules 4, 8 and 17 of the Beijing Rules—which, as is now common practice, were listed by the Court at the introduction to its judgment.[38] Article 6(1) provides express protection to 'juveniles' from a public trial, and it is clear from the ECtHR's judgment that it saw a strong connection between the right of the child to understand and participate in his or her proceedings and the placement of some limits on the public nature and publicity surrounding the trial process, as permitted by article 6.

Here, the ECtHR cross-referred to its consideration of the article 3 complaint (that subjecting the two young accused to criminal trial amounted to inhuman and degrading punishment) where it noted the strong international standards in support of the child's right to privacy. In particular, the ECtHR noted the 'minimum standard' set out in article 40(2)(b) of the CRC that recognises the right of children accused of crimes to have their privacy fully respected at all stages of the proceedings.[39] The Court noted that these standards demonstrate an 'international tendency in favour of the protection of the privacy of juvenile defendants'; it went on to note especially that the CRC is binding international law on the United Kingdom and all of the other member states of the Council of Europe.[40] Although it did not consider this standard determinative of whether the trial amounted to ill-treatment contrary to article 3, it was clearly relevant to its consideration of article 6.

In this regard, the Court concluded that the intimidating atmosphere, caused by the trial taking place with a packed public gallery and in the glare of intense media scrutiny, impeded the children's ability to understand and participate in the criminal proceedings. Crucially, and distinguishing the case from Stanford where the applicant could not hear some of the evidence given at his trial, the ECtHR held that it was highly unlikely that T (or V) would have felt 'sufficiently uninhibited, in the tense courtroom and under public scrutiny, to have consulted with [his lawyers] during the trial or, indeed, that, given his immaturity and his disturbed

---

[37] *T v. UK*, para. 84.

[38] *T v. UK*, paras. 43–47. Also cited were the Concluding Observations of the Committee on the Rights of the Child (calling on the UK to reform its youth justice system and raise the age of criminal responsibility), the Council of Europe Committee of Ministers of the Council of Europe Recommendation no. R (87) 2, and article 14(4) of the International Covenant on Civil and Political Rights, which requires that in juvenile justice the procedure shall be such as will take account of their age, and the desirability of promoting their rehabilitation.

[39] *T v. UK*, para. 74.

[40] Ibid., para. 75.

emotional state, he would have been capable outside the courtroom of cooperating with his lawyers and giving them information for the purposes of his defence'.[41] In conclusion, the ECtHR considered that both applicants were unable to participate effectively in the criminal proceedings against them and were, as a result, denied a fair hearing in breach of article 6(1).[42]

Although there was no mention of article 12(1) of the CRC in the ECtHR's judgments in either T or V. v. UK, the judgments are fully informed by the concept of effective participation that underpins this principle of the CRC. Choosing instead to rely on the protection afforded to a young offender by article 40 of the CRC and given expression in article 6(1), the ECtHR made its own connection between the right to a fair trial and the right to participate effectively in the trial process. In this way, the ECtHR can be credited with reinforcing the fundamental human rights from which children's rights are derived. The ECtHR's approach—to link the child's right to participate effectively in criminal proceedings with the fairness of those proceedings—is a persuasive restatement of the fundamental nature of these rights. The fact that the principle of effective participation, applied so eloquently to child offenders in the T and v. cases, was developed from the adult case of Stanford reinforces that the right to a fair trial is a core right to children too, while also highlighting that steps need to be taken to make this right effective for children.

The ECtHR went on to consider the concept of effective participation in *SC v. the UK*, which concerned the trial of a boy, also aged 11.[43] Explaining ECHR obligations in this context, the ECtHR accepted that article 6(1) does not require that a child on trial for a criminal offence should 'understand or be capable of understanding every point of law or evidential detail'.[44] Here, it noted that, as highlighted by article 6(3)(c), the right to legal representation is crucial. Drawing on the ECtHR's judgment in Stanford, it noted that

> 'effective participation' in this context presupposes that the accused has a broad understanding of the nature of the trial process and of what is at stake for him or her, including the significance of any penalty which may be imposed.[45]

Furthermore, the duty to ensure effective participation means that the accused

> if necessary with the assistance of, for example, an interpreter, lawyer, social worker or friend, should be able to understand the general thrust of what is said in court. The defendant should be able to follow what is said by the prosecution witnesses and, if represented, to explain to his own lawyers his version of events, point out any statements with which he disagrees and make them aware of any facts which should be put forward in his defence.[46]

---

[41] Ibid., para. 88.

[42] Ibid., para. 89.

[43] *SC v. UK*, no. 60958/00, 15 June 2004.

[44] Para. 29.

[45] Para. 29.

[46] Para. 29.

Significantly—and distinct from T and V v. UK—the applicant's arrest and trial were not the subject of high levels of public and media interest, nor was there evidence that the atmosphere in the courtroom was 'particularly tense or intimidating'.[47] Nevertheless, the ECtHR considered that the accused had not comprehended the situation he was in, had little comprehension of the role of the jury, and did not appear to have grasped that he risked a custodial sentence.[48] Taken together, and despite the efforts made to facilitate his participation in the proceedings, the ECtHR held that the applicant was not capable of participating effectively in his trial.

The Court's concern was clearly with the child's personal capacity to comprehend the proceedings. In this way, it is less about what steps can be taken to promote understanding of the trial process, and more about whether the process itself is comprehensible to those who labour under additional difficulties. Indeed, concerns about SC's cognitive and intellectual capacity were noted in the judgment, even though the ECtHR found no difficulty with the decision that he was fit to stand trial. In these respects, therefore, the judgments in T and v. and in SC are quite different, and concern different aspects of the effective participation concept.

Although article 12 was not mentioned in the judgments above, the issue of effective participation has been considered by the Committee on the Rights of the Child. In its General Comment on article 12, the Committee noted that 'a child cannot be heard effectively where the environment is intimidating, hostile, insensitive or inappropriate for her or his age. Proceedings must be both accessible and child-appropriate' (UN Committee 2009: para. 34). Moreover, in the context of juvenile justice, the Committee has held that

> [i]n order to effectively participate in the proceedings, every child must be informed promptly and directly about the charges against her or him in a language she or he understands, and also about the juvenile justice process and possible measures taken by the court. The proceedings should be conducted in an atmosphere enabling the child to participate and to express her/himself freely … the Court … should be conducted behind closed doors.[49]

Undoubtedly influenced by the case law of the ECtHR, the Committee's General Comment on Juvenile Justice contains a particular section on effective participation (UN Committee 2007). Notable in the extent to which it draws on the ECtHR's judgments in T, V and SC in particular, the Committee has noted as follows:

> A fair trial requires that the child alleged as or accused of having infringed the penal law be able to effectively participate in the trial, and therefore needs to comprehend the charges, and possible consequences and penalties, in order to direct the legal representative, to challenge witnesses, to provide an account of events, and to make appropriate decisions about evidence, testimony and the measure(s) to be imposed. Article 14 of the Beijing Rules provides that the proceedings should be conducted in an atmosphere of understanding to allow the child to participate and to express himself/herself freely.

---

47 Para. 30.

48 Para. 30.

49 UN Committee (2009), para. 60–61.

> Taking into account the child's age and maturity may also require modified courtroom procedures and practices.[50]

Through the adoption of this General Comment, the Committee has ensured that, just as the CRC can breathe new life into the ECHR, so too can the judgments of the European Court of Human Rights inform the interpretation of the CRC. In doing so, the ECtHR has drawn on CRC provisions concerning young offenders—especially article 40—rather than the more general participation principle in article 12. This may reveal a lack of understanding of the relevance of article 12 to this area, especially given that the Committee on the Rights of the Child's general comments on article 12 and on juvenile justice came later. Either way, reflecting the point made above, the value of the ECtHR's linking effective participation with the universal right to a fair trial, rather than to the child-specific (in international law, in any event) right to participation, may ultimately make states take it more seriously.

4 Conclusion

The above case studies examine the application by the ECtHR of the article 12 participation principle, and indicate that this particular provision of the CRC has had a clear impact on the case law of the ECtHR in the two areas of private family law and juvenile justice. So far, however, explicit references to article 12 within the ECHR case law are very limited, with the ECtHR choosing instead to draw on related provisions of article 40 (in juvenile justice) and article 9(3) (in family law). The reasons behind the Court's reluctance to use article 12 are not known, and could stem either from a lack of familiarity with the provision or a preference for the provision that is more context-specific.

Nonetheless, it is apparent that application of the ECHR in cases concerning children has been informed indirectly by both the principle and the substance of article 12 in the development of case law that supports children's participation in decision-making. The full potential of this approach is far from realised, and it could be supported by a more explicit reliance on the CRC as a treaty that binds all of the ECHR States parties. Cases concerning children should, as a minimum, state the CRC provisions that set the benchmark in the treatment of children. It is now common practice for the ECtHR to list the provisions of children's rights instruments relevant to the matter under consideration in the introduction to its judgment.

What is significant, and indeed positive, about the cases examined here—especially in the area of juvenile justice—is that the Court moved beyond listing these provisions to engaging with them more directly in its reasoning. The result was a genuine attempt to read the provisions together in an approach that has potential to advance further the understanding of children's rights. Based on these examples, the Court should be encouraged to integrate CRC provisions more fully into its

[50] UN Committee (2007), para. 46.

reasoning in children's cases, which would have the effect of highlighting coherence in international children's rights standards where that exists.

As is the case in the juvenile justice area, it is clear that the potential for interplay between the CRC and the ECHR is reciprocal and mutually beneficial; this is consolidated by the adoption in 2010 of the Council of Europe Guidelines on Child-friendly Justice. As the General Comment on Juvenile Justice shows, there is great potential for the Committee on the Rights of the Child to take cognisance of the case law of the ECtHR. The need for regional and international bodies to engage with and respond to each other's jurisprudence is increasingly important in view of the ever-expanding scale and detail of international standards. Directly integrating the CRC into the ECtHR's analysis serves to highlight where those standards cannot be reconciled. This is not without challenge and it may well reveal that conflict exists between these instruments, as is the case in ECtHR cases concerning application of the Hague Convention on Child Abduction (this was at its most acute in *Neulinger and Shuluk v. Switzerland* mentioned above). Nevertheless, this approach would enable the ECtHR to make a further, important contribution to the wider understanding of the application of children's rights in specific contexts.

References

Choudhry, S. (2009). Clashing rights and welfare: A return to a rights discourse in English family law. In M. Fineman (Ed.), *What is right for children: The competing paradigms of religion and human rights*. Aldershot: Ashgate.

Choudhry, S., & Fenwick, H. (2005). Taking the rights of parents and children seriously: Confronting the welfare principle under the Human Rights Act. *Oxford Journal of Legal Studies, 25*(3), 453–492.

Dickson, B. (2010). Positive obligations and the European Court of Human Rights. *Northern Ireland Legal Quarterly, 61*(3), 203–208.

Kaganas, F. (2013). A presumption that 'involvement' of both parents is best: Deciphering law's messages. *Child and Family Law Quarterly, 3*, 270–293.

Kilkelly, U. (1999). *The child and the European Convention on Human Rights*. Aldershot: Ashgate.

Kilkelly, U. (2000). The Human Rights Act: Implications for the trial and detention of young people. *Northern Ireland Legal Quarterly, 51*(3), 466–480.

Kilkelly, U. (2001). The best of both worlds for children's rights: Interpreting the European Convention on Human Rights in the light of the UN Convention on the Rights of the Child. *Human Rights Quarterly, 23*, 308–326.

Kilkelly, U. (2002). Effective protection of children's rights in family cases: An international approach. *Transnational Law and Contemporary Problems, 12*(2), 336–354.

Kilkelly, U. (2010). Protecting children's rights under the ECHR: The role of positive obligations. *Northern Ireland Legal Quarterly, 61*(3), 245–261.

Parkes, A. (2009). The right of the child to be heard in family law proceedings: Article 12 CRC. *International Family Law*, 238–244.

Parkes, A. (2013). *Children and international human rights law: The right of the child to be heard*. Oxford: Routledge.

Raitt, F. E. (2004). Judicial discretion and methods of ascertaining the views of the child. *Child and Family Law Quarterly, 16*(2), 151–164.

Stalford, H. (2012). *Children and the European Union: Rights, welfare and accountability*. Oxford: Hart.
UN Committee on the Rights of the Child (2007) General Comment No. 10, Children's Rights in Juvenile Justice UN. Doc. CRC/C/GC/10.
UN Committee on the Rights of the Child (2009) General Comment No. 12, The Right of the Child to be Heard. UN Doc. CRC/C/GC/12.
UN Committee on the Rights of the Child (2013) General Comment No. 14, The Right of the Child to have his/her Best Interests taken as a Primary Consideration. UN Doc. CRC/C/GC/14.

Chapter 13
The CRC in Litigation Under EU Law

Helen Stalford

Abstract The Convention on the Rights of the Child (CRC) has been adopted as a frame of reference to guide the development of EU law and policy affecting children. The extent to which the instrument informs actual interpretations and implementation of those measures, however, is highly questionable. This chapter examines how the EU's primary judicial institution, the Court of Justice, adjudicates on matters of EU law that relate to children. In particular, it explores the extent to which the Court uses the principles enshrined in the CRC and accompanying guidance to ensure compliance by the Member States not only with their obligations under EU law but with their obligations under the CRC. Moreover, it questions how the Court of Justice negotiates cases where the implementation of EU measures may undermine the principles and provisions of the CRC in the interests of pursuing and safeguarding the political and economic interests of Member States and, indeed, of the EU project more broadly.

1 Introduction

Children's rights occupy an increasingly prominent place on the EU legal and policy agenda. The EU now boasts a myriad of legislative, policy and research initiatives that seek to respond to the current and potential impact on children of a range of issues falling within the scope of EU competence.[1] Traditionally, the EU has

[1] For a detailed and critical analysis of the evolution, scope and substantive of the EU children's rights agenda, see Stalford (2012).

H. Stalford (✉)
European Children's Rights Unit, School of Law and Social Justice, University of Liverpool, Liverpool, United Kingdom
e-mail: stalford@liverpool.ac.uk

T. Liefaard and J.E. Doek (eds.), *Litigating the Rights of the Child*,
DOI 10.1007/978-94-017-9445-9_13

responded to children's rights-related issues in a largely ad hoc manner, as an aside to more pressing and mainstream political and economic preoccupations. This prompted criticism that the EU's children's rights mandate has evolved in something of an 'ideological vacuum' (McGlynn 2006; Stalford and Drywood 2009).

There is no doubt, however, that in recent years the EU institutions, particularly the Parliament and Commission, have sought to adopt a more ethical and ideologically robust approach to the development of children's rights measures. What has been key to the process is more explicit and routine endorsement of the principles and provisions of the CRC and its accompanying guidance. This is most evident in the EU's seminal Agenda on the Rights of the Child, which was adopted in 2011 and sets out concrete aims and priorities for EU action across a range of children's rights issues. Significantly, the Commission identified the CRC for the first time as the definitive framework within which to formulate and implement its children's rights strategy:

> The EU Agenda for the Rights of the Child presents general principles that should ensure that EU action is exemplary in ensuring the respect of the provisions of the ... UNCRC with regard to the rights of children.[2]

In the same vein, CRC-inspired references are now an increasingly routine feature of EU-level legislative and policy measures relating to children, especially in the context of EU free-movement law,[3] immigration and asylum law,[4] EU family law,[5] and policies seeking to tackle poverty and social exclusion.[6] Particularly noteworthy is the legislation enacted to address children's rights in a criminal-justice

---

[2] Commission, 'An EU Agenda for the Rights of the Child' (Communication) COM (2011) 60 final, at p. 3.

[3] See, for instance, Art 28(3) Dir 2004/38 on the right of citizens of the Union and their family members to move and reside freely within the territory of the Member States [2004] OJ L158/77, which prohibits the deportation of migrant children unless it is in their best interests.

[4] See, for instance, Art 25(6) Directive 2013/32/EU of the European Parliament and of the Council of 26 June 2013 on common procedures for granting and withdrawing international protection (recast); and Arts 13 and 16 Directive 2011/36/EU of the European Parliament and of the Council of 5 April 2011 on preventing and combating trafficking in human beings and protecting its victims, OJ L 101/1.

[5] See, for instance, a commitment to safeguarding children's article 12 CRC right to participate in decisions that affect them, in Arts 11(2), 23(b) and 41(2)(c) Regulation 2201/2003 concerning jurisdiction and the recognition and enforcement of judgments in matrimonial matters and the matters of parental responsibility [2003] OJ L338/1.

[6] Combating discrimination and child participation is a key feature of the Commission's anti-child poverty strategy, 'Investing in children: breaking the cycle of disadvantage' Commission Recommendation of 20.2.2013, C(2013)778.

context.[7] A directive aimed at establishing minimum standards on the rights, support and protection of victims of crime asserts from the outset that:

> [i]n applying this Directive, children's best interests must be a primary consideration, in accordance with the … United Nations Convention on the Rights of the Child. … Child victims should be considered and treated as the full bearers of rights set out in this Directive and should be entitled to exercise those rights in a manner that takes into account their capacity to form their own views.[8]

This commitment is reinforced through a number of more substantive provisions that point to the importance, inter alia, of adopting a child-sensitive approach to criminal proceedings involving child victims (articles 1(2) and 24), and to hearing the voice of the child (article 10).[9] Proposals for a new Directive seeking to put in place procedural safeguards for children suspected or accused in criminal proceedings[10] are even more comprehensive in their allegiance, not only to the CRC, but to the General Comment on Children's rights in juvenile justice.[11] It sets the scene as follows:

> When deprivation of liberty is imposed on children, they should benefit from special protection measures. In particular they should be held separately from adults unless it is considered in the child's best interest not to do so, in accordance with Article 37(c) of the United Nations Convention of the Rights of the Child.[12]

Thus, the proposed instrument aims to ensure that children are informed promptly about their rights (art. 4), are assisted by their parents or another appropriate person (articles 5 and 15), have mandatory access to a lawyer at all stages (art. 6), have the right to an individual-needs assessment and a medical examination (Arts 7 and 8), are detained only as a measure of last resort (art. 10), and have their privacy protected in the course of proceedings (art. 14).

The emergent body of binding EU measures dedicated to children, coupled with a growing preoccupation with accommodating children's rights in areas that intersect with EU activity, prompts some consideration of the role of the EU's main judicial office, the Court of Justice of the EU (hereafter the Court of Justice),

---

[7] See, notably: Directive 2011/36/EU of the European Parliament and of the Council of 5 April 2011 on preventing and combating trafficking in human beings and protecting its victims, OJ L 101/1; Directive 2011/93/EU of 13 December 2011 on combating the sexual abuse and sexual exploitation of children and child pornography, OJ L 335/1.

[8] Para. 14, Preamble.

[9] Directive 2012/29/EU of the European Parliament and of the Council of 25 October 2012 establishing minimum standards on the rights, support and protection of victims of crime, *OJ L* 315, pp. 57–73.

[10] Commission proposal of 27 November 2013 for a directive of the European Parliament and of the Council on procedural safeguards for children suspected or accused in criminal proceedings, COM(2013) 822 final.

[11] Committee on the Rights of the Child General Comment No.10 (2007) *Children's Rights in Juvenile Justice.* This General Comment heavily informed the Council of Europe's Guidelines on Child Friendly Justice, which are also a key point of reference for the proposed EU Directive.

[12] Para. 26, Preamble.

in facilitating actual enforcement of EU children's rights provision. As such, this chapter explores the extent to which the Court of Justice draws upon the provisions and principles of the CRC in interpreting and applying EU law.

The first section briefly describes the status of the CRC at EU level; it explains as well how the Court of Justice operates and how its role is defined in relation to the Member States' courts. Section 2 examines how claims are brought before the Court of Justice by and/or on behalf of children, and provides a short overview of the nature of the claims already litigated. Section 3 critically assesses the extent to which the Court uses (or, indeed, ignores or abuses) the CRC principles in considering specific children's rights claims or interests, and draws attention to factors that currently impede more fruitful application of the instrument. Finally, Sect. 4 considers alternative normative mechanisms in the EU context for litigating the principles and values inherent in the CRC.

2 The Status of the CRC at EU Level

Insofar as the EU is a non-State actor, it cannot become a party to the CRC,[13] nor can it ratify it, but that does not mean the instrument has no force at EU level. According to the general principles of EU law—that is, the written and unwritten principles drawn from the common, constitutional traditions of the Member States that supplement and guide interpretations of the EU Treaties[14]—the EU must adhere to the principles and provisions set out in international human rights law in relation to those matters that fall within the scope of EU competence. Respect for human rights has, therefore, been integral to the operation of EU law for almost as long as the EU has existed. The precise scope and impact of fundamental rights in an EU context has been the subject of dense judicial scrutiny since the late 1960s.[15] This has repeatedly confirmed that any obligations arising out of EU membership should accommodate international human rights treaties and

---

[13] Article 216 of the Treaty on the Functioning of the European Union (hereafter TFEU) does allow for the EU to accede to international treaties 'where the conclusion of an agreement is necessary to achieve, within the framework of the Union's policies, one of the objectives referred to in the Treaties'. A notable example of EU accession to an international convention on this type is the Convention on the Rights of Persons with Disabilities 2006, with plans afoot for the EU to accede to the European Convention on Human Rights (discussed further below at Sect. 4). However, insofar as the CRC contains measures that fall firmly outside EU competence, the prospect of EU ratification is highly unlikely. See further Haldorsson (2011).

[14] See generally Tidimas (2007).

[15] Case 26/69 *Stauder v. City of Ulm* [1969] ECR 419; Case 11/70 *Internationale Handelsgesellschaft* [1970] ECR 1125. For a more detailed analysis, see De Búrca (1993: 283, 2002: 131), Neuwahl and Rosas (1995), Weiler and Lockhart (1995: 51 [Pt 1] and 579 [Pt II]), Ahmed and de Jesús Butler (2006: 771).

conventions by which the Member States are also bound.[16] Indeed, the EU's commitment to upholding human rights within the scope of its activities is now constitutionally endorsed.[17]

It follows, therefore, that the CRC, as an international convention ratified by all 28 Member States, is equally embedded in the constitutional fabric of the EU, and that the EU is bound to adhere to the CRC's principles and provisions in relation to any EU activity affecting children. This relationship has been galvanised further by the introduction of the Charter of Fundamental Rights of the European Union in 2000,[18] which now has the same constitutional status as the EU Treaties.[19] The Charter comprises a detailed and explicit catalogue of the EU's fundamental rights obligations across a range of substantive areas, as underpinned by key principles such as equality, dignity and freedom. Significantly, the Charter manifests an explicit commitment to upholding the rights of the child, with its child-related provisions drawing heavily on the CRC.

Thus, the Charter grants children a specific right to: such protection and care as is necessary for their well-being; and the opportunity to express their views freely and an assurance that such views shall be taken into consideration on matters which concern them in accordance with their age and maturity [article 24(1)]. Article 24(2) further provides that 'in all actions relating to children, whether taken by public authorities or private institutions, the child's best interests must be a primary consideration'; while article 24(3) acknowledges the right of the child 'to maintain on a regular basis a personal relationship and direct contact with both his or her parents, unless that is contrary to his or her interests'.[20]

In addition to the general children's rights principles enshrined in article 24, the Charter states that discrimination on grounds of age is prohibited (art. 21), but it also acknowledges the many substantive rights protected by the CRC too: to receive free compulsory education [art. 14(2)]; to be protected from exploitative labour or harmful working conditions (art. 32); to be protected from undue interference in private and family life, home and communications (art. 7); and to enjoy legal, economic and social protection (art. 33). Moreover, the age-neutral provisions contained within the Charter resonate equally with those in the CRC dealing with, for example, the prohibition against torture and inhuman or degrading treatment (art. 4),[21] and the prohibition of slavery, forced labour and human trafficking [art. 5(1)].

---

[16] Case 7/73 *Nold v. Commission of the European Communities* (1974) ECR 491, para. 13.

[17] Article 6 Treaty on European Union (hereafter TEU). The terms 'fundamental rights' and 'human rights' are interpreted synonymously for the purposes of this discussion.

[18] OJ 2010/C 83/02.

[19] Article 6(1) TEU states: 'The Union recognises the rights, freedoms and principles set out in the Charter of Fundamental Rights of the European Union … which shall have the same legal value as the Treaties.'

[20] For a detailed analysis of article 24 of the Charter, see Lamont (2014).

[21] Applied successfully by the ECtHR in the context of corporal punishment under Art 3 ECHR; see *A v. United Kingdom* App no 25599/94 (1999) 27 EHRR 611.

The growing prominence of CRC-inspired provision within the EU Constitution, particularly the Charter, coupled with its now routine incorporation into child-related EU legislation and policy, has important implications for the status of children's rights at EU level, affording these rights greater coherence and legitimacy than has been the case hitherto. The benefits accrue, though, in the other direction too: embedding CRC provisions and principles within binding EU legislation technically provides a new channel through which the CRC can be enforced, one accompanied by proper justiciable mechanisms and sanctions for failure to comply with the obligations thereby imposed. This goes some way towards addressing what has been perhaps the biggest criticism of the CRC, namely that it lacks a proper enforcement mechanism. The Court of Justice is central to this process, and so it is to the functions, structure and procedural mechanisms associated with the Court that the discussion now turns.

3 Overview of the Court of Justice

The EU's main judicial institution, the Court of Justice, is composed of one judge from each Member State (currently 28) [article 19(2) TEU]. They are assisted by eight Advocates General who put forward independent non-binding opinions on cases prior to their being considered by the Court. Most cases are assigned to chambers of either three or five judges, but more significant cases, those where a Member State or EU institution is party to proceedings, are heard before the Grand Chamber of 13 judges.

The Court of Justice exercises jurisdiction in relation to two main types of action. First, it considers direct actions, which can be divided into four categories. These include:

- actions for annulment—essentially requests from the Member States or other EU institutions to annul a particular measure which is purported to have been adopted illegitimately (Art 263–264 and 266 TFEU);
- actions against a Union institution for allegedly failing to act when it was under a duty to do so (Arts 265 and 266 TFEU);
- actions for damages against the Union institutions; and
- enforcement proceedings brought by a Member State or the European Commission against another Member State for failing to fulfil its obligations arising out of EU law (Arts 258–260 TFEU).

The second type of actions brought before the Court of Justice are preliminary rulings (article 267 TFEU). A preliminary ruling is a process by which national courts call upon the Court of Justice to assist them in interpreting EU law relevant to domestic proceedings. The national courts are then obliged to apply the Court's interpretation to the facts of the case before them.

Underpinning both types of action the individual's fundamental right to judicial process, a right which is protected by article 6(1) of the European Convention on

Human Rights (ECHR) and confirmed by the Charter of Fundamental Rights[22] as well as the case law of the Court of Justice.[23] The right of access to judicial process thus applies for the benefit of all individuals, including children, whose Union rights are implemented through the national systems of judicial protection.

It is important to bear these key constitutional and procedural principles in mind when critically assessing how children's rights are litigated before the Court of Justice. Direct actions before the Court are notoriously difficult to pursue for any private individual, let alone children. Actions for annulment (essentially judicial review proceedings) are accompanied by stringent rules on standing which privilege Member States' authorities or the EU institutions (the Commission, Council or Parliament). 'Non-privileged' applicants can challenge the legality of an EU act only if it is cast in a particular legal form (a decision, as opposed to a regulation or directive), and if applicants can demonstrate that the measure affects them directly and individually due to their specific circumstances or characteristics.[24] To date, no EU children's rights measures have been articulated in the form of Decisions and are, therefore, unlikely to be vulnerable to an action for annulment; EU children's rights provision tends instead to be embodied in directives or, to a lesser extent, regulations, both of which are largely outside the scope of such proceedings.[25]

Given the limitations of the direct-actions route to challenging or enforcing children's rights at EU level, cases are far more commonly referred to through the intermediary of the national courts (through the preliminary reference procedure). Even then, a case will not reach a national court unless the relevant EU law (usually in the form of a Directive) has been implemented within domestic law and has affected individuals to such a degree that litigation is deemed to be the only route to ensure fulfilment of the entitlement set out therein.

In such a case, the national courts act as the main gatekeepers of individual access to EU-level justice, in that they retain the authority to initiate a preliminary reference to the Court of Justice for guidance on how to interpret the EU provision

---

[22] Individuals' right to judicial process is reflected (and, indeed, extended) in article 47 of the EU Charter of Fundamental Rights, which states: 'Everyone whose rights and freedoms guaranteed by the law of the Union are violated has the right to an effective remedy before a tribunal in compliance with the conditions laid down in this Article. Everyone is entitled to a fair and public hearing within a reasonable time by an independent and impartial tribunal previously established by law. Everyone shall have the possibility of being advised, defended and represented ….'.

[23] The Court of Justice first recognised in the *Johnson* ruling of 1986 (Case 222/84 [1986] ECHR 165) that the fundamental right of access to judicial process forms part of the general principles of EU law and is equally binding upon the Member States when acting within the scope of the Treaties. For an overview of relevant, subsequent case law, see Dashwood et al. (2011: 289–292).

[24] *Plaumann v. Commission* [1963] ECR 95. See also Arts 263–264 and 266 Treaty on the Functioning of the European Union (hereafter TFEU).

[25] The discussion returns further below to the legislative form in which children's rights are expressed.

at issue. In turn, the Court of Justice plays a significant role in guiding the national courts on the correct interpretation of that EU law at the domestic level—and its judgment will inform similar deliberations as to how the law should be applied in other Member States too. Where else might one hope to obtain a consistent and clear interpretation of EU measures that seek to impose uniform, often harmonised, standards across 28 different jurisdictions? Indeed, the Court of Justice has been accused of overstepping its interpretative function and creating new law and principles that extend well beyond its mandate.[26] Nowhere has the Court's activism and ingenuity been more pronounced than in the field of fundamental rights, which raises some hope that it might also hold the potential to advance children's rights in significant ways.

Disappointingly, however, in spite of all the developments that have taken place in the EU in the past 10–15 years, and notwithstanding the profound impact, actual and potential, of EU activities on children's lives,[27] the number of cases brought by, on behalf of, or even loosely related to, children before the Court of Justice is negligible—less than a dozen, in fact. This is even more marked when contrasted with the European Court of Human Rights (ECtHR): established at roughly the same time as the Court of Justice, it has delivered more than a thousand judgments concerned with children's rights.[28]

The disparity may be explained partly by the fact that the ECtHR has always been defined by a much more explicit and focused human rights mandate than the Court of Justice. Moreover, despite the absence of explicit children's rights provision in the European Convention on Human Rights, the ECtHR has shown far greater readiness to interpret broader, adult-framed human rights provisions in favour of children. The EU, by comparison, is a late-comer to children's rights in terms of enacting binding legal provision which forms the basis for judicial interpretation. Although a modest smattering of cases were heard in the context of free movement and citizenship law from the late 1980s onwards, most of the concrete grounds for litigation have emerged only since the turn of the millennium.[29]

---

[26] See further Adams et al. (2013), De Witte and Muir (2013).

[27] The impact of the EU on children is explored critically in detail in Stalford (2012).

[28] The first child rights case brought before the ECtHR was *Tyrer v. UK* (Application no. 5856/72) Judgment of 25 April 1978. See Chap. 12 of this book for a detailed account of use of the CRC in the ECtHR.

[29] Initially, EU cases that were of any relevance to children's rights responded to the claims of older (adult) children of EU migrant workers in the context of the free movement of persons provisions. See, for instance, Joined Cases 389 and 390/87 *Echternach and Moritz v. Netherlands Minister for Education and Science* (1989) ECR 723. Detailed fully in Ackers and Stalford (2004). Towards the late 1990s, cases relating to young children started to emerge. See in particular C-34/95 *De Agostini v. Konsumentombudsmannen* (1997) ECR I-3843, in which the Court held that Sweden could limit the broadcast of television advertisements originating in another Member State in the interests of protecting child consumers without falling foul of EU free-movement laws. None of these cases engaged directly with children's rights or the CRC.

Linked to this is the fact that until recently EU children's rights provision has been extremely difficult to litigate because of the detached nature and legislative form in which it is framed. Directives are the favoured format for children's rights. They impose binding obligations on the Member States regarding the broader objectives of the instrument, but leave a significant amount of discretion as to how these might be achieved through domestic legislation to accommodate the very diverse national contexts in which the legislation is transposed.[30] Regulations, on the other hand, give rise to direct rights for individuals that can be relied upon immediately by nationals before their domestic courts without the need for any national implementing legislation.[31] The few instances of children's rights measures contained in regulations tend to be relatively abstract requirements which are tangential to the focus of the instrument rather than aimed at imposing specific, binding obligations. As such, children's rights provision cast in regulation form typically defers to national mechanisms to give effect to it.

A good example of this is seen in the context of EU family-justice provision regulating recognition and enforcement of child custody and access arrangements.[32] It reinforces the right of children to be heard (subject to the standard age/capacity caveats) in relation to cross-border custody disputes, particularly those that culminate in parental child abduction. However, the Regulation only enforces this right in a manner that accords with national procedures for child consultation. It does not scrutinise whether such processes are comprehensive and accessible, nor does it impose any obligations on national authorities to enhance processes to make the exercise of children's right to be heard more feasible. At the very most, as the case of *Zarraga* tells us, it can call for states to put in place procedures that provide an 'effective opportunity' for the child to be heard.[33]

But the tide is turning. The pace at which EU legislative provision for children is currently unfolding is generating an increasing ensemble of rights that can be enforced by children and their representatives and that impose ever more specific obligations on national authorities to amend domestic laws, policies and processes to give effect to those rights. Take, for instance, the raft of EU measures developed to tackle cross-border criminal activities referred to above,[34] or to harmonise Member States' responses to the social, economic and security-related challenges

[30] According to article 288 TFEU, 'A directive shall be binding, as to the result to be achieved, upon each Member State to which it is addressed, but shall leave to the national authorities the choice of form and methods.'

[31] According to article 288 TFEU, 'A regulation shall have general application. It shall be binding in its entirety and directly applicable in all Member States.'

[32] Arts 23(b) and 41(2)(c) Regulation 2201/2003, above note 6.

[33] *Joseba Andoni Aguirre Zarraga v. Simone Pelz* (C-491/10 PPU) [2011] OJ C63.

[34] Detailed above at notes 10 and 11.

associated with immigration and asylum.[35] Both bodies of legislation are replete with references to children's right to protection, to appropriate representation and to be heard in proceedings, to expedited reunification with family members, and to immediate access to education, health and welfare services. Such rights can be fulfilled only if the national context in which they are articulated has sufficiently robust mechanisms in place to give them effect. It follows then that Member States that do not adapt domestic laws or processes accordingly may well be vulnerable to challenge before the Court of Justice for failing to give effect to their EU obligations in relation to children.[36]

Yet this raises the question of how the Court of Justice might respond to such claims, particularly given the paucity of child-related case law to have come before it. More specifically, how might the Court utilise the CRC to guide its interpretations of the relevant provisions at issue? An initial look at the cases to have come before the Court of Justice to date lends itself to some tentative responses to these questions.

4 How the Court of Justice Engages with the CRC

As noted, only a handful of child-related cases has been brought before the Court of Justice, and, of these, fewer still have prompted direct engagement with the principles enshrined in the CRC. It was not until 2006, for example, that the Court acknowledged that the CRC should be a primary reference point in assessing the compatibility of EU law with children's fundamental rights.[37] Prior to that, there had only been one cursory allusion to the CRC, in Advocate General Jacob's Opinion on a challenge to national rules governing people's surnames, a line of reasoning that at any rate was not pursued in the final judgment when it came to Court.[38]

All other cases involving a children's rights element have been pursued through the preliminary reference procedure, and there is only one example to date of the

[35] Directive 2013/33/EU of the European Parliament and of the Council of 26 June 2013, laying down standards for the reception of applicants for international protection (recast); Directive 2003/86/EC of 3 October 2003, on the right to family reunification, OJ L 251/12; Directive 2013/32/EU of the European Parliament and of the Council of 26 June 2013, on common procedures for granting and withdrawing international protection (recast); Directive 2008/115/EC of the European Parliament and of the Council of 16 December 2008, on common standards and procedures in the Member States for returning illegally staying third-country nationals, OJ L 348/98. A full summary of all EU-level children's rights measures is available at: http://ec.europa.eu/justice/fundamental-rights/files/eu_acquis_2013_en.pdf.

[36] Certainly this seems to be on the horizon as far as the Trafficking Directive is concerned (above note 5), with Commission scrutiny revealing patchy transposition across the Member States.

[37] Case C-540/03 *European Parliament v. Council* [2006] ECR I-5769.

[38] Case C-148/02, *Garcia Avello v. Belgium* [2003] E.C.R. I-11613.

Court of Justice engaging fully with, and attaching decisive weight to, the CRC.[39] The *Dynamic Medien* case concerned the lawfulness of German labelling restrictions on DVDs and videos that had been imported and already subjected to labelling controls in the UK. The Court concluded that the German checks constituted a lawful restriction of the EU's free movement of goods provisions (which otherwise precludes double regulatory processes of this nature), given that they were aimed at protecting the welfare of children. In drawing this conclusion, the Court referred to article 17 of the CRC, which encourages signatory states to develop appropriate guidelines for the protection of children from media-generated information and material injurious to their well-being.

Aside from the isolated example of *Dynamic Medien*, there is a persistent reluctance by the Court of Justice truly to engage with the CRC when charged with interpreting legislation relating to children. So why is it still the case, when the constitutional framework underpinning the Court's jurisdiction is now far more expressive in respect of children's rights, and when the culture and ideology of children's rights has been so vividly implanted in EU law and policy?

The preceding discussion alluded to the paucity of children's rights provision with which the Court has been presented; after all, it can work only with the tools at its disposal and cannot generate children's rights arguments out of a vacuum if they are not firmly and persuasively articulated by the legislation at issue. The first route to achieving more child-rights sensitive judgments, therefore, lies in addressing the quality and scope of the legislative provision on which such judgments are based.

But that is only part of the picture, and one suspects that even if it were to be presented with more explicit, far-reaching EU legislative provision for children, the Court of Justice might still struggle to deliver a judgment truly grounded in the CRC. Indeed, the Court has been presented with many claims in which reference to the CRC might have been extremely useful, and yet it has declined to do so.

The numerous cases brought by third-country nationals for entry or ongoing residence in a Member State based on their children's education or citizenship status offer useful illustrations in this regard. The Court's ingenuity in extending its interpretation of EU citizenship to children, and, in turn, in creating associated rights of residence for their primary carers regardless of nationality is well-documented and highly celebrated.[40] Nonetheless, a simple reference to children's education rights, enshrined in article 28 of the CRC, coupled with the right to pursue a relationship with parents (articles 5, 7, 9, 10 and 18 of the CRC), would have supplied obvious and persuasive scaffolding to support such arguments.

This perhaps points to the most obvious explanation for the Court's lack of engagement with the CRC: a simple lack of expertise when it comes to children's rights, out of which arises a distinct, albeit benign, indifference to the ideological

[39] Case C-244/06 *Dynamic Medien Vertriebs GmbH v. Avides Media AG* [2008] ECR I-505.

[40] Case C-413/99 *Baumbast v. R* [2002] ECR I-7091; Case C-200/02 *Chen* [2004] ECR I-9925; Case C-34/09 *Zambrano* [2011] ECR I-01177. Examined further in Stalford (2012): 73–78.

and normative arguments that might appeal to various aspects of EU law. This is less problematic when an equally favourable outcome for children might be reached through an adventurous interpretation of established EU principles such as citizenship and non-discrimination. In the case of *Kücükdeveci*, for example, the Court of Justice ruled that the principle of non-discrimination on grounds of age requires national employment measures to take into account periods of employment completed by an employee before reaching the age of 25 in calculating notice periods for dismissal. In other words, the ruling can be interpreted as requiring employers to take into account *all* periods of lawful work undertaken by employees, including those undertaken during their childhood, when determining notice and redundancy arrangements.[41]

What happens, however, when such alternative mechanisms do not exist, or when they are interpreted in a manner that fails to take into account the nuances of international children's rights perspectives? The decision in *Parliament v. Council of the European Union*,[42] the first instance in which the Court of Justice alluded to the CRC to guide its interpretation of EU law, offers a sobering illustration in this regard.

The case concerned the compatibility of specific provisions of the Family Reunification Directive[43] with fundamental rights, including children's rights. Specifically, article 4(1) allows Member States to impose 'a condition of integration' on children aged over 12 years old before authorising them to enter the host state and reside with their families. Moreover, under article 4(6) of the Directive, Member States can require families to apply for entry and residence for their children before they reach the age of 15 and, by implication, limit the entry and residence rights of children over 15 years of age. Finally, article 8 of the Directive allows Member States to preclude applications for family reunification until the migrant has resided in the host country for more than 2 years. The European Parliament requested that the Court of Justice annul these provisions on the basis that they undermined the best interests of the child and breached the right to family life as protected by the CRC and the ECHR, as well as the Charter of Fundamental Rights of the European Union.

The Court ruled (following a decidedly superficial reference to the CRC) that the provisions in question were justified. In particular, it determined that adopting 12 and 15 years as age thresholds for family reunification entitlement was based upon presumptions about children's capacity to integrate at these ages. Commenting on the decision, Drywood questions the empirical basis for the Court's conclusions, and notes that whatever the symbolic value of the reference to the CRC in this judgment, its

> … practical application of relevant international legal standards to the Directive raises doubts as to the Court's capacity and expertise in pursuing a children's rights agenda…. The Court never asks itself the question whether the disputed provisions ensure that the

[41] Case C-555/07, *Seda Kücükdeveci v. Swedex GmbH & Co. KG*, Judgment of 19 January 2010, ECR 2010, pp. 1–365.

[42] Case C-540/03 [2006] E.C.R. I-5769.

[43] Directive 2003/86/EC of 3 October 2003 on the right to family reunification, OJ L 251/12.

> child's best interests are a primary consideration, as a faithful interpretation of the provision would require. This approach is indicative of a frequently cited problem with the best interests principle: that although the question is posed from the child's perspective it is often answered from that of the adult (Drywood 2007: 396).

The Family Reunification decision is one instance where the rights of the child were clearly not at the forefront of the Court's reasoning in spite of its reference to the CRC. But the same could be said of cases where the Court has ostensibly been driven by a desire to uphold the interests of the child. Consider the decision in *Chen*, for instance,[44] which concerned the residence application of Chinese couple based on the fact that their baby was an Irish national (and by implication an EU citizen), having been born in Northern Ireland. The Court willingly supported the parents' associated claim for residence on the grounds that, as the baby's primary carers, their presence would enable the baby to remain in the host state and exercise her EU citizenship in her own right. Indeed, the Court went to some lengths in its decision to address the injustice of withholding EU citizenship entitlement from children solely on the basis that they are not yet old enough to exercise those rights independently.

A child-sensitive judgment indeed … or is it? Closer scrutiny by the Court of the facts of this case from a more explicit children's rights perspective would have resulted perhaps in a more nuanced response: keen to secure entry to and residence rights within an EU Member State, the mother made a conscious decision to give birth to the baby in Northern Ireland to exploit the Irish nationality laws at the time, thereby enabling the baby to acquire EU citizenship—yet nothing is made of the fact that the baby had an older brother in China. The parents, by pursuing EU citizenship for the baby, limited any future visits to China by baby Catherine to 30 days under a temporary visa, effectively excluding any possibility she might have of forging a meaningful relationship with her older sibling.

While this is not to suggest that the Court should usurp the function of parents in determining the legal, cultural and social context they deem most appropriate for raising their children, it highlights the superficial claims the Court has to developing a child-sensitive approach to EU citizenship. As such, the decision in Chen manifests a commitment to interpreting EU law in the political and economic interests of the parents (and, indeed, of the EU) rather than in the best interests of the child.

A further example in which the Court might be accused of failing to engage in a meaningful appreciation of children's rights is evident in the case of *Zambrano*.[45] In what has been hailed as a decidedly liberal and compassionate interpretation of EU citizenship, the Court recognised that refusing a residence permit to the third country national parents of two children born in the territory of the EU would deprive those children of any realistic opportunity of exercising their citizenship rights, both in the immediate and longer term. This was despite the fact that neither parent was an EU national, nor had they actually exercised

[44] Case C–200/02, *Zhu & Chen v. Secretary of State for the Home Department* (2004] ECR I-9923.

[45] Case C-34/09 *Ruiz Zambrano v Office National de l'Emploi* (2011) Judgment of the Court (Grand Chamber) of 8 March 2011.

free movement between two Member States (they had simply migrated from Columbia to Belgium, initially on a visitor's visa). In fact, such was the importance attached to the children's citizenship rights, the Court was prepared to overlook the fact that the father, as a failed asylum seeker, had resided and worked illegally in the host state for some time.

Not surprisingly, this judgment has been pounced upon by immigration practitioners seeking to support the ongoing residence claims of third county nationals who have children of EU nationality. In practice, what is emerging is a highly instrumental and disturbing manipulation of the rules that, in reality, may operate to the detriment of children. In the English High Court case of *Bent*[46] for instance, a Jamaican national sought to derive ongoing residence in the UK on the grounds that he was the primary carer of his old daughter who had been born to him and his ex-partner (whom he never married) in 2003. To bolster his claims that he was actively and equally involved in his daughters day-to-day care (a fact that had previously been vehemently and rightfully challenged), the father and mother organised for the child to be uprooted from her settled home with her mother and sibling, from her school and from her friends in London to move to the North of England to be cared for solely by her father. Fortunately, the judge in this case recognised the acute child welfare concerns arising out of the claimant's attempts to bring himself within the scope of a *Zambrano*-type scenario and, rejecting the claim, asserted:

> The obvious concern is that this change in Moesha's living, education and care arrangements may have been influenced by the issues affecting the claimant's long term desire to remain in residence in this country… My concern is that the welfare of Moesha does not appear at least to have been made known to, let alone considered…[47]

Examples such as *Chen* and *Zambrano* perhaps do not bode well for the Court's relationship with the CRC, particularly if national courts fail to carry out a more detailed assessment of the children's rights implications of EU citizenship and immigration law. Yet this does not mean the Court of Justice is altogether impervious to considerations of children's rights; alternative means have been developed for engaging with these rights beyond the CRC, means with the potential to yield equally favourable results for children. These are now addressed briefly.

5 Alternative Means of Interpreting and Applying the CRC

The Court of Justice has adopted alternative reference points when deliberating upon children's rights issues which, whilst not as comprehensive as the CRC, capture some key principles and jurisprudence that can uphold children's rights at EU

---

[46] *The Queen on the Application of Bent v. Secretary of State for Home Department* CO/2703/2012 ([2012] EWHC 4036 Admin).

[47] Above note, per Robert Owen HHJ, paragraph 123.

level and do so potentially with as much effect as reference to the CRC would achieve. Two of the best-preferred of these reference points are the ECHR and Charter of Fundamental Rights.

A long and extensive EU jurisprudence cements the influence of ECHR jurisprudence on EU matters, with the Court readily seeking guidance from the ECtHR where human rights concerns interact with the economic and political preoccupations of EU law. The Court's amenability to the ECHR over and above the CRC is attributable largely to its historical, institutional and legal relationship with the instrument, a relationship that will be constitutionally endorsed following the Treaty of Lisbon[48] which paved the way for the EU's accession to the ECHR.[49] As a consequence, individuals will be able to pursue the EU before the ECtHR in Strasbourg for alleged failures to observe their ECHR rights in the development and implementation of EU measures. This will potentially broaden individuals' access to European justice in ways that are, for the reasons mentioned earlier, simply not feasible in the context of Court of Justice proceedings.

What is perhaps most encouraging about this relationship is that the ECtHR has established a prominent and persuasive children's rights jurisprudence which is grounded very much in the CRC.[50] In that sense, the ECHR, by means of this fluid cross-referencing, can act as another channel through which the CRC could permeate the EU legal order.[51] It follows, therefore, that any EU measures that are deemed to undermine children's rights under the ECHR—or, indeed, that fail to positively uphold or promote children's rights under the ECHR—are likely to be open to more robust challenge in the future, and before a court significantly more amenable to reasoning based on children's rights than the Court of Justice.

That said, the process will have to concede to the reality that while fundamental rights have always formed part of the EU constitutional architecture, there are discernible tensions, between the human rights-based approach of the ECHR and what are the essentially economic and political goals of EU measures. In fact, existing jurisprudence attests to the willingness of the Court of Justice to undermine fundamental rights in favour of promoting market integration, leading one to ponder whether formal EU accession to the ECHR will make any difference at all to the level of rights-protection afforded at EU level.[52] Even in the family reunification case referred to earlier, the Court went to some lengths to respond to the

[48] Treaty of Lisbon amending the Treaty on European Union and the Treaty establishing the European Community, signed at Lisbon, 13 December 2007, 2007/C 306/01.

[49] Article 6(2) TEU and amended Protocol 14 ECHR.

[50] Detailed in Kilkelly's contribution to this collection (see Chap. 12) and, previously, in Kilkelly (2000: 87), (2001: 308).

[51] Discussed further in Stalford (2012: Chap. 2).

[52] Case C-341/05 *Laval un Partneri Ltd v. Svenska Byggnadsarbetareförbundet and Others* (2007) ECR I-11767 illustrates the ongoing tensions between accommodating fundamental rights (as expressed in the ECHR) and fundamental freedoms (as developed by the EU).

claims that its approach to minors' reunification with family members did not constitute a breach of articles 8 and 14 of the ECHR, insofar as such rights must always be balanced against the Member States' discretion to control the entry of non-nationals into their territory.

Perhaps a stronger channel through which the CRC might be enforced more effectively before the Court of Justice is the Charter of Fundamental Rights.[53] In matters relating to children, it has become the primary, and certainly the more comfortable, point of reference for Advocates General and the Court.[54] There is a growing body of case law in which the Court has sought inspiration in particular from article 24 of the Charter, which represents in turn an amalgamation of various CRC provisions (especially articles 3 and 12). The decision in *Zambrano*, referred to above, is a case in point. However, the degree to which this has stimulated more child-rights-sensitive judgments is highly questionable. In fact, there is much to suggest that the Court is merely paying lip-service to children's rights insofar as it remains reluctant to engage in any meaningful consideration of how such principles might be brought to bear on its adjudication of the facts at issue. In most cases, the Court tentatively acknowledges the relevance of children's rights principles, but then defers to the Member States' judicial, legislative and administrative processes to effect the necessary changes in the way that those rights are discharged at the national level.[55]

Consider the case of *Detiček*, for example, in which the Court was asked to clarify the meaning of certain child protection measures inherent in EU cross-border family law.[56] The facts related to a child who had been born in Italy to an Italian father and Slovenian mother. The parents sought a divorce when the child was 10 years old, upon which the Italian tribunal granted sole custody to the father and, for reasons not entirely clear from the EU Court of Justice's summary, ordered her to be placed temporarily in a children's home in Rome. On the same day as that decision was handed down, the mother, Ms Detiček, fled to Slovenia with her daughter, in clear violation of the Italian custody order. By virtue of EU legislation, the Italian order was declared automatically enforceable in Slovenia, and the mother was ordered to return the child to the care home in Italy.

Ms Detiček successfully appealed to the Slovenian court to overturn that decision on grounds that her daughter had become settled in her new environment and

---

[53] See the earlier discussion in Sect. 1.

[54] Examples of judicial references to Art 24 of the Charter include: Case C-149/10 Zoi Chatzi v. Ypourgos Oikonomikon 16 September 2010; C-491/10 PPU Joseba Andoni Aguirre Zarraga v. Simone Pelz (2011) OJ C63; Case C-400/10 PPU J McB v. LE [2011] WLR 699; Case C-403/09 PPU Jasna Detiček v. Maurizio Sgueglia (2009) ECR I-12193; and Case C-34/09 Zambrano v. Office National de l'Emploi [2011] 2 CMLR 46. In Case C-208/09 Ilonka Sayn-Wittgenstein v. Landeshauptmann von Wien [2011] 2 CMLR 28, the Court drew inspiration from Art 7 of the Charter (respect for private and family life).

[55] See, for instance Case C-400/10 PPU *J McB v. LE* [2011] WLR 699.

[56] Case C-403/09 PPU *Deticek v. Sgueglia* (2009) ECR I-12193. Specifically, the case concerned article 20 of Regulation 2201/2003, above note 6.

that any forced return to the children's home would be detrimental to her welfare. In addition, during the judicial proceedings in Slovenia, the daughter had expressed the wish to remain with her mother, a factor that the court was legally bound to take into account under the relevant EU legislation. The father appealed against that ruling to the Slovenian Court of Appeal, and it was at this point that the case was referred to the Court of Justice.

There are two notable features of its decision that characterise almost all such cases directly concerning children's rights. First, while the Court explicitly acknowledged the importance of respecting 'the fundamental rights of the child as set out in article 24 of the Charter' (paragraph 53) and of precluding Member States from interpreting EU law in a manner than disregards such rights (paragraph 55), the ultimate responsibility for assessing the substance and scope of children's rights lies with the domestic courts (and, in the Detiček case, with the Italian jurisdiction from which the child had been wrongfully removed).

It follows, then, that the incorporation of tailored children's rights provisions into the Charter does not extend in any way the Court's powers to enforce children's rights obligations in areas in which they are deemed to have limited competence, nor does it encroach on Member State sovereignty to determine the substance and scope of domestic child law. The Charter depends, rather, on the nature and scope of child-focused measures and processes that are already in place at EU level as well as on the amenability of domestic systems to give effect to them.

The result of this approach for the child in *Detiček* was an immediate return to Italy and, in that sense, was entirely consistent with the spirit and approach of the Hague Child Abduction Convention underpinning this legislation.[57] But further consideration by the Court of the currency of the child's objections or, indeed, whether a further upheaval following a settled period in Slovenia might be in her best interests—both of which are legitimate grounds for derogating from the principle of automatic return—would surely have assisted the Member States in determining the rightful outcome of this highly sensitive case.

A second, arguably more constructive, feature of the *Detiček* case that characterises many other cross-border family cases relates to the accelerated procedure commonly adopted by the Court to expedite decisions involving children, particularly in the context of parental child abduction. EU law imposes a 42-day deadline for issuing a decision on the return of an abducted child to his or her country of habitual residence,[58] a deadline that is simply unworkable if the parents are locked in protracted judicial proceedings. Such cases are now routinely expedited by the Court to afford the parties a reasonable chance of settling the matter and avoiding

---

[57] One would hope that, with the child having been returned to Italy, the Italian court would have fully reviewed the custody arrangements in the light of the child's change in circumstances and the objections she had raised to living in Italy. For more detailed discussion, see Stalford (2012: Chaps. 2 and 5).

[58] Regulation 2201/2003 above note 6, article 11(3).

further trauma and protraction for the child. It could be argued that inherent in this accelerated procedure is a concern to protect the best interests of the child, and, as such, it is perhaps one of the most positive, albeit much more subtle, endorsements of the rights of the child by the Court of Justice.[59]

These alternative pathways for integrating the CRC into the EU's jurisprudence are effective to some degree, but the illustrations above demonstrate their limitations in achieving more explicit and thoughtful judicial engagement with the CRC. Arguably, what the Court achieves by working through these alternative instruments is a refined, often inferior and usually more lacklustre interpretation of the original provisions. More generally, by recoiling from a fuller assessment of children's rights, even when the facts of a given case demand it, the Court misses the opportunity to breathe life into legislative measures that could significantly enhance the status and experiences of children implicated in such proceedings. As things stand, children's rights measures enshrined in EU legislation are worth little more than the paper they are written on until the Court offers fuller, more informed guidance on how they might be interpreted and applied in practice.

6 Conclusion

The CRC is now the primary point of reference for the ongoing development of children's rights at EU level. Efforts to integrate more extensive and explicit reference to substantive CRC provisions and principles into binding law and guiding policies are now being accompanied by an attempt to align EU children's rights with broader CRC processes and guidance. Most notably, efforts are underway in the NGO-led lobbying sector to develop a more coherent child-rights mainstreaming strategy, which resonates strongly with the CRC's General Measures of Implementation Framework.[60] As the latter explains, such a strategy is much more than simply an *ex ante* integration of children's rights provision into legislative texts; it demands considerable attention to the institutional and procedural factors that facilitate effective *ex post* enforcement of children's rights. The Court of Justice, as the key institution charged with upholding compliance with EU law by both the EU institutions and Member States, has so far evaded any serious scrutiny when it comes to the actual implementation of children's rights measures.

---

[59] For examples of such expedited cases which are replete with references to the best interests of the child, albeit in isolation from the CRC, see: C-400/10 PPU Judgment 05/10/2010 *McB*; C-491/10 PPU Judgment 22/12/2010 *Aguirre Zarraga*; C-497/10 PPU 22/12/2010 *Mercredi*; C-296/10 Judgment 09/11/2010 *Purrucker*; C-211/10 PPU Judgment 01/07/2010 *Povse*; C-403/09 PPU Judgment 3/12/2009 *Detiček*; C-195/08 PPU Judgment 11/07/2008 *Rinau*.

[60] Eurochild 'Mainstreaming Children's Rights in EU Legislation, Policy and Budget—Lessons from Practice' Brussels 2014.

Indeed, this discussion has revealed a pervasive reluctance by the Court to engage in any meaningful consideration of children's rights issues, even in matters that fall squarely within its competence. Instead it has leaned on rather vague, often inferior, iterations of children's rights principles and provisions enshrined in the Charter and the ECHR jurisprudence. The banal, vacuous statements of children's rights that result take us no further in achieving effective enforcement of EU children's rights measures when it really matters. This is perhaps not surprising, given the trickle of child-related cases to have reached the Court, but it is certainly untenable in the longer term, considering the proliferation of binding EU legislation that directly targets children, all of which will demand more rigorous assessment of its meaning and scope.

Surely the time has come for the Court of Justice to engage in more fruitful children's rights deliberations if it is not to undermine the increasingly significant efforts that are being invested in producing considered and sensitive EU children's rights legislation? The CRC and its accompanying guidance offer a vital, as yet untapped, source of inspiration to guide the Court in this process. If it would only take that creative leap and embrace the CRC more fully, the Court could provide an invaluable mechanism for stimulating dialogue between the Member States as to how they should apply uniform EU children's rights measures. It would, moreover, convey a powerful message to the Member States about the role of the EU in reinforcing—rather than reinventing or, worse still, undermining,—the international children's rights obligations by which they are all bound.

References

Ackers, L., & Stalford, H. (2004). *A community for children? Children, citizenship and migration in the EU*. Aldershot: Ashgate.

Adams, M., de Waele, H., Meeusen, J., & Straetmans, G. (Eds.). (2013). *Judging Europe's judges: The legitimacy of the case law of the European Court of Justice*. Oxford: Hart.

Ahmed, T., & De Jesús Butler, I. (2006). The European Union and human rights: An international perspective. *European Journal of International Law, 17*.

Dashwood, A., Dougan, M., et al. (2011). *Wyatt and Dashwood's European Union Law* (6th ed.). Oxford: Hart.

De Búrca, G. (1993). Fundamental rights and the reach of EC law.' *Oxford Journal of Legal Studies, 13*.

De Búrca, G. (2002). Convergence and divergence in European public law: The case of human rights. In P. Beaumont, C. Lyons, & N. Walker (Eds.), *Convergence and divergence in European public law*. Oxford: Hart.

De Witte, B., & Muir, E. (Eds.). (2013). *Judicial activism and the European Court of Justice*. Cheltenham: Edward Elgar Publishing.

Drywood, E. (2007). Giving with one hand, taking with the other: Fundamental rights, children and the family reunification decision. *EL Rev, 32*.

Haldorsson, O. L. (2011). *Governance fit for children: To what extent have the general measures of implementation of the UNCRC been realised in the EU Institutions?*. Brussels: Save the Children.

Kilkelly, U. (2000). The impact of the convention on the case-law of the European court of Human Rights. In D. Fottrell (Ed.), *Revisiting children's rights: 10 years of the UN Convention on the Rights of the Child*. Dordrecht: Kluwer.

Kilkelly, U. (2001). The best of both worlds for children's rights: Interpreting the European Convention on Human Rights in the light of the UN Convention on the Rights of the Child. *Human Rights Quarterly, 23*.

Lamont, R. (2014). Article 24: Children's rights. In S. Peers, T. Hervey, J. Kenner, & A. Ward (Eds.), *The EU charter of fundamental rights: A commentary*. Oxford: Hart.

McGlynn, C. (2006). *Families and the European Union: Law, politics and pluralism*. Cambridge: CUP.

Neuwahl, N., & Rosas, A. (1995). *The European Union and human rights*. The Hague: Martinus Nijhoff Publishers.

Stalford, H. (2012). *Children and the European Union: Rights, welfare and accountability*. Oxford: Hart.

Stalford, H., & Drywood, E. (2009). Coming of age? Children's rights in the European Union. *Common Market Law Review, 46*, 143–172.

Tidimas, T. (2007). *The general principles of EU law* (2nd ed.). Oxford: Oxford University Press.

Weiler, J., & Lockhart, N. (1995). Taking rights seriously: The European Court and its fundamental rights jurisprudence. *Common Market Law Review*, 32.

Chapter 14
The CRC as a Litigation Tool Before the Inter-American System of Protection of Human Rights

Monica Feria-Tinta

Abstract This chapter examines how the Convention on the Rights of the Child (CRC) has been used as a litigation tool before the Inter-American System of Protection of Human Rights. First, it argues that the CRC is used as a tool of litigation at the substantial level when construing the obligations of States Parties by the Inter-American Court of Human Rights in individual complaints under the American Convention on Human Rights. Secondly, the chapter examines the way in which the CRC is also effectively used at a procedural level. It is submitted that far from departing from traditional interpretative rules under Public International Law, the Inter-American Court's approach is, on the contrary, in accordance with the basic tools of treaty interpretation as enshrined in the Vienna Convention on the Law of Treaties. It is submitted that this is in agreement with keeping the unity of international law.

1 Introduction

Since 1999, when the first case with a particular focus on the rights of children emerged from the Inter-American Court of Human Rights (hereafter the Court), this international human rights court with jurisdiction for 21 countries in the American region,[1] has delivered sweeping judgments in contentious cases and an important legal pronouncement (Advisory Opinion) in the protection of the rights

[1] *Basic Documents of the Inter-American Court of Human Rights San José,* Secretariat of the Inter-American Court of Human Rights San Jose, Costa Rica, 2003, p. 59. Recently, however, the State of Venezuela took the step of denouncing the American Convention, the withdrawal taking effect since September 10, 2013.

M. Feria-Tinta (✉)
Member of Middle Temple (Inn of Court), London, United Kingdom
e-mail: monicaferiatinta@hotmail.com

T. Liefaard and J.E. Doek (eds.), *Litigating the Rights of the Child*,
DOI 10.1007/978-94-017-9445-9_14

of children under the American Convention on Human Rights. The Court has adjudicated cases alleging violations of children's rights in relation to countries such as Guatemala, Argentina, Peru, Paraguay, El Salvador, Dominican Republic, Honduras and Colombia.[2] Reparation orders have ranged from compensation measures, which included novel measures such as setting up investment funds and trust funds for beneficiaries who were minors, to measures of satisfaction such as naming schools or public spaces after children to honour their memory, and even the creation of a system of genetic information in the search for 'disappeared' children.

The CRC has played a crucial role in the creation of such precedents in the Inter-American System. The chapter discusses how this has come to be the case. It is argued that the CRC has been used in litigation in the Inter-American System at least in a twofold way. First, at a substantive level: *to construe provisions of the American Convention*, to the protection of the child. Second, at a procedural level: it is discussed the evidentiary use of the CRC reports (that is, examination by the Committee on the Rights of the Child of States parties' compliance with the CRC under its article 44) in litigation before the Inter-American System.

This jurisprudence on the rights of the child may strike some as 'progressive' in nature or regarded as the fruit of "judicial activism" in a region where an estimated 81 million children still live and are raised in poverty.[3] Contrasting with that view, it is argued here that in developing such jurisprudence, the Inter-American Court did not depart from the traditional interpretative rules set out in the Vienna Convention on the Law of the Treaties. Rather, the use of the CRC in the development of such jurisprudence reflects the application of such general rules in the Court's task of interpreting the American Convention, in particular the Convention's relevant provision on the rights of the child.

2 Individual Petitions Before the Inter-American System

Contentious cases on the rights of children can be brought before the Inter-American System under the American Declaration on the Rights and Duties of Man[4] (for those State members of the Organization of American States (OAS) that have not signed/ratified the American Convention on Human Rights), and for those who are party to the American Convention, under article 44 of the American Convention.

---

[2] For a thorough review of the jurisprudence on the Rights of the Child before the Inter-American Court see Feria-Tinta (2008).

[3] Organization of American States (OAS) data. Press Release E-345/13, 'OAS Assistant Secretary General Calls on Member States to Invest more in Children', 16 September 2013.

[4] The American Declaration of the Rights and Duties of Man contains a number of provisions particularly relevant for children rights *inter alia*, Article VI (Right to a family and to protection thereof), Article VII (Right to protection for mothers and children), Article XII (Right to education).

Any person or group of persons, or any non-governmental organisation recognised in one or more member states of the OAS may lodge petitions with the Inter-American Commission on Human Rights (hereafter the Commission) containing complaints of a violation of the American Convention by a State party. In other words, there is no 'victim requirement' to lodge complaints under the Inter-American System. A third party (such as an NGO), with or without the victim's knowledge or authorisation can denounce a violation.

Individual complaints are first dealt with by the Commission and if admissibility requirements are found to be satisfied, and a finding of a breach of the American Convention during the merits stage of the claim is made, the case is referred to the Inter-American Court unless the State party complies with the recommendations of the Commission, or the parties reach a friendly settlement during the proceedings.[5] The Court has jurisdiction if in addition to being a party to the Convention, the State party has accepted the optional jurisdiction of the Court.[6] Individuals do not have the right to submit a case to the Court though; only the Commission and State parties.[7] Although individuals cannot file a case before the Court, individuals enjoy today *locus standi in judicio* in the proceedings determining their rights; that is, the victim has direct access to make representations before the Court as a party once the complaint reaches the Court and she or he is notified of the commencement of the proceedings.[8] Victims can submit pleadings (written and oral), motions and evidence in an autonomous manner, before the Court.[9]

This has meant that the victim as a party have had the right to make an appraisal of the facts, or the law, different from the one made by the Commission in its analysis of the case, effectively contributing "to the better conduct of the proceedings" as acknowledged by Judge Cançado Trindade in his Separate Opinion (*Voto Razonado*) in the *Gomez Paquiyauri Brothers* case; a case concerning the rights of children, where the position of the victim as a party, helped to formulate a better statement of the law and correct comprehension of the facts at stake.[10]

---

[5] Article 33 of the American Convention on Human Rights establishes both the Commission and the Court as the competent organs with respect to matters relating to the fulfilment of the commitments made by the State parties to the Convention. See also Article 41 f, 44, 46–47, 48–51, and 61 of the American Convention.

[6] Article 62.1 of the American Convention. The following countries have accepted the jurisdiction of the Court: Argentina, Barbados, Bolivia, Brazil, Chile, Colombia, Costa Rica, Ecuador, El Salvador, Guatemala, Haiti, Honduras, Mexico, Nicaragua, Panama, Paraguay, Peru, Dominican Republic, Suriname, and Uruguay. (Venezuela and Trinidad and Tobago had given jurisdiction to the Court but subsequently denounced the Convention.)

[7] Article 61 of the American Convention.

[8] The Court introduced such changes originally, in its Rules of Procedure of 2000, which entered into force on 1 June 2001.

[9] See article 40 of the Court's current Rules of Procedure approved in November 2009.

[10] Int-Am. Ct H.R. *Case of the Gómez Paquiyauri Brothers vs Peru*, Series C: Decisions and Judgments No. 110, Judgment of July 8, 2004. Separate Opinion (*Voto Razonado*) of Judge A.A. Cancado Trindade, para. 32.

When a case is brought under the American Declaration only or when the State party has not given jurisdiction to the Court, the case ends at the Commission's level.[11]

3 The Use of the CRC as a Tool of Litigation at the Substantive Level Before the Inter-American System: Construing the Scope and Content of the Rights of the Child under the American Convention

The American Convention contains a provision with a specific focus on the protection of children, with no parallel in the European Convention on Human Rights, or the African Charter on Human and People's Rights. Article 19 of the American Convention on Human Rights states: 'Every minor child has the right to the measures of protection required by his condition as a minor on the part of his family, society, and the state.' As a result, the Inter-American Court of Human Rights has the jurisdictional power to pronounce itself on individual rights of children under complaint procedures, in a way no other international judicial body has been empowered to do. Not only it can issue binding decisions in that respect, but also, it can provide for a wide spectrum of reparation measures under article 63 of the Convention as will be discussed further below.

In order to interpret States parties' duties under article 19, the Court has resorted to general rules of interpretation on the Law of Treaties (article 31 of the Vienna Convention on the Law of Treaties) and the specific interpretative rules contained additionally in the American Convention, namely article 29. Unlike the European System, the Inter-American System does not have a

---

[11] See, for example, Inter-American Commission on Human Rights, Report No. 81/10 Case 12.562, *Wayne smith, Hugo Armendariz,* et al. United States, July 12, 2010, (a case of deportation from the United States). The case was brought under articles I (right to life, liberty and personal security), V (right to private and family life), VI (right to family), VII (right to protection for mothers and children), IX (right to inviolability of the home), XVIII (right to fair trial) and XXVI (right to due process of law) of the American Declaration on the Rights and Duties of Man. In its report on the merits the Commission stated among other things: '[…] the IACHR particularly emphasizes that the best interest of minor child must be taken into consideration in a parent's removal proceeding. Article VII of the American Declaration states, "all children have the right to special protection, care and aid." As a component of this special protection afforded children, in the context of legal proceedings that may impact a child's right to family life, 'special protection' requires that the proceedings duly consider the best interests of the child. (para. 56 of the Report)'. The Commission found the USA responsible for, inter alia, the violation of articles V, VI and VII of the American Declaration 'for failing to hear the [claimant's] humanitarian defense and duly consider their right to family and the best interest of their children on an individualized basis in their removal proceedings.' (ibid. para. 60).

'margin of appreciation' doctrine.[12] So, the approach taken by the Court, to the substantive interpretation of the rights of children in the system, is a reflection of essentially traditional rules under General International Law, that is, the same ones used to interpret any treaty under international law.

3.1 1969 Vienna Convention on the Law of Treaties, Article 31: General Rule of Interpretation

Article 31 of the 1969 Vienna Convention on the Law of Treaties states:

1. A treaty shall be interpreted in good faith in accordance with the ordinary meaning to be given to the terms of the treaty in their context and in the light of its object and purpose.
2. The context for the purpose of the interpretation of a treaty shall comprise, in addition to the text, including its preamble and annexes:
   (a) any agreement relating to the treaty which was made between all the parties in connexion with the conclusion of the treaty;
   (b) any instrument which was made by one or more parties in connexion with the conclusion of the treaty and accepted by the other parties as an instrument related to the treaty.
3. **There shall be taken into account, together with the context**:
   (a) any subsequent agreement between the parties regarding the interpretation of the treaty or the application of its provisions;
   (b) any subsequent practice in the application of the treaty which establishes the agreement of the parties regarding its interpretation;
   (c) **any relevant rules of international law applicable in the relations between the parties**. […] (Emphasis added)

In order to construe the duties of States parties towards children under article 19, both under its contentious procedures as well as under its advisory functions, the Inter-American Court has thus taken into account 'any relevant rules of international law applicable in the relations between the parties', including the legal obligations undertaken by the States parties under the CRC. In its first historic decision concerning the rights of children in 1999, *in the Villagrán Morales* et al. *case* (*Street Children* case)[13] for example, the Court had for the first time the task

[12] On the doctrine of margin of appreciation see Harris et al. (2009): 11–14. As explained therein, 'it means that the state is allowed a certain measure of discretion, subject to European supervision, when it takes legislative, administrative or judicial action in the area of a Convention right' (p. 11).

[13] Int-Am. Ct H.R. *Villagrán Morales* et al. case, Series C: No 63. Judgment of November 19, 1999.

of defining what is meant by the word 'child' under the American Convention. The Court observed that article 19 did not define the term. The content to be assigned to the word 'child' was determined by classic interpretative rules on the Law of Treaties such as article 31, bringing the definition enshrined in article 1 of the CRC to assist in the interpretation of article 19 of the American Convention. The Court thus held that for the purposes of the American Convention a 'child' was 'every human being who has not attained 18 years of age', 'unless, by virtue of an applicable law, he shall have attained his majority previously'.[14] The *Street Children* case was paradigmatic: at the time, a Non-Governmental Organization called Casa Alianza on its own, was handling domestically, 392 cases of alleged crimes against 'street children' perpetrated in Guatemala, of which approximately 50 were for murder. Of the 392 cases, fewer than 5 % had been finalised by the courts, and almost half of them had been simply filed away. The decision of the Inter-American Court in that sense broke with that climate of impunity concerning the fundamental rights of those children. Indeed, in the *Street Children* case the Court used the entire prevailing system for the protection of children in force at the time of the events, in order to assess the scope of the duties of the defendant State under the American Convention. In so doing, it reaffirmed a principle of interpretation already held in its earlier jurisprudence:

> This Court has said that "when interpreting a treaty, not only the agreements and instruments formally related to it should be taken into consideration (Article 31.2 of the Vienna Convention), but also the system within which it is (inscribed) (Article 31.3)".[15]

It proceeded to say that '[t]he Court has previously indicated that this focus is particularly important for international human rights law, which has advanced substantially by the evolutive interpretation of international protection instruments'[16] adding that

> [t]his evolutive interpretation **is consequent with the general rules of the interpretation of treaties embodied in the 1969 Vienna Convention**. Both this Court [...] and the European Court [...] have indicated that human rights treaties are living instruments, the interpretation of which must evolve over time in view of existing circumstances.[17] (Emphasis added)

Thus, starting from the understanding that both the American Convention and the CRC formed part of a very comprehensive international *corpus juris* for the protection of the child, the Court went on to establish the content and scope of the

---

[14] Ibid., at para. 188.

[15] Int-Am. Ct H.R. *The Right to Information on Consular Assistance in the Framework of the Guarantees of Due Process of Law.* Advisory Opinion OC-16/99 of October 1, 1999. Series A No. 16, para. 113 as cited in *Villagrán Morales* et al. case, Series C: No. 63., Judgment of November 19, 1999 at para. 192.

[16] *Villagrán Morales* et al. case, ibid., at para. 193.

[17] *The Right to Information on Consular Assistance,* para. 114, as cited in *Villagrán Morales* et al. case, ibid at para. 193.

general provision established in article 19 of the American Convention, relevant to this particular case, in the light of the various provisions of the CRC that threw light on the conduct that the State should have observed towards street children. It referred mainly to article 2, article 3, article 6, article 20, article 27 and article 37 of the Convention on the Rights of the Child.[18]

[18] The Articles read:

ARTICLE 2

1. States Parties shall respect and ensure the rights set forth in the present Convention to each child within their jurisdiction without discrimination of any kind, irrespective of the child's or his or her parent's or legal guardian's race, color, sex, language, religion, political or other opinion, national, ethnic or social origin, property, disability, birth or other status.
2. States Parties shall take all appropriate measures to ensure that the child is protected against all forms of discrimination or punishment on the basis of the status, activities, expressed opinions, or beliefs of the child's parents, legal guardians, or family members.

ARTICLE 3

[…]

2. States Parties undertake to ensure the child such protection and care as is necessary for his or her wellbeing, taking into account the rights and duties of his or her parents, legal guardians, or other individuals legally responsible for him or her, and, to this end, shall take all appropriate legislative and administrative measures.

ARTICLE 6

1. States Parties recognize that every child has the inherent right to life.
2. States Parties shall ensure to the maximum extent possible the survival and development of the child.

ARTICLE 20

1. A child temporarily or permanently deprived of his or her family environment, or in whose own best interests cannot be allowed to remain in that environment, shall be entitled to special protection and assistance provided by the State.
2. States Parties shall in accordance with their national laws ensure alternative care for such a child.

[…]

ARTICLE 27

1. States Parties recognize the right of every child to a standard of living adequate for the child's physical, mental, spiritual, moral and social development.

[…]

3. States Parties, in accordance with national conditions and within their means, shall take appropriate measures to assist parents and others responsible for the child to implement this right and shall in case of need provide material assistance and support programs, particularly with regard to nutrition, clothing and housing.

ARTICLE 37

States Parties shall ensure that:

(a) No child shall be subjected to torture or other cruel, inhuman or degrading treatment or punishment. Neither capital punishment nor life imprisonment without possibility of release shall be imposed for offences committed by persons below 18 years of age;
(b) No child shall be deprived of his or her liberty unlawfully or arbitrarily. The arrest, detention or imprisonment of a child shall be in conformity with the law and shall be used only as a measure of last resort and for the shortest appropriate period of time;

In the Court's view, these provisions allow 'to define the scope of the "measures of protection" referred to in Article 19 of the American Convention, from different angles'.[19] It stated that, among the CRC's provisions

> we should emphasize those that refer to non-discrimination, special assistance for children deprived of their family environment, the guarantee of survival and development of the child, the right to an adequate standard of living, and the social rehabilitation of all children who are abandoned or exploited. It is clear to the Court that the acts perpetrated against the victims in this case, in which State agents were involved, violate these provisions.[20]

The Court held finally that in cases where the State apparatus had to intervene in offences committed by minors, 'it should make substantial efforts to guarantee their rehabilitation in order to "allow them to play a constructive and productive role in society".'[21] The Court found that it was clear that the State had seriously infringed all these directives in the instant case. But the cases yet to come before the Court concerning Article 19, after the *Street Children* case, would allow the Court to elaborate further on the law concerning the obligations of States *vis-à-vis* children that were considered to be in conflict with the law.

The approach taken by the Court in this first case on the rights of children to construe the obligation of State parties under article 19 of the American Convention using the CRC as an important tool for those purposes, consistently continued in all the jurisprudence concerning the rights of the child to come under the Convention. In the case of the *Gómez Paquiyauri Brothers*, the first case concerning the rights of the child in times of armed conflict to be examined by the Court under the Convention, the Court explicitly reiterated in that sense:

> Both the American Convention and the Convention on the Rights of the Child are part of a broad international *corpus juris* for protection of children that aids this Court in

---

Footnote 18 (continued)

(c) Every child deprived of liberty shall be treated with humanity and respect for the inherent dignity of the human person, and in a manner which takes into account the needs of persons of his or her age. In particular, every child deprived of liberty shall be separated from adults unless it is considered in the child's best interest not to do so and shall have the right to maintain contact with his or her family through correspondence and visits, save in exceptional circumstances;

(d) Every child deprived of his or her liberty shall have the right to prompt access to legal and other appropriate assistance, as well as the right to challenge the legality of the deprivation of his or her liberty before a court or other competent, independent and impartial authority, and to a prompt decision on any such action.

[19] *Villagrán Morales* et al. case, op cit, at para.196.

[20] Ibid.

[21] Ibid, citing the *United Nations Minimum rules for the administration of justice for minors* (*'Beijing Rules'*). Adopted by the General Assembly of the United Nations in its resolution 40/33, of 29 November 1985, Fifth Part, Treatment in prison establishments, para. 26.1.

> establishing the content and scope of the general provision defined in Article 19 of the American Convention.[22]

The Inter-American Commission on Human Rights has highlighted that this *corpus juris* encompasses not only the text itself of the CRC, but also the decisions adopted by the United Nations Committee on the Rights of the Child in pursuit of its mandate such as General Comments, and Final Comments on the periodic reports under the CRC.[23] The Commission has stated in that regard:

> That approach represents a significant step forward that indicates not only the existence of **a shared legal framework in international human rights law as applicable to children** but also the interdependence that exists at the international level among the different international systems for protecting children's human rights.[24] (Emphasis added)

3.2 Article 29 of the American Convention on Human Rights

> The reference to the principle of "evolutive interpretation" referred to by the Court in the *Street Children* case,[25] has further support in article 29 of the American Convention containing and additional rule of interpretation. Indeed, the combination of the regional and universal human rights systems for purposes of interpreting the American Convention is based in addition to article 31 of the Vienna Convention, on article 29 of the American Convention.[26] Article 29 of the American Convention reads:

[22] *Gomez Paquiyauri Brothers* case, *supra* note 11, at para. 166 reiterating the same principle reflected in *Street Children* case, para. 194; Int-Am. Ct. H.R., *Juridical Status and Human Rights of the Child,* Advisory Opinion OC-17/02, August 28, 2002, Series A No. 17, para. 37 and 53; Int-Am. Ct. H.R. *Case of the Juvenile Reeducation Institute.* Series C No. 112, Judgment of September 2, 2004 at para. 148.

[23] IACHR, 'The Rights of the child in the Inter-American Human Rights System', OEA/SER.L/V/II.133 Doc 34, 29 October 2008, para. 53.

[24] IACHR, "Report on Corporal Punishment and Human Rights of Children and Adolescents", OEA/Ser.L/V/II.135, Doc 14, 5 August 2009, at para. 21.

[25] *Villagrán Morales* et al. case, at para. 192.

[26] IACHR, Report No. 41/99, Case 11.491, Minors in Detention, Honduras, March 10, 1999, paragraph 72. The Inter-American Commission on Human Rights pointed out therein in that sense: 72. For an interpretation of a State's obligations vis-a-vis minors, in addition to the provision of the American Convention, the Commission considers it important to refer to other international instruments that contain even more specific rules regarding the protection of children. **Those instruments include the Convention on the Rights of the Child and the various United Nations declarations on the subject**. This combination of the regional and universal human rights systems for purposes of interpreting the Convention is based on Article 29 of the American Convention and on the consistent practice of the Court and of the Commission in this sphere. (Emphasis added).

Article 29. Restrictions Regarding Interpretation
No provision of this Convention shall be interpreted as:

(a) permitting any State Party, group, or person to suppress the enjoyment or exercise of the rights and freedoms recognized in this Convention or to restrict them to a greater extent than is provided for herein;
(b) restricting the enjoyment or exercise of any right or freedom recognized by virtue of the laws of any State Party **or by virtue of another convention to which one of the said states is a party;**
(c) precluding other rights or guarantees that are inherent in the human personality or derived from representative democracy as a form of government; or
(d) **excluding or limiting the effect that the American Declaration of the rights and Duties of Man and other international acts of the same nature may have**. (Emphasis added)

This approach is thus not only reflected in cases concerning the rights of the child but it is indeed a general approach the Inter-American Court has in respect of rules of interpretation of the American Convention. In an *Advisory Opinion* not referring to the rights of the child, but highlighting this evolutive interpretation of Conventional rights, the Court stated:

> [t]he *corpus juris* of international human rights law comprises a set of international instruments of varied content and juridical effects (treaties, conventions, resolutions and declarations). Its dynamic evolution has had a positive impact on international law in affirming and building up the latter's faculty for regulating relations between States and the human beings within their respective jurisdictions.[27]

As a result of this interpretative approach having as basis both article 31 of the Vienna Convention on the Law of Treaties and article 29 of the American Convention, the Inter-American Court has been using the comprehensive existing international *corpus juris* for the protection of children developed to date, including the 1989 Convention on the Rights of the Child, the 1985 United Nations Standard Minimum Rules for the Administration of Juvenile Justice (the Beijing Rules), the 1990 United Nations Standard Minimum Rules for Non-custodial Measures (the Tokyo Rules) and the 1990 United Nations Guidelines for the Prevention of Juvenile Delinquency (the Riyadh guidelines) as well as the provisions relevant to the protection of children in times of war enshrined in the 1949 Geneva Conventions and 1977 Additional Protocols, in interpreting the American Convention. In addition, it has also taken into account provisions from regional instruments relevant in the analysis of a given case, such as the Additional Protocol to the American Convention on Human Rights in the Area of Economic,

[27] Int-Am. Ct H.R., Advisory Opinion OC-16/99, Series A. No 16, *The Right to Information on Consular Assistance in the Framework of the Guarantees of Due Process of Law*, October 1, 1999, para. 115.

Social, and Cultural Rights ('Protocol of San Salvador')[28] and the American Declaration of the Rights and Duties of Man (1948).

4 The Use of the CRC at the Procedural Level: The Evidentiary Use of the Work of the CRC Committee in the Litigation of Cases Before the Inter-American System

The results of the monitoring activities of the Committee on the Rights of the Child of the implementation of the CRC are an important source of information that can be used in the litigation of cases relevant to the rights of the child in the Inter-American System in order to prove existing patterns of systematic violations of rights of the child in a particular jurisdiction in the Americas. The Concluding Observations on the situation of countries, issued by the Committee on the Rights of the Child, is of particular importance in documenting the context, and proving factual information in a given case. The *Mapiripán* case[29] is an instructive example in that respect.

The Inter-American Commission on Human Rights had not included article 19 among the alleged violated rights under the Convention in its original complaint in the Mapiripán massacre case. It was raised, however, by the victims' representatives. Two children had been among the assassinated victims in Mapiripán. Likewise, of the 19 relatives identified throughout the litigation, nine were minors at the time of the events. The representatives argued in respect of this group that

(d) The development of those children was severely affected by their displacement, by their having to abandon their studies in order to start work or take on the responsibility for the care of their younger siblings or by having to be away from their families for the sake of their schooling, enduring hunger, lacking medical attention or adequate housing, amongst other situations, which constitute violations of the rights of the child. In accordance with the Convention, as well as with other international instruments, the State has the obligation to adopt special measures for boys and girls. Colombia failed to fulfill this duty by not preventing the displacement, not protecting the children during the displacement, not providing adequate humanitarian aid, not ensuring their return, resettlement or reintegration into dignified and safe conditions; and

---

[28] For example, the Court referred to articles 13, 15 and 16 of the said Protocol in its interpretation of article 19 in its *Advisory Opinion on the Juridical Condition and Human Rights of the Child,* Series A: No 17; Advisory Opinion OC-17/2002 of August 28, 2002, Requested by the Inter-American Commission On Human Rights.

[29] Int-Am. Ct. H.R., *Case of the Massacre of Mapiripán vs Colombia,* Series C: Decisions and Judgments No 134, Judgment of September 15, 2005.

(e) to date the victims are still living with fear and in situations of extreme precariousness. In spite of the duties that the State has towards this group of women and children, the families have not attained the dignity and the safety that they enjoyed before the massacre and the displacement.[30]

Colombia did not acknowledge responsibility for the violation of article 19.[31]

The Court reaffirmed its earlier jurisprudence in stating that article 19 must be understood as a complementary right that the American Convention establishes in favour of human beings that for their physical and psychological development need measures of special protection.[32] The Court held that in this matter the superior interest of the child, which 'is based on the very dignity of the human being, on the characteristics of children themselves, and on the need to foster their development, making full use of their potential, as well as on the nature and scope of the Convention on the Rights of the Child', takes precedence before any other consideration. In order to assess the content and scope of article 19 as applied to the case the Court referred to articles 6, 37, 38 and 39 of the CRC as well as pertinent provisions of the Protocol II of the Geneva Conventions.[33]

The brutality of the Massacre of Mapiripán had been an act of terror against a civilian population living in an area that paramilitaries aimed to control. It was an act perpetrated with the utmost savagery to provoke the forced displacement of such a population. The Court considered it necessary to reflect on the particular

---

[30] *Case of the Massacre of Mapiripán* at para. 148 d) and e). Translation by Barry Cheetham and revised by the author.

[31] Ibid at para. 151.

[32] Ibid at para. 152 citing Int-Am. Ct. H.R. Series C No 112; *Case of the Juvenile Reeducation Institute v Paraguay* ('*Case of the Children's Rehabilitation v Paraguay*'), Judgment of September 2, 2004 at para. 147; *Case of the Gómez Paquiyauri Brothers supra* note 11 at para. 164; and Int-Am. Ct. H.R. Series A: No 17; Advisory Opinion on the *Juridical Condition and Human Rights of the Child*, Advisory Opinion OC-17/2002 of August 28, 2002 at para. 54.

[33] Whereas Article 6 and 37 of the CRC refers to the right to life and freedom from torture, Article 38 and 39 provide:

Article 38

1. States Parties undertake to respect and to ensure respect for rules of international humanitarian law applicable to them in armed conflicts which are relevant to the child.
2. States Parties shall take all feasible measures to ensure that persons who have not attained the age of 15 years do not take a direct part in hostilities.
3. States Parties shall refrain from recruiting any person who has not attained the age of 15 years into their armed forces. In recruiting among those persons who have attained the age of 15 years but who have not attained the age of 18 years, States Parties shall endeavour to give priority to those who are oldest.
4. In accordance with their obligations under international humanitarian law to protect the civilian population in armed conflicts, States Parties shall take all feasible measures to ensure protection and care of children who are affected by an armed conflict.

Article 39

States Parties shall take all appropriate measures to promote physical and psychological recovery and social reintegration of a child victim of: any form of neglect, exploitation, or abuse; torture or any other form of cruel, inhuman or degrading treatment or punishment; or armed conflicts. Such recovery and reintegration shall take place in an environment which fosters the health, self-respect and dignity of the child.

consequences that such brutality had on the children who formed part of that community, who had been victims of such violence in the context of the armed conflict and who had been left orphans, displaced and had their physical and psychological integrity violated as a consequence. Among others, the Concluding Observations of the Committee on the Right of the Child to Colombia in 2000, served as evidence for the direct effects of the armed conflict in Colombia on the development of children. The Court referred:

> […] the United Nations Committee on the Rights of the Child has expressed its concern arising from the fact that "the direct effects of the armed conflict [in Colombia] have a very negative impact on the development of children and seriously hamper the implementation of many of the rights of the majority of children in the State party."[34] In particular, the armed conflict constitutes a "threat […] to children's lives, including instances of extrajudicial killing, disappearance and torture committed by […] paramilitary groups".[35] Likewise, the UN Special Representative of the Secretary General on Children and Armed Conflict has acknowledged that children who have been exposed to "violence and killing, displacement, violation or loss of loved ones carry with them the scars of fear and hatred".[36,37]

The Inter-American Court held that Colombia had failed in its duty of the protection of children before, during, and in the aftermath of the massacre:

> 159. In the first place, the State was fully aware that the region where Mapiripán is situated was characterized by high degrees of violence within the framework of the internal armed conflict (supra para 96.23), in spite of which it failed to protect the population of Mapiripán, particularly its boys and girls.
>
> 160. Furthermore, as has been established (supra paras. 96.36 and 96.55), the violence unleashed during the Mapiripán massacre affected the child population with particular intensity: many of them saw how their relatives—mostly their fathers—were taken away, they could hear their cries for help, they witnessed the remains of discarded corpses with throats cut or decapitated and, in certain cases, they knew what the paramilitaries had done to their relatives. Moreover, during the massacre the minors Hugo Fernando and Diego Armando Martínez Contreras, aged 16 and 15 respectively (supra para. 96.40) were either executed or removed, and there are also in existence affirmations of witnesses of the events that make reference to unidentified children who had been executed, including some only a few months old (supra paras. 75.1–96.52). In addition, there arises the case of the then children Carmen Johanna Jaramillo Giraldo, Gustavo Caicedo Contreras and Maryuri Caicedo Contreras who were threatened by the paramilitaries when they tried to follow or search for their relatives during the days of the massacre. In this connection,

[34] *Cfr.* Observaciones finales del Comité de los Derechos del Niño: Colombia, 16/10/2000, CRC/C/15/Add.137, 25° periodo de sesiones, Comité de los Derechos del Niño, párr. 10.

[35] *Cfr.* Observaciones finales del Comité de los Derechos del Niño: Colombia, 16/10/2000, párr. 34.

[36] *Cfr.* Informe del Representante Especial del Secretario General encargado de la cuestión de los niños en los conflictos armados. Doc. de la Asamblea General de Naciones Unidas A/54/430 de 1 de octubre de 1999, párr. 25.

[37] *Case of the Massacre of Mapiripán* at paras. 156 and 157. Free translation by Barry Cheetham and the author.

Gustavo Caicedo Contreras, 7 years of age at the time of the events, declared that "they [the paramilitaries] did not care if they were children or infants, they took them away for the sole purpose of asking about the relative [...] that they were after."[38]

161. Following the Mapiripán massacre, many families left the village and the vast majority of them have not gone back there. As is developed in the relevant chapter, the boys and girls, upon being displaced—[...]—were subjected to conditions such as separation from their families, the abandonment of their belongings and their homes, rejection, hunger and cold. For example, Carmen Johanna Jaramillo Girlado, at the time a minor, suffered threats from the paramilitaries just after the massacre (*supra* para 96.141). For his part, Gustavo Caicedo Contreras, aged 7 at the time of the events, declared that he had felt rejected "because when he was in Bogotá the people looked at him [...] in a strange way because he was a displaced person".[39] Furthermore, some of the displaced children had to live in "houses" made of tin cans and plastic, in addition to taking charge of their younger brothers and sisters, on account of their mothers needing to seek work in order to sustain the family. In this respect, Johanna Marina Valencia Sanmiguel, aged 8 at the time of the events, declared:

We had to endure hunger and my mother had to work so as to get hold of food. I had to begin looking after my brothers and sisters from the age of eight. I have a brother with special needs and I had to feed him from a feeding bottle and clean him. I also had to do the cooking [...].[40]

162. The obligation of the State to respect the right to life of every person under its jurisdiction presents special modalities in the case of children, and it becomes an obligation to "prevent situations that could lead, either by actions or dereliction, to the impairment of that right".[41] In the case that is *sub judice,* the massacre and its consequences created a climate of permanent tension and violence that impaired the right of the children of Mapiripán to a life of dignity. As a result, the Court considers that the State did not create the conditions or take the measures necessary so that the children in the instant case might have and develop a life of dignity, but rather that they have exposed them to a climate of violence and lack of safety.[42]

The Court found that the State of Colombia had violated article 19 in connection with articles 4.1, 5.1 and 1.1 of the American Convention to the detriment of the children whose names had been identified in the above description of their victimisation. In addition the Court also found that Colombia had violated article 19 in connection with articles 22.1, 4.1 and 1.1 of the American Convention to the

---

[38] *Cfr.* declaración jurada rendida por el testigo Gustavo Caicedo Contreras el 16 de febrero del 2005 (expediente sobre declaraciones rendidas o autenticadas ante fedatario público, folio 4566).

[39] *Cfr.* declaración jurada rendida por el testigo Gustavo Caicedo Contreras el 16 de febrero del 2005 (expediente sobre declaraciones rendidas o autenticadas ante fedatario público, folio 4567).

[40] *Cfr.* declaración jurada rendida por la testigo Johanna Marina Valencia Sanmiguel el 16 de febrero del 2005 (expediente sobre declaraciones rendidas o autenticadas ante fedatario público, folio 4577).

[41] *Cfr. Caso de los Hermanos Gómez Paquiyauri*, párrs. 124 y 171, y *Caso Bulacio*, párr. 138.

[42] *Case of the Massacre of Mapiripán* at paras. 159–162. Free translation by Barry Cheetham.

detriment of the children who had been displaced from Mapiripán as a consequence of the massacre and whose names had been individualised during the litigation.[43]

In another case, concerning a child soldier, the *Vargas Areco* case,[44] the Court referred to the evidential value of the Report Paraguay made before the Committee on the Rights of the Child when analyzing the individual case of Vargas Areco. In the said report Paraguay had 'acknowledged the existence of ill-treatment, forced conscription, and even wrongful death of children who take part in military service' in the country.[45] Paraguay accepted international responsibility in the case. However, this did not stop the Court from stating the law and in so doing using the Concluding Observations of the Committee on the Rights of the Child regarding the situation of children in Paraguay as factual statements, as evidence relevant to the case. It observed:

> 133. On June 18, 1997, the UN Committee on the Rights of the Child made its concluding observations on the situation of children in Paraguay and pointed out that, despite the legal restrictions imposed upon the recruitment of minors under the age of 18, "it is concerned that in practice this policy is not always enforced and that there are still under-age juveniles coerced or pressured into military service." Therefore, the Committee on the Rights of the Child encouraged the State party to enforce rigorously legislation in force.[46] The international body addressed the subject again in 2001, and recommended that Paraguay "put an end to the practice of recruiting children into the Paraguayan Armed Forces and national police."[47,48]

Evidential value of steps taken to comply with relevant observations made by the Committee on the Rights of the Child has also been considered by the Court—when assessing reparations orders in a particular case—as guarantees of non repetition. In the *Vargas Areco* case, the Court noticed, for example, that a recent statement made by the President of Paraguay on March 14, 2006, regarding the Optional Protocol to the CRC in relation to the involvement of children in armed conflict, which sets forth that minors under the age of

---

[43] *Case of the Massacre of Mapiripán* at para. 163.

[44] Int-Am. Ct. H.R., *Case of Vargas Areco v. Paraguay*, Series C: No 155, Judgment of September 26, 2006.

[45] Ibid., at para. 71.27 referring to the UN, Committee on the Rights of the Child, survey of the reports submitted by States pursuant to Article 44 of the Convention on the Rights of the Child. Paraguay Report. CRC/C/65/Add.12, of March 15, 2001.

[46] UN, Concluding Observations of the Committee on the Rights of the Child: Paraguay, June 18, 1997, CRC/C/15/Add.75, para. 17 and 36.

[47] UN, Concluding Observations of the Committee on the Rights of the Child: Paraguay, November 06, 2001, CRC/C/15/Add.166, para. 46(a).

[48] *Vargas Areco* case, supra note 45, at para. 133.

18 cannot be recruited into military service, 'constitute[d] a positive step to prevent events such as those that occurred in the instant case from happening again.'[49]

5 Reparation in Cases of Violations of Human Rights of Children in the Jurisprudence of the Inter-American Court of Human Rights

As mentioned before, the Inter-American Court not only has power to pass a binding decision when adjudicating a case but it is perhaps also the international human rights tribunal with most ample powers to grant reparation awards.[50] The measures ordered by the Court in order to redress violations of the rights of children as discussed above have ranged from restitutive measures (such as legal recognition of a name),[51] cessation of legal effects of violations[52] and compensation measures (moral and pecuniary damages) including setting up investment funds and trust funds for beneficiaries who are minors,[53] to guarantees of non-repetition (changes in legislation and policy)[54] and measures of satisfaction such as public apologies and acknowledgement of the truth as well as those who serve to honour the victims such as schools being named after

[49] Ibid., at para. 134.

[50] Article 63.1 of the American Convention states: 'If the Court finds that there has been a violation of a right or freedom protected by this Convention, the Court shall rule that the injured party be ensured the enjoyment of his right or freedom that was violated. It shall also rule, if appropriate, that the consequences of the measure or situation that constituted the breach of such right or freedom be remedied and that fair compensation be paid to the injured party.'

[51] As it was in the *Gómez Paquiyauri Brothers* case, where Rafael Gómez Paquiyauri (17) had left a pregnant girlfriend whose child could not take the name of her father since he was no longer there to recognise her as his child. The child, through her mother, requested before the Court, that as a way of restitution, the State should facilitate the registration of the name of the minor with the paternity of Rafael Gómez Paquiyauri acknowledged.

[52] See for example Int-Am. Ct H.R., *Molina Theissen vs Guatemala* case, Reparations, Judgment of July 3, 2004, Series C: No 108, Operative paragraph 7 at para. 106. The Court ordered the State of Guatemala to create an expeditious mechanism to obtain the declaration of absence and presumption of death for cases of enforced disappearances.

[53] See Int-Am. Ct H. R., Series C: Decisions and Judgments No 100; *Case of Bulacio v Argentina,* Judgment of September 18, 2003, operative paragraph 13 at page 61 and '*Gómez Paquiyauri Brothers*' case para. 248.

[54] This refers to entire changes in legal systems to bring State practice into compliance with the American Convention's standards such as in the *case of Juvenile Reeducation Institute" v Paraguay* (*'Instituto del Menor Panchito López'*) case. See also Operative paragraph 5 in the *Bulacio* case, ordering Argentina to adjust its domestic legal system to comply with international human rights provisions and make them fully effective.

children,[55] public places such as a square or a street being named after children,[56] and even setting up web pages for the search for victims, and the creation of a system of genetic information in the search for "disappeared" children.[57] The Court has ordered measures for addressing indifference and oblivion in the social milieu, as well as impunity.[58] All these measures have not only tried to 'help the survivors to live with their grief'[59] but also have stood as an issue of *order public*, to assert law over brute force: an attempt to organise human relations on the basis of *recta ratio*.[60]

6 Concluding Remarks

'Humanity must give children the best of itself', the Inter-American Court states in its Advisory Opinion on the *Juridical Condition and Human Rights of the Child*.[61] This legal pronouncement perhaps best encapsulates the Court's efforts in using general rules of treaty interpretation, traditional to public international law, to best serve its task of interpreting a 'living instrument' such as the American Convention, in particular its article 19. Not only is this in alignment with the basic tools of treaty interpretation as enshrined in the Vienna Convention on the Law of Treaties, it is also a way of keeping the unity of international law. A treaty, after all, is not an island. There *is* an existing legal framework within it is interpreted. In the CRC, the Inter-American system has found an important tool that has contributed to better state the law in the Americas. Other systems, in turn, may find the example of the Inter-American Court instructive in their approach to their own tasks.

---

55 See the *Villagrán Morales* et al. *case*, Reparations, 26 May 2001 at para. 103; Case of *Molina Theissen vs Guatemala,* Reparations, July 3 2004, Operative paragraph 6 at para. 106 and the '*Gómez Paquiyauri Brothers'* case, at para. 236.

56 See Int-Am. Ct H.R., *Case Servellón García and Others vs. Honduras*, Series C No 152, Judgment of 21 September 2006 at para. 199, in which the Court ordered Honduras to name a square or a street in Tegucigalpa in memory of the victims, two of whom were children. See also the *Vargas Areco vs Paraguay* case where the Court ordered Paraguay to put a plaque in the community where Gerardo Vargas Areco, a child soldier, had lived, to keep his memory alive. *Case Vargas Areco vs Paraguay, supra* note 45 at para. 158.

57 See Operative paragraph 8 at para. 106 in the *Molina Theissen vs Guatemala* Case, Reparations, July 3 2004 and Operative paragraph 7 at page 106 in the *Serrano Cruz Sisters* case; Int-Am Ct. H.R. Series C: No 120, Case of *Serrano Cruz Sisters vs. el Salvador*, Judgment of March 1, 2005.

58 See, in that sense, the remarks of Judge Cançado Trindade in his Separate Opinion in the *Bulacio* case, at para. 27–40.

59 Ibid., at para. 26.

60 Ibid., at para. 30.

61 See *Juridical Status and Human Rights of the Child,* Advisory Opinion OC-17/02, *supra* note 23, at para. 25.

References

Feria-Tinta, M. (2008). *The landmark rulings of the inter-American court of human rights*. Leiden: Martinus Nijhoff Publishers.

Harris, D. J., O'Boyle, M., Bates, E. P., & Buckley, C. M. (2009). *Harris, O'Boyle & Warbrick: Law of the European convention on human rights*. Oxford: Oxford University Press.

Chapter 15
Children's Rights Litigation in the African Region: Lessons from the Communications Procedure Under the ACRWC

Julia Sloth-Nielsen

Abstract This chapter describes and assesses the experiences to date of litigating children's rights under the African Charter on the Rights and Welfare of the Child (1990). The communications procedure under the African Children's Charter is explained with reference to the Charter itself as well as the rules of procedure developed in 2006 by the African Committee of Experts on the Rights and Welfare of the Child. The finding of the Committee in the first communication in which a finding was made, namely the so-called *Nubian Children* case, is discussed; so too is the decision in the second matter, which involved the government of Uganda. The chapter highlights a number of challenges and procedural issues; at the same time, it identifies good practice that can be used to inform children's rights litigation at the international and domestic level before national courts and other treaty bodies.

1 Introduction

This chapter describes and assesses the experiences to date of litigating children's rights under the African Charter on the Rights and Welfare of the Child (1990) (hereafter the African Children's Charter). The discussion begins with an overview of the communications procedure under the African Charter on Human and Peoples' Rights (1980) (ACHPR), which to all intents and purposes is the 'mother treaty' from which inspiration for the communications procedure of the Africa

J. Sloth-Nielsen (✉)
Faculty of Law, University of the Western Cape, Bellville, South Africa
e-mail: jsloth-nielsen@uwc.ac.za

J. Sloth-Nielsen
Department of Child Law, Leiden Law School , Leiden University, Leiden, The Netherlands

T. Liefaard and J.E. Doek (eds.), *Litigating the Rights of the Child*,
DOI 10.1007/978-94-017-9445-9_15

Children's Charter was drawn.[1] Thereafter, the communications procedure under the African Children's Charter is explained with reference to the Charter itself as well as the rules of procedure developed by the African Committee of Experts on the Rights and Welfare of the Child in 2006. The discussion turns to the finding of the Committee in the first communication in which a finding was made, namely the *Nubian Children* case.[2] The second finding, in respect of a communication brought against the government of Uganda, is outlined next.

A concluding section highlights challenges and raises some procedural issues, pointing at the same time to good practice which can be used to inform children's rights litigation at the international and domestic level before national courts and other treaty bodies.

2 The Communications Procedure Under the ACHPR

Although the ACHPR provides for both inter-state and individual communications, it is evident that the former has arisen only once in the two and a half decades of the existence of the Commission (the body which overseas implementation of the ACHPR).[3] It is therefore a reality that the Commission's protective mandate has been exercised almost exclusively through consideration of individual communications. In its jurisprudence, the Commission has developed a broad concept of *locus standi* that permits not only victims but others acting on their behalf to bring communications.[4]

---

[1] Amongst other Charter provisions. Notable amongst these is the article providing for the duties of the child (article 31), which takes its cue from the wording of a similar article in the mother treaty: see Sloth-Nielsen and Mezmur (2008): 159–189.

[2] This chapter refers variously to the 'decision' and the 'finding' of the Committee.

[3] *Democratic Republic of Congo v. Burundi, Rwanda and Uganda*, Communication 227/99. In relation to inter-state communications, the Commission found that the issue of exhaustion of local remedies does not arise where the alleged violations have been committed in the applicant state. Udombana explains in the following terms the reason why African States do not bring communications against each other: 'Diplomatic and economic ties between member states, plus the fact that African leaders tend to maintain intensive social relations among themselves, discourage the initiation of "hostile" actions.' See Udombana (2003): footnote 106.

[4] See *Malawi African Association, Amnesty international, Ms Sarr Diop, Union Interafricaine des Droits de l'Hommes, RADDHO, Collectif des veuves et Ayants–droits v. Mauritania and Association Mauritinienne des droits de l'homme v. Mauritania* Communications Nos. 54/91, 61/91, 98/93, 164/97 196/97, para. 78, 13th Annual Activity Report. 1999–2000, Annex V Addendum.

The seven admissibility criteria for individual communications before the African Commission are found in the body of the Charter itself, at article 55.[5] There is a rich history of litigation under the communications procedure of the ACHPR,[6] with at least 74 decisions having been taken on the merits, 84 ruled admissible and a variety of different outcomes being recorded in other matters (for example, postponed *sine die*, amicable settlement, and file closed or withdrawn).[7] However, at a recent Commission meeting in October 2013, it was lamented that many of the Commission's decisions remain unimplemented.[8]

3 The Communications Procedure Under the ACRWC

3.1 Background to the Charter

The African Children's Charter was developed in response to a continental view that African concerns had not been sufficiently assimilated during the CRC's drafting process, one in which only four African countries were represented.[9] It was intended to complement the CRC and further the enjoyment of children's rights in Africa (Bekker 2012: 249–263) by focusing on regional specificities concerning issues such as harmful cultural and social practices; the role of children in families and communities; child marriage; the position of children whose primary caregivers are imprisoned[10]; birth registration; the prohibition against the use of children aged below 18 years in armed conflict; and the duties and responsibilities of the child. In many respects, however, the Charter's provisions mirror those of the CRC. For instance, it enshrines the principle of the best interests of the child in

---

[5] Communications shall be considered if they: indicate their authors even if the latter request anonymity; are compatible with the Charter of the Organization of African Unity or with the present Charter; are not written in disparaging or insulting language directed against the state concerned and its institutions or to the Organization of African Unity; are not based exclusively on news disseminated through the mass media; are sent after exhausting local remedies, if any, unless it is obvious that this procedure is unduly prolonged; are submitted within a reasonable period from the time local remedies are exhausted or from the date the Commission is seized of the matter; and do not deal with cases which have been settled by the states involved in accordance with the principles of the Charter of the United Nations, or the Charter of the Organization of African Unity or the provisions of the present Charter.

[6] See, in general, Viljoen (2012).

[7] For further detail, see www.achpr.org/communications (accessed 30 June 2013).

[8] Personal communication from a delegate who attended the meeting.

[9] Only Algeria, Morocco, Senegal and Egypt had participated in the drafting process of the CRC: see Chirwa (2002): 157.

[10] This article of the Charter forms the basis of the first General Comment of the African Committee of Experts on the Rights and Welfare of the Child, adopted at its session in November 2013. See www.acerwc.org for the text of this General Comment.

regional treaty law, and reflects similarities in relation to children with disabilities, the administration of juvenile justice, and protection against various forms of abuse and exploitation (including within the family).[11] The Charter entered into force in 1999 after receiving the requisite number of ratifications. To date, 47 States parties have ratified the Charter, and, at the time of writing, universal ratification by all 53 member states of the African Union by the end of 2014 was not out of reach.

Oversight of the Charter's implementation is accorded to a Committee of Experts elected by the Assembly of Heads of State of the African Union (previously the Organisation of African Unity).[12] The first Committee of Experts took office in 2002 and set about drafting its rules of procedures, including guidelines for the submission of initial state party reports. Since the Committee in practice meets only twice annually, for a short period of a week at a time,[13] the criticism has been made that progress in implementing the Committee's mandate is slow (Viljoen 2000; Bekker 2012). Of late, however, this negative perception has started to improve, given that the Committee has become more active and visible in the African Union architecture.

3.2 *The Mandate of the African Committee of Experts*

The mandate of the Committee of Experts is set out in Chap. 3 of the Charter, in articles 42–45. It is clear from a cursory overview that the Committee has been awarded a more extensive role in the African treaty system than is the case with the UN CRC Committee, whose mandate is defined in articles 44 and 45 of the CRC to include receiving State party reports, reporting on its own activities to the UN General Assembly through the Economic and Social Council, recommending to the General Assembly to request the Secretary General to undertake on its behalf studies on specific issues relating to the rights of the child, and making suggestions and general recommendations based on information received.

The mandate of the African Committee extends beyond considering state reports submitted to it (which is provided for under article 43). Its broad mandate is prescribed by article 42 to include promoting and protecting the rights of the child enshrined in the Charter, collecting and documenting information, commissioning interdisciplinary assessments of the situation of children in Africa,

[11] For a full catalogue of the similarities and differences between the text of the African Children's Charter and the CRC, see Mezmur (2008); see too Chirwa (2002) and Olowu (2002). Note, however, that the Charter lacks the principle that deprivation of liberty be used as a last resort and then only for the shortest period of time (article 37(b) of the CRC).

[12] Chapter 2 of the Charter, chiefly set out in articles 32–37.

[13] The reasons have been lack of financial capacity as well as the crowded African Union meeting agenda.

organising meetings on child rights, and encouraging national and local institutions concerned with the rights and welfare of the child, as well as giving its views on child rights and making recommendations to governments (article 42(a)(i)).

In addition, the Committee is empowered to formulate and lay down rules aimed at protecting the rights of children in Africa (article 42(a)(ii)), and to cooperate with other African, international and regional institutions in connection with the promotion of children's rights and welfare; it may also interpret the Charter's provisions at the request of a state party or an institution of the African Union or 'any other person or institution recognised by the African Union or any State Party' (article 42(c)). The Committee is enabled by the treaty to perform such other tasks as may be entrusted to it by the Assembly of the Heads of State of the African Union, the Secretary General of the African Union or any other organs of the AU or the United Nations (article 42(d)). This conglomeration of capacities accorded the Committee of Experts is often referred to as the elaboration of the Committee's promotional mandate.[14]

Article 45 concerns the investigative mandate of the Committee, which may 'resort to any appropriate method of investigating any matter falling within the ambit of the Charter'. The Committee, in fulfilling this assignment, may request from the States parties any information relevant to the implementation of the Charter, and may also resort to any method of investigating the measures the State party has adopted to implement the Charter (article 45(1)). The capacity of the Committee to undertake investigations is relevant to the theme of litigating children's rights in the regional context, as will become evident below.

3.3 The Communications Procedure Under the Charter

The provisions of article 44 concern the Charter's communications procedure. It is noticeable that the article comprises of only two brief sections:

1. The Committee may receive a communication from any person, group or non-governmental organisation recognised by the African Union, by a member state, or the United Nations relating to any matter covered by this Charter.[15]
2. Every communication to the Committee shall contain the name and address of the author and shall be treated in confidence.

---

[14] See, for instance, Shehan (2010) and Lloyd (2008).

[15] Committee practice permits that NGOs and International Non-Governmental Organisations (INGOs) concerned with children's rights in Africa may apply to the Committee for Observer Status. Rules for the consideration of applications for observer status have been developed (see www.acerwc.org). To date, approximately seven such applications have been granted. Similarly, such organisations as are concerned with human rights on the continent may also acquire Observer Status before the African Commission on Human and Peoples' Rights which monitors the implementation of the African Charter on Human and Peoples' Rights.

From the above, it emerges that, as long as a communication relates to 'any matter' covered in the Charter, the Committee is given a broad remit as to who may submit it. (*Locus standi* to bring a communication is elaborated upon in Guidelines for the Receipt of Communications, discussed below). However, it is equally apparent from the Charter text cited above that the procedural niceties of any application are not directly evident. Such matters as the level of substantiation required to underpin a communication, the question of whether the victim or person or group whose rights have allegedly been violated must know about or consent to the communication being brought, the question of whether domestic remedies must first be exhausted, and the question of how communications brought to the Committee relate to the communications possibilities of the African Commission and the African Court on Human Rights (established in 2008), are not dealt with.

Hence, by the time of receipt by the Committee in 2005 of the first communication brought under the Charter, rules for the consideration of communications had to be drafted and adopted by the Committee sitting *en banc* before this complaint could be considered. Further, when it was agreed that all communications were to be submitted in the two languages of the Committee, namely English and French, the original communication (submitted only in English) had to be returned to the complainants for translation and re-submission before the question of admissibility could be decided.[16] Delays in communication between the Secretariat of the Committee and the complainants also exacerbated the length of time the process took, with the result that admissibility was decided only some five years later.

Once the communication was declared admissible, the 'offending' government had to be given the opportunity to respond to the allegations, which the responsible government indeed did, requesting an audience before the Committee. Thereafter, both the complainants and the government allegedly responsible for the violation were invited to address the Committee (separately) in support of their claims, an undertaking that proved inconclusive in view of the diametrically opposing points of view presented by the petitioners and the respondent.[17]

Unable to decide on the merits of the matter with the written and oral evidence at hand, the Committee proposed to undertake an investigative mission to the affected region to interview and consult with affected parties in situ. This was possible only after the relevant government had agreed to the visit and funds for the travel were sought and acquired. Ultimately, the delegation undertook the fact-finding mission only in 2013, which led to conclusive results insofar as the finalisation of the findings on the communication is concerned. The finding of this (first) communication is discussed briefly in Sect. 4.

---

[16] The Guidelines were adopted at the 8th Ordinary meeting of the African Committee of Experts on November/December 2006. For an overview of the proceedings of this meeting, see Mezmur (2007): 276–270.

[17] Own observation: the author was in attendance at the respective sessions.

3.4 The Guidelines for the Receipt of Communications

To return to the Guidelines for the Receipt of Communications developed by the Committee to guide its work, these commence with a definition of a communication, namely that it is 'any correspondence or any complaint from a State, individual or NGO denouncing acts that are prejudicial to a right or rights of the child'.[18] The Guidelines provide admissibility criteria in three domains: that is, with reference to the author; the form of the communication; and the content.

The 'author' requirements are contained, inter alia, in the quoted definition. They make clear that communications may be presented by individuals, including the victimized child and/or his or her parents or legal representatives, witnesses, a group of individuals or non-governmental organizations recognized by the African Union, by a Member State or by any other institution of the United Nations system. The author of the communication shall specify either to have been a victim of violations of the rights spelt out in the Charter, or to act on behalf of a victim or of other eligible parties. However, a communication may be presented on behalf of a victim without his or her agreement on condition that the author is able to prove that his or her action is taken in the supreme[19] in terest of the child. The victimized child who is able to express his or her opinions shall be informed of the communications presented on the child's behalf.[20]

Adherence to these principles concerning the authoring of communications is a requirement for the admissibility of the complaint. Bekker points out[21] that the broad *locus standi* provision incorporated in the communications guidelines of the African Committee of Experts and elaborating the briefer text of the African Children's Charter referred to in 3.3 above, is underpinned by a similarly broad jurisprudence which has been developed by the African Commission on Human and Peoples' Rights.

As regards the form of the communication, it is provided that no communication shall be considered by the Committee if it is anonymous; if it is not written; and if it concerns a State non-signatory to the Charter.[22]

In order to take a decision on the admissibility of a communication, the Guidelines require the Committee to ensure that:

- the communication is compatible with the provisions of the Constitutive Act of the African Union or with the African Charter on the Rights and Welfare of the Child;

---

[18] Article 1 of the Guidelines.

[19] This is likely the 'best interests' standard, derived from a literal translation of the French 'superior'.

[20] Chapter 2 article 1(1)–1(3) of the Guidelines.

[21] Bekker (2012).

[22] Chapter 2 II 1 of the Guidelines. There is an unusual savings clause that a Communication may be received in respect of a non- state signatory if this is in the best interests of the child; however, with near universal ratification of the Charter, it is only a remote possibility that this may arise.

- the communication is not exclusively based on information circulated by the media;
- the same issue has not been considered according to another investigation, procedure or international regulation;
- the author has exhausted all the available appeal channels at the national level or the author of the communication is not satisfied with the solution provided (the question of effectiveness of domestic remedies is discussed in more detail infra);
- the communication is presented within a reasonable period after appeal channels at the national level have been exhausted; and
- the wording of the communication shall not be offensive.[23]

These criteria are drawn pretty directly from prior jurisprudence of the African Commission on Human and People's Rights, which has a record spanning more than two decades of having received communications. It is significant, for the purposes of benchmarking an international standard, that the rule requiring exhaustion of local and national remedies has been placed in the Guidelines.[24] As noted, the exclusive jurisdiction requirement of Chap. 2 III (1)(c) is intended to avoid forum-shopping and a multiplicity of bodies adjudicating on the same issue with potentially divergent views or recommendations.[25] It also gives concrete effect to the principle of state sovereignty (Bekker 2012).

The communication will generally be considered by a working group of two or three committee members, who will consider the admissibility of the communication, will advise the outcome of this decision to the author and the state party concerned, and may request any further or additional information. The Committee's working group may request the presence of the author or authors, and the States parties concerned, to provide further clarification, and may conduct 'on the spot investigations'.[26]

The Guidelines provide some detail on the consideration of communication. For instance, there is a clause, dealing with the incompatibility of a member considering a communication, which provides that a committee member may *not* take part in the consideration of a communication:

- if the State Party on whose behalf he has been elected to the Committee is Party to the case;

[23] Chapter 2 III 1(a)–(f).

[24] See, however, the discussion of the *Nubian Children* case below.

[25] The jurisdiction of the African Court on Human Rights (which was established after both the Charter and the formulation of the Guidelines on Communications) does pose some new territorial dilemmas. Whilst the Rules of Procedure of the African Court on Human and Peoples' Rights do detail the respective relationship between the African Commission on Human and Peoples' Rights and the Court, they are silent on the position *vis-à-vis* the African Committee of Experts on the Rights and Welfare of the Child. See further www.african-court.org for the various statutes and protocols of the Court.

[26] See Guidelines Chap. 2 V 4, which uses this terminology.

- if the member has any personal interest in the case; or
- if he has participated in any decision-making process concerning the case relating to the communication.[27]

The Committee's actual deliberations on a communication are to be held in closed session—only general matters of a procedural nature pertaining to article 44 may be held in open session. This rule relates less to the fact that the communication may concern children than to the principle of respect for state signatories, and as such it echoes the practice of the African Commission on Human and Peoples' Rights. Moreover, this same principle explains why, even though a third communication is under consideration by the Committee at the time of writing, no information about the content or progress of the Committee's deliberations on it may yet be furnished.

The rules of procedure contained in the Guidelines give flavour to the concept of children's participation; Chap. 3 articles 3(1) and 3(2) record that 'the Committee should take measures to ensure the effective and meaningful participation of the child or children concerned by the consideration of the validity of the communications and its author', and that 'when the child is capable of expressing his opinions, he should be heard by a Committee member'. To date, practical effect has not yet been given to this injunction as it has not been deemed necessary in respect of either of the communications finalised by the Committee.

As far as remedies are concerned, the Guidelines are silent on what measures the Committee could institute or impose upon finding a violation of a Charter right. Given the fact that, as an international treaty body, it lacks any 'teeth' to implement a recommendation within the confines of a sovereign state or to force a country to abide by a finding, the usual route would be to issue advice to the infringing government about the violation[28] and possibly elaborate on the measures, if any, that the Committee would like to see as corrective action. The hope is that a State party's commitment to its good standing in the international arena and amongst other African States parties would result in the necessary compliance.

The Committee, of course, can use the state reporting procedure to address recalcitrance or enquire as to progress in implementing decisions; however, the Guidelines do contain a section dealing with monitoring, which requires a Committee member to be appointed for this purpose.[29] At a practical level, the Committee has also provided for follow-up visits to monitor the impact and operationalisation of its decisions.

---

[27] See Chap. 2 VI 1.

[28] Article 4(4) provides that '(t)he decisions of the Committee shall be submitted to the Assembly of Heads of State and Government of the African Union. The decisions shall be published after consideration by the Assembly and the State Parties concerned which shall ensure their dissemination in their countries, in conformity with Article 45, paragraphs 3 and 4 of the Charter'.

[29] Article 4(1).

4 The *Nubian Children* Case

This matter was the second communication to be received by the Committee (in 2009).[30] The complaint was brought by the Institute for Human Rights and Democracy in Africa (based in The Gambia) and the Open Society Justice Initiative. The complaint centred on a denial of Kenyan nationality to persons of Nubian descent born in Kenya,[31] a violation of articles 3 (non-discrimination) and 6 (right to name and nationality); consequential violations of socioeconomic rights to education and health care under articles 11 and 14 of the Charter were also alleged. At the 15th ordinary session of the Committee, the communication was deemed to be admissible. This was based on evidence that the matter had served before a High Court in Kenya for some seven years, with judgment not having been given. It was concluded, therefore, that local remedies were de facto 'exhausted' since they were not effective or efficient. The argument was put forward that the delay in adjudication of the case in the national courts rendered the local remedy ineffective.

In March 2011, a finding was made against the government of Kenya, *in absentia*. The government was advised through the appropriate official channels of the intention to consider the merits of the communication but had not taken the opportunity to present any argument or mount a defence.[32] The African Committee reasoned that children's best interests demanded that it consider the communication, and decided to be seized thereof and consider the communication on its merits. It could not be in children's best interests, it was opined, for the communication to be left in legal limbo for a protracted time. As a result, the Committee heard oral arguments by the complainants and scrutinised the validity, legality and relevance of such arguments through a series of questions.[33] A large volume of substantiating documentation, including statements from affected descendants, formed part of the complaint and supporting papers.

In the event, Kenya was found to be in violation of children's rights to non-discrimination, to nationality and to protection against statelessness. Consequential violations of their socioeconomic rights to health and education, as alleged, were also confirmed. Whilst Bekker (2012: 261) bemoans the fact that the Committee

---

[30] For a general discussion of the finding, see Durojaye and Foley (2012): 564–578.

[31] Originally the Nubians served in the British armed forces, and had stayed behind after independence in 1960. However, they were not granted land, and since descent is linked to ancestral land tenure, they were excluded from the civil registration system. This background is set out in the finding on the communication *Institute for Human Rights and Development in Africa (IHRDA) and Open Society Justice Initiative on behalf of Children of Nubian descent in Kenya v. The Government of Kenya* Decision: No 002/Com/002/2009, available at www.acerwc.org/wp-content/uploads2011/09/002-09-IHRDA-OSJI-Nubain-children-v-Kenya-Eng.pdf (accessed 10 June 2013) and in Durojaye and Foley (2012).

[32] See paras. 9, 10 and 11 of the communication. The finding indicates that a Note Verbale was sent in June 2010 and again in February 2011.

[33] Para. 12 of the communication.

took so long to decide on the communication submitted, and proposes that this may undermine the credibility of its ultimate judgment on the issues, other authors have welcomed the decision (Durojaye and Foley 2012: 565).[34]

Three salient comments can be made concerning this first decision of the Committee. First, the finding notes that the Charter requires the interpretation thereof to draw inspiration from 'international law, particularly from the African Charter on Human and Peoples' Rights, the Charter of the Organisation of African Unity, the Universal Declaration on Human Rights, the United Nations Convention on the Rights and Welfare of the Child, and other instruments adopted by the United Nations and by African countries in the field of human rights, and by African values and traditions'.[35]

This Charter provision is referred to directly in the *Nubian Children* finding,[36] and forms the basis (inter alia) for reliance in a number of respects on the jurisprudence of the African Commission on Human and Peoples' Rights. Hence, in the finding that local remedies were not effective, the Committee of Experts referred to the previous decisions of the African Commission that it is:

> only domestic remedies that are available, effective, and adequate (sufficient) that need to be exhausted.[37] In Communication Nos. 147/95 and 149/96, the African Commission held that a remedy is considered available if the Complainant can pursue it without impediment; it is deemed effective if it offers a prospect of success; and it is found sufficient if it is capable of redressing the complaint.[38]

Similarly, in concluding that the exclusion of the children of persons of Nubian descent from acquiring Kenyan nationality from birth violated the non-discrimination clause of the African Children's Charter, the finding refers to the prior jurisprudence of the African Commission:

> For a discriminatory treatment to be justified, the African Commission has rightly warned that 'the reasons for possible limitations must be founded in a legitimate state interest and … limitations of rights must be strictly proportionate (sic) with and absolutely necessary for the advantages which are to be obtained'.[39]

In the context of the alleged violation of the right to health of the affected children, the decision cites the *Purohit* case[40] in which the African Commission held that the right to health in the African Charter on Human and Peoples' Rights 'includes the right to health facilities, access to goods and services to be guaranteed to all without discrimination of any kind'.[41] It has been confirmed that the underlying

---

[34] See too Assefa (2012).

[35] Article 46 of the African Children's Charter.

[36] At para. 25.

[37] Referring to *Dawda Jawara v. The Gambia*, Communication Nos. 147/95 and 149/96, para. 32. See also paras. 31 and 32 of the ACERWC finding.

[38] Para. 28 of the Communication.

[39] Referring to *Legal Resources Foundation v. Zambia*, Communication No. 211/98, para. 67.

[40] *Purohit and Moore v. The Gambia*, Communication 241/2001, para. 80.

[41] Para. 59 of the finding.

conditions for achieving a healthy life are protected by the right to health: the *Zaire* case[42] stated that complementary determinants of the right to health such as the lack of electricity, drinking water and medicines can amount, too, to a violation of the right to health, and is referred to in the *Nubian Children* case.[43]

This reliance on the jurisprudence of the African Commission is a positive development which can only enhance the coherence of regional human rights standards.

Secondly, though, the findings do also (in accordance with the precepts of article 46 quoted above) refer to the CRC. Notably, the discussion of article 6 of the African Children's Charter is characterised by comparisons to the equivalent provision in the CRC (article 7(1))[44]; the CRC Committee's Concluding Observations to the Report of the Government of Kenya in 2007 are also cited.[45] In the context of the right to development, discussed under the rubric of the violation of the right to health, the decision of the African Committee refers to the right to survival and development provided for in article 6 of the CRC, as well as article 24, dealing with the right to health.[46] This enhances the complementary nature of the African Children's Charter as a regional instrument, whilst acknowledging the parallel obligations under the CRC. However, rather than deferring to the CRC provisions, the judgment seeks to interpret the regional Charter provisions in their own right. The 'jurisprudence' of the CRC Committee in the form of General Comments, was not relied upon, a factor noted by Durojaye and Foley (2012); this may well have been deliberate, insofar as the African regional jurisprudence is accorded a more prominent position.

The third comment relates not so much to form as to substance. The finding, it is submitted, advances child rights jurisprudence in four main ways. First, the Charter provision on the right to nationality and on birth registration has been purposively interpreted to mean that nationality rights must accrue from birth, noting that a system which requires a child to wait until he or she turns 18 until nationality is awarded cannot be seen as an adequate effort on the part of the State party to comply with its Charter obligations, broadly speaking.[47]

---

[42] *Free Legal Assistance Group and Others v. Zaire*, Communications No. 25/89, 47/90, 56/91, 100/93.

[43] At Para. 59 of the Communication.

[44] The Human Rights Committee and its General Comment No. 24 are also referred to in support of the discussion of the normative content of the right to acquire a nationality.

[45] Para. 40 of the finding.

[46] See footnote 26 of the finding.

[47] This being said, the Committee does accept that a state does not have an unqualified obligation to accord its nationality to every child born on its territory regardless the circumstances, and that states have the sovereign power to determine the conditions and rules for the award of nationality. Nevertheless, states are limited in their discretion to grant nationality by their obligations to guarantee equal protection and to prevent, avoid, and reduce statelessness (paras. 46–48 of the finding).

Secondly, the Committee regards the overall thrust of the violation as centrally linked to protection against statelessness, which is accorded substantial discussion in the body of the decision. This is of special significance in the African context, one characterised by large numbers of displaced and migrant people that include children. The decision notes that

> the root causes of statelessness are complex and multifaceted including state succession, decolonization, conflicting laws between States, domestic changes to nationality laws, and discrimination ... Whatever the root cause(s), the African Committee cannot overemphasise the overall negative impact of statelessness on children. While it is always no fault of their own, stateless children often inherit an uncertain future. For instance, they might fail to benefit from protections and constitutional rights granted by the State. These include difficulty to travel freely, difficulty in accessing justice procedures when necessary, as well as the challenge of finding oneself in a legal limbo vulnerable to expulsion from their home country. Statelessness is particularly devastating to children in the realisation of their socio-economic rights such as access to health care, and access to education. In sum, being stateless as a child is generally [an] antithesis to the best interests of children.[48]

Thirdly, the indivisibility of rights is a core theme of the Committee's decision. Not only is this evident in the way that rights generally regarded as civil and political rights (non-discrimination and violation of the right to registration of birth) flow seamlessly into what are termed 'consequential violations'[49] in the area of socioeconomic rights (the rights to health and to education), but the overarching point is that

> the implications of the multi-generational impact of the denial of right of nationality are manifest and of far wider effect than may at first blush appear in the case .... Systemic under-development of an entire community has been alleged to be the result.[50]

Indeed, the framework for adjudicating the normative content of justiciable socio-economic rights is, conversely, applied by the Committee to the civil and political rights at stake in the case:

> All Charter rights generate obligations to *respect, protect, promote and fulfil*. This is no less so in respect of the rights implicated when nationality and identity rights are violated.[51]

This typology is of some importance in the context (for example) of birth registration, which is overall at very low levels in Africa.[52] The establishment of a central birth registry is but one step in the implementation of the right, which frequently requires affirmative measures to reach rural and other populations, to address barriers and overcome obstacles. As the Committee notes, the right to birth registration creates not merely an obligation of conduct but one of result.[53]

---

48 Paras. 45–46.

49 At Para. 58.

50 Para. 68.

51 Para. 58. Emphasis added.

52 It is estimated that only 30 % of children's births in Africa are registered: information derived from the Civil Registration and Vital statistics conference, Gaborone, Botswana May 2013.

53 Para. 52.

Fourthly, the Committee draws on the unique provisions of article 31 of the Charter (the duties of the child) and links this to the denial of nationality to the children born of Nubian descent in the following manner:

> The Committee notes that Children of Nubian descent who have been born in Kenya are subject to the requirement of their serving their national community by placing their physical and intellectual abilities at the service of the nation, as well as preserving and strengthening social and national solidarity and the independence and integrity of his country. Although it cannot be suggested that the fulfilment of these duties is contingent upon their status as nationals and their identity as children of Kenya, the fulfilment of Article 31 responsibilities highlights the reciprocal nature of rights and responsibilities, which reciprocity is not fulfilled when Article 6 rights are not respected by the State concerned. The Committee wishes to emphasise that national solidarity and African unity are best achieved in an environment which eschews discrimination and denial of rights.[54]

Arguably, this is a significant *entrée* into a conceptual terrain in which rights (from the top down and the bottom up) are intertwined with reciprocal responsibilities.[55]

In sum, the *Nubian Children* case represents a promising start to litigation for children's rights at the continental level. It has been mentioned that the Guidelines of the Committee in respect of the receipt of communications provide for monitoring and follow-up of decisions taken regarding communications and that the Committee is required to designate one of its members to be responsible for monitoring its decisions as well as reporting to the Committee. A visit to Kenya to investigate the measures adopted in consequence of the decision in the *Nubian Children* case has already been undertaken.[56]

5 The *Ugandan People's Defence Force* Case

As mentioned previously, this was the first communication received by the Committee. It spans the period, specifically 2002–2005, during which the Lord's Resistance Army (LRA) waged its war of terror in northern Uganda, but the main thrust of the complaint against the government of Uganda and the Ugandan Peoples' Defence Force relates to the recruitment of children under 18 into the armed forces in this period in violation of article 22 of the African Children's Charter, which contains a 'straight 18' prohibition on the participation of children in hostilities. Subsidiary complaints included the exposure of girl children to sexual violations by members of the armed forces as well as violations of the rights to health, to education and to an adequate standard of living of the children who (together with their families) had been moved into camps to enable better protection from the raiders.

---

[54] Para. 66.

[55] Assefa (2012) notes that the interpretation of article 31 went beyond what the applicants requested.

[56] The visit was undertaken in 2013, to the personal knowledge of the author.

As noted in Sect. 3, the consideration of this communication was delayed by some years whilst the Guidelines on the receipt of communications were prepared, the communication was translated, the complainants and the government of Uganda gave oral submissions before the Committee, and, finally, the working group of the Committee undertook a site visit to determine the veracity of the allegations.[57] By this time, the war was long since over, the people of northern Uganda had moved out of the camps which had been set up for their protection and had been resettled, and the reconstruction of the north was moving apace. It was, therefore, an issue as to whether the complaint was not moot, given the length of time that had elapsed since the perpetration of the alleged violations. However, the working group proceeded on the basis that the issue was not moot, given the high prevalence of child-soldier recruitment on the continent and the importance of setting guidelines for States parties in this sphere.

In the event, representatives the government of Uganda conceded there had been a breach of the 'straight 18' position in several ways. Notably, the Ugandan Defence Force had used children previously abducted by the LRA as scouts to lead the Defence Force soldiers back to hideouts and lairs, thereby exposing them to risks. In addition, local militias had not adequately ensured proof of age before permitting recruits to join.

The finding of a violation was accepted at the 22nd ordinary meeting of the African Committee of Experts on the Rights and Welfare of the Child in the first half of 2013. This was also communicated to the government of Uganda at the AU Heads of State meeting that followed shortly after the 22nd meeting of the Committee. However, a reasoned decision setting out the bases for the relevant findings has not yet been published or communicated to the government concerned. Therefore, it cannot be stated definitively what the consequences of the Ugandan decision will be or what contribution to child rights jurisprudence the Committee will make as a result of this communication.

6 Concluding Remarks

The experience under the African system of children's rights affords a number of insights. First, the processes that delayed the consideration of the first two communications received by the Committee are regrettable, more so because the best interests (not to mention physical security) of the children of Uganda demanded that their plight be addressed with the requisite urgency.[58] Furthermore, the period

---

[57] The author of this chapter was a member of the working group and participated in the site visit.

[58] The Guidelines do make provision for the issuing of provisional measures: 'When the Committee decides to consider a Communication, it may forward to the State party concerned, a request to take provisional measures that the Committee shall consider necessary in order to prevent any other harm to the child or children who would be victims of violations.' However, the lapse of time rendered this provision futile.

of time that elapsed (almost eight years) meant that the issue came dangerously close to being moot, given that, at the time of consideration, the tide had turned decisively and that reconstructing the events was not easy.

Secondly, referring again to the communication relating to Uganda, it is apparent that treaty bodies are not courts of law and lack the forensic tools of adjudication which courts have at their disposal (evidence, cross-examination, the ability to call witnesses, and so forth). Hence, when two contradictory versions surface, the treaty body is not in a position to challenge one or the other version in terms of its usual processes of dialogue with States parties and presenters of shadow reports. Further to this, the need to travel to northern Uganda on a fact-finding mission was not underpinned by clear rules as to when site visits are required or how they are to be conducted.

The decision in the *Nubian Children* case does break new ground in elaborating a nascent jurisprudence on children's rights under the African Charter and fashioning a remedy that, arguably, is not unachievable in the context of the country against which the finding was made and in view of the fairly limited group of affected beneficiaries. However, the matter of remedies is an issue that merits further thought and which has occupied children's rights litigators at national level.

As noted, the African Children's Committee is fortunate to have provided explicitly for follow-up on its decisions and to have introduced such monitoring in its emerging practice. This moves the agenda beyond the 'violations approach' that for two decades characterised the practice of the African Commission on Human and Peoples' Rights, which had limited its decisions to making a finding without exploring a concrete remedy. However, the Committee must still grapple fully with the boundaries of its mandate as far as remedies are concerned. The easy answers are to be found in injunctions that require states to amend their laws or policies, to adopt new laws, to include the excluded, and to end practices which violate the Charter. Yet addressing many of the violations will hinge on resource mobilisation and the progressive implementation of socioeconomic rights. Even the establishment of birth registries, for instance, requires considerable human, technical and financial capacity. Thus, some guidance may have to be sought from domestic litigation on children's rights, as well as from comparable regional and international bodies. The Committee's monitoring approach could become a process akin to the use of structural interdicts at national level.

With the first two decisions under the belt and a third communication awaiting consideration, there is a need for awareness to be raised of the communications procedure under the Charter. The submission of only three communications in the 14 years in which the Charter has been in force is worryingly low. There also is some concern that academic institutions or the larger of the NGOs[59] will monopolise the platform provided by a communications procedure to the exclusion of individuals, grass-roots organisations and child complainants themselves. The latter

---

[59] The Nubian Children case was brought by a large INGO in concert with a supranational NGO operating on continental level. The other two communications were brought by the Centre for Human Rights at the University of Pretoria.

grouping might well lack the technical and financial resources required to pursue litigation successfully first at national level and, thereafter, before the regional body.

With the Third Optional Protocol to the CRC having entered into force and for the first time permitting communications to be brought under the CRC, it is hoped that the experiences of children's rights litigation under the African Children's Charter will be instructive.

References

Assefa, A. (2012, April 13). Will Nubian children have to go to the African Court? *AfricaLaw*. http://www.africalaw.com.

Bekker, G. (2012). The African Committee on the Rights and Welfare of the Child. In M. Ssenyonjo (Ed.), *The African regional human rights system: 30 Years after the African Charter on Human and Peoples' Rights* (pp. 249–263). The Netherlands: Brill Publishers.

Chirwa, D. (2002). The merits and demerits of the African Charter on the Rights and Welfare of the Child. *International Journal of Children's Rights, 10*(2), 157.

Durojaye, E., & Foley, E. (2012). Making a first impression: An assessment of the decision of the Committee of Experts of the African Children's Charter in the *Nubian Children* communication. *African Human Rights Law Journal*, 564–578.

Lloyd, A. (2008). The African Committee of Experts on the Rights and Welfare of the Child. In J. Sloth-Nielsen (Ed.), *Children's rights in Africa: A legal perspective*. Dartmouth: Ashgate.

Mezmur, B. D. (2007). Still an infant or a toddler? The work of the African Committee of Experts and its work on the 8th ordinary session. *African Human Right Law Journal, 7*(1), 270–276.

Mezmur, B. D. (2008). The African Children's Charter versus the UN Convention on the Rights of the Child: A zero-sum game? *SA Public Law/Publiekreg, 23*, 1.

Olowu, D. (2002). Protecting children's rights in Africa: A critique of the African Children's Charter on the Rights and Welfare of the Child. *International Journal on Children Rights, 10*, 127.

Shehan, F. (2010). *Advancing children's rights: A guide for civil society organisations on how to engage with the African Committee of Experts on the Rights and Welfare of the Child.* Save the Children (UK).

Sloth-Nielsen, J., & Mezmur, B. D. (2008). A dutiful child: Article 31 of the African Children's Charter. *Journal of African Law, 2*, 159–189.

Udombana, N. (2003). So far, so fair: The local remedies rule in the jurisprudence of the African Commission on Human and Peoples' Rights. *American Journal of International Law, 97*, 1.

Viljoen, F. (2000). The African Charter on the Rights and Welfare of the Child. In C. J. Davel (Ed.), *Introduction to Child Law in South Africa*. Juta: Cape Town.

Viljoen, F. (2012). *International human rights law in Africa* (2nd ed.). Oxford: Oxford University Press.

MIX
Papier aus verantwortungsvollen Quellen
Paper from responsible sources
FSC® C105338

If you have any concerns about our products,
you can contact us on
ProductSafety@springernature.com

In case Publisher is established outside the EU,
the EU authorized representative is:
Springer Nature Customer Service Center GmbH
Europaplatz 3, 69115 Heidelberg, Germany

Printed by Libri Plureos GmbH
in Hamburg, Germany